Preface

"How long," Hamlet asks of the Gravedigger, "will a man lie i' th' earth ere he rot?"

In selecting the essays for this anthology, the editors have more than once indulged in Shakespearean paraphrase, wondering how long a playwright must lie in the minds of his critics before he ripens.

There is no clear answer, at least in terms of the criteria by which these essays were chosen. Essays which would offer the reader a sense of the central direction of the important writers for the modern theatre and of major contemporary critical reinterpretations of their immediate forerunners were not easy to discover.

Neither Sean O'Casey nor John Synge, for instance, has been the subject of a decisive critical interpretation, so far as the editors can discover, and some brilliant young writers who have achieved success both in the critical journals and on the stage are so on the move that they cannot yet be fully assessed, even in terms of a single play.

Omissions acknowledged, however, this book offers a group of essays which hopefully will lead the reader to grounds on which he may continue his own exploration. Here are streets both broad and narrow. Some essays, those of William Arrowsmith or Robert Corrigan, for instance, focus on the total work of an author, describing and evaluating his thought or his technique in a long view. Others, such as Jean-Paul Sartre's essay on Genet's *The Maids* or John Gassner's critique of *A Streetcar Named Desire*, imply the whole view in the examination of a particular work of art. Essays on older playwrights, Strindberg, Ibsen, Chekhov, Pirandello, Shaw, have been chosen because they reflect new critical problems and new shapes of assessment.

A few of the essays—those by Ugo Betti, Arthur Miller, and William Oliver, discuss not a playwright or a work, but modes and problems of the modern theatre. These men who write from the widest perspective are all, in the first instance, playwrights. Something of the quality of their work as dramatic artists can perhaps be inferred from their criticism.

The picture this volume suggests is of an unusually serious and vital drama and of responsive and aware critics. In the twentieth century, at least in the theatre, it is good to be alive.

Our gratitude is owing to Miss Diane McDonald and Miss Linda Neel for their assistance in preparing the manuscript.

University of California   T.B.
Berkeley, California   W.I.O.
October 1964

Contents

The Absurdists   Between Absurdity and the Playwright BY WILLIAM I. OLIVER, 3

Jean Anouilh   Obsession and Technique in the Plays of Jean Anouilh BY S. BEYNON JOHN, 20

Ugo Betti   Religion and the Theatre BY UGO BETTI, 43

Bertolt Brecht   How Epic Is Bertolt Brecht's Epic Theatre? BY HEINZ POLITZER, 54

Anton Chekhov   The Drama of Anton Chekhov BY ROBERT W. CORRIGAN, 73

Friedrich Duerrenmatt   Friedrich Duerrenmatt and the Tragic Sense of Comedy BY ADOLF D. KLARMANN, 99

Thomas Stearns Eliot   The Comedy of T. S. Eliot BY WILLIAM ARROWSMITH, 134

Jean Genet   *The Maids* BY JEAN-PAUL SARTRE, 152

Jean Giraudoux   Theatre as Proposition: Jean Giraudoux BY JACQUES GUICHARNAUD, 168

Henrik Ibsen   Kindermord and Will in *Little Eyolf* BY JAMES E. KERANS, 192

v

Federico García Lorca   *Don Perlimplín:* Lorca's Theater-Poetry BY
                            FRANCIS FERGUSSON, 209

Arthur Miller   The Family in Modern Drama BY ARTHUR
                    MILLER, 219

Eugene O'Neill   O'Neill's *Long Day's Journey into Night* and
                     New England Irish-Catholicism BY JOHN
                     HENRY RALEIGH, 234

Luigi Pirandello   Pirandello and the Nature of Man BY
                       HUBERT C. HEFFNER, 255

Jean-Paul Sartre   The Problem of Acts BY FREDERIC JAMESON,
                       276

George Bernard Shaw   The Making of a Dramatist (1892–1903)
                          BY ERIC BENTLEY, 290

August Strindberg   Male and Female in August Strindberg BY
                        ROBERT BRUSTEIN, 313

Thornton Wilder   The Comedy of Thornton Wilder BY TRAVIS
                      BOGARD, 355

Tennessee Williams   *A Streetcar Named Desire:* a Study in Am-
                         biguity BY JOHN GASSNER, 374

William Butler Yeats   The Later Plays of W. B. Yeats BY THOMAS
                           PARKINSON, 385

MODERN DRAMA
Essays in Criticism

WILLIAM I. OLIVER

Between Absurdity and the Playwright

Few spectacles in the history of theatre have been more amusing
than the current Babel raised upon the grounds of absurdist drama.
The voices that cry out in many tongues issue from all walks of life
(from expert and amateur, critic and playwright) and the appalling
humor of it is that in all but a few instances—a very few instances—
what they tell us is incomplete, opinionated, or downright balder-
dash. Clear and lucid thought on the subject of absurdist drama is
indeed rare, and even then, as in the case of Esslin [1] or Coe,[2] it is
marred by excessive sympathy or partisanship.

No one can write about absurdist playwrights and their craft
without first defining in some way the nature of their subject: absurdity. It is their subject and not their craft that effectively distinguishes
them and, at the same time, relates them to the stream of world
drama. It is precisely because so many critics have attempted to define the absurdists from the point of view of craftsmanship that we
have created the situation I have called a critical Babel. Perhaps
the most serious critical limitation of Mr. Esslin's otherwise excellent
work, *The Theatre of the Absurd*,[3] is precisely this tendency to focus
too quickly and exclusively on the stylistic breed without stressing
the philosophical genus.[4]

The absurdist playwrights believe that our existence is absurd be-

Reprinted from the *Educational Theatre Journal* (XV, 3), by permission
of the American Educational Theatre Association and the author.

cause we are born without asking to be born, we die without seeking death, we live between birth and death trapped within our body and our reason, unable to conceive of a time in which we were not, or a time in which we will not be—for *nothingness* is very much like the concept of infinity: something we perceive only in so far as we cannot experience it. Thrust into life, armed with our senses, will and reason, we feel ourselves to be potent beings. Yet our senses give the lie to our thought and our thought defies our senses. We never perceive anything completely. We are permitted to entertain committedly only one perspective of any object, fact, or situation: our own. We labor to achieve distinction and permanence only to find that our assessments are perspectively incomplete and therefore never wholly effective. All of our creations are doomed to decay as we ourselves are doomed to death. We create in order to identify ourselves in some semblance of permanence, but our creations become autonomous facts the instant we have created them and do not identify us except in so far as we pretend what they do. Therefore, the more we strive for definition and permanent distinction, the more absurd we are. Yet, the only value we can affirm with certainty is a self-defeating complex that we do not understand: our life. If we despair of definition, of ever achieving a sense of permanence, and we contemplate suicide, we are put in the absurd situation of sacrificing our only concrete value, life, for a dream of power and permanence that no man on this earth has ever experienced. On the other hand, if in despair we turn to religion or illusion *of any sort* we betray and deny our only means of preception: our reason. If, in a transport of ecstacy, be it mystical or sensuous, we feel at one with power and permanence . . . we are forced to admit the illusionistic aspect of this transport and we must confess that our sense of power, permanence and definition is achieved at the sacrifice of our reason. If it is impossible for us to act with complete efficacy, to perceive with complete accuracy, to create anything definite and lasting that expresses exactly our intentions, we must also remember that it is impossible for us to cease acting as long as we live. This then is the condition of man that we of the twentieth century call "absurd." It is the same state of being that Aristotle labeled as "ignorance." It is this complex of self-defeating paradoxes, this even check and balance of power and impotence, knowledge and ignorance, attunement and alienation that is the subject of the absurdist playwrights of all ages, no matter what form or style they may have chosen to express it.

If we begin our definition of absurdist drama with an examination of its subject matter rather than its style, we create an instantaneous bond between all manner of writers such as Beckett, Ionesco, Genet, Adamov, Miller, O'Neill, Brecht, Pirandello, Unamuno, Sartre, and Camus. Furthermore, we find no difficulty in making comparisons between the works of the current generation of absurdists and their historical ancestors: the Greek tragedians and farceurs as well as the great dramatists of the English Renaissance (including Shakespeare). What more explicit statements of man coming to terms with the absurdity of his condition than that of Oedipus, Hamlet, Lear, Vendice, D'Amville, Phaedra, Oreon, Hippolytus, Orestes, and Prospero?

It is possible that there are some who object to such a broad and inclusive definition. However, it must seem clear that if absurdity has any worth at all as a concept, it is precisely because it embraces anagogically the whole of human existence . . . it defines the condition of man, today, in the past, and into the future. Within this circle of absurdity man may change his conventions of behavior and belief but he will not break out of the encompassing definition. Any writer who attempts to define the nature of man and proceeds reasonably and empirically will take an existential posture that in some way expresses man's confrontation with absurdity. It is precisely because of the accuracy and soundness of its postulates that absurdity can be used as a means to distinguish between those assertions about the nature of man that are dogmatically entertained and those that are the result of empirical assessments. Critico-philosophical tools such as the concept of absurdity which help us correlate diversity of artistic expression, are every bit as essential as those which help to establish the distinctions that isolate these expressions. The style of absurdist drama will change many times but the content will remain very much the same until man ceases to be man by becoming God, or by losing his power of reflection and becoming a beast. Absurdist drama then, is not new; it is as old as tragedy, as old as farce—for farce and tragedy are indeed the double mask of absurdity.

The absurdists of today write in such diverse styles that one hesitates to compare them in anything but their philosophical categories. However, some generalizations can be made. The modern absurdists, almost to a man, determinedly resist the traditional separation of farce and tragedy. The subject of farce is the same as that of tragedy: the terrible or comic discovery of man's absurdity, ignorance and impotence. The essential difference between the two forms is one of

e arouses laughter and tragedy draws our tears—tragedy
r sympathy, while farce dispels our sympathy and frees
y.[5] The absurdists of today, as Euripides once did, com-
he qualities of farce and tragedy, making us laugh at that
n hurts us most, making us weep at that which is most foolish
in our nature.[6] They are all, in the best sense of the word, ironists.

Of necessity, an absurdist playwright is one who is predominantly
thematic in his dramaturgy. That is to say, these are dramatists of a
philosophical bent who place the greatest value on their thematic
statement. Consequently, their plays are constructed and polished in
such a fashion as to call attention to their intellectual content, and
this in spite of the fact that their thought refuses to be narrowly
systematized. This tends to make their works more presentational
than the works of authors less concerned with universals and more
inclined to create a drama of sensuous experience, of realism. Now,
the drama has had many authors of a philosophical bent, of an intellectual disposition, but they have never produced plays quite like
these. What one must emphasize is the degree to which these modern absurdists mean to be intellectual, ideological, objective, and
cerebral; and, concomitantly, the extent to which they want their
audiences to accompany them on their cerebration. Only the authors
of Medieval allegory have called attention to their thought as noisily
as do the absurdists of today.

The tendency toward presentational drama is another pattern
which identifies the creative posture of the absurdist. If there is one
quality that marks the major trends of modern art and certainly the
art which burgeons out of Paris, it is the movement toward pure art,
or "de-humanized art" as Ortega y Gasset puts it.[7] Modern artists
and absurd playwrights in particular seem concerned with creating
works that proclaim their independence from the traditional neo-
Aristotelian strictures of imitation or representationalism. These
playwrights want a drama that proclaims, "This is not life! It is my
work of art about life!" or even, "This is life itself that I've created
. . . mad-made life . . . ersatz life." In order to achieve a level of
abstraction sufficiently pronounced to evince such a response from
their audiences, the absurdists have resorted to various devices, none
of which are new to the theatre. They have taken up every conceivable symbolical device employed in allegory and dramatic expressionism. Furthermore, several of them have discarded psychology
as a control of action.[8] The action of these plays is intended to dem-

onstrate symbolically the ideas of the playwright and to create the dramatic temperature necessary to maintain the interest of the audience. At first glance some of their plays appear to be utterly illogical until we realize that the logic of the author's thought is not directly expressed but rather symbolically stated in action. One might well question this procedure on grounds of deliberate obscurantism— "Why not come out and say what you mean?" The answer is simple and didactically sound. If one has an important body of thought to purvey one must beware of presenting it too facilely, lest the "student audience" simply *recognize* it and fail to *learn* it. Finally, the absurdists are not afraid of obscurity in art since they employ it as a direct symbol of the obscurity they find in life.

The tendency to dehumanize their art has another rather interesting application in the absurdists' understanding of the function of the actor. The founding fathers of absurd drama (Beckett, Ionesco, and Adamov) were not theatre people. It is significant that none of these men had any marked respect for the practice of theatre as they found it. They objected to the realistic drama of their youth on grounds that realism was an irritating, if not inferior, form of art that enslaved the artist in a photographic relationship to life. Ionesco, the most outspoken of the absurdist elders on technical matters, felt that realism reduced the actor to a puppet. When these men finally brought themselves to write their new drama, they had a revolutionary motivation that was not entirely philosophical: they were out to liberate the theatre and emancipate the actor from the bonds of naïve imitation.[9] Their revolution has not been entirely effective. The more naïve and bold their allegorical expressionism, the less imaginative room they afford the actor. Only when the playwright is capable, as are Beckett and Genet, of creating plays which are microcosms in and of themselves, with their own peculiar behavioral rules and emotional responses, only then is the actor permitted some imaginative freedom and given an opportunity to speak through his emotional-intellectual attitudes and his states of being. Plays such as Ionesco's *A Maid to Marry* reduce the actor to absolute puppetry and enslave him interpretatively to the author's ideas in a way that he was never bound in realism to the imitation of life.[10]

The question of intelligibility referred to earlier is one which is further complicated by a popular concern amongst the absurdist playwrights: their distrust of language. Believing as they do that man's powers of perception, expression, and self-identification are pathetically limited by the fact of his individualistic perspective of anything and everything, it is only natural that they should question our means of communication. They are not inspecting semantic phenomena as semanticists. Rather, they are defining the gulf of misunderstanding that exists between our desire and our definition of it, between our expression of ourselves and its apprehension by others. This certainly is a dramatic concern, but the absurdist expresses the problem by forcing his language to nonsense. This device when added to the absurdist's general tendency to express himself in allegorical and expressionistic symbols, simply increases the difficulty of understanding their plays. The number of people who have difficulty catching secondary dialogue in the works of Chekhov [11] is surprising; one can well imagine their difficulty when confronted by something like *The Bald Soprano*.[12]

There is another important generalization that can be made about the absurdists: they are, almost without exception, ironic proselytizers. Their picture of the human condition, reasonable though it is, is not a very popular view. If it was clearly put in readily identifiable language, the majority of their audience would find the absurdist's view to be nihilistic. They would simply say, "Oh no! How dreary! That's all wrong!" and then make a mental note never to see another play by that horrible author! Yet a confrontation with the absurdity of one's condition is an inescapable prerequisite if one hopes to live sanely, that is to say, reasonably. How then to administer this view to an audience optimistically rooted in the certainty of faith—be it in God, or culture, or even in the potency of their own individuality? The answer is simple: pretend to give them something else. Make the play as amusing and sensational and surprising as possible *but* bury the message in symbols. Get the audience to swallow the comedy-coated pill of absurdity by letting them believe it as all harmless comedy or sensationalism. This ironic approach to life and dramatic action is justified rhetorically since most of the audience find it difficult to equate the farcical cavorting with anything as disturbing as absurdity. Furthermore, this approach is also justified thematically since the absurdist thinks of life in the light of a tragic joke or comic tragedy.

On the negative side of the critical ledger of absurdist drama we find that these plays are no longer thought of as the drama of the future. Absurdist drama is, in fact, dated. It is now *the* fad across the country and is imitated by an alarming number of young student playwrights in our colleges. Somewhat like boogie woogie, absurdist drama has become the vogue with the neophyte at precisely the moment when its creators indicate that they are beginning to tire of their creation. Adamov now writes quite conventional social realism à la Brecht. Ionesco has moved steadily toward longer, more psychological plays. Only the slow-writing Beckett has remained more or less faithful to his original pattern . . . perhaps because his works, more than any other absurdist's, were rich intellectually and experientially to begin with. It is no accident that some of the young writers in the absurdist camp, such as Pinter and Albee, have chosen to write in a far more realistic vein than did the first masters of the form. It is quite easy to write a realistic allegory of the absurdist statement, and furthermore it accomplishes some, if not all, of the intents of the original absurdists without resorting to tedious expressionistic symbols. Audiences who have the thematic key to the play can understand it as readily as they understood the earlier works. Audiences who don't have the key to the absurdist code are nonetheless given greater opportunity for empathic or emotional response to the drama.

One of the so-called advantages of the expressionistic control in absurdist drama is its power to alienate the audience, keeping it alive to the ideological byplay of the symbols. Esslin, correctly enough, says that the absurdists have succeeded in achieving this alienation effect more completely than its so-called inventor, Bertolt Brecht.[13] Beholding an action that is symbolic, the sequence of which is determined ideologically rather than psychologically and representationally, the spectator is supposed to have no recourse but to remain objective and analytical. But I have watched audiences ignorant of Mr. Esslin's assertion sit delightedly through *Waiting for Godot*, laughing as uncritically as though they were watching the Keystone Cops. The alienation-effect works beautifully in Brecht's plays where it is needed: a representational action is interrupted or qualified by all manner of presentational devices in order to draw the audience's attention to the ideological issues of the play. Alienation in absurdist drama is often, though not always, an effect incompatible with the play itself. If, for example, the author has rejected a linear approach to his plot, as well as psychological reality, the sequential structure of his theme—if, in effect, he is asking us to do a line-by-line, gesture-by-gesture analysis of his play in the manner of modern or new criticism—then the theatre is not the place for him.

He should be content with the printed page. The cerebration demanded by such plays, and Beckett is the worst offender, is no longer a question of theatrical response, but of scholarly industry. The alienation-effect is justified when you provide the audience with an abundance of emotional representational action to be distanced, as it were, in order more clearly to perceive its meaning. It seems cruel, if nothing else, to confuse an audience to such an extent that the only way they have of saving face is to laugh uproariously at what they mistakenly presume to be sheer nonsense.

Working with allegorico-expressionistic devices, the absurdists demand of their audiences a skill in symbolic thought that they do not possess. In fact, if there is one major deficiency in our ability to perceive drama on the stage (as opposed to drama on the printed page) it is a lack of skill in interpreting symbolic action.[11] We must commend any effort to strengthen our ability in this interpretative function. On the other hand, this predisposition toward a totally symbolic drama demands of the absurdists that they themselves be masters of the symbol. Some of them are not. The most notable example of symbolic bungling in the canon of absurdist masterworks is the end of *The Chairs*. Why, having gone to great lengths to establish the emptiness of the illusion of the oldsters, must Ionesco bring on that claptrap figure of the Orator? Why not let the old couple introduce a nonexistent orator, and allow the audience to sit facing the empty chairs until they realize the play is finished and that the emptiness of the stage is a symbol, an idea made concrete? The Orator completely negates the allegorical frame of the play. Not long ago I had occasion to meet Arrabal and I questioned him about his *Automobile Graveyard*. I wondered why the figures of the mother and her athlete son so clearly established in the first part of the play emerge in the last portion of the play as policemen. I had several explanations, none of which completely satisfied me. Arrabal shrugged and answered succinctly enough, "Because I needed policemen." I suggest that this is puerile writing.

Another danger that grows out of this density of symbols is that it makes it difficult to identify a sound work from a fraudulent one, the serious play from the spoof. If I'm not mistaken, Mr. Kopit meant *Oh Dad, Poor Dad, Mamma's Hung You in the Closet and I'm Feelin' So Sad* to be something of a parody of absurdist drama. Upon close inspection I find this play every bit as sound as many seriously recognized pieces in the absurdist field. Like jazz, or any other extreme artistic expression, absurdist drama will not bear parody, for the parodies often appear as good as the work parodied. I have also been amused by the ease with which my beginning playwriting students can ingeniously concoct plots that would pass for a good absurdist action. The plain truth of the matter is that writing an acceptable absurdist play is not difficult at all.

One of the dilemmas most frequently encountered by the absurdist is the problem of overcoming the boredom of depicting monotony. This is really a new problem to the theatre. Even in the works of Chekhov the problem depicted is boredom, not monotony. Any playwright of moderate sensitivity can make boredom dramatic if he focuses upon the agony and irritation of the person who endures it. Monotony, on the other hand, is altogether a different problem. As used by the absurdists, it is not a term which connotes an emotional response; it is, rather, a philosophical assessment, the absurdist assessment of the value of all action. All value in life must logically be predicated from the point of view of the individual and is, therefore, more a question of individualistic bias imperfectly formed than it is a question of abstract truth. This assessment *does not deny absolute truths*—it simply states that no human being's vital response to a truth is utterly comparable to another's. From a reasonable point of view—that is to say, from the vantage point of abstract thought that allows one to compare the values of the individual against the standards of the absolute truth—all action, all value, all hope is absurd because it is imperfect, transitory, or illusory. This absurd pronouncement reduces all actions to a hypothetical monotony of value. Running for president and running to the bathroom, loving and hating, killing and curing, striving and drifting, believing and not believing—when assessed from an individualistic and experiential view, are all reduced to the same plane, since no single action is worth more than the next, except in so far as that imperfect, perishable, and only partly reasonable figure, man, chooses to believe that it is. The rational hierarchy of ideals is leveled flat by the subjectivity of their employment in the life of the individual. This then is the monotony so crucial to the absurdist's statement. He must define the ignorance and impotence that undermine all our choices while at the same time he must point out the ironic distance that exists between our subjective opinion and our assessments of absolute truth. In order to do this he writes from a totally empirical and amoral vantage point. Unfortunately, this concept creates a technical problem in the drama which is singularly difficult, for the absurdist must make his statement comprehensive and, at the same time, demonstrate it in terms of action. The result is the destruction of plot and the boredom of the audience. One tires of the non-dramatic reduction of plot to the level of a dreary catalogue of equivalent actions.[15] Yet if the playwright doesn't demonstrate *an exhaustive variety* of values in the light of absurdity, the audience may justifiably think that the playwright means to attack only one set of values and this, of course, could be interpreted as a non-absurdist affirmation of absolute value. The absurdist is therefore always in dramatic danger of foundering his play on one of the crucial tenets of his theme: the monotony of value. This danger increases as the structure of the play becomes more simple and shallow. For these reasons Ionesco always appears to write plays that are half again as long as they should be.[16] Monotony of the sort described is often expressed by repetition of gestures and situations, time and time and time again within the course of one play (note the shoe and hat business of *Waiting for Godot.*) This creates a terrible problem for the actors and directors of the plays, for too bald a representation of this repetition is a sure way of being thematically clear, yet dramatically boring.

Again the most important thing that can be said against the practice of the absurdists is not primarily technical in its nature. One can accuse a good number of these playwrights of failing to extend their role of philosopher-playwright beyond the initial confrontation and definition of absurdity. If, as Kierkegaard says, "Authorship is and ought to be a serious calling implying an appropriate mode of personal existence. . . ."[17] and, if I am just in describing the absurdists as ironic proselytizers, then I am free to criticize their didactic intentions. Time and time again absurdist plays carp at us that the human condition is absurd, as though the confrontation of absurdity were some sort of agonizing process that paralyzed our ability to act, that corroded our will, destroyed our hope, and sapped our imagination of all vigor. Granted, one's realization of absurdity is a terrible thing, but if this realization doesn't shock us into suicide we do go on living. We write plays, we build bridges, we run for public office, we fall in love, we raise families, we may even become religious! *Granted, no action we take after this confrontation or realization will be enacted with naïve and implicit faith in its existential rewards of definition and permanence.* The realization of absurdity makes ironists of all of us who undergo it and continue to live in action—but note that it is enlightened action in the sense that the action of Oepidus is enlightened once he has blinded himself to the optimistic vanities of man. One may even love God through disillusion! It was Unamuno who believed that the true saint was the man tortured by his inability to believe in God.[18]

Generally, absurdist writers with the notable exception of Beckett and a few of the younger hybrid absurdists such as Mortimer, fail to give us a picture of man living beyond his confrontation with the abyss of ignorance and impotence. Even Beckett has a way of presenting this action in a particularly depressing and dreary light, as though all life after the confrontation suffered from a spiritual and emotional leukemia. Most of the absurdist writers limit their plays to dramatic definitions of absurdity or to depicting the plight of the immediate or naïve man who entertains illusions of power and definition without knowing that he is absurd. Having written one or two such plays, an author should at least begin to prepare himself to write about the engaged man who has sought to live actively in the knowledge of his own absurdity. Failing to develop in this direction casts the playwright in the unsavory role of a gloating harpy that delights in the misery of others—*for notice that the absurdist playwright is already engaged in the game of value by the very fact of his playwriting.* This strain of sentimentality and sadism is evident in the absurdists' fondness for images of man's impotent degradation. There was a time when I found these images startling and sensational but I have now wearied of them. I have developed an aesthetic allergy to men who gobble bananas, men who vomit, figures who have difficulty excreting or urinating, bums, perverts, human beings who are phenomenally unclean, bloody handkerchiefs, smelly feet, and climactic scenes of castration. I am so irritated with this sentimental ghoulishness that I have begun to make ironic parodies of it within the context of my own plays.

As I suggested earlier it is virtually impossible to generalize effectively about the absurdists of today because of the divergence of technique and contrast of interest that exist between one author and the next. Obviously no one virtue or flaw that I have alluded to is applicable to all absurdists. I have tried to cull out the main values in the thought and practice of those absurdists that write a more or less allegorical and expressionistic drama. It is my conviction that absurdity is best expressed in representational drama. Absurdity is a significant fact of life as we live it. It loses its impact in a "world" where women have three noses and people live buried in the sand or in garbage pails. Absurdity is something which is inextricably fused to our process of living! Absurdity as a theme is best served then, by the representational playwright. However, the title of *absurdist* has fallen not upon the men who state it best but upon those who have chosen to express it through the allegorical-expressionistic mode. I have avoided, therefore, reference to the plays of writers who have retained an allegiance to the conventions of representational drama such as O'Neill, Sartre, Brecht, Camus, Ghelderode, etc.

It was my original intention simply to state some of the significant virtues and flaws of that rather controversial group of playwrights founded by the awesome three. However, I now find my initial intent somewhat unsatisfactory. If there is any value to an aesthetic approach in the instance of absurdist drama, it lies in the freedom afforded me to correlate the artistic practice of the absurdist with the content of his plays, and, in turn, with the impact of these plays upon the mind of the beholder. I know of no better way to do this and, as it happens, to conclude this essay, than to give you what I consider to be a definition of the ideal absurdist playwright of the allegorical-expressionistic inclination.

The absurdist as a thinker: This man is convinced of the absurdity of the human condition. He is, therefore, certain of his own absurdity. He believes that a recognition of absurdity is essential in order for one to live a life of reasonable expectation and vital responsibility. He believes that without this recognition man is a puppet dangled on the strings of dogma and illusion. He knows that absurdity is a bitter discovery for all men, but believes that it is the only assessment which will accurately define man's power of perception, action, and accomplishment. Absurdity is, ironically enough, the only ground upon which man's reason can stand secure.

The absurdist as a social force: This man tries to awaken his audience to the logical conclusion of absurdity. He does this, not to attract notoriety, but for the good of his audience. Knowing that the greater portion of his audience is not in sympathy with his assessment of the human condition, he cannot assault their convictions with jeremiads. Such an approach would prompt his audience to brand him as a nihilistic crank. He knows that their illusion of optimistic attunement can never be destroyed directly, that only by indirect means can he successfully dispel this illusion. A direct assault only strengthens his audience in their optimistic conviction. He must know, as Kierkegaard knew, that in order to help his audience effectively, he must understand more than they—yet first of all, surely, he must understand what they understand.[19] He must present his audience with the need to confront the absurdity of their own existence in order that they may no longer be unnecessarily vulnerable to the vicissitudes of life. He must eventually show them the reasonable advantages of absurd living in order that they may be induced to leave their nests of dogma, illusion and superstition. In short, he illustrates for the audience the unbreakable relationship of reason to courage in the face of ignorance.

The absurdist as a technician: This playwright has one major technical criterion: he will choose those devices that allow him to express his ideas and his intent indirectly. Until his audience becomes an absurdist one he must continue to use the devices of indirect communication, be they those of expressionism, allegory or irony. If he discards these three modes of expression, he will no longer be an absurdist, in our conventional use of the word; he will simply become a tragedian or a farceur. He may write representationally only if he maintains a strong allegorical or ironic control over his material. His major dilemma will be one of maintaining the dramatic temperature of his plays. He must never let the symbols or the thematic density of his play dampen his philosophical and social purposes. His drama must *induce* or *shock* a philosophical response from the audience— it must never openly demand such a response. In the light of these statements, we can say that the absurdist playwright will seek a form and style which, first of all, act as a disguise of his assertions rather than a direct and compatible expression of them. Yet this stylistic and structural disguise must never be so complete as to make it unnecessarily difficult for the audience to chance upon the proper perspective of interpretation that will reveal the true contour of the playwright's thought. Finally, the ideal absurdist will never present his views in symbols and action which connote that the confrontation with absurdity is a nihilistic experience. If he does this he becomes guilty of entrenching the uninitiated in their conviction that absurdists are nothing more or less than a pack of exhibitionistic misanthropes. A playwright guilty of this error will have defeated aesthetically his philosophical posture as an absurdist, by unwittingly revealing to his audience the fact that he is unable to accept and espouse the irony of the view he advocates.

NOTES

1. Martin Esslin, *The Theatre of the Absurd*, (New York, 1961).
2. Richard Coe, *Eugene Ionesco*, (Edinburgh, Scotland, 1961).
3. Early in his work Martin Esslin makes the stylistic division between the absurdist and the representationalist, "This sense of the metaphysical anguish at the absurdity of the human condition is, broadly speaking, the theme of the plays of Beckett, Adamov, Ionesco, Genet, and the other writers discussed in this book. But it is not merely the subject matter that defines what is here called the Theatre of the Absurd. A similar sense of the senselessness of life, of the inevitable devaluation of ideals, purity, and purpose, is also the theme of much of the work of dramatists like Giraudoux, Anouilh, Salacrou, Sartre, and Camus himself. Yet these writers differ from the dramatists of the Absurd in an important respect: they present their sense of the irrationality of the human condition in the form of highly lucid and logically constructed reasoning, while the Theatre of the Absurd strives to express its sense of the senselessness of the human condition and the inadequacy of the rational approach by the open abandonment of rational devices and discursive thought. While Sartre or Camus express the new content in the old convention, the Theatre of the Absurd goes a step further in trying to achieve a unity between its basic assumptions and the form in which these are expressed. In some senses, the *theatre* of Sartre and Camus is less adequate as an expression of the *philosophy* of Sartre and Camus—in artistic, as distinct from philosophic, terms—than the Theatre of the Absurd." Esslin, pp. xix–xx.
4. The most brilliant definition of absurdity is Albert Camus' *The Myth of Sisyphus* (New York, 1959).

   One of the most moving statements of absurdity in dramatic literature is found in the last long speech of the father's in Fernando de Rojas' *La Celestina*, published in *The Classic Theatre*, Vol. III, ed. Eric Bentley, trans. James Mabbe (New York, 1959); or, Rojas, *La Celestina* (Buenos Aires, Argentina, 1938).
5. One of the best essays on the interrelationship of farce and tragedy: Wylie Sypher, "The Meanings of Comedy," in *Comedy*, ed. Wylie Sypher (New York, 1956).
6. For interesting references to absurdist premises in the tragedy of Euripides, see: William Arrowsmith, "The Criticism of Greek Tragedy" (*Tulane Drama Review*, New Orleans, March, 1959).
7. José Ortega y Gasset, *The Dehumanization of Art* (New York); also Ortega y Gasset, *The Modern Theme* (New York, 1961).
8. Arrabal has written a play, *Orchestration Théâtrale*, in which "he has tried to create a dramatic spectacle consisting entirely of the movements of abstract three-dimensional shapes, some of which were mechanical

devices, while others were moved by dancers. The formal world of this strange spectacle was based on the inventions of Klee, Mondrian, Delauney, and the mobiles of Alexander Calder," Esslin, p. 190.

9. Esslin makes several references to the initial approach to the drama experienced by Adamov, Beckett, and Ionesco. On page 1 we have a quote from *Murphy* which neatly sums up Beckett's antagonism to realism. Adamov's original purgative and chimerical approach to the drama is indicated in his fondness for Strindberg's dream plays. See page 56. Ionesco is quoted amply throughout the Esslin book, but on page 87 we find a statement in which Ionesco reveals the embarrassment aroused in him by representational drama. However, on page 91 we find another quotation from Ionesco in which we are given a glimpse of the delightfully frightening sensation he experienced when he realized that he had, finally and in turn, become the puppeteer. Esslin, p. 1; p. 56; p. 87; p. 91.

10. This presentational, thematic and symbolic determination of character has another major aesthetic limitation: it does not produce memorable figures; it creates, at best, naïve or gauche archetypes. Memorable figures such as Don Juan, Quixote, Hamlet, Oedipus, Medea, Lear, Falstaff, Sancho, are composed of highly specific and unique qualities which are fused with almost eternal norms of human behavior. The norms would be dull and unpalatable without the particularizing eccentricities of the individual. By and large absurdists provide the actor with the normative pattern and expect him to supply what little particularization is needed from his own (the actor's) being.

11. In this connection it is interesting to note Adamov's excitement at what he thought was a new technical discovery in the theatre. Some time later Adamov realized that his so-called discovery was nothing more nor less than the tried and true device of secondary dialogue. This rather amusing incident is another indication of the dramaturgical inexperience of some of the most prominent absurdists. Esslin, p. 56.

12. The absurdist distrust of language as an instrument of definition extends to the point where Esslin says of Beckett's use of language, "Where there is no certainty, there can be no definite meanings—and the impossibility of ever attaining certainty is one of the main themes of Beckett's plays." (p. 44).

Again, with regard to Beckett's language, Mr. Esslin quotes *Murphy*: "When we hear Beckett's characters using language, we often feel like Celia when she was talking to Murphy; '. . . spattered with words that went dead as soon as they sounded; each word obliterated, before it had time to make sense by the word that came next; so that in the end she did not know what had been said.' . . . And in fact the dialogue in Beckett's plays is often built on the principle that each line obliterates what was said in the previous line." (p. 43).

This distrust of the communicative efficacy of language may be one of the strongest factors in predisposing the absurdists to employ or rely upon physical action to a degree seldom before known in the drama. Some, notably Beckett, have written exercises in pure mime. Esslin, p. 44; p. 43.

13. Esslin, "The Theatre of the Absurd" (*Tulane Drama Review*, New Orleans, Summer, 1960), p. 5.

14. "The twentieth century may be the heir of all the ages, but so far as literary criticism goes it has preferred not to use all of its inheritance. . . . I. A. Richards has observed that a characteristic of plays during the Elizabethan age was the 'possibility of being enjoyed at many levels.' T. S. Eliot is more explicit about such 'levels of significance' when he explains that, in a mature play, 'For the simplest auditors there is the plot, for the more thoughtful the character and conflict of character, for the more literary the words and phrasing, for the more musically sensitive the rhythm, and for auditors of greater sensitiveness and understanding a meaning which reveals itself gradually. . . .' If it is true, as R. P. Blackmur claims, that the modern audience badly needs instruction in the 'lost skill of symbolic thinking'—and it seems true —then one crucial problem for modern criticism will continue to be what it has been since Coleridge's time: to re-educate modern readers in the ways metaphor works. Thus far, the larger audience has gained little of its lost skill, and an interest in metaphorical language has been confined to coteries of scholars, critics, and other unacknowledged legislators." Edward B. Partridge, *The Broken Compass* (New York, 1958), pp. 37–38.

Mr. Partridge's views apply largely to metaphorical language, but, if one is sufficiently mature in one's theatre experience, it is possible to apply his comments with even more vigor to the understanding of what I call "gestural metaphor" or "action metaphor"—a metaphor constructed not only out of words but deeds, situation, and character as well. Our ability to understand drama on this level is perhaps lamentably limited to the expert.

15. One of the most striking examples of this philosophically engendered boredom is the response evinced by the recent French film, *Breathless*, in which we witness assault, robbery, sex, pursuits, betrayal, and murder. These actions are so presented as to emphasize their monochromatic values. The movie leaves one not breathless with excitement but with boredom—a boredom which is the more singular since it grows out of an action that one might readily mistake for a cops-and-robbers film.

16. Next to its ending, the most distressing aspect of *The Chairs* is the naïveté of its structure. The play is little more than a catalogue of values undermined by the irony of absurdity. This catalogue of values is thoroughly compiled and makes the play excessively long. The actors

and directors who attempt this piece find little sequential intricacy with which to engage the audience's interest. They are forced, therefore, to rely almost entirely on virtuoso acting. Even the best productions of the play tend to stretch the audience interest until, like a piece of chewing gum, it begins to sag of its own weight.

17. Sören Kierkegaard, *The Point of View for My Work as an Author* (New York, 1962), p. 44.

18. Migual de Unamuno, *Saint Emmanuel the Good Martyr* in *Abel Sanchez* (Chicago, 1956).

19. Kierkegaard, p. 27.

S. BEYNON JOHN

Obsession and Technique in the Plays of Jean Anouilh

Obsession supplies the motive power of Jean Anouilh's plays. It is a creative obsession since it invents, and successfully imposes on the public, a fictional world, coherent in itself and characterized by a distinctive vision, sensibility and idiom. The real power of such an obsession is inseparable from the imaginative form in which it has been cast. If it is impressive, it is because of a total *aesthetic* effect. The animating ideas in Anouilh's drama are feeble enough once they are divided from their peculiar dramatic form, but, communicated through that form, they hold the attention and involve the emotions in a singularly compelling fashion.

Anouilh's plays do not reflect reality in the sense of fidelity to the detail of common, everyday experience. They do not attempt an explanation of human motive in terms of psychological realism or involve themselves in the social problem. They express instead a significant distortion of reality, a distortion conveyed through extremely stylized dramatic conventions. Much has been written about Anouilh's obsession with purity, but what has been neglected is the way in which this obsession acts as a unifying and organizing principle in his work, determining the structure of his plays and

Reprinted from *French Studies* (XI, 2), by permission of the author and the publisher.

intimately related to the character of the dramatic conventions which he exploits.

Some analysis of the nature and force of this notion of purity will help to illuminate its dramatic function. The claims of purity are at their most absolute in the earliest plays and, though they are expressed in accents that reveal a spontaneous and lived experience, they establish from the outset a false and stagey antithesis between absolute purity and absolute corruption which recalls the sensibility of Jansenism.[1] In Anouilh's drama one of the most characteristic acts of his heroes is their rejection of society. Significantly, his heroes and heroines live a sort of marginal existence. They are rarely engaged in any purposive or connected work and, if they pursue a trade or profession at all, it is usually casual and precarious. Thus Thérèse of *La Sauvage* plays in a shabby and insecure café orchestra; Orphée, the hero of *Eurydice*, is an itinerant musician, little different from the buskers of theatre queues; Gaston, the amnesic ex-soldier of *Le Voyageur sans bagages*, by the very fact of his amnesia, inhabits a social vacuum; Jeannette, the fey creature of *Roméo et Jeannette*, lives as wild as a bird. Medea in her gipsy caravan represents their most extreme type, since she is endlessly in exile.

This lack of vital contact with normal society, this absence of social density in his heroes, makes Anouilh's drama essentially a-social. Anouilh implies no faith and little interest in social relations as such. The mark of his heroes is to live in that austere solitude to which their own intransigent standards condemn them. Social ties and obligations are nowhere envisaged by his heroes and heroines as offering the possibility of a larger and richer life. They are conceived exclusively as sources of contamination and corruption. Anouilh's outbursts against the rich and his passionate sympathy for the poor are not the pleas of the reformer anxious to change society. Social satire implies some belief in the value of society, at least of a society purged of abuses, and some insight into the nature and sources of social conflict. Anouilh conspicuously lacks any such social grasp and so his bitter satirical portraits of the aristocracy are moral rather than social in content. Anouilh fails to realize the Duchess, in *L'Hermine*, or Lady Hurf, in *Le Bal des Voleurs*, as social types. Rather they represent the quintessence of arrogance, callous frivolity and insincerity. They are caricatures of their own moral failings. In the same way, all the references to poverty are fierce because they spring from the experiences of humiliation and human estrangement, rather than because they are related to notions of social utility or reorganization. Thérèse's protest against poverty touches on religious sensibility, but without, in any sense, springing from religious conviction. In her reference to poverty as "ce manteau saignant," she exploits a language close to the devotional. She speaks like an avenging angel of the poor, with a savage indignation that recalls Léon Bloy: "Je me sens grosse ce soir de toute la peine qui a dû serrer, depuis toujours, le cœur des pauvres quand ils se sont aperçu que les gens heureux ne savaient rien, qu'il n'y avait pas d'espoir qu'un jour ils sachent!" [2]

How uncertain is the social aim of these attacks upon privilege may be gauged from the ambiguous rôle played by money in Anouilh's drama. Money is mainly envisaged as the symbol of society's corruption. Those who possess great wealth—the Duchesse de Granat or Messerchmann, the fabulous financier of L'Invitation au Château, for example—are usually odious or lamentable. The sterility of money is caricatured in that feverish and oddly pathetic scene when Messerchmann and Isabelle make confetti of thousands of francs, watching the pieces flutter down, with an initial joy that soon gives place to a sense of exhaustion and futility. But, if too much money corrupts the rich, too little helps to degrade the poor. The free and willed acceptance of poverty is rare and heroic. Thus, the repudiation of money, implied in Thérèse's rejection of Florent in La Sauvage, attains a moral grandeur that is almost unique in Anouilh's plays. Involuntary poverty, on the other hand—the condition of Thérèse's parents or of Orphée's father—is responsible for a whole gallery of pitiable, vulgar and abject characters. The scene between Isabelle and Messerchmann has its counterpart in that ugly scramble which Florent provokes in La Sauvage when he gaily scatters his money on the café floor before the avid and horrified eyes of Thérèse's parents. The last twist of irony here is brilliantly supplied when Thérèse too joins in the scuffle to recover the money and so symbolizes in a single painful moment the gulf which divides her from Florent's world.

Even more remarkable as evidence of the essentially a-social character of Anouilh's attitude to money are the reactions of the young lover, Frantz, in L'Hermine (1931), the dramatist's earliest success.[3] Frantz wishes to marry Monime whom he loves devotedly. The marriage is impossible since he is too poor to be able to take Monime away without the consent of her aunt, the Duchesse de Granat, a sour and egotistical tyrant, who controls Monime's fortune and does not intend to permit any misalliance with Frantz, originally her doctor's son. Frantz is humiliated but he rejects any notion of love in a cottage with Monime. Wealth alone can secure for the lovers a privileged sanctuary against the corrupt and degrading influences of society. It alone can protect them from the "contagion of the world's slow stain." Frantz insists: "Mon amour est une chose trop belle, j'attends trop de lui pour risquer qu'elle le salisse, lui aussi. Je veux l'entourer d'une barrière d'argent." [4] This alone will keep love "immaculate." Subsequently, Frantz batters the Duchess to death in circumstances that seem peculiarly gratuitous since they occur *after* he has received a telegram from the American business-man, Bentz, assuring him of a modest but adequate income. He then justifies his action, and his willingness to implicate an innocent and idiot servant, by declaring that the Duchess's death was the "prix exact" of the young lovers' purity. Such an explanation lends all the colour of pagan sacrifice to his act. It is as if he suggested an almost supernatural relationship between the Duchess's wealth, her blood and the purity of the lovers. The whole episode, unique in Anouilh's drama, is an extreme illustration of his intense reactions to money. Money is not the economists' cash-nexus, not the drab symbol of economic functions. It is an animating and theatrical spirit: "Pour Anouilh, l'argent n'est pas une chose, un bien qu'on peut utiliser à son gré; c'est un mythe, une idole dont on ne se rend jamais maître, dont on ne possède que les signes." [5] Money, then, tends to elude judgments based on social utility or social justice, and this is true in spite of the spontaneity of Anouilh's revolt against poverty. The absolute power of money emphasizes the dichotomy Anouilh tends to establish between his heroes and the debased society which contains them; between moral man and immoral society. That is why he occasionally sounds like a Rousseau of the *boulevards* and why his caricatures of the aristocracy suggest that, if all society corrupts, high society corrupts absolutely.

If, however, Frantz's crime hints at an almost superstitious view of the power of money, his defence implies a justification which draws its force from the nature of the love which unites Frantz and Monime. This love, the property of heroes, is inseparable from the notion of purity, of which it offers the highest expression. Such a love is rare, rare enough for those who experience it to constitute the Elect. M. Henri in *Eurydice* hits off their distinctive qualities in an ironical speech: "Mon cher, il y a deux races d'êtres. Une race nombreuse, féconde, heureuse, une grosse pâte à pétrir, qui mange son saucisson, fait ses enfants, pousse ses outils, compte ses sous, bon an mal an, malgré les épidémies et les guerres, jusqu'à la limite d'âge; des gens pour vivre, des gens pour tous les jours, des gens qu'on n'imagine pas morts. Et puis il y a les autres, les nobles, les héros." [6] The distinction is almost Racinian. In French classical tragedy, the birth and station of the main protagonists exempted them from vulgar cares, set a distance between them and normal society, afforded them a purer and more intense emotional life. In Anouilh, the almost hypnotic virtues of money are intended to produce similar conditions for the lovers. They justify this desperate stratagem, so flagrantly in contradiction with the general spirit of Anouilh's attack on money, precisely because they *are* the Elect and touched with the special grace of a love that is the embodiment of purity. That love is a state of grace is not too extravagant a claim to make for it. Frantz can declare, with proper humility: "Mon amour est imparfait, mais je sens tout près, *dans l'invisible*, un autre amour *aux ailes immenses* qui sera peut-être à moi si je sais le mériter." [7] The imagery faithfully reflects a profane theology and is consistent with the language employed elsewhere by Lady Hurf, a very different character: "Ma petite Juliette, elle, *sera sauvée* parce qu'elle est romanesque et simple. C'est une *grâce* qui n'est pas donnée à toutes." [8]

Purity involves sincerity and the cult of sincerity in Anouilh is not without its embarrassments. It tends to assume that sincerity is enough, irrespective of its objects and this leads, almost inevitably, to a confusion between sincerity and truth. Even so, the passion for sincerity creates some of the most moving and compelling scenes in Anouilh's plays. All his heroes and heroines manifest in their pure love a profound need for *authenticity* (to borrow the now fashionable expression of the existentialists). Like Sartre, Anouilh conducts an endless guerrilla campaign against self-deception and the social shams in which it so often reveals itself. The long effort towards sincerity shapes the course of a number of his plays. It informs the charming trifle, *Cécile ou L'École des Pères* (1949), in which each of the characters indulges in the social comedy as a sort of defensive strategy. Each assumes a conventional mask, appropriate verbal forms and gestures and each is revealed in his true nature only after a protracted process of unmasking. Their failure to realize their true potentialities is expressed neatly by Monsieur Orlas: "Parce que je suis votre père et que vous êtes ma fille, nous nous croyons obligés l'un et l'autre de jouer des rôles tout faits." [9] The same struggle, more painfully realized, determines the development of *Colombe* (1950). Julien pursues sincerity at any cost and is driven to expose his young wife, Colombe, in the artifices she has adopted out of love for him. Essentially a-moral and pleasure-loving, she has assumed the more rigorous and pure character Julien has imposed upon her, only to discard it when his absence allows her opportunities to develop freely. Similarly, in *Eurydice*, the supernatural encounter in Act III between Orphée and the 'dead' Eurydice is the culminating and crucial point in their attempts to reach the bed-rock of sincerity. Orphée desperately needs to achieve an authentic relationship with Eurydice, beyond all deception and reticence. He feels he can only test the truth of her answers by looking into her eyes. Thus the rage for absolute sincerity breaks the supernatural pact which would have restored Eurydice to life.

There is something terrible about love conceived in terms of such moral rigour and it is significant that the chosen lovers who commit themselves to purity at its highest tension and pursue it to its logical end reach the final impasse of death. Orphée joins Eurydice in death; Hémon follows the immured Antigone; the tide rises and swallows up both Frédéric and Jeannette. Anouilh's Elect share in common the experience of suffering. There is no election without suffering. The capacity to suffer also distinguishes those lovers, equally committed to purity and to the total gift of self, who renounce the possibility of realizing their love at the moment it falls within their grasp. Marc, in *Jézabel* (1932), rejects the devotion offered by Jacqueline; Thérèse walks out of Florent's life as his music floods effortless, beautiful, assured into the room. What animates these striking examples of abnegation? It is a feeling of responsibility for others, an obscure but powerful sense of human solidarity that will not allow these characters to reach out for the fulfilment of their love. The need for absolute purity and sincerity passes over into a sort of *charity* that owes nothing to belief in a loving and merciful God. They choose to suffer *with* others because they have suffered themselves. Thus Marc rejects Jacqueline, even though he expected to find in her love mitigation of this burden of responsibility for others: "Parce que c'est elle qui m'a montré pour la première fois qu'on pouvait se reposer sur une épaule, qu'on pouvait ne pas être obligé de toujours sauver les autres. Penser aux autres." [10] In rejecting her, he also refuses any escape from responsibility.

It is idle here to insist, as some critics have done, that Anouilh is a Catholic in spite of himself. In fact, Anouilh's is a drama from which God is conspicuously absent. If he does appear, it is as an ironic afterthought. Lucien is the first of Anouilh's characters to enter into a spirited and ironical combat with God, but he regards Him (in *Roméo et Jeannette*) as a malignant and unappeasable God of wrath who nods occasionally while men cheat.

We have now examined the range and implications of Anouilh's obsession with purity and the complex of ideas and sentiments which crystallize about it. These, taken together, attract their opposites by a sort of moral pull and it is in the system of attractions and repulsions thus created that the recurring pattern of Anouilh's plays is to be found. This whole system is, however, governed by Anouilh's profound need to show that the thirst for purity is a doomed passion.

The passion for purity moves in almost ritual phases to its predestined defeat. These phases, obvious enough in Anouilh's serious plays, tend to become blurred and confused under the play of fancy which marks his fantasies, though, even here, they can be glimpsed at critical moments.

The first stage in this unfolding pattern of fatality is the evocation of the world in all its vulgarity and corruption. *L'Hermine*, for instance, opens with a barely concealed duel between the moral absolutism of Frantz and the sceptical materialism of Bentz. The dominant note is one of cynicism, and this is intensified when Mrs. Bentz's offer to intercede with her husband on Frantz's behalf is revealed to be prompted by the desire for a promiscuous *affaire* with the young idealist. *La Sauvage* not only opens against the background of seedy café life, but soon plunges us into the squalid detail of the relationship which exists between Gosta and Madame Tarde.

Into this desert of waste and shame, which Anouilh creates with a sort of fascinated loathing, there enter the "ill-starred" lovers—the cliché is peculiarly appropriate to his intentions. Occasionally, as with Frantz and Monime, each lover is a chosen exemplar of the rage for purity, each endowed equally with the grace of love. More often, the moral capacities of the lovers are very disparate. Thérèse's agony of mind has no counterpart in Florent's effortless mastery of life. Orphée's struggle to establish the conditions of purity evokes a fitful and rather bewildered response in Eurydice. Julien's austere mission to live without compromise fills Colombe with blank misgiving. Yet, however disparate, the lovers always represent the possibility of redeeming the cowardice and corruption of the society which surrounds them.

Between the possibility and the realization, the world intervenes in its opacity, inertia and hostility. Anouilh's Elect now enter the next phase in the ritual: they are subjected to a series of *confrontations*, all of which brutally juxtapose the aspirations of his heroes to the standards of the "normal" world. In their concreteness and particularity, these confrontations represent the negation or the parody of the heroic ambitions nursed by the chosen lovers. The inventiveness, ironical power and savage verve with which Anouilh manages these confrontations give evidence of his immense technical assurance as a dramatist.

The system of confrontations hinges on the play of opposites: past against present, resignation against revolt, happiness against the suffering that comes of recognition of human solidarity, lies and social shams against naked sincerity, promiscuity and vulgar sensuality against fidelity and pure intensity of feeling. The effects created out of this clash of incompatibles are ironical in varying degrees, ranging from the whimsical to the savage. These effects reach their greatest power in the devices of caricature and parody.

The irreversibility of time and the impossibility of redeeming the past are recurring themes in Anouilh's work. On the rare occasions in the plays when a major character successfully escapes from the burden of his own past, the elements of fiction and artificiality are very pronounced. In *Le Voyageur sans bagages*, Gaston's exit with the little Madensale boy is a perfectly gratuitous scene of tender fantasy, quite at variance with the tone and implications of all that has gone before. Similarly, in *Roméo et Jeannette*, Lucien's personal dilemma is resolved on a note that is almost indecently flippant, coming as it does immediately after the drowning of Frédéric and Jeannette. The postman who brings the long-awaited letter that allows Lucien to escape to a new life in Africa is altogether too casual a *deus ex machina*. Usually, however, the potentialities of the present are destroyed by the force of the past.

Thérèse, confronted by her abject and panic-stricken father and by a desperate and pathetic Gosta, realizes that they represent, in their very defects and shame, her own inescapable past. Faced with

these two humiliated creatures, she rejects the happiness proffered
by Florent so as to identify herself with them. Gaston, in spite of his
factitious escape, is at the centre of a series of confrontations between
his uncertain present and his conjectural past. Through the eyes of
the servants, then through the recollections of his family, he is
brought face to face with a past utterly unlike the one he had
imagined for himself in the loneliness of his amnesia. This imaginary
idyllic past, full of friendship, candour and innocent pastoral pleasures is confronted with the detail of his real past: his sadism towards
small creatures, his brutal attack on a childhood friend, his seduction
of a servant-girl and, later, of his brother's wife, his fraud practised
on a respected friend of the family, his estrangement from his
mother. This succession of confrontations is handled with remarkable pace and bite.

The resigned and the unreconciled are constantly brought face to
face in Anouilh's plays. Frantz's revolt against society is set in opposition to his friend Philippe's acceptance of the social norms—as
represented by women, politics, literature. Philippe is half-ashamed
of his involvement in normal society, but feels that resignation and
the acceptance of social responsibility are inevitable. If Philippe is
feeble (judged by Frantz's absolute standards), he is in no sense
ignoble, as are the majority of the apologists for resignation in
Anouilh's drama up to the appearance of *Roméo et Jeannette* (1945)
and *Médée* (1946). Thérèse gives her name to the play because she
is "la sauvage," that is, recalcitrant to the social comedy. For her,
purity is revolt; to be human is to be in revolt. Her most typical
gestures are those of defiance of the compromises and shams of
society. Hence, she tries to prevent her own father from exploiting
Florent's love for her by his attempt to induce the brilliant young
musician to play for a drunken client in the deserted café. Tarde
himself is an abject figure of fun whose characteristic gestures are
those of complicity with all that is most vitiated and false in society.
Thérèse's grand gestures of defiance are juxtaposed to his acts of
shabby buffoonery. It is, of course, Antigone who symbolizes the
most extreme form of revolt and her encounter with Creon represents
the most intense and sustained confrontation between revolt and
resignation that can be found in Anouilh's plays. Anouilh, in fact,
adheres to the form of the Greek myth, as found in Sophocles, but
utterly changes its substance. Removed from its Greek context of
religious piety, belief in a divine law and respect for human law, the

tragedy of Antigone becomes an amputated tragedy. But this is necessarily so since Anouilh is not concerned with the classical values. He
has simply found a vehicle for expressing the *Romantic revolt*. In
Antigone's person, Anouilh seems to envisage disobedience as the
highest moral law. She is moved neither by religious conviction nor
by the need to protest against political tyranny. She revolts against
the world *as it is*—that is to say, in its impurity.

What precipitates Antigone's final spasm of revolt is, significantly,
the prospect of being spared so as to become a candidate for vulgar
happiness. Creon's psychological error, after disarming Antigone of
her conventional arguments, is to evoke the life of social compromise
and humdrum happiness that awaits her, Antigone regains her nerve
and contemptuously dismisses this "sale espoir." In this way, the
play rejoins its forerunners. It sets happiness, the object of vulgar
feeling, against the suffering which is inseparable from the quest for
purity-in-love. It is true that a sort of happiness seems to be intended
for Anouilh's chosen lovers, but its quality is so rigorous as to deserve
the epithet "terrible" which is so frequently applied to it. Happiness
is above all "terrible" because its successful pursuit can only be
achieved at the expense of others or through indifference to them.
Thérèse recognizes this: "Ce qu'il faut, c'est ne jamais penser qu'il
y en a d'autres qui vivent, qui se battent, qui meurent." [11] It is for
these reasons that she rejects happiness: "Vous me dégoûtez tous
avec votre bonheur! On dirait qu'il n'y a que le bonheur sur la terre.
Hé bien, oui, je veux me sauver devant lui. Hé bien, oui, moi, je ne
veux pas me laisser prendre par lui toute vivante. Je veux continuer à
avoir mal et à souffrir, à crier, moi!" [12]. Happiness is almost confined
to fantasy in Anouilh's plays, as *Léocadia* (1939) and *L'Invitation
au Château* (1947) confirm.

The confrontations that are most brilliantly and memorably
handled are those in which sincerity and purity are humiliated. The
disappointed idealist lampoons the world with which he is at odds.

Anouilh's heroes, whether they are the very types of sincerity or
whether they are struggling painfully to achieve it, are frequently
brought face to face with those most admirably realized of his minor
characters: the third-rate repertory actors. Anouilh creates these with
a wealth of just observation and controlled malice. The habit of acting has imperceptibly destroyed their authentic personalities, leaving
behind a bundle of ill-assorted gestures, mannerisms and fragments
of dialogue from plays in which they have appeared. They thus

represent the total dissolution of the ideas of personal integrity and sincerity. They are vivid caricatures of all that is most false and unauthentic in human experience. Lost in factitious rôles, they have become completely dissociated from their real selves. When Robert in *Le Rendez-vous de Senlis* (1937) is attempting to create a synthetic past for himself, he employs a couple of seasoned actors to play the rôles of his mother and father. Mme de Montalembreuse calls upon her long experience of the stage to play before Robert the "perfect mother." She evokes dignity, tenderness, understanding, as Robert supplies her with the background material against which to react. Robert is profoundly impressed and inquires whether she has ever had a similar interview with her own son. Her manner changes abruptly and she reveals herself in all her obtuseness and vulgarity. It is, however, Julien in *Colombe* who is confronted by the most finished example of unauthenticity in his own mother, the celebrated tragic actress, Mme Alexandra. Julien's rage for sincerity is brought up sharply against her endless play-acting. Having farmed out Julien as a child, Mme Alexandra, who sees him rarely, visits him on one occasion only to find him in a condition of shocking neglect. Returning to the theatre the same evening, she plays her current rôle—of a mother who abandons her baby on the steps of a church—with immense effect! Both *Cécile ou L'École des Pères* (1949) and *La Répétition ou L'Amour puni* (1950) are nothing but an extended system of confrontations between sincerity and insincerity, between a desire to achieve an authentic relationship with others and the tendency to adopt the social comedy. Thus, in *La Répétition*, Tigre, the Comtesse, Héro and Villebosse are all engaged in an elegant, alert and perpetual dance before mirrors. For all his cruelty, Horace, in *L'Invitation au Château*, attracts some sympathy when he decides to reveal Isabelle's lowly origins to his assembled guests. His stratagem derives from a double compulsion: to humiliate Diana, whom he loves, but who is engaged to his twin, Frédéric, and also to humiliate his guests by putting a bomb under the social comedy and exposing the falsity of social conventions.

The defeat that Anouilh everywhere implies for pure love gives to his encounters between true love and its parodies or caricatures a corrosive quality. The meeting between Anouilh's chosen lovers touches off the hidden need for purity and fidelity in each. There is a strong undercurrent of puritanism in love as conceived by Anouilh's Elect. The sexual content of their relationship is attenuated. If

Eurydice and Orphée consummate their love in a shabby hotel room, it is only as a necessary prelude to an ill-defined but curiously desexualized relationship: "Comme s'il avait fallu notre lutte et notre nudité sur ce lit en désordre pour que nous devenions vraiment *deux petits frères*." [13] Anouilh's vocabulary is peculiarly significant in this respect. Lovers are constantly recalling moments when they have lost their sexual identity in a common non-sexual tenderness, usually likened to the relationship between brothers or between military comrades ("mon petit soldat"). Disgust of the body pervades *Médée* and is evoked in imagery of almost clinical precision. Medea equates sexual intercourse with the experience of being wounded ("cette blessure que j'implorais"). She speculates nostalgically on the *male* Medea she might have been or seeks to dissociate herself from her sex by objectifying her pudenda. But, in spite of her disgust, she cannot resist the physical. Sexual appetite goads her on to promiscuous relationships. It transcends the personal in the sense that it belongs to the world of nature, the realm of necessity, and rejoins the massive, undifferentiated forces of animal instinct. From this notion, Anouilh obtains some of his most powerful effects, for he sets the pure aspirations of his chosen lovers against the immense and obscene *caricature of sex* that is incarnated in the life of nature. For Anouilh, nature is not the world of vegetal innocence nor are its plants and insects the symbols of harmonious growth. It is the omnipresent caricature of human pretensions over love. Such a conviction animates Lucien's gibe in the face of Frédéric and Jeannette: ". . . c'est la loi depuis toujours, depuis qu'il y a des hommes et des femmes et que l'amour les colle un matin, deux à deux *comme des mouches*." [14] Medea too is intensely aware of the life of nature in its great, instinctive rhythms: "C'est cela qu'ils appellent une nuit calme, les hommes, ce grouillement géant d'accouplements silencieux et de meutres." [15] But the most potent and terrifying confrontation between human love and the activity of nature is created by the half-crazed wife of General Saint-Pé in *Ardèle ou La Marguerite* (1948). This is the more effective in that it is thrust before a household which is wholly involved in love affairs. In particular, Madame Saint-Pé's pathological awareness of the activity of nature brings the young, ardent and idealistic couple, Nathalie and Nicolas, brutally up against a humiliating caricature of their own passion. Madame Saint-Pé raves: "Non, je ne rentrerai pas! Le paon appelle lui aussi. Et les belettes et les blaireaux et les fouines et les renards dans la clairière et les insectes, les millions d'insectes, en silence, partout. Tout jouit et s'accouple et me tue. Je sais quand les fleurs même se détendent soudain et s'entr'ouvrent, obscènes, au petit matin. Tous ignobles, vous êtes tous ignobles, avec votre amour." [16] Nature mocks purity and fidelity.

Pure love is also confronted with its *parodies*. It is brought face to face with the sensibility of café ballads. For example, while Thérèse and Florent embrace, they are discovered by Monsieur and Madame Tarde who accompany this scene with a wealth of winking and nudgings. They confront the young lovers with a gross parody of love. Prince Albert, in *Léocadia*, enters the room at the very moment when Amanda and the butler are mimicking the walk and deportment of his beloved actress. As the notes of Orphée's violin herald the encounter of the predestined lovers, the vulgar sentimentality of Eurydice's mother is given expression in a series of contrapuntal dialogues with Vincent, her lover. The purity and exigency symbolized by the notes of the violin are parodied by the nostalgic recollections of this ridiculous couple. When, at the end of their first encounter, Orphée and Eurydice embrace, there is an immediate transition to a dialogue between Eurydice's mother and her lover which is nothing more than a comic burlesque on all the platitudes of romantic love. But the parody of love with which Orphée is confronted in his own father is infinitely more raw and painful. In Act IV, after Eurydice's death, he has to submit to the recollections of this libidinous old buffoon, who recalls his past conquests, his shabby amours and celebrates the glory of the body by a grotesque spasm of physical jerks.

The opposition between love as purity and love as habit or appetite or vanity is nowhere depicted with more ferocious irony than in the cumulative series of confrontations through which the play *Ardèle* progresses. Ardèle, for whom her aristocratic family have complacently envisaged a spinster's future, has fallen desperately in love with a hunchback of no social standing. Finding her brother, the lecherous General Saint-Pé, totally unsympathetic, she has locked herself in her room, prepared, if necessary, to die for love. She remains unseen and unheard throughout the play and this brilliant device helps Anouilh to establish her as an overriding symbol of absolute purity and devotion. Ranged against this exigent image of love, other versions of love in the family emerge as parodies of it. Ardèle's sister, Liliane, is estranged from her husband, the Count, and has a ridiculous lover in Villardieu. For her, love is vanity; an endless attempt to rediscover her lost youth in the eyes of her lovers. For Villardieu, love is a form of the social comedy and the beloved a form of property. The Count himself, a more lucid and ironic commentator of the situation, is also involved in a highly theatrical and rather comic *affaire* with a person we gather to be very commonplace. General Saint-Pé, tied to a supposedly paralysed wife, whose jealousy is pathological, maintains furtive relations of lust with a maid. But, if Ardèle's presence in the house is a constant, silent challenge to the ideas of the family, the actual confrontations which suggest Anouilh's despair over the fate of purity are those in which the defenders of purity and the moral absolutes—in this case, Nicolas and Nathalie—see played out before them a concrete and dramatic parody of their ideals. The house is in darkness and Nicolas waits to meet Nathalie. He witnesses a series of nocturnal encounters. Toto, one of the General's young children, creeps in and filches some adult clothes from the hall. The Count, returning from a theatrical dash to save his mistress from suicide, is met on the landing by Liliane. They discuss their estrangement, only to be interrupted by Villardieu who, by playing the rôle of the outraged husband, reduces the whole scene to a farcical parody of love. The trio have scarcely regained their rooms when Ada, the maid, appears on the landing in her nightgown and enters the General's study. The General leaves his wife's bedroom to join her. Their furtive movements mime a degraded parody of love. Nathalie joins Nicolas in the shadows but their tryst is interrupted by the arrival of Ardèle's hunchback lover. Nathalie, confronted with this disconcerting symbol of love, can only find in it further evidence of crude physical compulsion. Hence she compares the hunchback to a dog after a bitch. He intensifies for her the atmosphere of sexual promiscuity which surrounds this country-house. At this point, Madame Saint-Pé appears on the landing, in the terrifying scene I have already analysed, confronting this young couple with an overpowering caricature of sexual attraction, as present in nature. Still raving, she insists that Ardèle and a man are engaged in the sexual act. The General, the Count and Villardieu eventually break down the door. When General Saint-Pé emerges from the room, it is to announce that both lovers are shot dead. This situation confronts Nathalie with an extravagantly theatrical parody of love, the effect of which is revealed in the significant comment she makes to Nicolas, from their hiding-place under the stairs: "Nous n'avons même pas à nous tuer, tu vois. Eux qui ne devaient que faire rire, ils l'ont fait." [17] The children, Toto and Marie-Christine, now enter upon the empty scene, dressed up in the clothes Toto had filched earlier. They mimic the rapturous reactions of their elders in love, rivalling each other in protestations of devotion and eventually falling into a vicious scuffle, punctuated by insults. This derisive parody of love confronts no one except the audience. It is as if Anouilh suddenly deserts the creatures of his imagination so as to confront us directly with this bitter parody.

To arrive at the final stage in Anouilh's pattern of fatality—the triumph of the world in the defeat of purity—his Elect have to pass through this system of confrontations. In each play, these confrontations involve a *test* for his heroes and this test implies desperation. It is desperate because it springs from an obscure need, on the part of the hero or heroine involved, to embrace defeat. The relief which Antigone and Jeannette alike feel when they have placed themselves in an impossible position comes, it seems to me, from this craving to know defeat, from the surrender to fatality. The test in Anouilh's plays is almost invariably self-imposed and goes beyond the limits of what is necessary.[18] Thus, Frantz puts himself to a test by murdering the Duchess, in *L'Hermine*, immediately after hearing that Bentz has relieved him of his worst financial anxieties. In *Jézabel*, Marc, confronted with Jacqueline, the girl of his choice, repudiates with every confession he makes the happiness which, he is convinced, she holds out for him. He reveals his relations with the vicious maid, Georgette; confesses his sexual need of her and then induces his abject mother to drink in Jacqueline's presence. Jacqueline persists in her love for him and this knowledge seems to drive Marc on to the most desperate self-imposed test of all. Urged by Jacqueline to declare his ignorance of his mother's murderous intention in leaving a poisonous fungus among the mushrooms prepared for his father's meal, he vehemently asserts—without any vestige of truth—that he was her active accomplice. This appalling gratuitous act alienates even Jacqueline and consummates the destruction of all the hopes Marc had placed in their life together. Marc seems to be motivated by an obscure sense of complicity with his mother and by a profound feeling of responsibility for her. In *La Sauvage*, Thérèse, who is assured of Florent's devotion and who longs to leave the squalid world in which she has lived since childhood, is nevertheless driven to invent a series of self-imposed tests, each of which threatens to make impossible the realization of her love for Florent. Invited to

Florent's elegant home, she deliberately brings her father, confident that his conduct will outrage Florent and perhaps alienate him. Tarde lives up to these expectations. While descanting on his bourgeois origins, he attempts to pick the lock of the wine-cupboard. At dinner, he is gluttonous and prone to belching. But Thérèse incites him to worse. She encourages his tippling, shrieks with vulgar gusto when he almost mistakes the finger-bowl for a drinking receptacle, and urges him on to indecent songs. Later still, she abuses Florent's books, insults his mother's portrait, fakes an anonymous letter in which she accuses herself of being Gosta's mistress, and, lastly, invents a positively Zolaesque finale, involving an abortive illegitimate birth. In all these self-imposed tests, Thérèse appears to experience the need for self-abasement. She invokes fatality. It is these tests above all which lend to Anouilh's serious drama a sort of moral anguish.

The obsession with purity and the ritual stages through which it progresses on its way to defeat are contained within a framework of highly stylized dramatic conventions. These are the conventions of melodrama, farce and fantasy.

The focal point of Anouilh's originality as a dramatist seems to me to lie in his disconcerting fusion of the crudest dramatic themes and conventions with a concern for moral and even metaphysical issues which is normally remote from the exercise of such conventions. In fact, Anouilh is the knowing and lucid manipulator of these conventions, using them as pretexts for communicating his personal vision of life. The degree to which this drama is deliberately conventional is to be judged not simply by Anouilh's robust exploitation of all the themes and situations of melodrama, farce and fantasy, but also by certain special devices. The first of these is his tendency to signal to the audience over the heads of the actors, thus conveying to them the notion that he is manipulating an illusion and that they may enjoy the illusion, conscious of its real nature. Hence, when the maid in *La Valse des Toréadors* (1951) reads out loud Ghislaine's "farewell" letter to General Saint-Pé, she comments admiringly to the audience on its literary merits. She is clearly intended by this piece of by-play to provoke in the audience an amused awareness of the author's sly self-advertisement. She confirms them in their conscious enjoyment of an illusion. An even more remarkable example of this device occurs in the very middle of that welter of melodramatic incidents leading up to, and following upon, Frantz's murder of the Duchess in *L'Hermine*. His journalist friend, Philippe, enters in search of the real story and comments on Frantz's pallor. The reply is significant: "C'est exactement la question que le comparse pose dans les mélodrames. L'autre ne répond pas. Il s'appuie au dossier d'un fauteuil, tres pâle, comme tu l'as finement observé. Et le comparse se doute de quelquechose . . ." [19] It is as if Anouilh were engaged in self-parody, in a caricature of the situation he has himself created. In this way, he shows an ironic awareness of the conventions he has adopted and conveys to us that he is not their dupe.

The second device which emphasizes the highly conventional nature of Anouilh's plays is his use of a deliberately repetitive vocabulary. For example, he persistently uses certain epithets with certain nouns: "sale bonheur," "sale espoir." Similarly, "dure" and "exigeante" are often applied to his heroines, whilst purity and innocence are evoked by references to nakedness ("toute nue sous votre petite robe de quatre sous"). This device has at least superficial affinities with French classical models—say, the usage of Racine. Anouilh's intention seems to be for these words to achieve by repetition an accretion of significance. Finally, in using certain familiar proper names drawn from literary classics—Juliette for the winsome young heroine of *Le Bal des Voleurs*, Capulat for the lady's companion in *L'Invitation au Château*, Lovelace as General Saint-Pé's outraged description of Gaston or Paméla as the name of his new maid—Anouilh obviously intends to recall his audience to what is consciously *literary* and hence, conventional, in his plays. In one other way, his depiction of the very aristocratic or the very rich, Anouilh emphasizes that he has chosen to work within certain, clearly defined, *popular* limits. One critic sums it up: "Duchesses et richards sont peints tels qu'une midinette se les représente." [20]

When Anouilh adopts the conventions of melodrama, he does not hesitate before any extravagance. *L'Hermine* involves a faithful old family servant (Marie-Anne), a Duchess who is the essence of all Duchesses, a brutal murder, an idiot servant, a police interrogation that fairly crackles with drama and, finally, a last-minute confession. *Jézabel* offers a drunken nymphomaniac, a crude and elementary poisoning by poisonous fungus and a blackmailing maid. In *Le Rendez-vous de Senlis* there is some play with a pearl-handled revolver and a piece of heroic deception in which the wounded Georges conceals his wound from Isabelle. *Eurydice* exploits that most theatrical of all conventions—the supernatural encounter of lovers after death—epitomized in Sutton Vane's *Outward Bound*. Apart from this, the play contains two young lovers who are "destined" for each other, a gross and vulgar seducer (Dulac), the transmission of a secret note by means of a bribed servant, a sudden and violent death (Eurydice's) which does not disfigure, and an ambiguous and sinister character (M. Henri) who may be Death itself. In *Roméo et Jeannette*, Jeannette, trying naïvely to compete with the legendary wife of Poctus, comes down the stairs of the derelict lodge in the woods wearing a bridal-gown of virginal white, stained by the blood which oozes from a self-inflicted gash in the arm.

What does Anouilh intend by so complete an acceptance of the conventions of melodrama? Monsieur Henri suggests part of the answer by assimilating these conventions to life: "Cette pitrerie, ce mélo absurde, c'est la vie. Cette lourdeur, ces effets de théâtre, c'est bien elle." [21] This implies that life can be defined in terms of the elements which constitute melodrama: violence and accident, the two faces of the *arbitrary*. Anouilh's use of melodramatic conventions may therefore be seen as a method of conveying the absurd order of the world, and it is thus comparable with Camus's exploitation of the themes of Grand Guignol in *Le Malentendu*.

More important still, Anouilh's self-consciousness in exploiting these conventions does not prevent them from corresponding to certain of his most profound and spontaneous feelings. The character of these conventions is peculiarly apt for a theatre of extreme situations and it is precisely this sort of theatre that results from Anouilh's central antithesis between purity and corruption. The conventions of melodrama, in their very extravagance, are the most appropriate vehicles for conveying his moral absolutism and perfectionism.

By using popular and familiar dramatic conventions, Anouilh is enabled to exclude the exigencies of realism so as to concentrate on *intensity* of feeling, especially in so far as the themes of love and purity are concerned. By exploiting the conventions of melodrama, he reduces the element of surprise and so forces attention upon the sensibility and idealism of his main characters. In this way, he makes more vivid and memorable their tragic thirst for the absolute. By insisting upon stock themes of melodrama, Anouilh induces a readier "suspension of disbelief" in all that concerns his heroes. By selecting the *milieu* of the theatre as the background for several of his plays— *Eurydice* and *Colombe*, for instance—he removes their content one step further from real life. This device of *aesthetic distance* creates perspectives more favourable to the extremes of thought and feeling which characterize Anouilh's work.

A similar function is reserved for farce. If comedy is often anger deflected, farce is a more extreme form of comedy in which the anger is too savage, intense and unforgiving to be accommodated within the limits of comedy. Farce, like melodrama, is the vehicle of extreme situations. Though different in tone, it shares with melodrama a tendency to show men and women at the end of their tether. The ferocity of attack that is possible in farce makes it an admirable weapon for the wounded idealist. It is part of Anouilh's talent to have fastened on these possibilities and to have filled certain situations, which would have been immensely popular at the *Théâtre de l'Ambigu*, with different overtones and a different significance. Certainly, he races with abandon through all the stock situations of farce. For instance, Marc's nymphomaniac mother, rummaging through the drawers in search of money while her poisoned husband's corpse is hardly cold, represents a stock device of French farces on peasant avarice. But the most developed use of farce occurs in *Ardèle* and *La Valse des Toréadors*. There could be few more farcical variations on the "eternal triangle" than the situation between Liliane, the Count and Villardieu. In the first place, as Anouilh's stage directions make clear, husband and lover are intended to be virtually identical in dress, appearance and manner, a detail which emphasizes the irrelevance of Liliane's choice. *Ardèle* opens with a scene of the crudest vaudeville (in which General Saint-Pé fumbles lecherously with the maid) and continues intermittently in the same vein. But, of the altered significance which Anouilh intends these farcical situations to have, there is no more illuminating an illustration than in the scene where the Count, the General and Villardieu still reeling from Madame Saint-Pé's deranged outbursts, attempt to break down Ardèle's door. The key to Anouilh's intentions is again supplied in his stage directions: "*Le comte, Villardieu et le général se jettent sur la porte d'Ardèle. On les entend souffler. Ils sont ridicules et inopérants. Ils se bousculent, cela doit presque être un numéro de clowns, malgré l'angoisse.*" [22] Farce is clearly envisaged here as the vehicle of intense and painful feeling. *La Valse des Toréadors* is a burlesque on the themes and situations of romantic love. Eternal fidelity is burlesqued in the person of Ghislaine and "dying for love" in the ludicrous attempts at suicide made by Madame Saint-Pé, Ghislaine and the General's fatuous daughters.

Madame Saint-Pé, for example, lies on a railway-crossing in the confident knowledge that no train is due for another twenty-four hours. The General's antics as he struggles to unhook his duelling sabres from their decorative position on the wall or to unbutton his trousers so as to compare paunches with the Doctor, produce scenes of uninhibited slapstick. Yet, involved in both plays is a sort of moral masochism: Anouilh jeers at his own ideals out of despair of seeing them realized.

Both melodrama and farce, then, involve the trial of purity. Farce and melodrama alike rise to moments of extreme and painful tension and Anouilh's recourse to fantasy is an admission that this tension cannot be sustained. Fantasy represents Anouilh's constant temptation towards irresponsibility, an irresponsibility which is, perhaps, an instinctive and necessary defence against the extreme pressure of his obsession with purity. It is true that the highly artificial endings to those diluted melodramas, *Le Voyageur sans bagages* and *Le Rendezvous de Senlis*, imply a moral break-down that prepares us for the process of evasion common to the fantasies. Elements of the test and the confrontation do, in fact, occur in *Le Bal des Voleurs*, *Léocadia* and *L'Invitation au Château*, but in shadowy and attenuated form. The issues are transposed into a different key and subordinated to disinterested creative play. These thieves disguised as Spanish grandees, whose entries are marked by musical obligatos (*Le Bal des Voleurs*); that park with its deserted restaurant, weed-tangled taxi, its musicians suspended endlessly in false postures, its identical butlers (*Léocadia*); this country mansion with its twin brothers (intended to be played by the same actor), its lavish ball, its disconsolate millionaire roaming through the conservatory, its minor characters who break into music-hall couplets (*L'Invitation au Château*)—all point to an omnipotent creator, indulging the private pleasure of manipulating his creatures according to his whim. Confident in his talent, Anouilh responds to what W. B. Yeats once called "the fascination of what's difficult." We pass from the moral plane to the aesthetic.[23] No graph of Anouilh's production would reveal this as a simple progression, for his tendency is to oscillate between moral melodrama and the various modes of escapism. There are some gains in this conversion to the aesthetic. For instance, if it is true that Anouilh exploits the conventions of melodrama only to distort them with wilful and sophisticated irony, this does not always save him from the defects of his models. He is sometimes too close

to the original for comfort and so his successes with melodrama tend
to be adulterated successes. In turning to farce and fantasy in his
later plays, he acquires greater control over his material, but technical assurance and deftness, indulged too far, bring their own
pitfalls. Anouilh has learned too well Giraudoux's dictum about
emotion in the theatre being a mechanical effect. Like Giraudoux,
Anouilh is occasionally over-fascinated by the theatrical machine.
Thus, *L'Alouette* (1952), Anouilh's ambitious attempt to recreate
the legend of Joan of Arc, is fatally damaged at its centre because of
an irresistible urge to exploit mere technical effect. The central
dramatic device of the play is a form of cutting and "flash-back"
common in films. Joan relives her past life in a series of dramatic
episodes which are inserted into the progress of her trial. This device
is brilliantly successful in making vivid and actual the incidents and
words which are now embedded in the charges brought against the
Maid. So long as these episodes—a sort of play within a play—follow
the proper chronology of Joan's life, they seem naturally integrated
with the course of the trial. Difficulty arises when the past inset-
scenes culminate in the trial's present and in Joan's conviction. Joan
confesses her guilt, recants, is condemned to the stake. The audience
at the trial raises a pyre on the stage. The faggots are lit. At this
critical moment Baudricour charges on and complains that, in enact-
ing Joan's past, the crowd have overlooked the Coronation at
Rheims, the summit of her exertions. The pyre is hastily dismantled,
an altar raised, and the coronation re-enacted with all pomp and
colour, so that the curtain falls on a graphically satisfying tableau in
which Joan is petrified for ever in the conventional posture of story
books ("cette belle image de livre de prix"). The agony at the stake,
the long ordeal of the individual conscience pitted against authority
are both obliterated in the posthumous reputation. Whatever the
merits of this interpretation—and it seems to me to lessen greatly
the tragic force of Joan's career—Anouilh's methods border on the
frivolous. Technique triumphs over feeling. By reversing the normal
order of events at the very moment of the burning, Anouilh powerfully reinforces in the minds of his audience the notion that they
have witnessed, not some tragic and exemplary passion in which they
were sympathetically involved, but the adroit manipulation of a
theatrical illusion. Attention has been diverted from the creature so
as to fall on the creator.

Anouilh's melodramas are fanatically partial, prone to hysteria and self-pity. The fantasies are cooler, more detached, more urbane, but these civilized virtues are purchased at a price, which is: loss of contact with what is most vital and relevant to the human predicament. The fantasies are more humane, but the melodramas, though grossly flawed, have more humanity. Melodrama is Anouilh's puritan conscience; fantasy, the release from it.

NOTES

1. On the "almost Jansenist" attitude of Anouilh to his heroes and heroines, a suggestive comment is made by Merlin Thomas, "Anouilh and the French Classical Tradition," *The Listener*, February 7th, 1952, p. 218.

2. *La Sauvage* in *Pièces Noires*, Paris, Calmann-Lévy, 1951, p. 210.

3. All references to the dates of plays are intended to refer to the dates at which they were *written*. In this respect, I adopt the information tabulated at the end of Edward Owen Marsh's *Jean Anouilh: Poet of Pierrot and Pantaloon*, London, W. H. Allen, 1953, pp. 200–201.

4. *L'Hermine* in *Pièces Noires*, p. 49.

5. Pierre de Boisdeffre, "Jean Anouilh ou l'enfance en exil," *Métamorphose de la littérature de Proust à Sartre*, Paris, Éditions Alsatia, 1952, p. 176.

6. *Eurydice* in *Pièces Noires*, p. 440.

7. *L'Hermine* in *Pièces Noires*, p. 50. My italics.

8. *Le Bal des Voleurs* in *Pièces Roses*, Paris, Calmann-Lévy, 1951, p. 45. My italics.

9. *Cécile ou L'École des Pères* in *Pièces Brillantes*, Paris, La Table Ronde, 1951, p. 507.

10. *Jézabel* in *Nouvelles Pièces Noires*, p. 85.

11. *La Sauvage* in *Pièces Noires*, p. 238.

12. Ibid., p. 194.

13. *Eurydice* in *Pièces Noires*, p. 418. My italics.

14. *Roméo et Jeannette* in *Nouvelles Pièces Noires*, p. 315. My italics.

15. *Médée* in *Nouvelles Pièces Noires*, p. 397.

16. *Ardèle ou La Marguerite*, Paris, La Table Ronde, 1949, pp. 109–10.

17. Ibid., p. 115.

18. It is tempting to see in Anouilh's use of the test a more profound affinity with Marivaux than that which is offered by Anouilh's obvious concern for a mannered and poetic style and by his affectionate tribute to Marivaux in *La Répétition*. It is at least arguable that Marivaux's use of the device of a test, as epitomized in his *L'Épreuve*, is part of a conscious effort to reach sincerity. See Gabriel Marcel's Preface to *Marivaux: Théâtre Choisi*, Paris, Éditions du Loisir, 1947, pp. 9–12.

19. *L'Hermine* in *Pièces Noires*, p. 108.

20. R.-M. Albérès, "Jean Anouilh et la recherche de la pureté," *La Révolte des écrivains d'aujourd'hui*, Paris, Éditions Corrêa, 1949, p. 143.

21. *Eurydice* in *Pièces Noires*, pp. 500–501.

22. *Ardèle ou La Marguerite*, p. 114. Italics in the text.

23. Anouilh's drift towards the aesthetic is suggestively plotted by Bernard Pingaud, "Anouilh ou la Tentation de la frivolité," *La Table Ronde*, février 1952, p. 171. Pingaud thinks *La Répétition* marks an especially important moment in this development.

UGO BETTI

Religion and the Theatre

To approach a subject like this in a truly meaningful way, it seems
to me that it is necessary first to force oneself to a humble objectivity
and even to a certain detachment. This subject is too important and
we are bound to it by too jealous a commitment to allow ourselves to
dismiss it with pat solutions or lyrical effusions. It is necessary to
examine it with a dispassionate eye instead of imagining what we
would like it to be. The point is to understand to what extent the
movement which is drawing the theatre towards religious, Christian
themes is authentic.

I am speaking, of course, of the theatre of today, which is history
in the making, a phenomenon still in the process of taking shape. In
my opinion, only the theatre of today is in every respect truly theatre, that is, actual collaboration between speakers and listeners in
the common effort to formulate the dialogue of our epoch and to give
expression to its aspirations.

In the meantime, there is indeed one point worthy of consideration: that such a subject—Christ and the theatre, and even more
generally, religion and the theatre—has assumed, in the conscience
of many, a new importance precisely at a time when large areas of

Translated by Gino Rizzo and William Meriwether. Reprinted from the
Tulane Drama Review (V, 2), by permission of Mrs. Ugo Betti, the trans-
lators, and the *Tulane Drama Review*. Copyright 1960 by the *Tulane
Drama Review*.

disbelief, or at least indifference, seem to spread both in the individual soul and in the world.

At least, such is the appearance. Nonetheless, it is precisely now that a confused instinct leads many playwrights and many audiences to converge on themes, problems, figures, and events which, consciously or not, revolve like the wheels of a mill, spun by the visible or hidden current of the same stream: Religion.

This may be religion viewed as a good already attained, which must now be exalted and asserted; or as a good yet to be attained, towards which one is moved by an indistinct desire if not by a precise aim; or as the inner reëlaboration of certain principles in order to make them alive and integral; or even religion viewed as an enemy to be attacked, but not without a wealth of distress and remorse.

Many contemporary plays are indeed religious in an obvious way, and since they represent edifying episodes and settings which are peculiarly sacred, they could, in fact, be performed just as well in a church square as on the stage of a theatre. In general, these works are so well known that I find it unnecessary to name them. Their titles are frequently displayed on the billboards, and audiences, even in the most sophisticated cities, and perhaps especially here, flock to see them.

But if we wish to interpret this religious character in broader terms, the field is considerably widened. One may go so far as to say that it is above all the theatre which corroborates an observation that is only surprising at first sight: If our epoch has affinities with any other, it is more with the passionate Middle Ages than with the brilliant and tolerant Renaissance. In some respects, our epoch, too, is eager for universal systems, and it is not so much preoccupied with living and prospering in them, as in fighting for them, in asserting that they *are* universal and absolute: in a word, religious. This need for universal systems often demands to be heard in the theatre, although through very different and frequently incongruous voices. But, if considered as an indication, perhaps the more these voices appear incongruous—incongruous because they are unconscious: a spontaneous movement and not a preëstablished plan—the more their importance as a symptom must be recognized. We are concerned with the theatre, that is, with an art. This is not an area where a rigorous, logical consistency—critical, political, or philosophical—is essential; here, what is often alive and positive is precisely that which, on the plane of logic and orthodoxy, may seem unclear.

That part of the contemporary theatre which is insensitive to this need may be said to consist of plays which are little above the level of entertainment and, if listened to attentively, sound to us a little out of tune with the times, and basically antiquated. What truly sets these plays in motion, perhaps under the pretense of real problems, is a basic indifference to any problem whatever, an air of routine which is at times good-natured, at times impertinent, and fundamentally nihilistic even though gay on the surface. It is, in short, the survivor of the facile, post-romantic hedonism of the nineteenth century under a different guise, scarcely modernized by a certain irony. They are anachronistic plays; although numerous, they are not part of the picture. The true picture, surveyed in its entirety, induces us to conclude that all, or almost all of the contemporary theatre that counts draws its life from needs which, although variously expressed, are essentially religious.

The basic authenticity of these needs seems to me unquestionable. They are born, ultimately, of the ineradicable need of modern man to feel reassured by certain hopes. But it is equally unquestionable that such a deep authenticity is combined with countless other heterogeneous motives which contaminate it and at times end by overwhelming it.

The first of these contaminations is that of "religiosity," I mean a religion which is no longer a precise issue and necessity—and maybe even a painful error—but a benign substitute, a flexible fall-back, a comfortable *flou* which evades precisely the dilemmas that are well defined (the "either-or," the clear-cut boundaries between good and evil, the responsibility towards others and towards ourselves), a poetic way of making us always right and never wrong. Closely related to this is the vague humanitarianism with which the modern age pads every edge a little, and, pushing them towards a meaningless philanthropy, has diluted all principles and relationships of politics, family, justice, and, naturally, religion. It is used to make us all feel good and at peace with our conscience, without any great effort. How much shrewdness, even if unconscious, under this sugar-coating! In the theatre we can taste its flavor towards the third act, in the reconciliations and effusions which resolve everything, and perhaps a grand finale accompanied by organ music. Not that I am disturbed by the sound of organs or by the effusions at the end, quite the contrary. But I think that one has to pay for those results and suffer for them; and when I see them given away free, I become suspicious. This extreme need for love, this great flame—Christ—is, I think, something else.

Another contamination comes from the decadent self-gratification by which an emotion, originally religious, is little by little cherished and nurtured in and for itself, a perturbation savored like a quivering sensation, a rare experience: confessions in which suddenly glow the oozings of I don't know what sexuality; martyrdom, guilelessness, ecstasy, whose cruelty or self-annihilation is pierced (even though very remotely) by some kind of inversion. (I cannot avoid thinking of certain moments in *The Cocktail Party*.)

Next to this there is the trap of the décor. The religious issue often implies, especially for us Latins, an ostentatious background. Gold, music, purples, rays falling from high stained-glass windows, angels' tresses on frescos; one feels, at times, that the poet writing, let's say, *The Martyrdom of San Sebastian*, or the director staging an *auto sacramental*, has ended by being more attracted to all this than to the rest—more to gestures, colors, and drapery than to the sentiment.

Another contamination, it seems to me, is the one caused by the intellect: too intently bent on its inner polemics, on its own way of "being Christian," on more and more subtle doubts and hypotheses expressed through self-questioning and increasingly more labyrinthine crises so that these gradually fascinate the intellect, but perhaps more for their complication and subtlety *per se* than for their substance. Then, once the contact with facts has been weakened, the self-revelations and the polemics come close to resembling an agonizing chess game of words, a dry equation of algebraic signs. In all this, apart from a certain gratification, there is no want of a real ferment which I would also call useful if I didn't see that certain scrupulous self-examinations end, almost without exception, by acknowledging their own inanity and by characteristically returning to the initial propositions, which would indicate a certain lack either of courage at the conclusive moment or of concreteness in the premises.

Not even the theatre seems to me immune from such indulgences, whose real place is in diaries and essays, although the physical weight and near coarseness, peculiar to the theatre, reject by their very nature all that is of little weight, and easily reveal, in the harsh brightness of the footlights, the quasi-arbitrariness of certain arabesques: arabesques that are almost a luxury (whether or not literature, as action, fulfills a commitment of a religious nature); antitheses that are mainly verbal ("he will bear, then, the martyrdom of not having suffered martyrdom"); complications that are refined and, I would say, marginal (martyrs who spend their last vigil in self-contemplation, examining with subtle syllogisms their own spiritual experience—whether it is one of fear, of pride, of forgiveness, or what have you). Inquiries of this kind are certainly not superfluous, but since they deal with exceptional cases, they evade the real, important issues, the central ones, those shared by everybody —the issues of the people we meet on the street, whose conscience, in regard to religion, is not preoccupied with such fine points, but with other problems which are humbler and probably more important and, in the end, more meaningful and universal; with other and far more dangerous doubts which, finally, are also our own doubts and dangers; with other and truer anguishes.

Such an excess of subtlety, such an eagerness to attach importance to the least coils of one's conscience—in short, such a lack of coarseness—probably betrays a certain lack of seriousness, in the moral sense of that word—a nursing of one's own perturbation, which, from the beginning, carries within it the punishment of sterility. Nevertheless, in spite of all its errors and lack of concreteness, there is something positive in all this. Undoubtedly, there is the need to discuss certain situations anew, to react to passive resignation, to live one's faith and not to accept it as a free gift, to enrich it with a suffering and an effort of one's own. Indeed, there is in all this a rich possibility, and an important one, which can be understood especially by comparing it with another of the dangers which threaten the authenticity—let us say it: even the usefulness—of the religious issue in art, and specifically in the theatre: the opposite danger, which I will call habitual complacency.

But at this point I must honestly admit that these pages (I realize it as I go on) cannot avoid being, above all, a confession. In the long run, all the issues inevitably confront me already conditioned by my preoccupations as a writer. The confusions and misrepresentations to which the originally religious impulse of a play is subject, the contaminations of which I have spoken so far, are contaminations which beguile me too; they are the traps that I should like to avoid and to which, when I have finished writing, I suspect, once again, I have succumbed. Religiosity without rigor; the extreme need to love and be loved which, however, remains so indolent; an accommodating and soft humanitarianism; the sensation more alluring than feeling; the frame which enamors more than the picture; the condescension in showing or believing one's own intelligence and in putting oneself on display; certainly, all these faults are mine too, for it would be strange if I were immune to the malaise affecting practically all the literature of our age. On the other hand, precisely the fact that I am tainted with these faults (and the fact that I am involved, as an old craftsman, in such difficulties), precisely this gives me the right, my only right, to have my say, although a crude and unqualified theoretician, in the tremendous subject of this essay.

It is in this spirit of making a confession that, coming now to speak of the danger represented by habitual complacency, I will begin with a humble disclosure: rarely, after seeing a religious play, especially if explicitly and programatically religious, rarely, I say, have I returned home and gone over it in my mind without experiencing a certain dissatisfaction—but not because I had been irked by the "contaminations" of which I have already spoken. In general they were works without faults, works entirely dedicated to the humble—and lofty and ancient—task of being religious and nothing else; interpretations of glorious miracles; representations of edifying sacrifices; vicissitudes of Carmelite nuns led to the scaffold or of Jesuits put to the test; by and large excellent works, and unobjectionable in every respect. And yet I experienced a sense of disappointment.

This disappointment was due first of all, if I may say so, to reasons of pure dramatics. From the first scene it was altogether too obvious how the whole thing was going to end. No matter how cleverly or ingenuously the author had shuffled his cards, everything happened exactly as it had been arranged and also, unfortunately, as it had been foreseen. Battles were won and lost at the very outset—won, naturally, by the good cause and lost by the evil, won by the spiritual and lost by the material, won by faith and lost by disbelief. But, in a religious work, what other solution can conflicts of such a nature have? The posing of such conflicts is enough to give us their solution. Perhaps the fault (I am still speaking from a dramatic point of view) of the plays which disappointed me consisted precisely in this: from the very beginning every passion and every character appeared already labeled and defined, or (if the author had ably managed to deceive us) they had been labeled and defined in the author's own mind.

They entered into the plays, then, already judged and without hope, judged *a priori* and not brought in to struggle with real alternatives of victory and defeat, but to run through a fixed (and, therefore, habitual) trajectory, measured by a yardstick which allows no error. (I repeat once more that I am speaking from a dramatic point of view.) That's why plays which had Freedom as their goal seemed to the man of the theatre somewhat lacking in freedom, why plays having Life as their subject matter seemed in want of life. Don't misunderstand me: those plays did not lack emotive power. The great crosses shedding their light on the darkness, the sacred chants rising above Error, those immolations, those miracles, those heroic deeds—sublime flowers of a sincere, and severely tried, faith—had the power of making the lady next to me wipe away her tears and even of filling my heart with palpitations. I do not wish to sound irreverent, but such an emotive power seemed to me somewhat automatic and physical. If you will forgive me the analogy, it re-called to my mind the emotion by which, undoubtedly, both young and old are assailed when they watch the flag go by from a crowded sidewalk, and behind the flag the marching step of an heroic troop amidst the sounding of trumpets and the roll of drums. A slight shiver runs automatically through the crowd, but it is a slight shiver that remains such: not one of those who experience it would dream, a moment later, of leaving his own business to join the army, heaven forbid, or of immolating himself. Thus the tears that flowed down the cheeks of the lady at my side left me with the suspicion that they would have very little influence on what she would do once she was back home. Those tears did not change that woman. The sacri-fice of the Carmelite nuns had certainly moved her, but, nonetheless, it would not occur to her the next day, or six months hence, to re-frain from certain actions and habits. In sum, that emotive power and those plays fell short. The conventional targets they reached no longer amount to much. The true targets, the dangerous targets of today—that is, certain objections widespread in the world, certain disbeliefs, certain discouragements—are probably beyond the range of fire, and the sacrifices of the Carmelites or of Thomas à Becket cannot even scratch them.

That contrast between good and evil, then, had a very mediocre effect on a world whose characteristic is precisely this: to believe very little in the real existence of good and evil. For some time the world has suspected that vice and virtue are only products like vitriol and sugar, that certain moral conflicts are mere conventions sanctioned by smart people to keep the fools in check. Above all, I fear that several of the ladies in the audience, or several of their friends, are rather sceptical about what Someone said to each and every one of them: "Verily I say unto thee, Today shalt thou be with me in paradise." I am of the opinion that today many people are scarcely convinced that they will be resurrected after death in order that they may be judged. At any rate, they don't believe in it strongly enough to conform their actions to such a conviction. That is all. It is very simple: one must try to convince them again.

In regard to such a situation, what is the thinking of many Catholics, particularly writers and critics? Their thinking strikes me as curiously rosy. I say "curiously" because the reality of today, on the crust of the world, from the big atheisms to the small indifferences, from the apocaleptic thundering in the far away horizon to the most trivial episodes of everyday exchange and intercourse, the reality of today does not seem to me to encourage a great optimism, but rather, it appears such that persons in a position of high responsibility solemnly avow their concern over it, and even speak of crusades. The optimism of a complacent conscience, however, does not allow concern. What strikes one and causes one to envy them is a kind of soft, quiescent contentment, always repeating that "all is well"—the words of those who live off the fat of the land, and know it. The frame of mind that is at the bottom of this acquiescence seems to me the same as that of the critic who concluded that "tragedy" ended the very moment in which Christ spoke, because wars stop when victory begins. That critic was speaking only of the theatre, but his words leave us nonetheless perplexed. Then wars would be over for mankind; which would mean, to remain in the field of art and the theatre, that Art and Theatre are over too, if it is true that art is always tragedy. With Art and Theatre finished, we are left with only an elegant delight with which to garland our leisure. Leisure, nothing but leisure, if everything were said and done; and our efforts and conflicts would be, to a great extent, superfluous since we have been given the Truth which resolves them once and forever.

I am speaking with the timidity of one who is groping through a maze of problems that are too big for him, and who, at this point, sees himself reduced to the modest resource of a hesitant common sense. We were indeed given a final victory and truth. This is sure.

But why these landslides around us, then? And still others announce their coming with far-off thundering. Why these defeats here and there? And why, today and perhaps again tomorrow, this flood of cruelty and hatred, greater than ever before in history? What is the dam that gave way? And, on the other hand, this giving way—was it useless? Is this vast perturbation which is in us and in many others, useless too?

Is error useless—totally useless—and is this effort in our time to fight against it, but at the same time to know it and therefore to love it and extract from it a beneficial suffering, useless too? Should the fact that we have already arrived make our journey useless? We have arrived, but are we surrounded by the everlasting calmness of a haven, by the still waters of a harbor? Why, then, should Bernanos' abbess say to her novice, "Our rules are not a refuge. It isn't the rules that guard us, but we who guard the rules"? Has the danger ceased to exist; is vigilance useless; is doubt itself forbidden, even though it was allowed Christ when He said, "Remove this cup from me," or when he cried with a loud voice at the ninth hour, "Eli, Eli, lama, sabachthani"? Is it a lie, then, this hope we have that Man's life is useful, that it is an ascending, even though difficult, path towards the ever fuller, more intimate, and enlightened discovery of that Truth? Granted the stability and perfection of that Truth, how is it possible not to think that our humble ways, the ways in which we, frail men, gradually become convinced of it and prove to ourselves its eternal validity, may change with time, just as, with time, they lose their efficacy? And don't we see around us so much weakness and bewilderment, and, indeed, a pressing need to be convinced on a new basis in the face of certain new objections, thus more firmly reassuring ourselves of those certainties without which we cannot live? Happy are they who are calm, sure, strong, and no longer need anything, or at least think they don't. But how can we avoid thinking, also, of those who are weak, without faith, and without hope? Is it not true that we must think of them before all?

When I think of men without hope an image often comes to my mind. I imagine them as inhabitants of an arid planet, without water or earth. Since these two elements—the source of life and the place where it exists—are totally unknown to the senses of these men, they are also totally unknown to their minds. But one day, having split, by chance, the rock on which they live, they discover some strange objects that are embedded in it. These objects are also rocks, but different from the others. These men cannot even fathom what a grain of wheat or a fish is, but what they now have before their eyes is a petrified grain and a petrified fish, and they do not know it. Their wise men carefully examine and re-examine those curious scales, those peculiar shapes, those inexplicable formations. And finally these very same shapes and formations, irreconcilable with all other hypotheses, will necessarily and of themselves create an hypothesis which is almost unbelievable, and yet the only one possible. Each one of these two fossils cannot but presuppose a certain unknown element. One will call forth the sea, the other, the earth. Bent over those scales, these men will finally behold what they never have and never will see in their mortal lives, but which, somewhere, if those scales exist, must certainly exist as well—the blue, infinite ocean, the green, marvelous pastures: Life.

No other way could have convinced them: not even an oath. It would have been an inane declaration, words of an unknown language. Only now are they convinced, since they themselves have discovered those scales.

I fear that it is not always possible or useful to speak of faith to those who despair, or to describe that fresh water, that earth in flower, to them. They do not know, and perhaps they do not want to know, what freshness and gardens are. They do not live in such a world, or they do not believe they do.

However, it can be demonstrated that they do belong to it. But demonstrated, perhaps, in one way only. One must enter their refuge and dig into it and know it. In order to do this, we must go to that rocky land and accept it as it is. The proofs must be found there, for it would be of no use to bring them from outside. I believe that by studying man carefully one will undoubtedly discover that, just as the grain of wheat presupposes the earth and the fish, the water, man presupposes God.

I realize that, even at this point, these are nothing but justifications. The means whose validity I am supporting are none but the means which, in writing for the theatre, I, myself, have tried to follow, although in part, unconsciously. But what else should I uphold if not these confused efforts—more than ideas—which have impelled me for so many years? All I can do is try clumsily to prove again certain things to someone, starting from zero. I believe, truly believe, that if we search untiringly at the bottom of all human abdications we will always end by finding, under so many "no's," a small "yes" which will outweigh every objection and will be sufficient to rebuild everything. One must not be afraid of that desert. On the contrary, everything must actually be razed to the ground first, one must find himself on that arid planet, and must have gone there without panaceas in his pocket. When we have truly suffered and understood human baseness, we will find at the bottom (since in error not all is error) several illogical and, I would say, strange needs: "illogical" because they cannot be measured by the yardstick of human reason, "strange" because unknown or, rather, opposed to the mechanism and the advantage of the world in which we live and in which we have discovered them. They deny this world and paint a different one, revealing a "bewildering incongruity between our existence and what it ought to be according to the aspirations of our soul." (I wrote these words twenty-five years ago as an introduction to my first play.)

They are inexplicable needs. But in the soul of the unjust man, and even in the soul of the judge who betrays justice, we will discover that, in the end, he, himself, cannot breathe or survive without justice. Underneath the most hardened bitterness we will, at a certain point, discover in the cruel, selfish, lost souls, a need for mercy, harmony, solidarity, immortality, trust, forgiveness, and, above all, for love: a mercy and a love which are far greater than the pale imitations offered by this world. This is a thirst which all the fountains of the earth cannot quench. Each of these mysterious needs is one side of a perimeter whose complete figure, when we finally perceive it, has one name: GOD.

HEINZ POLITZER

How Epic Is Bertolt Brecht's Epic Theater?

When Bertolt Brecht died in East Berlin, on August 14, 1956, he
left behind an impressive literary work, a new method of producing
and acting plays, as well as a theory of the drama. Even his enemies
admit that his better poetry and drama has made an impact on the
contemporary literary scene. However, his most ardent admirers
cannot close their eyes to the often fantastic unevenness of his performance as a writer. He was as erratic as the era of revolution and
war which he witnessed and depicted. Since he saw himself living in
the "jungle of cities," he more than once adopted the law of the
jungle as an aesthetic principle.

He succeeded, to some degree. Today, nearly six years after his
death, Brecht's theatrical style is being perpetuated by the Berlin
Ensemble am Schiffbauerdamm. There the actress Helene Weigel,
Brecht's widow, guards the practical techniques and theoretical pol-
icies which Brecht developed for modern stage production. Guest
performances around Western Europe have established the fame of
the Brecht troupe as a potent germinating force in the theater of
today. To be sure, this style—which is both austere and grotesque—
has remained a very personal achievement of its creator and defies
any easy imitation. Therefore, Brecht's followers have to rely on his
theory, the idea of the epic theater.

Brecht claimed that his idea was universally valid. "Modern the-

Reprinted by permission from *Modern Language Quarterly* (XXIII, 2).

ater is epic theater," he announced as early as 1930 when, still gropingly, he sketched the general principles of his theory in the notes to the opera, *Rise and Fall of the Town of Mahagonny*.[1] After his return, twenty-five years later, from an exile which had driven him across half the globe, he asked more modestly: "Is it possible to reproduce the modern world in the theater?" To this he answered:

> I have (before me) all the possibilities but I cannot say that the dramaturgical ideas which I . . . call non-Aristotelian, and the epic manner of acting they entail, represent the one and only solution. However, one thing has become clear: the modern world can be described to modern men only when it is described as an alterable world.[2]

It was the old and somewhat tired Brecht who spoke; furthermore, since his statement was directed to a group of people who were discussing the theater outside of Eastern Germany, it had to be toned down considerably. Nevertheless, Brecht made it perfectly clear how he wanted the rather elastic term, "alterable world," to be understood. To him, "alterable" indicated no more nor less than the state of readiness for a change in the structure of society. Therefore, he wrote: "You will not be surprised to hear from me that I consider the question: can the world be described, to be a sociological issue." [3] Since it is Brecht in East Berlin who has raised the issue, the nature of this sociological description will be determined by Marxist theory. We know from his biography that Brecht's conversion from a bitterly exuberant anarchist to an orthodox Marxist preceded his first declaration of the principles of the epic theater by only two years. After this he was adamant in stressing the organic connection between dialectical materialism and his aesthetic theory.

No one knew better than Brecht himself that the influence of his epic theater reached much farther than the Communist countries. In fact, the activities of the Berlin Ensemble and its leader were tolerated rather than approved by the East German regime, whereas the (London) *Times Literary Supplement*—certainly no Marxist outpost—declared editorially in 1956: "The broad aims in which Brecht believes are sound and good and of general relevance: and where he sticks to them he is unmistakably a great writer." [4]

In spite of the Cold War and the Berlin crisis, we seem to be headed today for a Brecht boom as bullish as was the Kafka craze ten or fifteen years ago. For five consecutive years a not altogether authentic version of *The Threepenny Opera* had been running off Broadway, to be replaced recently by a *Brecht on Brecht* show. College and university theaters have tried their hands at *Mother Courage* and *The Caucasian Chalk Circle*. There are two full-fledged critical studies of Brecht in English,[5] and a highly ornate edition of seven of his plays has recently been published in this country by Eric Bentley.[6]

How are we to reconcile Brecht's political creed with the interest in his work which is displayed by the West? The vast majority of his critics have declared themselves firmly opposed to the political consequences he appears to draw in his didactic plays. Is it possible then that Brecht's non-Aristotelian poetics do not rest as solidly on Marxist grounds as he himself proclaimed time and again? Or do his plays continue to fascinate their audiences in spite of his theory rather than because of it? The following remarks attempt to sketch preliminary answers to both these questions.

What is the epic theater? First and most important, it is, as Eric Bentley noted, a "misnomer."[7] It is certainly non-Aristotelian in so far as it upsets the sequence of time which Aristotle presupposed as one of the constituents of tragedy. As the early Brecht stated in the notes to *Mahagonny*, "narrative" is to replace "plot." Instead of being "a part of the whole" each scene is to be "an entity in itself," moving in "jerks" rather than in the "evolutionary necessity by which one follows from the other" (*evolutionäre Zwangsläufigkeit*).[8] But the negation of Aristotle's sequence of time does not yet turn the dramatic theater into an epic one. If Aristotle defined the epic as a narrative form in which "many events simultaneously transacted can be represented," he did not exclude coherence and consistency. The epic, Aristotle notes, "should have for its subject a single action, whole and complete, with a beginning, a middle and an end."[9] Yet this is precisely what Brecht attacked when, in the notes to *The Round Heads and the Pointed Heads* (1931–34), he demanded that "certain incidents in the play should be treated as self-contained scenes and raised—by means of inscriptions, music, and sound effects, and the actor's way of playing—above the level of the everyday, the obvious, the expected."[10] It is here that he mentions the *Verfremdungseffekt*, or Alienation Effect, which propels the spectator from a merely passive—or, as Brecht was fond of saying "culinary" —attitude into one of genuine participation. Instead of resting comfortably in his seat, the spectator is expected to take a stand, both literally and figuratively. Or, as Brecht put it, by the "culinary" theater "the audience is entangled in the action on stage," a process which is bound to "exhaust their power of action." The epic theater, on the other hand, arouses their power of action and "extorts decisions from them." [11]

It cannot be denied that some of the shock techniques of his Alienation Effect have contributed greatly to the success of his plays both am Schiffbauerdamm and off Broadway. He uses boards and streamers across the stage to indicate the time and place of the action, to give summaries of the action which is to follow (thus eliminating the "culinary" element of suspense), to contradict the action on stage (thus forcing the spectator to think for himself), or to address the audience in the way a street orator addresses a crowd. The dramatic action is suddenly and illogically interrupted by shrill songs, very often only tenuously relevant to the plot itself. Cruel gags alternate with practical jokes, which are occasionally rather sophisticated. The mechanics of the stage remain visible and function as a play outside the play.

These tricks, which follow one another in rapid succession, do not allow the spectator a moment of respite. They spread an air of excitement such as children might experience when they visit a circus. They seldom fail to impress even the connoisseur, who recognizes them as important steps in the liberation of modern theater from the limitations of realistic stagecraft. Brecht's most exciting Alienation Effect, however, lies in the human sphere. He likes to present characters who are alienated from themselves and from one another. His figures often seem to move in a vacuum where the most unexpected must be expected. Man is shown as "an animal with a peculiar smell";[12] his words belie his feelings, his deeds belie his words. The dialogue proceeds erratically, the figures bluff each other as well as the audience. In this world without human mercy, even the good is possible—as an Alienation Effect.

Although Brecht claimed to be "the Einstein of the new stage form" [13] (thereby comparing, by implication, his non-Aristotelian drama to Einstein's non-Euclidean geometry), he was far from being the originator of a new dramaturgy. One has only to remember the epic elements in Strindberg's dream and ghost plays where the balanced construction of the realistic stage is already willfully and consciously disrupted. Reaching back into his romantic heritage, the great Swedish innovator used quite a variety of Alienation Effects but did not choose to attach any "sociological" strings to them.

Strindberg, in turn, was one of the moving forces of German expressionism, in the wake of which Brecht moved along during his formative, pre-Marxist, days.

Nor was Brecht's activism foreign to the writers of the expressionist generation, who rose up in arms against their fathers and charged them with the guilt of World War I and social injustice. They too countered the passive enjoyment of art with the active demand for social Utopia. "We are against music," wrote Ludwig Rubiner in his manifesto, *Man in the Middle*, of 1917, "we are against music,—and for man's awakening to community. . . . We are against novels,—and for instruction in living; we are against dramas,—and for instruction in doing deeds; we are against images,—and for examples." [14] With this pronouncement Brecht's later declaration of principles shares one decisive aspect: he too knew very well and defined clearly what he was against. A certain ambiguity prevailed, however, when he had to declare what he was for. Let us take, for example, the following sentences from the "Little Organum for the Theater," which he published in 1948:

> The ancient and medieval theaters alienated their characters by using masks of people and animals, and the Asiatic theater still uses musical and pantomimic Alienation Effects. These effects undoubtedly prevented empathy; yet the technique rested on hypnotically suggestive foundations. . . . The social aims of the ancient effects were entirely different from ours. . . . The new effects have nothing bizarre about them; it is an unscientific vision which immediately stamps the alien as bizarre. [15]

By 1948 Brecht had learned a lot about the theater, especially the Eastern one; he was quite prepared to acknowledge the existence of Alienation Effects before and outside of his epic theater—and to declare them unacceptable. But what about the "scientific" newness of his own achievements? Peachum, in *The Threepenny Opera*, considers the organization of his army of beggars. During his monologue a large board comes down from the flies bearing the inscription, IT IS MORE BLESSED TO GIVE THAN TO RECEIVE,[16] while at the same time Peachum's real intentions, which are directed toward a personal profit, become more and more apparent. Later in the play Peachum is told by his daughter Polly that she has married Mackie the Knife; she sings a song which says nothing about her marriage but instead is quite candid about her loss of innocence. While she sings, she is steeped in a most incongruous golden light. An organ is lit up. Three lights come down on a bar, and a board is lowered which spells out the very news she herself is keeping from her parents. Since they know their offspring, they catch on immediately.[17]

In the opera's finale, Mackie the Knife is saved from the gallows by the appearance, on horseback, of the corrupt John Brown, sheriff of London, who brings a completely unwarranted pardon from the queen. Peachum moralizes: "Mounted messengers from the queen come far too seldom, and if you kick a man he kicks you back again. Therefore never be too ready to oppose injustice." [18] Sense makes nonsense, and nonsense sense. The opposite is always true. But you cannot even rely on this kind of truth, for truth is set spinning around its own axis and vanishes amidst the laughter which its dizzying revolutions have evoked.

Are not these Alienation Effects bizarre? No, says Brecht, they are not; they only seem so to eyes unaccustomed to the perspectives of dialectical materialism. Yet, one can easily counter Brecht's apodictic assertion with Eric Bentley's observation that "there was a small production of *Threepenny Opera* in Russia some thirty years ago! Despite the visit of the Berlin Ensemble in 1957, the Russians are still (1960) not doing any Brecht plays." [19] Could it be that Russian eyes, adjusted as they are to the vision of dialectical materialism, miss the superb fun spread by these Alienation Effects, and for this very reason remain impervious to the epic theater as a whole?

About dialectical materialism, or "the method of the new science of society," Brecht says in the "Little Organum":

> This method, in order to show how society is susceptible of change, treats social conditions as though they were "on trial" and convinces us of all their contradictions. Before this method nothing exists unless it is changing and is thus in disharmony with itself. The same is also true of the feeling, opinions, and attitudes with which people express their current modes of living together.[20]

Brecht's claim to have put social conditions "on trial" is doubtless justified. He has done so with great aplomb in his *Galileo* (1937–39), where the Inquisition of Pope Urban VIII offered an easy target and at the same time an ample arsenal of characters and artistically convincing symbols.

The same method, it may be noted, has failed him dismally in
The Resistible Ascent of Arturo Ui, a political cartoon parodying
Hitler's career, which Brecht never released for the stage and which
was performed only after his death. How was it possible that the
same method, based on scientific insights, should lead to such divergent results? Had he not chosen the scientific approach as a
safeguard against artistic debacle? The answer may lie in the observation that in *Galileo* not only the social conditions are "on trial," but
the human condition of the hero as well. To be sure, Galileo, who
succumbs to the Inquisition, publicly abjures his theories, and yet
gains immortality by smuggling the manuscript of his *Discorsi* out of
Italy, is a dubious hero. But the very ambiguity of his character, that
is, his humanity, secures him the interest of the spectators. After all,
he defeats the society against which he is pitted, not by bravery, but
by cunning. Western audiences have grown tired of victors, unless
they are at the same time defeated, and, as G. B. Shaw has demonstrated time and again, they succumb more readily to a display of
intellectual versatility than to the exhibition of character. Charles
Laughton, who collaborated with Brecht in translating the script,
played Galileo and could be relied upon to act out fully, as Brecht
had asked him to do, the determination of this man "to find the
easy way and to employ his reason in low pursuits as well as high." [21]

Galileo shares his cunning with many of Brecht's other heroes—
with the judge, Azdak, in *The Caucasian Chalk Circle,* for example,
or with Mother Courage—and, in the final analysis, with Bertolt
Brecht himself. Walter Jens has related an incident from Brecht's
high-school days which foreshadows the Alienation Effects the writer
was to use later on the stage. According to this story, Brecht and a
classmate were about to fail a course. Both wrote highly unsatisfactory examinations. The classmate erased a few mistakes and complained. The teacher held the bluebook against the light, discovered
the erasures, and had the student expelled from school. Brecht, on
the other hand, added a few red marks, complained, and proved to
the teacher that he, the instructor, had committed the worst error
authority can commit by making a mistake himself. The teacher
conceded "clerical errors," Brecht passed the course and was saved.[22]
The friend had taken the teacher's authority for granted; he felt put
on trial and acted accordingly. By trying to extricate himself from
his predicament, he sealed the verdict the teacher was all too ready

to pronounce. Brecht, on the other hand, reversed the position by putting authority on trial. He realized that the most vulnerable spot in authority's system was its feeling of invulnerability. There he attacked and succeeded.

The professor's "social condition" determined his thinking to such an extent that he unwittingly fell into the trap the smart student had set for him. This incident anticipates the thoughts of Brecht's Mother Courage, who reflects, while the soldiers lead her son to the execution: "I think they'll let us have him. Thank goodness, they are bribable. They're no wolves, they're human and after money. . . . Corruption is our only hope. As long as there is corruption, so long will there be mild judgments, and even the innocent can survive his trial. . . ." [23] Again, it is not the accused who is on trial here. It is the accusers who are accused. Quite plausibly Mother Courage expects their "social condition" to corrupt their thinking and the bribe to save her son. Yet she miscalculates and Swiss Cheese is shot; but it happens only because Mother Courage's love was still more corruptible than the justice of the judges, and her greed for money had dwarfed theirs. She forgot that she, too, was "on trial."

Brecht, however, never forgot. In 1934 he composed a pamphlet which was to be distributed illegally throughout Hitler's Germany. He called it "Five Difficulties Incurred while Writing the Truth," and prefaced it with the following sentences:

> He who wants today to fight ignorance and to write the truth, has to overcome at least five difficulties. He must have the *courage* to write the truth, although it is suppressed everywhere; the *smartness* to recognize it, although it is hidden everywhere; the *tricks of the trade* [he said "*Kunst*," which means "art"] to make it operative as a weapon; the *judgment* to select those in whose hands it will be effective; and the *cunning* to spread it among the chosen ones.[24]

Cunning is mentioned last, for it is, at least in Brecht's mind, the basic requirement to be expected from those who fight for truth.

But what, again, is this truth? In Hitler's Germany it could easily be defined as the exact opposite of everything the regime stood for. Outside of Nazi Germany and after the war, Brecht was ready to answer: dialectical materialism. But what would happen if dialectical materialism itself were betrayed by those who professed to realize it in their politics? Bentley reports that "Stalin's pact with Hitler in 1939 was a baffling blow" to Brecht,[25] and I know of at least one poem in which Brecht turned the full force of his wit and anger against the East German authorities whom he had chosen as his masters after 1948. Among the papers in his estate, the following lines were discovered, written under the impact of the rioting on the borders of East and West Berlin, June 17, 1953:

THE SOLUTION

After the uprising on June 17th
The secretary of the Writers' Union
Had handbills distributed on Stalin Boulevard
On which it said that the populace
Had lost the confidence of the government
And could regain it only by doubling
Its output. In view of this would it be
Not simpler if government
Dissolved the populace and elected
Another people? [26]

The East German Writers' Union and the administration they served were just as much conditioned by their social status as Brecht's middle-class high-school teacher had been some forty years before. Needless to say, the official attitude Brecht adopted after the East Berlin uprising was one of loyalty to the Communist party. But his cunning may have reached further than this. It is at least think-able that he constructed his brilliant and incisive theory of the epic theater in order to be protected not only as a private citizen, but also as a creative playwright—protected, that is, from those whose ranks he had joined. Having made cunning, as he understood it, the indi-vidual's supreme weapon in the struggle for existence, he would have been a fool and—what was worse in his eyes—a dilettante, had he not secured himself and his work against his political friends as well as against his enemies. Unlike his Mother Courage, he proved clair-voyant: in spite of all official misgivings, the Soviet Union gave him the Stalin Peace Prize in 1954, and East Germany still seems to subsidize the Theater am Schiffbauerdamm.

In saying this, I do not intend to minimize the contribution which Brecht's non-Aristotelian theater has made to the development of the modern stage. Along with Strindberg and O'Neill, Pirandello and

Antonin Artaud, Brecht belongs to those who have reconquered the reality of imagination for the contemporary drama. What I question is merely the relevance of his political thinking to his aesthetic theory. Being the most dynamic dramatist Germany had produced since the days of Grabbe and Büchner, he could hardly be satisfied with coming to rest in as closed a system as Marxism is, in spite of its dialectics. More likely, the Marxist superstructure of his theory may have served him as a last camouflage.

The trouble with Brecht is that he was so cunning that he succeeded in outwitting even the most cunning among his critics, right or left. He was a cryptic man and a champion in the art of leaving unwelcome questions open. When his work is at its best, it is just as inscrutable as he was. As a result, The Caucasian Chalk Circle (1943–45), his last major effort, has been hailed as both "the outstanding example of the technique of the 'epic' drama" [27] and a "Parable for the Theater," [28] which, at least on the surface, are somewhat contradictory classifications.[29] Yet both descriptions are very much to the point.

The Chalk Circle is epic theater primarily because it consists of three loosely connected parts: the prologue, the story of Grusha the kitchen maid, and the story of Azdak the village recorder. The prologue is set in Soviet Russia and occurs, as Bentley points out, "at a date later than the year when Brecht started work on the play." [30] Russian peasants who return to a village destroyed by the Germans are engaged in a discussion bordering on a quarrel: one group claims the valley as a homestead, the other plans to irrigate it and to use it for vineyards and orchards. The latter group wins out. To celebrate the reconciliation, the play of the Chalk Circle proper is performed.

Its first part describes Grusha's rescue of the Governor's deserted child, her flight before the revolution, her marriage to a peasant who is supposedly dying, and finally the return of the Governor's wife and her claim for the child. The second part traces the career of Azdak from village recorder to judge, for he becomes the magistrate who tries the case of the child. Not only do the two actions cover roughly the same span of time—both begin with the revolution which set the Governor and his wife to flight and started Azdak on his career —but they also receive equal comment from the Story Teller, who takes the stage at the end of the prologue. A crossbreed between Greek chorus and personified Alienation Effect, the Story Teller also has the final words:

> Take note what men of old concluded:
> That what there is shall go to those who are good for it,
> Thus: the children to the motherly, that they prosper
> The carts to good drivers, that they are driven well
> And the valley to the waterers, that it bring forth fruit.[31]

These words hark back to the prologue, and their moral adds the distinction of *Lehrstück* or didactic play to those of epic drama and parable.

But in order to arrive at this moral Brecht had to change radically the old story of the chalk circle. This story, incidentally, did not come to him from Chinese sources, as the prologue claims, but from *Der Kreidekreis*, written in 1925 by the expressionist playwright, Klabund. In Brecht's version it is not the physical mother who is discovered by the Solomonic judgment of the chalk circle. Instead Azdak awards the child to Grusha, his foster mother, who had saved him by sacrificing her personal happiness and risking her life for his rescue. In this scene the parabolic elements of the plot stand out in bold relief. Furthermore, it is a modern parable in that it is told not to exemplify a doctrine, but rather to reveal a paradox: Grusha's sacrifice is recognized as superior to the natural ties which bind the Governor's wife to her own child.

As if to stress the climactic character of this scene, Brecht constructed the two parts of the play so that the life histories of both Grusha and Azdak are crowned by it. The time sequences of both actions converge here and break the parallel structure of the epic drama. The courtroom scene stands all by itself in an atmosphere of timelessness, the air of the parable. All the conditioning forces—social distinctions, revolution, and war—recede to reveal the exemplary deeds of the maid and the model wisdom of the judge. Moreover, Azdak, who really is a cunning rogue very much after Brecht's own heart, is all but transported into immortality:

> And after that evening Azdak disappeared and was not seen again.
> The people of Grusinia did not forget him but long remembered
> The period of his judging as a brief golden age
> Almost an age of justice.[32]

Cleverly inserting the words "brief" and "almost," Brecht fortified his play against all critics who would charge him with "hero worship."

It depends entirely on the spectator's reaction to the prologue and his evaluation of it, whether he will consider the *Chalk Circle* to be a didactic play in the epic manner or a dramatic parable presented with all the persuasiveness of the modern imaginary theater. In the former case it is the valley that matters, and not the child; the future of the commonweal prevails over the individual's longing for his past; and the rights of motherhood, like the possession of a few plots of land, can be decided by arbitration. In the latter case it is Grusha's human virtue—to use a word which would have made Brecht cringe with distaste—which leads us to accept Azdak's judgment. Her victory is, after all, a victory of goodness and charm over the wickedness and frigidity of the real mother.

If we argue Grusha's case on the human level, however, we shall find it hard to accept the living child as symbol of a valley, which is an inanimate thing, no matter how much fruit it may produce after irrigation. Nor shall we be able to identify the full-blooded personality of the kitchen maid with the flat figures who populate the prologue. Grusha, who is humble and dignified, naïve and witty, as peasant women often are—and Brecht has given her some of his most lyrical lines—hardly fits in with those Russian peasants who speak like editorials and act as the party line expects them to act. In other words, although the prologue lives up to its ideological intentions and proclaims the Marxist moral of this epic drama, as a work of art it belongs among the worst Brecht has ever written.

The real question is, however, whether in this prologue Brecht's imagination was stifled by his desire to conform with the philosophy of the Communist party, or whether he actually wanted the prologue to be so poor a specimen of writing that it lost all power when it was actually presented on the stage. Performances in the West have omitted the prologue without doing harm to the artistic effectiveness of the play. Moreover, Brecht himself included in the prologue the highly ambiguous question: "You arrange the redistribution of vines and tractors, why not of songs?" [33] Did he want to say here that Russian literature, the officially sponsored "Social Realism," was in need of a revision?

The prologue itself pays lip service to the state, and even to Stalin, since it is set in Stalin's homeland, Georgia; but the drama, in its playfulness, defies the limitations of state-controlled art. Or was Brecht secretly poking fun at the very idea that someone would be so Philistine as to think that one could redistribute songs—and construct plays—like tractors? Did he wish to regain his independence and dignity as a writer simply by asking a silly question? If he did, then this line would indeed rank among the most cunning of his Alienation Effects. Tongue in cheek, he would have justified the prologue where he treats literature as one treats tractors, and he would have pointed to the play, where he produces literature in the only possible way—namely, as literature. Then, the play would have succeeded as obviously as the prologue failed, and yet he would have done nothing more than pose a question.

In any case Brecht does not confine his question to the prologue; in the play of the *Chalk Circle*, Brecht continues to ask questions, but they become so infinitely more complex that it is difficult to find an answer at all. What becomes of Azdak? And, more important, can his judgment be upheld? The true mother should be the one who can pull the child out of the circle. However, the trial establishes Grusha as the mother, Grusha who, contrary to the traditional story, refuses to hurt the child. Although she has done more than her duty, and even her love, had required her to do, she is certainly not the true mother of the child. What is the truth behind this truth? Brecht has persuaded us to agree with Azdak's judgment, but our "Yes" is a stunned and puzzled one. It continues to affect and afflict us and invites us to return again and again to the play and to reopen the case. Doing this, we only follow Brecht's bidding.

The Good Woman of Setzuan ends altogether with a question:

> In your opinion, then, what's to be done?
> Change human nature or—the world? Well: which?
> Believe in bigger, better gods or—none?
> How can we mortals be both good and rich?
> The right way out of the calamity
> You must find for yourselves. Ponder, my friends,
> How man with man may live in amity
> And good men—women also—reach good ends.
> There must, there must, be *some* end that would fit.
> Ladies and gentlemen, help us look for it.[34]

A convinced Marxist may be able to answer the first set of Brecht's questions; the second set ("How man with man may live in amity . . . ") is—undoubtedly on purpose—phrased in a way so general that it remains tantalizingly open. This "open" ending of Brecht's play is, on the surface, nothing but the logical consequence of his aesthetic theory which was meant to "extort decision" from the spectators. One excellent way to do so is to force them to answer "Yes" or "No." But was Brecht so sure that they would give him the expected answer? The bourgeois audiences which, in the early thirties, exposed themselves willingly to the titillations of *The Threepenny Opera* were far from being converted to Brecht's dialectical materialism. Today it is downright impossible to imagine a West German braving the Berlin wall and crossing over into the Eastern sector for good, in response to the questions put to him by *The Good Woman* or any other Brecht play he has read or seen performed at home.

Was Brecht the playwright superior to Brecht the theoretician in that he granted his audiences complete freedom, the freedom to say "Yes" or "No"? It almost seems so, for his questions became more and more unanswerable the more his stature as a dramatist grew. To side with the progressive peasants in the prologue to the *Chalk Circle* demanded no important decision, especially when one heeded the party line. But it took all of Brecht's skill and inventiveness as a dramatist to make us side with Azdak and Grusha at the end of the parabolic part of the play, and even so we answered only with a very tentative "Yes." One could almost say that the later Brecht singled out the plays which he wanted to survive by basing them on questions that were difficult to answer, if they could be answered at all.

This is especially true of *Mother Courage* (1938–39). In the final scene dumb Kattrin sacrifices herself to save the children of the city of Halle from a night attack. She stakes her life, just as Grusha risks hers to rescue the Governor's son. Moreover, Kattrin is killed, whereas Grusha is rewarded—Grusha keeps both her life and the child. Kattrin's death is bound to carry the audience along by way of the same process of empathy, or identification, against which Brecht's theory of the epic theater is directed. The cunning Brecht did what he could to brake the emotional force with which he had informed the climax of his best-known play. In the program notes to *Mother Courage*, he published a double picture, the right side showing Kattrin, sitting on the straw-thatched roof of a peasant hut, drumming and braving the fatal salvo; on the left side, however, he had juxtaposed a photo from a French newspaper, with the following caption:

Raymonde Dien faces a French Military Court in Bordeaux. She has been accused of having thrown herself before a train carrying arms to the war in Vietnam. She declared: "I have stopped the train because there are already enough mothers who have lost their sons. I am prepared to repeat this action any day." [35]

This prime example of an extended Alienation Effect is, of course, a double falsification: ideologically, dumb Kattrin does not roll the drum because she is an antimilitarist, but because she cannot bear the thought of innocent children being slaughtered wholesale. Raymonde Dien acted as an agent, deliberately, perhaps on orders from headquarters; dumb Kattrin, on the other hand, acts on the spur of the moment, desperately, as a human being, mustering her last strength to break through a lifelong solitude. Raymonde Dien served as the model for a politically effective poster; dumb Kattrin performs a tragic act. And Raymonde Dien stayed alive, as the newspaper clipping of her trial proves, whereas dumb Kattrin paid for her pity with a sacrificial death.

Obviously stunned by the tragic impact he had produced, Bertolt Brecht declared rather lamely: "The spectators may identify themselves with dumb Kattrin in this scene; they may feel empathy with this human being and be happy to observe that such energies are extant in them,—however, the process of empathy will not be complete here ("jedoch werden sie sich nicht durchaus eingefühlt haben").[36] The playwright retires behind the dogmatist who assures him that his creative genius did not "completely" pierce the systematic cobweb of his theory. What else was this retraction but a security measure, not unlike the one by means of which Brecht's Galileo saved his own skin, abjuring his discoveries? Both Galileo and his author are men who, with a twinkle in their eyes, agree to the proposition that "if there are obstacles,, the shortest line between two points may be the crooked line." [37]

Was Brecht so anxious to uphold his theory and be foolproof against the Inquisition of his day? Or was he, conversely, so sure of the tragic force emanating from Kattrin's death scene that he did not mind one more intellectual sleight of hand? Albrecht Schöne has called this scene "the self-alienation of Brecht's Alienation tendencies." It shows, he says, "the unconditional and presents compassion as a force beyond any dispute; it grows into a parable of human behavior which is no longer in any way subject to the criticism from the viewpoint of any following period." [38] One can put it much more simply: Kattrin's sacrificial death is unabashedly moral.

Is the epic theater perhaps a "moral institution"? Brecht himself asked this question, quoting a speech young Schiller had delivered in 1784 before the Prince Elector's Academy in Mannheim and published later under the title, *Die Schaubühne als eine moralische Anstalt betrachtet*. Schiller, the popularizer of Kant and educator of the German middle classes, had always been a thorn in Brecht's side. His play, *St. Joan of the Stockyards* (1929–31) is, among other things, a vicious parody of Schiller's romantic *Maiden of Orleans*. And yet, although Schiller's drama appeared to him as the epitome of "culinary" stagecraft, he could not completely detach his epic theater from the ethics of Schiller's dramaturgy.

> We spoke [Brecht says], not in the name of morality but on behalf of the damaged. These are really two different things, because the damaged are often told, with moral authority, that they have to make do with their conditions. In the eyes of these moralists the people are there for the sake of morality, instead of the other way round. Be this as it may . . . you will understand from what I said to what extent and in what sense the epic theater is indeed a moral institution.[39]

Brecht is begging the question here; instead of facing Schiller's revolutionary idealism, he argues against his feeble nineteenth-century followers ("these moralists"), who watered down and obfuscated Schiller's principles and are forgotten today. Brecht's last sentence, the "open ending" of his statement, however, does not completely close the loophole by which morality could sneak even into his plays.

It is doubtful whether Brecht read any more of Schiller's essay than its title. Critics of the drama who did were able to establish more subtle connections. Ernst Bloch, for instance, speaks of the epic theater as a "paradigmatic" rather than a "moral" institution.[40] The distinction is a rarefied one. If Brecht wanted the underprivileged and "damaged" to profit from his plays, then he was coming dangerously close to Schiller's precept that the stage is "to teach us to wield greater justice towards the miserable and to judge them with increased clemency. Only when we fathom the depth of their oppression are we allowed to adjudicate upon them." If the paradigms in Brecht's didactic plays are meant to establish a healthy balance between the society of the future and their rulers, then he could have found the idea of this kind of *Lehrstück* anticipated by Schiller:

> The stage could be used to correct the opinions of the nation about their administration and executives, provided that the chiefs and guardians of the state would grasp this opportunity. On the stage the legislature would talk to the subjects through alien symbols, would answer their complaints even before they were uttered, and would favorably prejudice their doubts without seeming to do so. Even tradesmen and inventors could and would be inspired by the stage if the poets would take the trouble to be patriots and the state would deign to hear them.

Here Schiller envisages the stage less as a moral institution than as a subtle propaganda machine working for the balance of the utopian state of the future. Brecht's Communist state, on the other hand, was far from being utopian. It hardly ever listened to him. Therefore, he had to hide behind the more extreme demands of his theory, lest he be forced to change the text of his plays, as indeed he was in the case of his opera, *The Trial of Lucullus* (1951).

In the final analysis Schiller, too, persuaded his spectators to come to a decision. This decision, with which he concludes his essay, is "to be human." [41] Deeply convinced of man's inhumanity, Brecht harangued his audiences through his Alienation Effects, urging them to *become* human. It is this dynamic that distinguishes the epic theater from Schiller's drama. Inasmuch as this dynamic shows man to be "on trial" and "in the process" of becoming, Brecht's epic theater is a legitimate offspring of the expressionist revolution of the twenties and of European theatrical history in general. Since his aesthetic theory is a mechanism, both of offense and defense, it may well be recognized for what it is: the intellectual mimicry behind which a creative mind hid from outward persecution and inward doubts.

This creation at times leaves its "epicality" behind to grow into theater, great theater, pure and simple. Whether the greatness of these individual scenes will bestow lasting life upon them, only history can tell; and it is harder in Brecht's case than in many another to predict the outcome of time's selective processes.[42] Brecht himself threw in his lot with Marxism, as if he were banking on its ultimate victory. But so far it has been the free West which has welcomed this writer, discussed him, learned from him, and performed his plays. Paradoxically, Brecht's survival may depend on the survival of the West which he, by all ordinary standards, had tried so hard to prevent.

NOTES

1. Bertolt Brecht, *Schriften zum Theater* (Frankfurt, 1959), p. 13. Hereafter *SCH*. Translations are my own, unless otherwise indicated.
2. Ibid., p. 8.
3. *SCH*, p. 9.
4. *TLS* (March 17, 1956), p. 142.
5. John Willett, *The Theatre of Bertolt Brecht: A Study from Eight Aspects* (New York, 1959); Martin Esslin, *Brecht: The Man and His Works* (Garden City, 1960).
6. *Seven Plays by Bertolt Brecht*, edited and with an introduction by Eric Bentley (New York, 1961). Hereafter *SP*.
7. *SP*, p. xxxi.
8. *SCH*, pp. 19, 20.
9. S. H. Butcher, *Aristotle's Theory of Poetry and Fine Art* (London, 1895), pp. 87, 83.
10. Bertolt Brecht, *Stücke VI* (Frankfurt, 1957), p. 221; Willett, p. 179.
11. *SCH*, p. 19.
12. Bertolt Brecht, "Vom armen B. B.," *Hundert Gedichte* (Berlin, 1952), p. 59.
13. Mordecai Gorelik, "Brecht: 'I Am the Einstein of the New Stage Form,' " *Theatre Arts*, XLI (March, 1957), 72; Willett, p. 178.
14. Quoted from Albert Soergel, *Dichtung und Dichter der Zeit*, Neue Folge. *Im Banne des Expressionismus* (Leipzig, 1925), p. 370.
15. Translated by Beatrice Gottlieb, *Accent*, XI (1951), 26.
16. *The Modern Theatre*, Eric Bentley, ed., I (Garden City, 1955), 114.
17. Ibid., pp. 137–8.
18. Ibid., p. 192.
19. *SP*, p. xxxvii.
20. *Accent*, XI (1951), 27.
21. Ibid., p. 35.
22. Walter Jens, "Protokoll über Brecht: Ein Nekrolog," *Merkur*, X (1956), 944.
23. Bertolt Brecht, *Stücke VII* (Frankfurt, 1957), pp. 124–5; *SP* p. 290.
24. Bertolt Brecht, *Versuche 20–21* (Berlin, 1950), p. 87.
25. *SP*, p. xlix.

26. Marianne Kesting, *Bertolt Brecht in Selbstzeugnissen und Bilddoku-menten* (Reinbek, 1959), p. 141.
27. Esslin, p. 311.
28. Bertolt Brecht, *Parables for the Theatre: Two Plays*, trans. Eric Bentley and Maja Apelman (New York, 1948), cover.
29. Brecht himself speaks occasionally of a "parabolic type of non-Aristotelian drama," e.g., in the notes to *The Round Heads and the Pointed Heads* (*Stücke* VI, p. 213).
30. *SP*, p. xlvii.
31. *SP*, p. 587.
32. Ibid., pp. 586, 587.
33. *SP*, p. 503.
34. *Parables for the Theatre*, p. 106, but omitted in *SP*.
35. *Theaterarbeit* (Dresden, 1952), p. 273.
36. *Theaterarbeit*, p. 244.
37. *SP*, p. 398.
38. Albrecht Schöne, "Bertolt Brecht: Theatertheorie und dramatische Dichtung," *Euphorion*, LII (1958), 272–96.
39. "Ist das Theater etwa eine moralische Anstalt?" *SCH*, pp. 71, 72.
40. Ernst Bloch, *Das Prinzip Hoffnung*, I (Berlin, 1953), 441 ff. See also Marianne Kesting, *Das epische Theater* (Stuttgart, 1959), p. 57 ff. Kesting also refers to her paper, "Das Theater als eine marxistische Anstalt betrachtet," *Augenblick* (December, 1956), which was inaccessible to me.
41. *Schillers sämtliche Werke*, X (Leipzig, n.d.), 46, 48, 49.
42. Otto Mann's verdict, "It is impossible to appreciate Brecht as a dramatic writer because he failed to follow the tradition and to present (dramatic) worlds" (*B. B.—Mass oder Mythos?* [Heidelberg, 1958], p. 110), attempts to eliminate the Brecht problem instead of solving it.

ROBERT W. CORRIGAN

The Drama of Anton Chekhov

In our times no playwright is more respected and less understood than Anton Chekhov. For most theatre people he is like Faulkner's Miss Emily—"a tradition, a duty, and a care; a sort of hereditary obligation." His plays are thought to be moody, complex, soulful, vague, and impossible to do successfully on the American stage. For the most part, readers and audiences have agreed with that critic who, on seeing the famous Cornell-Anderson-Gordon production of *The Three Sisters* in 1942, remarked that she "could not see much sense in three adults spending four acts in *not* going to Moscow when all the time they had the price of a railroad ticket." But since then conditions have changed, and today Chekhov's plays seem to have a startling and refreshing contemporaneity; they reflect as few plays do the spirit of our time. What accounts for this belated popularity? Why, a hundred years after he was born, do we think Chekhov has something significant to say to us today?

Part of the answer lies in the fact that all of his plays reflect the mood of spiritual discouragement which permeates the anxieties of the mid-twentieth century. In an age dominated by the fear of nuclear war, the tension of cold war diplomacy, and the insecurity of a defense economy, people wonder what, if anything, can be done

This essay serves as the Introduction to Mr. Corrigan's *Six Plays of Chekhov*, Holt, Rinehart and Winston, 1962. Reprinted by permission of the author and the publisher.

to resolve the apparently insoluble problems of life. All of his life
Chekhov, too, despaired of the fact that he was unable to answer
life's important questions. "Life," he said, "is an insoluble problem."
At the end of the first act of *The Sea Gull*, Dorn—one of the many
doctors in Chekhov's plays—is trying to comfort the distraught and
unhappy Masha, but all he can find to say is "But what can I do,
my child? Tell me, what can I do? What?" This question, "What
can I do?" runs like a leitmotiv through all of Chekhov's works. This
is the clue to Chekhov's great modernity.

Chekhov more than any dramatist of the late nineteenth and early
twentieth centuries was very conscious of the existential loneliness
of the human condition. In fact, the central theme of all his plays
is estrangement. He was conscious of man's helplessness before the
overpowering forces of circumstance; he was aware of man's little-
ness, his insignificance in a gigantic and impersonal universe; he
knew that no matter how closely men huddled together they could
never really communicate. In short, he was aware of the fact that
the very conditions of life doom man to failure and that there was
nothing anyone could do about it. He knew the utter impossibility
of finding an answer to the question "What can I do?"

In their ontological solitude, Chekhov's characters are like those
helpless travelers described by Kafka in his *Notebooks*:

> We are in the situation of travelers in a train that has met
> with an accident in a tunnel, and this at a place where the
> light of the beginning can no longer be seen, and the light
> of the end is so very small a glimmer that the gaze must
> continually search for it and is always losing it again, and,
> furthermore, both the beginning and the end are not even
> certainties. Round about us, however, in the confusion of
> our senses, or in the supersensitiveness of our senses, we
> have nothing but monstrosities and a kaleidoscopic play of
> things that is either delightful or exhausting according to
> the mood and injury of each individual. What shall I do?
> or: Why should I do it? are not questions to be asked in
> such places.

The train of Chekhov's characters' lives has been wrecked too; there
is no continuity upon which they can depend; everything seems
ludicrous and absurd, painful and hopeless. Ivanov cannot extricate

himself from the morass of his lassitude; nobody succeeds in finding love in *The Sea Gull*; no one achieves his goal in *Uncle Vanya*; the sisters do not go to Moscow (and it would not have solved their problems if they had); and the cherry orchard is not saved. In short, there is nothing one can do in such a situation, and we notice that increasingly, as Chekhov matures, nothing is even attempted. Ivanov's and Treplev's suicides are at least solutions, albeit negative ones, to their problems. Uncle Vanya is incapable of even such a negative solution. In *The Three Sisters* the nearest attempt is Irina's and Tusenbach's decision to get married and at least try to make a new life. But even this fails, for despite man's best efforts, a meaningless and mocking fate will destroy him even before he begins. (And we must remember that the couple's approaching marriage was not anticipated joyfully, for Irina did not love Tusenbach.) Finally, in *The Cherry Orchard* nothing is attempted. The sending of Gaev to the auction is little more than an afterthought, a pitiful reminder that nothing can be done, for the cherry orchard—the symbol of their lives—is doomed, no matter who owns it, from the beginning.

But this is not the whole story. If it were, Chekhov's plays would be little more than unrelieved pictures of gloom, and this we know they are not. This is so because Chekhov, in spite of his realization that man was alone and doomed to failure in all of his attempts to find meaningful relationships and meaningful action, never abdicated his sense of responsibility for human life. Even though Chekhov knew there were no solutions, all his life he sought to find an answer, and his plays are a record of that quest. Thomas Mann, in his perceptive essay on Chekhov, in *Last Essays* (Knopf), was conscious of this when he wrote:

> One has to face the fact that man is a failure. His conscience, which belongs to the spirit, will probably never be brought into harmony with his nature, his reality, his social condition, and there will always be "honorable sleeplessness" for those who for some unfathomable reason feel responsible for human fate and life. If anyone ever suffered from this, it was Chekhov the artist. All his work was honorable sleeplessness, a search for the right, redeeming word in answer to the question: "What are we to do?" The word was difficult, if not impossible, to find.

This, I believe, was the central and creative tension in all of Chekhov's life and work. His own life was filled with the kind of experience that made him ever aware of the inevitability of failure and the absurdity of a man's attempts to triumph over his fate. All of his early years—and he did not have many years to live—were spent in an erosive struggle against poverty, and only shortly before he died did he achieve any kind of personal and financial independence. Finally, after years of hard work, he succeeded only to discover—before he could enjoy the fruits of his labor—that he was dying as a young man of tuberculosis. All of his life was a constant and quiet search for love, and he finally seemed to have found it in his marriage with the great actress Olga Knipper. But their happiness was at best sporadic—their careers kept them apart much of the time—and was never free of the engulfing shadow of his approaching death, a death which came less than three years after they were married. The same characteristic was true of his relationship with Stanislavsky and Danchenko at the Moscow Art Theatre. Without the encouragement and support of these two men, Chekhov very likely would never have succeeded as a playwright; in fact, it is doubtful that he would have written his last three plays. But his relationship with Stanislavsky was never a happy one and was a constant source of frustration to him, for Stanislavsky never understood what Chekhov was trying to do in the theatre and "ruined" his plays in production. Finally, his approaching death itself, which Chekhov as a physician was the first to diagnose, and the reality of which, because he was a physician, he could not escape in the mists of illusion, made the playwright ever aware of the loneliness and absurdity of his own existential nature. Death, and therefore, as we shall see, life also, was not an abstraction for Chekhov. He, like all men, was born to die; but unlike most of us, Chekhov lived his life with the full awareness of his unique, dying self.

Yes, Chekhov had good reason to know that life is loneliness, failure, and absurdity, but as I said earlier, that is not the whole story and this second aspect of his life is the source of strength for the other half of that creative tension which informs his plays. Chekhov countered the reality of his death with an equally powerful weapon —his own life. He met his dying life with honesty, reserve, integrity, and simplicity; and above all, as an artist, a doctor, and a man he had great sympathy for others and an abiding respect for the dignity of human life. Chekhov's career both as a dramatist and a physician took its nourishment from a single source: his great capacity to observe and cherish life; not life as an abstraction or as an ideal, but as a doomed phenomenon of which he was a part. His tolerance, sympathy, wisdom, and his hard-headed vision made it possible for him to achieve, as few writers do, an unflinching but generous perspective on life; a perspective which is a victory over our absurdities, but a victory won at the cost of humility, and won in a spirit of charity and enlightenment. Maxim Gorky, Chekhov's younger colleague, caught some of this when he wrote of Chekhov:

> I think that in Anton Chekhov's presence every one involuntarily felt in himself a desire to be simpler, more truthful, more one's self. . . . All his life Chekhov lived in his own soul; he was always himself, inwardly free, and he never troubled about what some people expected and others—coarser people—demanded of Anton Chekhov. . . . Beautifully simple himself, he loved everything simple, genuine, sincere, and he had a peculiar way of making other people simple.

And thus we find in his plays, as in his life, a regard for his characters' pathetic destinies, and a nobility in their attempts to change or overcome that destiny. Goethe once wrote: "It occurs to me that the hope of persisting, even after fate would seem to have led us back into the state of nonexistence, is the noblest of our sentiments." And this is the quality that informs Chekhov's characters. Vanya is a ridiculous, fumbling, grumbling, ineffectual, self-pitying man, and yet we take him and his plight seriously (we must or the play would collapse); we do, I think, because for all his weakness he never loses his sense of dignity. Tusenbach is a funny little man with his three names, his ugly appearance, his pampered childishness, and his ridiculous talk about the brickyards. He knows this, and he also knows that life has no meaning and will not change. But this does not keep him from making the effort, from asserting the validity of life in the face of death. In his last speech, when he knows he is going to be shot in the duel with Solyony, when he is fully aware that just as all his dreams are about to be realized he will be deprived of them, he is still able to say:

> Really, I feel fine. I feel as if I were seeing those pine trees and maples and birches for the first time in my life. They all

seem to be looking at me, waiting for something. What
beautiful trees—and when you think of it, how beautiful
life ought to be when there are trees like these! *Shouts of
"Halloo!" are heard.* I've got to go . . . Look at that tree,
it's dead, but it goes on swaying in the wind with the
others. And it seems to me that in the same way, if I die,
I'll still have a part in life, one way or another. Good-bye,
my darling . . . *Kisses her hands.*

We could continue this catalogue: the three sisters themselves, Nina,
Lyubov, Gaev, in fact, just about every character Chekhov ever
created. But the point is this: the creative tension of Chekhov's
work spring from his recognition that in all men there is a great
disparity between the facts of their animal existence and the aspiring
ideals by which they attempt to live. But he accepted both, and he
saw the life of a man as the meaningful and at the same time
pathetic, ludicrous, and tragic attempt to bridge this gap. In
Chekhov's plays this conflict is seen in his characters who embody
both a terrible earnestness of purpose and an awkward and ridiculous
acting out of that purpose. In his own life this conflict is reflected in
the very act of writing itself. For Chekhov, as Thomas Mann has
pointed out:

> Work, pursued relentlessly to the end with the awareness
> that one has no answers to the final questions, while one's
> conscience pricks one for throwing dust in the eye of the
> reader, remains a strange obligation in spite of all. It comes
> to this: One "entertains a forlorn world by telling stories
> without ever being able to offer it the trace of a saving
> truth." To poor Katya's question (in "A Tedious Tale"):
> "What am I to do?" one can but answer: "upon my honor
> and conscience, I don't know." Nevertheless, one goes on
> working, telling stories, giving form to truth, hoping darkly,
> sometimes almost confidently, that truth and serene form
> will avail to set free the human spirit and prepare mankind
> for a better, lovelier, worthier life.

One of the reasons that Chekhov's plays seem so difficult to audiences and critics alike is the fact that they are so different. Until
recently, with the advent of the plays of Beckett, Ionesco, Adamov,

Albee, and Pinter on our stages (Chekhov, I believe, is the legitimate father of the so-called "absurdist" movement in the theatre), we went to the theatre expecting to see a story about someone doing something, "character in action" is the way the critics put it. This story also usually involved some kind of "message" or "statement" about an aspect of human experience: Life can be good if we are honest with ourselves (*Pillars of Society*); life is always doomed because our irrational drives are at variance with our conscious aims (*Ghosts* and a host of other plays); one's marriage is doomed if as a husband you act and react like a soldier (*Othello*). In short, one of the things that we expect of a dramatic action is that it express some kind of completion to the statement: "Life is ———!"

Shortly before he died, Chekhov's wife asked him what he thought the meaning of life was. He replied: "You ask me what life is? It is like asking what a carrot is. A carrot is a carrot, and nothing more is known." Herein lies the basic secret, both in meaning and form, of Chekhov's drama. He did not believe that "life is something"; all of his plays are expressions of the proposition that "life is." This is what he meant in his often quoted and usually misinterpreted remark about what the nature of the theatre should be:

> A play ought to be written in which the people should come and go, dine, talk of the weather, or play cards, not because the author wants it but because that is what happens in real life. Life on the stage should be as it really is and the people, too, should be as they are and not stilted.

Such an idea of the theatre has tremendous implications for the drama, and we are just now becoming aware of them. First of all, it abolishes the traditional linear plot because Chekhov was not interested in presenting an action in any Aristotelian sense, but rather he was dramatizing a condition. Whenever one asks what the central action of a Chekhov play is, he comes a cropper. Is it Treplev's suicide? Vanya's attempted murder? The three sisters' attempt to go to Moscow? The sale of the cherry orchard? The answer in each case must be "no," for these are only small parts of the plays and everything that happens in the plays is not directly related to these events; "action" for Chekhov was an artificial concept. He was concerned with showing life as it is, and in life there is no central action, there are only people and the only thing that is basic to each individual is the ontological solitude of his being. As one of my students put it recently: "Chekhov's plays do not tell stories. What do stories have to do with life? To be about life, a story must either be myth, invention, or chronicle; it must have a protagonist or center. But then it becomes a personal narrative or history, either real or imaginary. Chekhov, on the other hand, is not interested in describing a personal history: he has no Oepidus, no Lear, no Macbeth. In showing us life as it is, he has no use for seeing particular men in particular world systems. Chekhov's subject matter is life itself, not 'the life of a great man named Othello,' or 'the life of a school teacher named Medvedenko.'" As a result, Chekhov sought to create in his plays a situation which would reveal the private drama that each man has inside himself and which is enacted every day in the random, apparently meaningless, and undramatic events of our common routine.

But because Chekhov is more concerned with the inner lives of his characters and is not interested in presenting an action, his plays seem lifeless, timeless, static. Such plays of "wrecked travelers" are bound to be the antithesis of an Aristotelian action. Like the characters in the novels of Kafka, Proust, and Joyce, the people in Chekhov's plays talk and plan a great deal, but they do nothing. In fact, part of each play's meaning derives from this disparity between language and action. And we notice that as he develops as a playwright, Chekhov increasingly seems to doubt the possibility of meaningful action (even negative) at all. Ivanov, Uncle George, and Treplev are able to commit suicide, but Uncle Vanya fails in his attempt at murder; in *The Three Sisters* and *The Cherry Orchard* nothing happens, and in the latter play not even a gun is fired and no one dies. All of the traditional ingredients of dramatic action— love, murder, suicide, revenge—are present in the Chekhovian drama, but they are used differently, used to serve different ends. They are not ends in themselves or plot devices to further the action but are used as indirect means of focussing our attention on the inner lives of the characters themselves.

Or again, we notice the quality of timelessness in the plays. This is a strange effect, for all of the plays are structured within a variation of an arrival-departure pattern and there is a great specificity of time in each of the plays; we are conscious of dates, ages, the passage of years, the time of day, the seasons. We know that the cherry orchard is to be sold on August 22nd; Irina, Masha, and Olga are respectively twenty, twenty-two, and twenty-eight at the beginning of *The Three Sisters*, they are twenty-four, twenty-six, and thirty-two at the end; the carnival party will be coming at nine; and the daily routine of the Serebryakov estate with "tea at eight, dinner at one, and supper in the evening" has been upset by the Professor's arrival. And yet, in spite of this frame of a time pattern, we have no real sense of time passing. Chekhov for all his apparent attention to temporal concerns has been interested only in revealing more and more fully the continually shifting and changing state of consciousness within each of the characters. And when the characters, if they do, come back momentarily to temporal reality, they show painfully as Vanya does:

> But, my God! Why are my thoughts so entangled? Why am I so old? Why won't she understand me? I despise all that rhetoric of hers, that indolent morality, that absurd talk about the destruction of the world. . . . A *pause*. Oh, how I have been deceived!

Or they sob with Irina:

> Where. . . . Where has it all gone? Where is it? Oh, God! I've forgotten. . . . I've forgotten everything . . . Everything's so confused . . . I don't remember the Italian for "window" or for "ceiling" . . . Every day I'm forgetting more and more, and life's slipping by, and it will never, never return . . .

"Where has it all gone?" and in between these moments of painful discovery, they have not been concerned with time. Most of Chekhov's characters are like the three sisters, ageless and no age at all. Only those characters whose inner life Chekhov was not interested in revealing are conscious of time and change. The Natashas, Lopahins, and Yashas for the most part live only in the world of events and appointments to be kept; they make things happen, they are interested in time. Natasha asks what time it is; Lopahin is constantly looking at his watch. But most of the characters in Chekhov's world have no sense of time; as Kulygin points out to the three sisters, their clock "is seven minutes fast."

Further, Chekhov made it quite clear that what his characters do want in time is really nothing at all, only an illusion: Astrov's planting of forests, Nina's achievement on the stage, Serebryakov's articles,

Irina's desire for work and dreams of true love, Vershinin's happiness in two or three hundred years, the trip to Moscow, finally the cherry orchard itself. If the orchard means so much to Lyubov, why does she do so little to save it? The fact is that Lyubov loves the orchard and at the same time does not care about it at all. It is her life, but her life is meaningless. The orchard is at once the great cause, and nothing at all. All of Chekhov's characters finally arrive at that point where their most deep-felt needs are nothing, that existential nothingness which confronts Kafka's wrecked travelers. They want to be free of time; in fact, they wish to be free of life itself.

Finally, what it all boils down to is this: for Chekhov to show "life as it is," each of his characters must be defined by his solitude and estrangement from life and not by his participation in life. Each man's existence is ultimately solitary, and his unique self can only be known, if it ever can, only after all of his social contexts have been stripped away. And yet, although this may be true, no man can exist in the vacuum of self, albeit Chekhov's characters try to. Each of them attempts to build and then operate in his own little world, with no sense of social responsibility, totally unaware of the sufferings of others. Each character has his own thoughts and problems with which he is usually morbidly consumed. As a result, the people in Chekhov's plays never seem to hear or notice one another. Each has room only for himself and each acts in a social vacuum. And yet it is not always easy to keep the walls of these private worlds from breaking down. We notice that Chekhov generally sets his characters in restricted areas. The interiors are always closely confined rooms; the exteriors are usually attached to the house or are nearby. For this reason, if none other, Chekhov's characters are always in contact with each other and it is sometimes difficult to maintain a complete self-centeredness. As a result, each of his characters must have one or more protective escapes to which he can resort if too much is demanded of him. The plays are filled with escapes from social reality; for some it is drinking, for others, like Sonya, it is blind religious belief; for Vanya it is sleep; for Astrov it is beauty; for Gaev it is billiards and gum drops; for Andrey it is his violin, his books, his gambling; and for many it is work. No matter what the nature of the escape may be, they are all means whereby Chekhov's characters can return to their own little private worlds when outside demands become too great.

But Chekhov did not stop here. If he had, his characters would

be little more than selfish and unattractive. And although we know
this is true of them, we also know they are more than that. Chekhov's
most profound insight was that in addition to knowing that each
man is alone and that he seeks to maintain his solitude, he also knew
that for each man solitude is unbearable. Man is aware that finally
he is alone in the universe and that he is incapable of being alone.
The essential drama of the human condition as it is expressed in
Chekhov's plays lies in this tension between the uncertainty of each
man's relationship to others and the uncertainty of his relationship
to himself.

As we indicated earlier, Chekhov's plays are different from most
plays we are accustomed to seeing or reading, and we suggested that
this was because he was attempting to say something different and
this required new dramatic forms and techniques. Therefore, we
must now say something about certain dominant aspects of Chekhov's
dramaturgy. From the very beginning we are faced with a difficult
problem: it is impossible to use any of the usual procedures of dramatic criticism—narrating the plot line, describing the characters,
thematic analysis—because the texture and density of a Chekhovian
play defies such methods. To analyze these plays properly one would
have to begin with the opening speech and then, making cross-
relationships, work through the entire play until the final curtain
in much the same manner one would give a critical reading of a
poem. Such a procedure would not be to our purposes here; rather,
I shall illustrate some of the major devices used by Chekhov to
achieve his dramatic effects.

However, before we do this, we must discuss in greater detail the
more general problem of form in a Chekhovian play. Earlier, we
said that these plays were not imitations of an action in any Aristotelian sense. Chekhov was dramatizing a condition, and therefore
he needed a dramatic form which, as Ionesco put it, "progressed not
through a predetermined subject and plot, but through an increasingly intense and revealing series of emotional states." Such a drama
must from the beginning then dispense with the traditional linear
plot. The traditional plot is sequential; it starts at a certain moment
in time and then moves through a series of events to a conclusion.
Everything that occurs in this kind of play—each speech, every
action, any symbols—is a part of the play's forward movement and
is causally related to the sequence of events. It is this sequential
nature of dramatic action, of which plot is the first form, that

Aristotle was referring to when he said that tragedy is an imitation of an action "which has a beginning, a middle, and an end."

But as we said, Chekhov was not interested in "imitations of actions," he wanted to show "life as it is." Life as it is lacks the direction, the external causality, the cathartic effect of completed events. Like so many painters, composers, poets, novelists, and now, fifty years later, playwrights, Chekhov was aware that the crises which are so neatly resolved by the linear form of drama are not so neatly resolved in life. To be alive is to be in a continual state of crisis; in life as one crisis is resolved another is always beginning. He wanted his plays to express the paradox, the contradiction, and the incompleteness of experience; he wanted to suggest the raggedness, the confusion, the complexity of motivation, the "discontinuous continuity," and the basic ambiguity of all human behavior. Chekhov believed that the drama as he knew it could never express the "is-ness" of experience because it was under the destructive tyranny of a sequential and chronological structure. So in its place he invented a form which might be called, to use the terminology of the new criticism of poetry, a contextual or concentric action. (It is hardly fitting to use the word plot here, for, because of its usual connotations, it can only be misleading.) The structure of a Chekhovian play is epiphanic; its purpose is to reveal—literally, "to show forth"—the inner lives of his characters. In such a drama the plot has been twisted into a situation that is to reveal the psychic lives of the characters. There are many dramatic situations in a plot; here a single situation has been stretched to take the place of the plot. This inflation of the situation into the source of the dramatic action so that it replaces the plot is the vital secret of Chekhovian dramaturgy. To capture "the aimless, unclimactic multiplicity" of his characters' lives, Chekhov has created a form based on what Marvin Rosenberg has called "the tensions of context, rather than direction, of vertical depth, rather than horizontal movement." Chekhov takes a situation and then develops it concentrically, like a series of inscribed but tangential circles. For example, in *The Cherry Orchard* the situation at the beginning of the play is simply that Lyubov has arrived home because the cherry orchard is to be sold; at the end of the play the orchard has been sold and everyone leaves. Nothing happens really, the situation is single and static; but in the four acts in which the situation takes one—and the only one—forward step, Chekhov has revealed a great deal about the way "life is" for twelve people as they are related to that situation.

This is a new kind of drama and the devices which Chekhov used to create it and achieve meaning through it will appear by traditional standards to be untheatrical or, to use the language of his present-day followers, "anti-theatrical." And yet, as we pointed out earlier, Chekhov does use the techniques of the earlier realistic drama; only he uses them for different reasons and in different ways. It is quite proper, therefore, that his plays have been called "dramas of indirection."

Before examining the techniques of indirection, however, I should like to make one more point. In discussing the use of time in the plays, we noticed that there was a great specificity about time. This is but one example of the great specificity which informs Chekhov's drama, and this fact does much to account for the enduring quality of his art. The biggest danger that faces an artist when he is dealing with man's inner life is that in his presentation of that life he will of necessity become too private, too personal, too subjective, since such a life is the ultimate in subjectivity; but such subjectivity tends to cancel out all communication. If, as Chekhov maintains, all men are solitary and ultimately unknowable, how can the equally solitary reader or member of an audience enter into the private worlds that are being presented on the stage? How and why should they have relevance for us? Who really cares—except perhaps our psychiatrist —about the *psyche* of another, and even if we might care, how can we ever comprehend it? I believe Chekhov does much to overcome this problem—and it is a lesson that Beckett and Ionesco would do well to learn—by enclosing his subjective "actions" in an objective frame of specific external details. He was trying to capture the private inner lives of each of his characters, but he did it by means of those every-day events, objects, and expressions that as human beings, in all places and in all times, each of us shares. Chekhov was the great observer, and his plays are filled with the details of his observation. As a man Chekhov cared deeply for all of his fellow human beings; as an artist he always maintained complete objectivity. It is the fusion of these two characteristics that makes his plays great and, more important, makes them work as plays.

Keeping in mind, then, that all of Chekhov's plays are framed in great specificity of detail, what are some of the techniques of indirection which he employed to reveal the inner lives of his characters? The most obvious was his refusal to use the big scene, the stereotyped dramatic situation. There are no "obligatory" scenes or great denouements in a Chekhov play. Traditionally, such scenes were used to reveal through action the truth about a play's central characters. But for Chekhov, the truth is not dramatic in this way nor is it necessarily full of consequence; more likely, it is quite commonplace. We are accustomed to the "big" scenes and have come to expect them; when Chekhov refuses to give them to us we feel cheated. But Chekhov was not trying to fulfill our conditioned expectations and responses, he was showing "life as it is." We are moved by Othello's "Soft you; a word or two before you go" as his universe crashes down upon him, but in life our universes, if they do cave in, do not usually do so quite so dramatically; rather such times are hushed and of no great consequence to most people. So *The Sea Gull* ends with Dorn taking Trigorin aside and quietly telling him: "The fact is, Konstantin Gavrilovich has shot himself. . . ."

But the very muted and underplayed quality of the scene is precisely what gives it its effect. It may not be as theatrically exciting as Hedda Gabler's suicide, for instance, but it is much truer to life and in the long run its impact upon us is probably more lasting and horrible. Chekhov had a great distrust of the artificiality of the conventional big curtain scenes of the well-made play, and his work shows that he gradually discarded it altogether. In his early plays (*Platonov*, *Ivanov*, and *The Wood Demon* are for the most part structured according to the conventions of the well-made play) he uses the big curtain. For example in *Ivanov*, Act I ends with Anna's decision to follow her husband to the Lyebedevs', Act II ends with her discovery of Ivanov and Sasha in each other's arms, Act III with Ivanov's brutal revelation to his wife that she is soon to die, and Act IV with Ivanov's suicide. But Chekhov gradually came to see that such scenes were phony and while he was working on *The Wood Demon* he wrote:

> The demand is made that the hero and the heroine should be dramatically effective. But in life people do not shoot themselves, or hang themselves, or fall in love, or deliver themselves of clever sayings every minute. They spend most of their time eating, drinking, or running after women or

men, or talking nonsense. It is therefore necessary that this should be shown on the stage.

The Sea Gull is the first play to manifest this change of attitude. The suicide is still there, but, as we have shown, it was used in a very different way. The only "dramatic" event in *Uncle Vanya* is Vanya's botched attempt to shoot Serebryakov near the end of the third act. In *The Three Sisters* Tusenbach is shot by Solyony in a duel, but his death is off-stage and the shot is muffled. Finally, in *The Cherry Orchard* none of the traditional dramatic events take place and even the sad departure of Lyubov and Gaev is undercut by the final appearance of the bumbling Feers. But more important than the gradual elimination of such theatrically effective scenes is the fact that when Chekhov uses them they are no longer ends in themselves but rather they serve as pointers to the more powerful, albeit less theatrical, drama that is taking place within the characters who are on the stage. By underplaying the big, exciting, dramatic events we are better able to see the drama and the complexity of the seemingly trivial, the inconsequential, and the simple that is the very tissue of the human situation. Chekhov had learned well the wisdom of *Hamlet:* "By indirections find directions out."

Chekhov's use of obligatory scenes, then, was ironic, and this leads us to another aspect of his dramaturgy. Throughout his life Chekhov constantly made the statement that "the truth about life is ironical," and since he was showing "life as it is," almost all of his dramatic devices were ironic. This is best seen in the disparity between what his characters say and what they do. Thus we find in all of his plays characters making brilliantly incisive remarks about themselves and other people, and yet they are said in such a way and are put in such an incongruous and ludicrous context that we do not stop to take them seriously when we hear them. The force of these statements is driven home cumulatively; we are suddenly aware as the play ends that the characters have done just the opposite in their actions to what they have expounded they should do in their dialogue. These flashes of self-revelation have been more than static, isolated, and disconnected statements of opinion; despite all their apparent ludicrousness, they have become ironically true. Thus, Yelena says to Sonya in the second act of *Uncle Vanya:* "You mustn't look at people that way. It isn't right. You must trust and believe in people, (*pause*) or life becomes impossible." Even at this point in the play we know that this is precisely what Yelena does not do. We tend to laugh at the incongruity of the situation; but as we leave the theatre our stomachs begin to squirm as the truth of her statement begins to sink in. Look at Yelena and one can see in dramatic terms just how impossible life can really become. But Chekhov has achieved his effect indirectly.

We find something similar in the third act of *The Cherry Orchard*, when Trofimov is telling Lyubov: "You mustn't worry, and above all you mustn't deceive yourself. For once in your life you must look the truth straight in the face." To be sure, Trofimov has spoken the truth about Madame Ranevsky, but it tells us very little about the Russian equivalent to our perpetual graduate student. After all, it is easy for almost anyone to make that observation about Lyubov (Lopahin has been telling her the same thing from the beginning of the first act); what is more important in the scene is how Trofimov reacts when Lyubov rebuffs him: "This is dreadful . . . I can't stand it. I'm going. . . . *Goes out, but returns at once.* Everything's over between us!" By exaggerating (one of Chekhov's chief ironic techniques) his reaction, Chekhov points up the melodramatic quality of his exit and in so doing shows Trofimov as a comic butt. He underscores this by having Trofimov run out of the room and fall down the stairs in the midst of a chorus of laughter.

Or, to take a final example of this kind of ironic disparity between speech and action, let us look briefly at Treplev in *The Sea Gull*. Treplev is a typical adolescent writer—today we find his counterpart taking courses in creative writing and going to "writing workshops" in the summer. Treplev has lofty ideals, but he is a bad writer. (Chekhov makes this clear by contrasting him to Trigorin, who, although not great, is a good craftsman.) We learn of Treplev's ideals when he attacks the theatre:

> But in my opinion our theatre's in a rut. It's nothing but clichés and shopworn conventions. When the curtain opens on those three-walled "living rooms," and I see those famous and talented actors, those high priests of that sacred art, parade about in their costumes in front of the footlights showing the way people eat, drink, make love, and walk about; when I hear them try to squeeze a moral out of com-

> monplace phrases and meaningless events—some cliché that
> everyone knows and is suitable for home consumption; when
> they give me a thousand variations of the same old thing
> over and over again. . . . I have to leave! . . . we need
> new forms, and if we can't have them, then it's better to
> have nothing at all!

Now all this may be true, but the fact that he says it does not make
him a playwright. That Treplev is a bad writer is made very clear when
his own play is produced:

> Men, lions, eagles, and partridges, horned deer, geese,
> spiders, and the silent fish of the deep, starfish, and creatures
> which cannot be seen by the eye—all living things, all living
> things, all living things, having completed their cycle of
> sorrow, are now extinct. . . . I am alone. Once in a hun-
> dred years I open my lips to speak, and then my voice echoes
> mournfully in the void, unheard by all. . . . You, too, pale
> spirits do not hear me.

This is drivel (it seems to foreshadow the plays of the bad expressionists) and the disparity between what Treplev says about the
theatre and what he writes for it is part of Chekhov's point. I think,
as much as anything, it is Treplev's recognition of this fact that
drives him to suicide. (But already I am aware that such analysis as
this has falsified the significance of his death, for it tends to reduce
the many interlocking meanings of the play to a single action.) We
notice just before Nina's final appearance that the young writer is
struggling over a description of moonlight:

> And the description of the moonlight is no good either.
> Trigorin's worked out his own techniques, so it comes easily
> for him. . . . He'd just mention the neck of a broken bottle
> glittering in a mill stream and the black shadow of the mill
> wheel—and he's got a moonlight night. But for me it's the
> shimmering light, the silent twinkling of the stars, and the
> distant sounds of a piano, dying away in the still, fragrant
> air . . . It's terrible!

We know from a letter written by Chekhov to his brother Alexander
in 1886 that the playwright approves of the "Trigorin method," for

in that letter he uses word for word the example of the moonlit night that appears in Konstantin's speech. And, finally as Nina leaves him, she not only confesses that she still loves Trigorin but also goes out the door reciting the lines of Treplev's ill-fated play. The final truth about Konstantin Treplev is very sad and pathetic, but it has been revealed to us indirectly by the ironic devices of Chekhov's method.

We have already indicated that Chekhov often achieves his irony by the use of an undercutting speech. Such a device does much to give the plays their comic quality (we shall discuss the nature of Chekhov's comedy presently), but it also is a means whereby Chekhov can reveal some truth about the inner lives of his characters. For instance, in the first act of *Uncle Vanya*, Vanya has been arguing with his mother and he is finally shut up. An awkward pause follows, and to relieve the tension of this pause Yelena remarks: "What a fine day! Not too hot." Vanya self-pityingly replies: "Yes, a fine day to hang oneself!" This line is immediately followed by Marina's coming in to look for the chickens. She says: "Here chick, chick, here chick." In her world, in which she is doing her job, this is a perfectly logical line; however, coming as it does immediately after Vanya's ironic self-dramatizing, it is not only immensely funny but it acts as a commentary on Vanya's line. The result is a kind of grotesque humor which makes us laugh with a lump in our throat. It is funny until we realize the total implications of our laughter.

We find much the same thing in the opening act of *The Cherry Orchard*. Lyubov has just arrived and she is gushing about her "dear, beautiful nursery," Gaev is talking about efficiency, and exactly at this point Charlotta, in a conversation with Pishchik, announces that "my dog eats nuts, too." In short, all this talk is just so much gabble. Or to take a final example, in the opening scene of *The Three Sisters* Olga and Irina are talking about how wonderful it would be to go back to Moscow. Tusenbach, Chebutykin, and Solyony are carrying on their own conversation in the adjoining room; we catch only snatches of their talk, but notice how Chekhov uses it:

> OLGA: I wanted so much to go home again. Go home to Moscow!

> CHEBUTYKIN: *Sarcastically to* SOLYONY. A small chance of that!

> TUSENBACH: *Also to* SOLYONY. Of course, it's nonsense.

A few lines later the dialogue goes as follows:

> IRINA: Go to Moscow! Sell the house, leave everything here, and go back to Moscow.
>
> OLGA: Yes, to go back to Moscow! As soon as possible.
> CHEBUTYKIN *and* TUSENBACH *laugh.*

No more need be said; from the beginning of the play the sisters' talk of returning to Moscow is an idle dream, but it has been shown to us by the ironical device of the undercutting speech.

I should like to point out one more ironic device. It is a commonplace that Chekhov's characters are addicted to making speeches. Gaev makes a speech to the bookcase; Trofimov is constantly carrying on about the "brave new world" that is approaching; Vershinin and Tusenbach, when they have nothing better to do, philosophize; Vanya is continually making speeches; and so on. But, beginning with Stanislavsky, many interpreters of Chekhov have missed the point of this speechifying. T. S. Eliot was very perceptive on this point when he wrote in his essay "Rhetoric and Poetic Drama":

> Speechmaking in a play can serve useful dramatic ends. Genuine rhetoric is a device of great effect when it occurs in situations where a character in a play *sees himself* in a dramatic light. In plays of realism we often find parts which are never allowed to be consciously dramatic, for fear, perhaps, of their appearing less real. But in actual life, in many of those situations in actual life which we enjoy consciously and keenly, we are at time aware of ourselves in this way, and these moments are of very great usefulness to dramatic verse. They are valuable because they give us a new clue to the character, for we discover the angle from which he views himself.

"We discover the angle from which he views himself"—not the way we see him, or the other characters see him, or the playwright sees him. Thus by contrasting the way the characters see themselves with what they do and with the way the other characters view them, Chekhov, again by indirection, is able to reveal the way life really is.

A few words should probably be said about Chekhov's use of symbols. It has often been noted that the modern drama, beginning with Ibsen, has been increasingly dependent upon non-verbal symbolism and the imagery of inanimate objects (what Cocteau refers to as "poetry of the theatre") to achieve emotional depth within theatrical conventions which are, for the most part, committed only to external reality. Ibsen, beginning with *A Doll's House* and *Ghosts*, and most explicitly in *The Wild Duck*, used symbols to give a metaphoric meaning that a predominantly naturalistic theatre denied him. Chekhov also used this kind of symbolism, but in a fashion different from his contemporaries (or, indeed, those that followed him). Unlike Ibsen's "ghosts," Chekhov's symbols are never abstractions, nor are they simply analogous to the play's action; they are always concrete, they are a part of the life of the people in his plays; in a word, they are organic to the texture and meaning of the play. Nor, like the "wild duck," are they bizarre superimpositions on the action. (I believe the wild duck symbolism works, but the Ekdal attic stretches conventions of naturalistic verisimilitude almost to the breaking point. What is more crucial, one has the feeling that the wild duck metaphor existed prior to the writing of the play, as a kind of symbolic framework, and that Ibsen then created an action to fit the frame.) There are big, almost all-inclusive symbols—the sea gull, Astrov's forests, Moscow, the cherry orchard—in a Chekhovian play, and these symbols do give meaning and depth to large segments of the plays of which they are a part. But these extending symbols are effective because they grow out of the action and are not imposed upon it, and, more important, because they rest upon the less noticeable but more significant symbolic underpinning of the whole play. For example, Moscow is the symbol of the three sisters' dream of happiness. This we know is an illusion and their belief in this illusion shows how out of touch with reality they are. And yet the play is filled with less obvious symbols that make it clear that everyone in the play—with the exception of Natasha—has to some degree lost touch with reality. These lesser symbols support the over-arching Moscow symbol and, what is more, give it its organic quality. To point out but one instance, as the play opens Irina is celebrating her birthday (more exactly the anniversary of her baptism) and old Dr. Chebutykin, who perhaps more than all the others has lost touch with reality, with great ceremony brings Irina her present—a silver samovar. Everyone gasps, and with protestations of "you shouldn't have done it" and "it costs too much money," the incident is dropped as quickly as possible. The point is that in Russia a silver samovar is the traditional gift of a husband to his wife on their silver wedding anniversary. Nothing could have more effectively nor more completely shown just how out of touch with reality the doctor had become; nor, we might add, have revealed the lifetime of pain and disappointment that was the result of Irina's mother's decision to marry Brigadier General Prozorov rather than young Dr. Chebutykin.

In *Uncle Vanya* we notice how Chekhov uses a symbol to achieve another effect. Several of the plays have references to the watchman's rattle or stick. In the nineteenth century Russia the watchman would go about the estate clacking his sticks—much as our present-day nightwatchmen make the rounds with clock and key; the purpose of this was both to frighten any prowlers that might be about and to let the members of the household know that they were being protected. But Chekhov did not include this effect for verisimilitude alone; he also used it as a thematic symbol.[1] Such is the use of the watchman at the end of the second act of *Uncle Vanya*: Yelena and Sonya have just had an honest talk with each other and because of it they are capable of feeling. The windows are open, it has been raining, and everything is clean and refreshed. Yelena thinks she can play the piano again; as Sonya goes to get permission, the watchman's rattle is heard; Yelena has to shut the window—the source of refreshment —and Serebryakov says "no." Their whole life of feeling has been so protected by the "watchmen" of their lives that they have no feelings left.

There are countless examples such as these in the plays. All of Chekhov's symbols have this same kind of organic quality; they deepen and enhance the play's meaning, but more importantly they too serve as a means of pointing, indirectly, to that inner drama which is at the heart of each of the plays.

There is one more aspect of Chekhov's art which I should like to discuss: the tendency on the part of his characters to aestheticize life. All of the people in Chekhov's plays are shown to be either consciously or unconsciously aware of their own inadequacies as people. They realize that in one way or another they have failed as human beings, and they therefore attempt to make their lives like the more perfect world of art. This desire to identify with art manifests itself in various ways. The most obvious is the tendency on the part of several of the characters to identify with great artists of the past or with great heroes from literature. Serebryakov as he suffers from the pains of old age and a life of retirement (not to mention the probable realization that his life and work as a scholar may have been as

meaningless as Vanya says it was), identifies with Turgenev, when
he says at the opening of the second act of *Uncle Vanya*: "They say
Turgenev got heart trouble from gout. I'm afraid I'm getting it too."
In *The Three Sisters*, Solyony is constantly insulting and antagoniz-
ing people because he feels inferior to them. In a quiet moment with
Tusenbach, whom he later kills, he confesses: "When I'm alone
with someone I'm all right, I'm just like everybody else. When I'm
in a group of people, I get depressed and shy, and . . . I talk all
sorts of nonsense." This shy captain wears the mask of Lermontov—
he is always quoting the Russian Byron; he has been in several duels;
and he will brook no rivals in love. Vanya, unable to stand the final
disillusionment of his life's work, shouts: "My life's ruined! I'm
gifted, I'm intelligent, I'm courageous. . . . If I'd had a normal life,
I might have become a Schopenhauer, a Dostoyevsky. . . ." Finally,
in *The Sea Gull*, Treplev, out of the despair of his mother's rejection,
identifies himself with Hamlet.

This aestheticizing tendency is also seen in the way Chekhov's
characters are more conscious of *how* they say things than what they
say. In the third act of *The Cherry Orchard*, Epihodov says to Varya:
"I wish you'd express yourself more delicately." He does not care
what is said so long as it is said beautifully. Or, in *The Three Sisters*,
Vershinin has just made one of his typical speeches about how
beautiful life will be in two or three hundred years, and Irina, obliv-
ious to the meaning of what he has said, says with a sigh: "Really,
someone should have written all that down."

The desire for beautiful expression is directly related to the many
quotations and literary allusions which we find in the plays. There are
quotations from Shakespeare, Pushkin, Krylon, Lermontov, and
Gogol, to name but a few, and allusions to Ostrovsky, Balzac, Bat-
yushkov, and Turgenev. Chekhov's characters are always quoting and
talking—in short, finding comfort in words. They are attempting to
give a meaning to their otherwise empty and meaningless lives
through words by giving their words artistic form.

Finally, and most profoundly, the aestheticizing of life is carried
to its limit by those characters who seek to make their own lives into
works of art. Consider Astrov's remarks about Yelena in the second
act of *Uncle Vanya*:

> In a human being, everything ought to be beautiful: face
> and dress, soul and thoughts. She is very beautiful, there's

> no denying it, but, after all, all she does is eat, sleep, go for
> walks, fascinate us by her beauty and—nothing more. She
> has no duties, other people work for her.

Later, he says to Sonya:

> I am old, tired, unimportant; my feelings are dead. I could
> never care for any one again. I don't love anyone, and I
> don't think I shall ever love anyone. The only thing that
> appeals to me is beauty. I just can't remain indifferent to it.
> If, for example, Yelena wanted to, she could turn my head
> in a day.

Finally, he forces the affair with Yelena; his outburst is not one of
physical passion but a reaction to her beauty which culminates in his
asking her to keep a tryst in a beautiful forest arbor. We are reminded
of Hedda Gabler's request that Lövborg shoot himself beautifully—
through the head. Thus the man who has failed, who is incapable of
loving anyone, attempts to substitute an erotic picture of idyllic love
for a mature and demanding relationship. It is a relationship that is
symbolized by the "autumn roses" Vanya brings to Yelena; such roses
—like all the love affairs in Chekhov's plays—are very beautiful, but
they discolor and disintegrate the moment they are touched.

This tendency is most fully developed in Trofimov in *The Cherry
Orchard*. Like Astrov, he has become a walking vegetable, an emotional turnip. He loves life and the beauties of nature, but he hates
anything animal or physical. Thus his whole relationship with Anya is
vegetative. He wants to look at her, but even the slightest trace of
physical desire is repulsive. "We are above love," he says. He cannot
accept the responsibility of human animal existence and must escape
into the ideal world of art which is bloodless but extremely beautiful.
This, then, is but another of the dramatic processes of indirection
which Chekhov employs to reveal the absorbing drama of "life as it
is," as opposed to the tendency toward statement which is so prevalent in the modern theatre.

Finally, something must be said about Chekhov and comedy. Critics
are continually telling us that Chekhov is funny, and also we know
that both *The Sea Gull* and *The Cherry Orchard* were called comedies
by their author, and that he conceived none of his plays (despite Stanislavsky's interpretations) as tragedies. But Chekhov's plays are so
unlike most of the comedies we know that we are not sure we should

trust even the author's assurances that they are. Perhaps a better way of understanding what is meant when Chekhov is referred to as a comic writer is to recall that he was writing a drama that was to show "life as it is." Another way of describing "life as it is" is expressed in Santayana's statement, "Everything in Nature is lyrical in its ideal essence, tragic in its fate, and comic in its existence." This provides a very important insight into the form of Chekhovian drama, and it also accounts for the complex overtones that are present in the plays, for Chekhov's characters respond to all three of Santayana's levels with an especial intensity. They are comedians by necessity, smitten with a tragic sense of life, lyrically in love with the ideal in a world poorly equipped to satisfy such aspirations.

The essential quality of the "is-ness" of life is, as we said earlier, its absurdity, its futility. Some would argue that this is tragic, perhaps the most tragic condition of all, but as Dorothy Sayers has wisely pointed out: "The whole tragedy of futility is that it never succeeds in achieving tragedy. In its blackest moments it is inevitably doomed to the comic gesture." Thus, when man comes to see his existence as absurd, that it is governed by the irrational, the inexplicable, and the nonsensical, he moves into the realm of the comic. For comedy presupposes such a world, a world being made and turned upside down. As Gautier put it, "Comedy is the logic of the absurd," and thus it can admit the disorderly and the improbable into the realm of art. Chekhov was aware that the fragmentary, schizoid life that each of us lives is an existential comedy. His plays suggest that man lives in the midst of so many irreconcilable forces—both within and without— that the only way life can be given form in art is in comedy. But it is a special kind of comedy, a grotesque kind of comedy, which makes us, as I said earlier, laugh with a lump in our throats. This is so because for all of its awareness of the absurdity of experience, it is also extremely conscious of the suffering, struggle, and failure of experience. Christopher Fry wrote in his essay "On Comedy" (*Tulane Drama Review*, Vol. 4, Spring, 1960):

> I know that when I set about writing a comedy the idea presents itself to me first of all as tragedy. The characters press on to the theme with all their divisions and perplexities heavy about them; they are already entered for the race to doom, and good and evil are an infernal tangle skinning the fingers that try to unravel them. If the characters were not

qualified for tragedy there would be no comedy, and to some extent I have to cross the one before I can light the other. In a century less flayed and quivering we might reach it more directly, but not now unless every word we write is going to mock us.

Chekhov, I think, would have seen the applicability of Fry's remarks to the plays in this volume, for they too contain such a vision of life, a vision that may be summed up by the closing prayer of Joyce's *Finnegans Wake*:

> Loud, heap miseries upon us yet entwine
> Our arts with laughters low. In the name
> Of the former and of the latter and of
> Their holocaust, All men.

And yet, somehow, I am not content to stop here. Traditionally we think of tragedy as a form which celebrates man's capacity to suffer and aspire even though he is doomed to destruction by the inexorable workings of fate. Comedy, on the other hand, celebrates man's capacity to endure. It is *terribly* conscious of the resilience of the human spirit. Fry, in the essay just quoted, distinguished the two forms in this way:

> The difference between tragedy and comedy is the difference between experience and intuition. In the experience we strive against every condition of our animal life: against death, against the frustration of ambition, against the instability of human love. In the intuition we trust the arduous eccentricities we are born to, and see the oddness of a creature who has never got acclimatized to being created.

Perhaps this explains the mysterious quality of affirmation that we sense in Chekhov's plays. There have been many playwrights in the modern theatre who were conscious of the doomed nature of human experience, but I know of none who accepted this fact and still had such trust in the enduring qualities of those "arduous eccentricities we are born to" as did Anton Chekhov.

NOTE

1. Chekhov did not believe in verisimilitude for its own sake. He was constantly quarreling with Stanislavsky over just this point. The famous

director was always trying to introduce realistic touches—the croaking of frogs, the barking of dogs, crying children—that served no organic function in the play. When Stanislavsky defended his actions by saying that such effects did occur in real life, Chekhov replied: "Quite true, but the stage demands a certain amount of convention. You have no fourth wall, for instance. Besides, the stage is art; the stage reflects the quintessence of life. Nothing superfluous should be introduced on the stage."

ADOLF D. KLARMANN

Friedrich Duerrenmatt and the Tragic Sense of Comedy

1

From its origins in the *comos* and *mimos* to the complicated gyrations of the Paris *avant garde*, the term comedy has come to mean different things to different people. Taking a glance at its development in modern literature, we discover that the very basis of comedy is tragic; indeed, the modern playwright no longer cares to separate his worlds into tragedy and comedy but prefers to use the term tragicomedy or, like Brecht, omit any designation altogether. However, we need not be too surprised if we remember the tragic background of *The Birds* or *Lysistrata*, *The Merchant of Venice* or *The Tempest*, *The Misanthrope* or *Georges Dandin*. The reason for calling a play a comedy or a tragedy frequently is historical or personal. Were *Wozzeck* to be written today it certainly would have been called something like a tragicomedy. After all, Eliot's *The Cocktail Party* is a comedy. Beckett's *Waiting for Godot* is a tragicomedy and Ionesco's *The Chairs* a tragic farce.

The optimism which prevailed at the end of World War I is dissipated as a result of the sobering bitter years thereafter, leading to a largely nihilistic attitude among the generation born between

First published in the *Tulane Drama Review* (IV, 8). Reprinted by permission of the author and the *Tulane Drama Review*.

99

1910 and 1920. It is symptomatic that both in Europe and in America the frame of the drama becomes largely diffused, the genres merge and the stage is in full flight from reality in form or content or both. The revolution that started with Strindberg's *Dream Play* has come to fruition. The voices of dramatists that reach out from the past generation are those of Strindberg, Pirandello, Giraudoux, Cocteau, Wilder, Eliot, Kaiser, and Brecht. Just as in painting the fauvists, expressionists, cubists, futurists, surrealists, and abstractionists maintain their influence on the younger generation, so do their literary counterparts challenge the metarealistic or abstract theatre of such contemporaries as Anouilh, Aymé, Marceau, Sartre, Beckett, Ionesco, Genet, Adamov, Shehadé, Tennessee Williams, Arthur Miller, Osborne, Frisch, and Duerrenmatt. In their own ways they all struggle with the apparent meaninglessness or nothingness of existence. They are suspended above the dreadful and tempting pit of blackness, of death, some trying to infuse a purpose and to defy the absurdity of life by its very affirmation. The Sisyphus of Camus smiles as he starts again and again to push the stone uphill, and it is perhaps his happiness that lends essence to the modern comedy.

Common to all modern comedy is its devotion to the theatrics of the stage, to play acting, to the spectacle, to distraction. The play is the thing, and the moral, if any, though not necessarily secondary, must be so well integrated in the whole that the audience does not become aware of it, or if it does, that it reacts with a Brechtian kind of "alienation." In contrast to the naturalistic concept of the theatre as an illusion of reality with the fourth wall removed, the modern theatre, especially since Strindberg, Wedekind, and Pirandello, establishes the reality of illusion. With a sovereignty of spirit, kindred to romantic irony, the new drama creates a world of its own which denies accepted laws of rationality and recognizes only those of its own making. The *homo ludens* knows that he is playing and that the *ratio ludendi* need not be identical with the *ratio agendi*. Antonin Artaud in his *The Theatre and Its Double* calls for a "total" theatre without logic and rationalism. This implies an inherent danger of a contest between drama and stage. The stage takes over completely, reducing the drama to something like a scenario. The spectacular productions of the baroque stage are a case in point. The contemporary scene, too, is replete with such efforts; the pantomimic theatre in the German or French neo-romanticism of a Vollmöller or Maeterlinck, or more recently the Piscator productions in Berlin of *Hoopla, We Live!* or *Drums in the Night* with their impact on young Toller and Brecht, not to mention the earlier experiments of Expressionism, and in our time, Brecht, Anouilh, Genet, George Shehadé, Max Frisch are all fully aware of the splendid autonomy of the stage. And of these, it is difficult to imagine a greater display of theatrical pyrotechnics than those unleashed by Duerrenmatt. Figures appear out of trap doors, enter through windows and clocks, scenery flies up and down in full view, torture wheels are outlined against the sky, moon dances are performed on roofs, angels alight on chandeliers, chickens run across the stage, in short, every conceivable trick of the trade of the theatre, of the cabaret, the burlesque and the movies is applied with a lusty abandon.

Friedrich Duerrenmatt and Max Frisch are the realization of the age-old Swiss dream of producing dramatists of European rank. They are generally accepted as the most important living playwrights writing in German, and Duerrenmatt's fame reached some sort of an apogee with the New York production of *The Visit*, Maurice Valency's deviate adaptation of *The Visit of the Old Lady*. And yet, Duerrenmatt's contempt for the literary historian and his odd predilection for the detective story—"the only sure way of escaping critical attention"—makes it difficult when one attempts to arrive at a critical evaluation of his work.

Considering his age and fame, Duerrenmatt's literary output is anything but remarkable. He has published six full-length plays, at least five plays for the radio, and some remarkable prose which ranges from the short piercing outcries of unredeemed existential loneliness to social satire and the detective story. But two facts stand out, even upon a casual examination of his plays. Almost all have been reworked at least once, and almost all bear unusual baroque titles and subtitles in which, as may be expected, the term "comedy" predominates in one form or another. *It Is Written* (1945–46) and *The Blind Man* (1948) have no subtitles. *Romulus the Great*, "an unhistorical comedy" exists in two versions (1949 and 1957). *The Marriage of Mr. Mississippi*, "a comedy," produced in New York early in 1958 as *Fools Are Passing Through* in an adaptation by Maximilian Slater, has two versions (1952 and 1957). *An Angel Comes to Babylon*, "a fragmentary comedy in three acts," has three versions (1948, 1953, and 1957). *The Visit of the Old Lady*, "a tragicomedy in three acts," of 1956 was originally to have the sub-title "a bullish comedy."

Comedic elements also prevail in his short pieces, most of them "Radio Plays." Only two come to mind, where the theme is tragic throughout. The first *The Vega Enterprise*, printed in 1958 but broadcast a few years earlier, this much admired and discussed science-fiction thriller, ends pessimistically with the atomic bombing of Vega, the penal colony of the Earth, where in the dire effort of mere survival the separative forces of earthly prosperity have vanished and have yielded to a soberly exalting feeling of solidarity of one for all and all for one. The other is *A Nocturnal Conversation with a Despised Man*, "A Course for Contemporaries" (1957), a beautifully written dialogue between the secret executioner and the idealist and a dirge on the futility and eternity of self-sacrifice, on the art of dying and of humility. All his other radio plays share the grotesqueness and bizarreness of his full-length plays and, because of their necessarily greater concentration, exceed them in humor. They are: *Hercules and the Augean Stable* (1954) and *Stranitzky and the Nationalheld* (1956), two entirely different plays on the common theme of the professional hero, a character particularly objectionable to Duerrenmatt, though he does show some sympathetic understanding for his Hercules. Then there is the very funny *The Trial of the Asses' Shadow*, "a radio play based on Wieland, but not too much so" (1957), a tragicomedy of causality, and *An Evening in Late Autumn* (1957), a ragout of comedy, "who-done-it," and spoofing the literary admirer, wherein the Hemingway-like author, Korbes, writes crime stories with such convincing verisimilitude, as if he had committed them himself—which he has.

His nondramatic prose includes one full-length novel, the delightful *Greek Youth Seeks a Greek Maid*, "a prose comedy" (1955); three detective stories, which some critics consider in the tradition of Schiller, E. Th. A. Hoffmann, Poe, Chesterton, and Graham Greene: *The Judge and His Executioner* (1952), *Suspicion* (1953), and *The Promise*, "A Requiem for the Detective Novel" (1958); a collection of short stories, *The City* (1952), which contains pieces of uneven quality written from the depth of existential blackness, composed for the most part between 1943 and 1946. He considers them early attempts to come to grips with himself; finally, there is the significant story, *The Flat Tire*, a "Still Possible Story" (1956), with the theme of the awakening sense of responsibility for one's deeds and the ensuing self-execution after a grotesquely drunken all night session in which Traps, like Ill of *The Visit of the Old Lady*, accepts the death sentence as an expiation.

2

The main concern of this study, however, is Duerrenmatt's comedy. For this we must first turn to "Problems of the Theatre," an essay which is a statement of his dramatic principles as well as a confession of faith. In it he raises the question of whether the present world can be presented at all in the theatre. This man, now in his thirties, who has lived through all the falsehoods and empty promises of the years after 1930 has little faith in man as redeemer. As for great tragic heroes, what would they be doing in an age of automation that only knows impersonal institutions? The heroic drama cannot deal with boards of directors, or secretaries of nebulously anonymous executives. It needs a hero; and this is an unheroic age. Tragedy is essentially optimistic, it believes in the perfectibility of man. That faith is gone now. Life is and remains absurd, and there is—but for the unpredictable grace of God—no salvation. If this be nihilism, make the best of it. Yet this realization does not call for despair. On the other hand, the modern author can no longer write in the grand tragic tradition, for:

> Tragedy presupposes guilt, despair, moderation, lucidity, vision, a sense of responsibility. In the Punch-and-Judy show of our century, in this backsliding of the white race, there are no more guilty and also, no responsible men. It is always, "We couldn't help it" and "We didn't really want that to happen." And indeed, things happen without anyone in particular being responsible for them. Everything is dragged along and everyone gets caught somewhere in the sweep of events. We are all collectively guilty, collectively bogged down in the sins of our fathers and of our forefathers. We are the offspring of children. That is our misfortune, but not our guilt: guilt can exist only as a personal achievement as a religious deed. Comedy alone is suitable for us. Our world has led to the grotesque as well as to the atom bomb, and so it is a world like that of Hieronymus Bosch whose apocalyptic paintings are also grotesque. But the grotesque is only

a way of expressing in a tangible manner, of making us perceive physically the paradoxical, the form of the unformed, the face of a world without face; and just as in our thinking today we seem to be unable to do without the concept of the paradox, so also in art, and in our world which at times seems still to exist only because the atom bomb exists: out of fear of the bomb.

But the tragic is still possible even if pure tragedy is not. We can achieve the tragic out of comedy. We can bring it forth as a frightening moment, as an abyss that opens suddenly; indeed many of Shakespeare's tragedies are already really comedies out of which the tragic arises.

After all this the conclusion might easily be drawn that comedy is the expression of despair, but this conclusion is not inevitable. To be sure, whoever realizes the senselessness, the hopelessness of this world might well despair, but this despair is not a result of this world. Rather it is an answer given by an individual to this world; another answer would be not to despair, would be an individual's decision to endure this world in which we live like Gulliver among the giants. He also achieves distance, he also steps back a pace or two who takes measure of his opponent, who prepares himself to fight his opponent or to escape him. It is still possible to show man as a courageous being. . . . The world (hence the stage which represents this world) is for me something monstrous, a riddle of misfortunes which must be accepted but before which one must not capitulate. The world is far bigger than any man, and perforce threatens him constantly. If one could but stand outside the world, it would no longer be threatening. But I have neither the right nor the ability to be an outsider to this world. To find solace in poetry can also be all too cheap; it is more honest to retain one's human point of view.

Duerrenmatt's concept of comedy then, is the result of an overall *Weltanschauung*. Since, however, its life blood remains tragic, it is essential to investigate by what means an inherently tragic subject may assume the form of a comedy and a nonheroic character heroic dimensions.

In his excellent introduction to the third volume of the German edition of Anouilh's plays, Gerhart F. Hering underscores the critical nature of modern comedy and its function as the conscience of the age by its tendency to overstate reality to the point of clowning. The cathartic impact of the comedy is achieved by its expansion into the macabre-grotesque, "as used again among the contemporary dramatists by Friedrich Duerrenmatt as an aggressive stylistic device in gratefully acknowledged discipleship of Frank Wedekind" (p. 14). The grotesque is undoubtedly the most striking and immediately apparent aspect of Duerrenmatt's comedy. One is tempted to invoke Strindberg's famous introduction to his *The Dream Play*, where everything can happen, everything is possible, time and place cease to exist, fancy goes weaving new patterns from an insignificant bit of reality into a tapestry made of memories, experiences, ideas, improbabilities and incidental writing.

In Duerrenmatt's love of the macabre, there is a definite kinship to Kafka and E. Th. A. Hoffmann and a spiritual affinity to the graphic art of Alfred Kubin in the conceptualization of a situation as well as in its *mise en scène*. Duerrenmatt visualizes scenes with the eye of an experienced draftsman before he translates them into the idiom of an imaginative stage, as for instance the moon dance scene at the end of *It Is Written* or Akki's abode under the Euphrates bridge in *An Angel Comes to Babylon*, to pick but two examples. Hence also his preference for the stage settings of Teo Otto: "I have little use for a theatre that uses black curtains as was the fashion once upon a time, or for the tendency to glory in threadbare poverty which some stage designers seem to aim for."

It Is Written, the play about the Anabaptists in Münster, in spite of its immaturity and its lack of economy and discretion, best demonstrates Duerrenmatt's characteristic dramatic devices. In form and subject matter it is a kindred spirit to such divergent plays as Goethe's *Götz von Berlichingen*, Hauptmann's *Florian Geyer*, Sartre's *Le Diable et le bon Dieu*, and Cocteau's *Bacchus*. It also shows Duerrenmatt's love for Nestroy and the Viennese folk theatre, "This most wonderful phenomenon in the German theatre." A discussion in greater detail might therefore be indicated.

The play's tragic theme of man's search for God is introduced in shocking terms: As the stage lights go on, three Anabaptists are kneeling in front of the curtain invoking in a baroque poetic form

their involuntarily humorous apocalyptic visions. A stage direction
warns us not to take them seriously:

> One needn't take these scoundrels seriously enough to
> construct a special scene for them, God forbid; it is enough
> to let them appear in front of the curtain. The director and
> the actors are welcome to make use of their own ideas for
> we are only supplying a few scanty notes and touches toward
> a colorful world which yesterday looked exactly like today
> and tomorrow.

We note the primacy of the stage and the reintroduction of improvisation as practiced in the commedia dell'arte and in Viennese folk
theatre. The "Idea" has a prominent place in the Duerrenmatt design. Here, as in other instances, it sometimes takes over the play and
carries the author merrily and recklessly to a burlesque exuberance—
he calls it "Übermut"—which he considers an essential condiment of
the comedy. Words, he says, are of great but not of exclusive importance. Almost as important are stage "Ideas" (Übermut), the
rhetorical gesture which he loves so dearly and which according to
him was lost for the world of drama when a naturalistic actor with
bad memory could not remember his part. Striking also is his varied
use of the Tieck-like touch of romantic irony: for instance, the
author's addressing the reader in his stage direction or in the very
next scene the monk's speaking out of character directly to the audience as he criticizes the preceding action and at the same time
introduces himself in a long monologue of rhythmic prose. This is a
trick common to the oriental theatre as well as to Nestroy and Brecht
and is used extensively by Duerrenmatt. The device of the monologue
is very important here as well as in the next few plays. It serves several
purposes: first, it introduces a character in the manner of a *conférencier*, who comments on actions past and future with conscious
anachronism, e.g., here when the monk states that he is neither
historical nor, fortunately, has he ever lived:

> I appear only a few times in this play, two or three times,
> perhaps. Why, it even happens once in a while that I don't
> have to appear at all, because the director has cut me out
> to shorten the play or because he is one actor shy. Even now,
> as I am talking to you, I am not much more than a silence

filler. To be sure the curtain has gone up and all eyes are on the stage, but no one quite knows how it goes from here.

Here is the second function of the monologue as the time filler, the substitute for a curtain between scenes, and also as the *raconteur*, and the obliterator of time and space. The monologue may also, in an expansiveness of language, grow into something like a couplet or *chanson*, a *Liedeinlage* à la Nestroy, as for example, later on in the play, Bockelson's recital of his multifarious regal culinary or connubial joys. (Sometimes, however, to the boredom of the audience, Duerrenmatt allows himself to be intoxicated by his own eloquence.)

The introduction of Bockelson is a hilarious bit of buffoonery in the best tradition of the folk theatre. The recital of Bockelson's several survivals reminds one of Nestroy's Knieriem, and the watchman with his *judico ergo sum*, and the learned street cleaner who has absorbed at least as many faculties as Faust, are of the same species. Even the first appearance of Knipperdollinck, the richest man and truly pious leader of Münster, the earnest Godseeker and the antithesis of the self-seeker Bockelson, still follows the pattern of the folk-comedy. He has qualms about his wealth, in view of the Biblical statement about the rich man and the eye of the needle. As Bockelson makes his harlequin entrance demanding a share of his host's wealth, we have again an example of mixing the serious and the comic. Knipperdollinck is revealed as the tragic character who presumes to fathom God's will.

The shoving onto the stage in a wheel chair of the centenarian bishop is another bit of macabre drollery. There follow again a lengthy address to the audience, references to the stage as a stage, allusions to the stage present as contrasted with historical time, and a striking sample of romantic irony anticipatory of future action:

> If you get to see things that appear too cruel and too nonsensical to you, don't get too scared: Believe me, the world can endure any wound and on the whole it does not matter so much, whether man is happy or not; for happiness was not given to him; and he has it only because of a great act of grace. Above all, it is necessary that he exists, stumbling on earth. I know there is much misery down here and much despair and confusion without end. Yet if we do not seem to take it all too seriously here on stage, it is not in

order to mock your misfortune and ours, but because we want to show man's actions a bit disengaged from the gravity of earth and in the light of those regions in which the lines are more distinct and less blurred, and in which the forms rise in clean contrast from the background. All of us, or at least all of us here on stage, lived four centuries before you . . . etc.

This parodistic anachronism is exceeded later on by the expatiation of the class-conscious proletarian vegetable woman on the importance of onions for the propagation of mankind if it is to survive:

for the dark Middle Ages have barely passed and ahead still lie the Thirty Years' War, The War of Succession, the Seven Years' War, the French Revolution, Napoleon, the Franco-Prussian War, the First World War, Hitler, the Second, Third . . . Twelfth World War. This is why children are needed! Ladies and gentlemen, and corpses too! Help the course of the world, consider the future and eat onions, what difference does a little stench more or less make?

The shift from the comic to the tragic comes too abruptly for its own effectiveness. Thus the discourse on religion between the Bishop and Knipperdollinck loses a good deal of its impact by the preceding parodistic introduction to the Bishop. Matthisson, the fanatical Anabaptist leader, suffers a similar theatrical fate. He literally pops up from a trap and gives vent to his dislike of the play and its frivolous attitude, saving his strongest censure for the hapless playwright of this dubious and impudent parody on Anabaptism, who is nothing but a

. . . literally uprooted Protestant, afflicted with the boil of doubt, suspicious of the faith which he admires because he lost it, a kind of mixture of hollow clichés and a scurrilous enjoyment of indecencies. He does not shrink from tucking in his tail even before the Pope, the arch enemy of religion, only to renew his monstrous attacks upon us from that front, too.

This is one of his best displays of romantic irony, an honest bit of self-persiflage, and a humble confession. For, as will be seen later,

Duerrenmatt comes to grips here with man's greatest glory and even greater tragedy: his incomprehension of and impatience with the design of the world order and his foredoomed attempts at correction in the role of the self-appointed savior. This is also the crucial problem of *The Marriage of Milord Mississippi* and *An Angel Comes to Babylon.*

The next scene introduces the trick of flying scenery, which performs an important function here as everywhere. The stage directions are couched in typical ironical *Übermut:*

> The camp of the mercenaries, painted on wrapping paper, is lowered in front of the two Anabaptists [of the previous scene] who are sitting motionless. The sky on it is dark blue with a yellow three-quarter moon, a few splotches in all colors, which are supposed to represent stars, and a medium sized not too expensive comet. One can also recognize the planet Saturn with its ring and Mars with a few canals, on which sailing boats ply. Two magnificently and martially attired men step in front of this wrapping paper. Their visors are closed and must be raised every time they speak, whereupon they drop again, covering their faces.

After Matthisson's vainglorious death, Bockelson takes over the defense. Instead of introducing battle scenes in a Shakespearian manner, Duerrenmatt has him jump out of the orchestra pit to where the conductor might stand, "raised and jutting into the audience," and keeping his sword pointed at von Büren, the commander of the mercenaries. The lights go out and music and darkness substitute for "the impossible stage battles." Scene follows scene in quick succession giving a snapshot view of both the epic progression of action as well as the crystallizing contours of the main protagonists. Nothing and nobody is safe from Duerrenmatt's absurdly irreverent parody and ironic buffoonery, not even the majesty of Charles V: "With great skill the make-up man has made me look like my picture by Titian which is hanging in the Münster Pinakothek." Or the impossible scene with the Turkish chronometer or the chamberlain's dusting off the Emperor with a feather duster. An out and out farcical introduction leads again to most serious reflection, which, in turn, is interrupted by the intrusion of burlesque, as the backstage howling regularly emitted by the two month old Infante Philip upon every mention of torture, hanging, and quartering.

The second half of the play seems to be little more than an arbitrary proliferation of wild scenes which put the most virulent Storm and Stress of a Klinger or Lenz to shame. The tempo obviously intends, by its rising breathlessness, to convey the quickening of the pulse of the action, but all it actually achieves is the embarrassingly short breath of asthma. The revelatory soliloquies multiply without adding the zest of a new "Idea." As the play approaches the end there is the scene of the mutual judgment between Knipperdollinck and Bockelson culminating in the macabre moon dance of life and death; the last moment of the two on the wheel with the return to the grotesque humor of the beginning and the final summing up of the senseless sense of this tragedy in the discourse of the Bishop and the Landgrave as they stand before the wheels:

>   LANDGRAVE: They have paid for their guilt.
>
>   BISHOP: Guilt, expiation. What small words . . . Man's deeds are the rack to which God has bound him.
>
>   LANDGRAVE: They were fools for trying to fly before they learned walking.
>
>   BISHOP: Were they able to stand when Luther sought to teach them how to walk? . . .
>
>   LANDGRAVE: A life without sense! Despised by all!
>
>   BISHOP: The sense lies in their torment.
>   For what ever happens manifests Thy infinity, O Lord! The depth of my despair is but a symbol of Thy justice and my body lies in this wheel like in a cup which Thou fillest now with your grace to the brim!

Summing up Duerrenmatt's first dramatic effort, we see certain tendencies come to the fore which—with greater skill and discretion —remain typical for his drama: the grotesque setting of a tragicomedy with strong emphasis on the bizarre and macabre; ample variations of romantic irony by the *conférencier* method, by parody, by anachronism, and by exaggeration; the yielding to idea and exuberance (*Einfall* and *Übermut*); the broad use of the soliloquy for purposes of persiflage, epic link, curtain, elimination of time and space, and intensification into a *chanson*; the use of choral speaking and similar vaudeville techniques; the preëminence of the stage by every conceivable trick of the trade; and the consistent mixture of the tragic and the comic in the shocking contrasts of sequences.

The next play, *The Blind Man*, never appeared in a trade edition. This version of the Job story, set at the time of the Thirty Years' War with the Italian nobleman Negro da Ponte playing the part of Satan, is the story of a faith which is stronger than all efforts to maintain it by deceit, or deny it, or destroy it. By means of its epigraph from Matthew 9:29, "Then touched he their eyes, saying according to your faith be it unto you," Duerrenmatt approaches the ramparts of unprotesting acceptance which our age has lost. At the outbreak of the war the Duke has become desperately ill, and now having recovered, he is completely blind and completely happy; for what greater miracles could have happened to him than his recovery, his blindness that opened his eyes, and the sanctuary of his domains, which by Divine grace have been spared from the ravages of the war. He is aided and abetted in his belief by the pious connivance of his Hamlet-like son Palamedes who without faith, with little love and much sadness had created an illusory world for his father. The Duke has faith in da Ponte, whom he makes governor over all his domains, but he misjudges as weakness and selfishness his son's efforts to defend the blind man's world against the frivolous design of da Ponte. He yearns for the love of his daughter Octavia, who has renounced the world of father and brother and has given herself to da Ponte in her search for his beautiful Italy, his paradise lost, to which he can never return nor can she find the way! The Duke's blind happiness and trust in him is da Ponte's great temptation. He must destroy this world of faith which has escaped all delusion and despair. This is his calling and this his conspiracy with the scum of the war, the actor and his fellow derelicts. With their aid he prepares to destroy the Duke's faith:

> I cast him to you, my rabble, as one casts a bone to the dogs. He shall not be broken by the greatness of the world, but he shall perish from its ludicrousness which is the same as his. Inflict all troubles upon this blind man, drive away his sleep . . . His foot shall never rest, and when he collapses cast him down in anguish. Then you will see what

man is: A screaming mouth, two broken eyes in which nothing is reflected anymore.

But the Duke's faith is stronger than Palamedes' nihilistic self-accusation and condemnation, stronger than the daughter's death in empty despair, stronger than the court poet Gnadenbrot Suppe's realistic truth which the Duke chokes to the silence of death, stronger than all the diabolical visitations of negation by the actors, stronger, alas, than Satan himself, who in the end must admit defeat. In his blindness the Duke sees a higher sense in creation in spite of all absurdity:

> The time has come when men are standing with empty hands, gathered like animals about sealed springs . . . We must grow silent, only then shall we hear . . . What we once possessed has been taken from us . . . What was between man and God has been broken; like shard lies man's greatness about us, and the road which we must travel is hewn into our flesh like into a rock. Thus we have received what is our due; thus we are turned back to the place that we must occupy; thus we lie shattered in the face of God; and thus we live in his truth.

> DA PONTE: Then the seeing are blind and the blind are seeing.

> DUKE: Become blind and ye shall see.

> DA PONTE: I have been vanquished at the hands of one who will not defend himself. For he who opposes me, falls prey to me and whoever resists is lost. I leave you now just as Satan left Job, a black shadow.

And the Duke speaks the final words of the play: "Go hence from me in the name of God."

This play blends tragic and grotesque rather than comic elements. The satanic retinue of da Ponte and their make-believe world for the benefit of the Duke is reminiscent of Wedekind's *King Nicolo* with the many scenes of grotesque crudeness. On the whole, the stage is rather tame; the set is the ruin of the Duke's castle throughout, and eerie changes are achieved with lighting.

Though the play is heavy-footed, with its flirtations with *King*

Lear, Hamlet, King Nicolo and German Neo-Romanticism, it is still noteworthy for its poetry. Its concern with man's lot in a world without faith places it in the main stream of twentieth-century drama. We need but think of Hofmannsthal's *The Tower,* of Werfel's *Paul Among the Jews* and *The Kingdom of God in Bohemia,* and of the great symbolical plays of Barlach of three decades ago, or more recently, Giraudoux's *Sodome et Gomorrhe,* Valéry's *Mon Faust,* Cocteau's *Bacchus,* Sartre's *Le Diable et le bon Dieu,* T. S. Eliot's *The Cocktail Party,* and Wilder's *The Skin of Our Teeth.*

If *The Blind Man* is Duerrenmatt's most Shakespearean play, then *Romulus the Great* is his most Shavian. This persiflage of history again follows a pattern important in modern drama, namely the use of classical, Biblical, or historical subjects to reflect contemporary concerns. As far as the bizarre and spectacular are concerned, *Romulus the Great* makes the least demands on the stage and easily falls into its four acts. Purely from the point of view of constructing a viable play, it is probably his most successful. It is clever, witty, graceful, full of fine repartée and irony. There are few if any stage tricks, and Nestroy's impact is felt in the cleverness of the dialogue and in the conception of certain characters. The play, in its travesty on the military in the dying Roman Empire and on the humorless, mission-ridden submissiveness of the future idol of Germanic hero worship is also a good example of Duerrenmatt's characteristic irony.

However, a different type of comic character is introduced in the person of Cäsar Rupf, a tremendously wealthy trouser manufacturer who is determined to dress the Roman Empire in pants come what may, either by bribing Odoaker to leave or siding with him against the Empire. Irony turns here to mordant satire.

The third act, set in the Emperor's bedroom approaches burlesque. And yet, as in his first play, Duerrenmatt uses burlesque as a frame for the central serious action—the destiny of Rome. When finally Odoaker appears, he looks like a tourist and knows more about Rome, its history, its culture and its beauty than the Emperor himself. (Shades of German tourism!) He is a pleasant peace-loving farmer who started out on a war because of nationalistic pressures. Now he fears that one of these days his presently loyal and respectful nephew, the abstemious and chaste Theoderich, will assassinate him to become the great national idol and will lead the German people to ever greater and more destructive victories.

Here Duerrenmatt performs a most daring intellectual *salto mor-*

tale. To forestall this dreadful future, Odoaker has come to surrender to the Roman Emperor, who for the same reasons has taken no action in order that the empire might be destroyed by the Germans. We witness the amazing attempts at mutual persuasion, the one begging for the acceptance of surrender, the other for his own death. The impasse culminates in a compromise solution: Odoaker is proclaimed King of Italy, and in a remarkable switch in the party line the Emperor receives the official homage of the German generals and accepts retirement and a pension from the victorious Germans who submit to an official surrender. Who is the winner and who the loser? There are no winners—all human schemes at shaping destiny fail before its own irresistible force. Fate will not be bargained with:

> ROMULUS: My dear Odoaker, I wanted to *play* fate and you
> wanted to *avoid* yours. It now has turned out to be our fate
> to be shipwrecked politicians. We thought we could just
> drop the world out of our hands, you your Germany and I
> my Rome. Now we have to attend to the wreckage which
> we cannot just drop. I executed Rome because I feared its
> past, you executed Germany because you shuddered at its
> future. We allowed ourselves to be persuaded by two ghosts;
> for we have no power over that which was, as little as we
> have power over that which will be. We only have power
> over the present which we did not consider and which now
> causes our failure.

Reality has corrected their ideas. "Bear the bitter lot and try to put some sense into all this senselessness. Give the world a few peaceful years, Odoaker, which history will, of course, skip because of their lack of spectacular feats of heroism. Let us finish out our comedy. Let us pretend that the impossible equation has a solution, that the spirit has won out over the matter Man." History informs us of the German succession to the glories of the great Roman Empire.

The next two plays return to the more or less complicated symbolical stage business of *It Is Written*. They apply it, however, with much greater skill and discretion. The first, *The Marriage of Milord Mississippi*, is a *Lehrstück* (Learning Play). It owes something to Wedekind (particularly *The Marquis of Keith*); it shows evidence of linguistic affinity to Sternheim's annihilating satire of the correct bourgeois; and in its quality of "demonstration" it is closely related to Brecht. Yet, in spite of all these associations, it is very much the author's play, and the comparisons are coincidental rather than derivative.

The play starts with what is really its ending: Saint-Claude's execution, and then it proceeds to demonstrate how it got to that point, by having each one of three protagonists present by illustrated monologue his version of the story. This does not imply the use of a flashback technique, although there is a similarity. The element of self-justification, or perhaps better, of defense before a higher tribunal (inherent in all of Duerrenmatt's plays), is particularly strong in this one and brings to mind the technique of the medieval mystery, especially in the concept of the test, or *"Bewährungsprobe."* (The "hundred per centers" of ideologies, as Henry Hewes calls Mississippi and Saint-Claude, also bring to mind Ibsen's *Brand* and Sartre's *Les Mains sales.*)

How great a part is played by the stage as symbol and as vehicle of the tragicomedy is evident from the extensive stage directions. It is spiced with such remarks as, "the room smells to high heaven" with its bourgeois lack of taste. There are two windows in the background; their view: confusing. Right, a Nordic city with apple trees and Gothic cathedral; left, a cypress, ruins of a classical temple, a bay, a port. The explanation of this confusion is given in "Problems of the Theatre" where Duerrenmatt speaks of the dematerialization not only of the stage set but even more so of the locus of the drama:

> . . . in *The Marriage of Milord Mississippi* . . . I expressed the indefiniteness of the locale (in order to give its spirit of wit, of comedy) by having the right window of a room look out upon a northern landscape with its Gothic cathedral and apple tree, while the left window of the same room opens on a southern scene with an ancient ruin, a touch of the Mediterranean and a cypress. The really decisive point in all this is that, to quote Max Frisch, the playwright is making poetry with the stage, a possibility which has always entertained and occupied me and which is one of the reasons, if not the main one, why I write plays. But then—and I am thinking of the comedies of Aristophanes and the comic plays of Nestroy—in every age poetry has been written not only *for,* but *with* the stage.

(Similarly in *An Angel Comes to Babylon,* the stage has to indicate the two loci of the drama, heaven and Babylon, heaven as the mysterious point of departure and Babylon as the place of action. To indicate the vastness and the incomprehensibility of heaven he prescribes a gigantic drop of the Andromedae nebula as might be seen at Mt. Palomar and to stress the ubiquitousness of the metropolis he designs a Babylon somewhere between New York and Paris.)

As the play opens we find Saint-Claude, already having been executed, informing the audience "partly like a manager of a second rate stock company, partly like a Mephisto" that for therapeutic reasons the last scene of the play is put first, because thereby one of the worst scenes of the play is gotten out of the way, and further, the play is not only about the marriage of Mr. Mississippi but also about the fate of three men—at this point three "pathetic portraits," Saint-Claude's, Übelohe's, and Mississippi's, the two on either end draped in black crepe, descend and remain hovering in the background—three men, "who proceeding from different methods . . . got it into their heads . . . to change the world and in part to save it. They had however the cruel misfortune of encountering a woman, (Picture of Anastasia, likewise draped in black crepe, descends and hovers between Übelohe and Mississippi) who was neither to be changed nor to be saved, for she loved nothing but the moment . . . and therefore one could just as well have called this comedy . . . *Mrs. Anastasia and her Lovers.*" The play could also start differently, for instance with the Rumanian revolution against King Michael, or Übelohe performing an appendectomy in some rotten hole in the interior of Borneo (both scenes descend). The locus of the play is undetermined; the author thought first of the South, then of the North. At any rate, we have to go back five years: over the hall clock there hangs now the picture of the recently deceased husband of Anastasia. The maid is showing Mr. Mississippi in just as Saint-Claude is climbing out through the window on the left.

And so the play really starts. Mississippi, the man of law of the Old Testament, of an eye for an eye, the prosecuting attorney, the fanatic of strict justice for whom modern laws are too humane, the absolute and uncompromising moralist, the reformer through severe punishment, proposes marriage to Anastasia as the most perfect expiation. For she has poisoned her husband for his infidelity with Mississippi's wife. He, in his turn, has just poisoned his wife for the same reason. In either case the poison was procured under false pretenses from Übelohe, who, realizing what Anastasia has done, has fled to Borneo in order to protect her by his absence. Of course, the plot gets much more involved until truth seems unobtainable.

The *conférencier* style has been enriched by the "Moritat" element of telling a gory story with the aid of illustrative material. Next, Mississippi presents his side of the story as *raconteur* of the five years of marriage with Anastasia, "the Angel of prisons," a perfect, self-denying penance—or so he thinks. His friend the minister Diego enters unseen by Mississippi through the hall clock. (Duerrenmatt points to this as an example of "*Übermut*.") He has come to ask for Mississippi's resignation since his fanatically murderous sense of justice is causing popular unrest, fomented, as we soon find out, by the communist agitator Saint-Claude. Duerrenmatt uses at this juncture an interesting device to demonstrate the relativity of truth; for had the protagonist of this scene known what the protagonist of the same scene retold knows, the outcome would surely have been different. This situation should not, however, be confused with the certain knowledge of the eternally inexorable necessity under which Pirandello's characters live. Here, as in Kleist's *The Broken Pitcher* the audience is informed while the players are groping for the truth to the end. In a way it resembles the Aeschylean Fate, with comic implications.

The situation at the entrance of Saint-Claude is no different in principle: "Could the audience be wrong if it seems to them that Saint-Claude were just coming from Anastasia whose hand he is kissing as he enters?" In the ensuing scene he tries to blackmail Mississippi into accepting the leadership of the Communist party since, because of his three hundred and fifty executions, he has the best qualifications. Next we learn of the origin of the two in the absurdly factitious story told with the mock-seriousness and pathos of a Sternheim *Colportage*. Mississippi is not as we thought the natural child of an Italian princess and an American general celebrated for his cruelty, but, like Saint-Claude, a product of the gutter. He has studied at Oxford with the money earned at a brothel which both of them ran. Mississippi had learned by reading in a stinking cellar from a Bible he found there:

> Would I have stayed alive another day had not this vision
> of the law consumed me like an ocean of fire which swept
> into our darkness so that from that moment on everything

I did, the lowest humiliation and the meanest crime served only one purpose: To let me study at Oxford in order to reintroduce as public prosecutor the law of Moses, driven on by the realization that humanity must go back three thousand years in order to progress again.

Saint-Claude, on the other hand, had a similar catharsis with a copy of *Das Kapital* which he found in the pocket of a murdered pimp: "Have I not endured this dreadful life which was forced upon us only to proclaim some day the world revolution? We are the two last great moralists of our times." Both redeemers are possessed by their one and only truth. The one upholds the justice of heaven, the other, the justice of the earth: "You wish to save an imaginary soul and I a real body." Mississippi remains adamant. Saint-Claude will call a general strike against him.

Sorrowfully Saint-Claude leaves through the window with a lyrical farewell:

> Farewell, I disappear again. We were brothers who were seeking one another in a night that was all too dark, alas. We have cried for each other but we did not find ourselves. It was the only chance but the hour was impropitious. . . . We had everything, you the intelligence and I the strength, you the terror and I the popularity, and both of us had an ideal background. What a history making pair the two of us would have made!

Stones begin to fly through the window, Anastasia enters in a nightgown: "You are all I have left, Madame, the angel of the prisons, a shield with which I defy all humanity." Curtain, lights—Übelohe steps quickly in front of the curtain, begging the audience not to leave for the intermission until they have witnessed his scene.

Now comes the third soliloquy with its Pirandellesque version of personal truth. Some of Duerrenmatt's best writing and most gripping thinking goes into Übelohe's recitation of his struggle with his author for a different fate and a worthier love than Lilith-Anastasia, but in vain, for the author is infatuated with his fate as if it were his own. In this wonderful bit of romantic irony which touches on the question of all destiny Übelohe pleads with the audience:

> A question must be raised at this critical juncture of the action, into which you, ladies and gentlemen as spectators,

and we here on stage have been written by an insidious author, namely, what share he had in all of it; whether he allowed himself to drift without a plan from idea to idea, or whether he was guided by a mysterious plan. Oh, I am willing to believe him, that he did not conceive me frivolously and that he was primarily concerned to investigate what happens when certain ideas collide with men who take such ideas truly seriously and who strive with courageous energy and raging madness as well as with an inexhaustible cupidity for perfection to translate them into reality. . . . I am also willing to believe that the curiosity of the author was concerned with the question of whether the spirit in one form or another is capable of changing a world which only exists and which has no idea whether the world as matter is incorrigible. . . . It remains however a most lamentable fact that he [the author], once he had created us, no longer interfered in our fate. . . . And so he created me, me, the only one whom he loved with his whole heart, because I alone in this play take the adventure of love upon myself, that sublime task which to fulfill or in the cause of which to succumb represents man's greatest distinction.

And instead of giving him a Beatrice with whom a good Catholic author would have rewarded him, he gave him that image of earth, that "Frau Welt" Anastasia.

So this lover of cruel tales and good-for-nothing comedies . . . this tough writing Protestant and lost visionary smashed me in order to taste my pith . . . and he dishonored me lest I resemble a saint for whom he has no use but rather that I become like him; to cast me into the melting pot of his comedy not as victor but as vanquished, the only position into which man gets again and again—and all this only in order to ascertain whether Divine Grace in this limited world of ours really is without limit, our only hope.

This is followed by a sequence of scenes of bizarre grotesqueness far exceeding the exaggerations of Wedekind's Lulu plays. The stage again is central. There is a wonderful confusion of tricks: A canvas descends; Mississippi in front of it protests Anastasia's loyalty and behind it two pairs of legs indicate a clinch—Anastasia and the minister. The inebriated Übelohe just back from the tropics breaks in—more confusion, more burlesque (the minister must not be seen here), divulgence of Anastasia's past five years, Übelohe faints, comes to, wants to tell Mississippi the whole truth; she is full of terror; the scene is interrupted by the representatives of the clergy who have come to express in choral speaking and Faustian verse their admiration and gratitude to Anastasia—they leave. Anastasia wants to run away with Übelohe, but he will stay and wait for the miracle. And down comes the curtain again to end part one.

The second part does not quite measure up to the first. The scene remains the same and changes are only apparent through the windows. As the action begins, an insurrection is going on. Mississippi collapses from a bullet under an apple tree; he crawls through the window into his house and finds Anastasia and Übelohe together. Übelohe, who has returned from Borneo a ruined alcoholic but retaining his holy and mad zeal, is waiting for the miraculous moment of truth. Mississippi proceeds to address Übelohe in his flawless, deliberate, unnatural, super-refined language: "I welcome you home," are his very first words. The entire conversation about Anastasia's and Übelohe's love is carried on in this tone—part of the time on the floor because of the flying bullets. Mississippi refuses to believe that Anastasia had been Übelohe's mistress when, out of love for him, she had poisoned her first husband. The shooting stops, the insurrection is quelled. There follows the confrontation with Anastasia who swears that she never loved Übelohe. Doctors enter through all the doors and windows to take Mississippi to the insane asylum on orders from the new premier. Anastasia and Übelohe are again alone. He forgives her, for he knows that fear may be greater than love. The miracle for which he had been waiting has happened, they are free, but now separated forever. Nothing is left but the love of a ludicrous fool. To the last he will carry this great love, which can no longer belong to only one person, into all the market places of the world, a laughingstock, a last Christian.

> Henceforth I shall call out your name like the cry of the
>> pestilent
> Which warns the wanderer, I shall call it into the night into
>> which
> I disappear. You have cursed me but I love you. Yet hence-
>> forth

I turn away from you.
You shall never look again in my face.
I leave you forever.
But I take with me
My love for you;
This love which never grows weaker,
The love that burned me out and killed me
And in whose name I arise again and again.
I bury it into the lands through which I now wander, wearily,
A ruined count, derelict from booze,
Sharing this love with every beggar.
Thus I am ejaculated upon an earth which no longer can be
     saved,
And I am nailed to the cross of my ludicrousness;
I am affixed to that beam
That mocks me,
Raised toward the face of God,
Unshielded,
A last Christian.

The canvas presenting an airplane in which Anastasia dreams of escaping to the only country of safe refuge, Chile, descends, as the now beardless Saint-Claude steps in front of it in full dress. There is no sense in Anastasia's wasting any further thought on Übelohe. The insurrection has been quelled and he is in disgrace with the party. The Soviets are after his head. The Premier is getting married in a great public ceremony. (A tableau descends depicting that scene to snatches from Beethoven's Ninth.) We see Mississippi in an asylum uniform climbing and disappearing into Anastasia's room. Anastasia returns from her vain quest for the Premier and whether she likes it or not she is going to go underground with Saint-Claude, who will return her to her true calling, and, who knows, one of these days he may work himself up again to the proprietorship of a brothel. Coffee is being served. She drops something white out of her medallion into his cup. He does not drink but rushes her to get dressed for the reception at the American Ambassador's, for this is the only way of evading the attention of the Russian executioners. He leaves to steal a car for the escape. Alas, he was too sure of his disguise or he would have noticed three suspicious figures.

Mississippi in the robes of his office of prosecutor enters the empty stage to interrogate his wife. He notices the cups, puts poison into one. Anastasia returns dressed in a red evening gown and assures him that she was expecting him. In a pathetic speech he insists she tell him the truth, for if he has not converted her to the necessity of atoning, then his whole life—from gutter to insane asylum—has lost all justification. They drink the coffee, and even in the face of death she maintains her innocence. A great triumph for Mississippi who is also feeling the pangs of death:

> Then the law is not senseless? Then it is not senseless that
> I have killed? The wars are not senseless, the multiplying
> revolutions that condense themselves to one single fanfare
> blast of death? Then there is sense to the Last Judgment?

Why did Anastasia lie to the last? Is it that as a woman she could not hurt the man so deeply? Or did she, the woman, believe in a truth which did not follow the absolute standards of men but was the truth for the moment? No clear answer is given to Mississippi or to us. What remains is the palliative of pious consolation.

Saint-Claude at once realizing the truth, paints to the dying Mississippi a picture of a new and promising future running a brothel. He rings for coffee. Instead of the maid, three raincoated men with armbands appear—we know the rest. The Grand Guignol is finished. But not the play: Sitting up, Mississippi announces: This is our story, this is how we died, hangmen and hanged for our own deeds. Through the window enters the Premier. He covets nothing but power, hence the world belongs to him, as does Anastasia who rises and embraces him, "a whore that goes through death unchanged." The macabre ensemble of a musical comedy reaches a crescendo of a sort in the nihilistic duet of Saint-Claude and Mississippi singing of their eternal return. Their illusion of striving for a better world hides from them their true motivations: their desire for revenge on society and for acceptance by society. The fate of the unwanted outcast knocking in vain at the doors of bourgeois respectability is their great tragedy:

> SAINT-CLAUDE: Yet, whether we are lying here in this ruin,
>
> MISSISSIPPI: Whether we die against a whitewashed wall, or
> on a slowly sinking pyre tied to a wheel, between heaven
> and earth,

SAINT-CLAUDE: We return again and again as we always returned,

MISSISSIPPI: Forever in new forms yearning for ever more distant paradises;

SAINT-CLAUDE: Ostracized from your midst again and again,

MISSISSIPPI: Nurtured by your indifference,

SAINT-CLAUDE: Thirsting for your brotherliness,

MISSISSIPPI: We sweep over your cities;

SAINT-CLAUDE: Panting we turn the mighty wings

MISSISSIPPI: Driving the mill that grinds you to grist.

Taking his cue from the world *"Mühle"* (mill), Überlohe grotesquely attired, a new Don Quixote of the absurd age, appears in the window, ridiculous yet moving, desperate yet not conquered, Don Quixote the sweet and chivalrous knight, the eternal promise and hope of Duerrenmatt, as he is of Unamuno. And he intones his sad and brave finale which brings down the curtain:

> Often cudgeled, often mocked and
> Yet defiant.
> Well, then!
> As Thou raise us with Thy swirling hand,
> Horse and man, wretched both,
> As you smash us against the glittering
> Silver of the glassy sky:
> Riding on my nag
> I fall
> Over Thy greatness
> Into the flaming abyss of infinity.
> An eternal comedy.
> So that Thy glory may shine
> Fed by our impotence.

There is no end to men's quest and folly. Settings may change, but man remains the same. There are always the Bickelsons and Saint Claudes, and the Knipperdollincks and the Mississippis; but the temporary victories will go to the uncommitted, to the Diegos, and forever will the Überlohes break their spears on the mills of fate, riding on, loving without hope. Thus ends a spectacle in which Duerrenmatt's stage virtuosity reaches its apex.

According to the notes which Duerrenmatt appended in his *Comedies*, *An Angel Comes to Babylon* essays to interpret the motivation for the building of the Tower of Babel. It is his belief that we are deeply involved in a similar folly. His original plan called for a sequel, *Die Mitmacher* (*The Conformists*) in which everybody is against the Tower, yet it gets built. The allusion to our own atomic extravaganza is obvious. In tone and spirit this play comes closest to the Volksspiel quality of Nestroy. Its objectivity is pointed up by the exclusion of the *conférencier*. The stage directions are filled with ironic gags and anachronisms as "Old-Babylonian gas lantern" or "Old-Babylonian streetcar." The action has a double setting: heaven and Babylon. (The setting of the second act under the Euphrates' bridge reminds one of Giraudoux' *The Madwoman of Chaillot*.) Again, we experience an amusing variety of stage business, bordering occasionally on slapstick.

Akki is Duerrenmatt's stroke of genius, with his brusque sentimentality, his wit, his intelligence, his embarrassed charity, his decency and his love of freedom and the world of make-believe. (Similarities between Akki and Azdak in Brecht's *The Caucasian Chalk Circle* indicate the influence of Nestroy on both dramatists.) Vienna somewhere between Raimund and Nestroy could well have evoked that rare atmosphere of fairy tale and irony which Duerrenmatt creates by bringing down to earth a professional angel—an empiricist pedant, utterly confused by the duplicities of the earth and enthralled by its scientific oddities—whose mission is to deliver a creation of Divine whimsy to the poorest of mortals, the last beggar of Babylon. Nestroy's sharp tongue can be heard in the social satire of the good-natured wickedness of the people, the banker, the merchant, the prostitute, the laborer, as well as in the constant allusions to the present. Bureaucracy comes in for a ribbing, whether in the form of the typically Central-European policeman or the rank-conscious hangman, nor does the clergy with their petty foppery and greed escape attention. But Duerrenmatts' sharpest satire is reserved for the perfect state, the Mussolini-like, super-welfare state, where happiness is decreed and begging is outlawed as treason and as a disgrace to the fatherland.

The Angel is to deliver to earth Kurubi, a gossamer creature spun of the finest dreams of a Raimund, whom God in a moment of almost absent-minded sympathy, had made out of nothing by rubbing His palm—a sliver of Divine grace. According to the reliable calcu-

lation of our academic Angel only Akki, the last remaining beggar
of the great empire of Nebukadnezar, can be the recipient. Having
conquered all of the known world, the king systematically proceeds
to establish human happiness by outlawing poverty. He and Nimrod,
his constant counter-king, know full well that their people would be
better off if they got after the bankers, but since they are too powerful
the kings concentrate on prohibiting begging instead: They decree
the absorption of all beggars into the state's mammoth bureaucracy.
Akki is the last to hold out, and therefore the king himself disguised
as a beggar has come to persuade Akki, for he after all, challenges the
system of perfect happiness. This explains the consternation of the
Angel who is now confronted by two beggars. To whom should he
give Kurubi, the divine girl? It must be to the beggar of Niniveh—
the disguise chosen by Nebukadnezar—for he is easily defeated by
Akki in the amazing contest in the art of begging. And thus the
disconcerted Angel gives Kurubi to Nebukadnezar with a bourgeois
avuncular admonition: "Go on begging diligently. And do it de-
cently. Not too much, not to little. It is sufficient if you beg your
way up to the status of a respectable middle class." So it comes to
pass that Kurubi falls in love with the beggar of Niniveh and not the
King of Babylon—a lovely and sad parable, for when he is finally
faced with the choice of love and personal happiness on the one
hand, and might and glory on the other Nebukadnezar abandons
Kurubi to the people who have come to demand that he make her
their queen. Since only a beggar can have her love, the self-same
people who wooed her ardently in the second act turn in righteous
indignation against the witch who would deprive them of their
precious egotisms and surrender her to the executioner. In vain are
her entreaties to the Angel. The lovable pedant of an angel is noteworthy for his incomprehension of the Divine design to which he is
as much subject as the mortals, or perhaps even more so, for he
consistently draws the wrong conclusions and fails to see the most
obvious truths. He understands, however, his own limitations and
the inscrutability of the ways of heaven: "We never understand
what comes out of the hand of Him who made you [Kurubi]."
Hence also his embarrassed attempt at covering up heavenly incon-
sistencies: "Heaven never lies . . . It finds it occasionally difficult
to make itself intelligible to man." Duerrenmatt's God remains inscrutable even to the Angel, but Divine grace, unexpected and
unearned, is always a possibility, and the gates of heaven remain open.

As Kurubi is about to be executed, she is saved by Akki. In contrast to Indra's daughter in Strindberg's *The Dream Play*, she does not return to her heavenly father to report on the state of human misery, but in deep sympathy with the senseless lot of man—"Man is unhappy"—she stays on earth, entrusted to the Akkis, the unheroic victors over the worldliwise and powerful. They are poor because they know the transitoriness of all material attachment:

> To withstand the world the weak must understand it, lest he get onto a path which leads nowhere, and lest he run into danger which leads to death. The powerful are powerful; it is base to disregard this truth and to dream up tomfooleries how to conquer the powerful without having arms at one's disposal to which they would succumb. Heroisms make no sense, they only give away the impotence of the weak man, and his despair makes the powerful laugh. Listen to a beggar now, tortured, in tatters and harried by hangmen: The powerful in this world takes what he likes; now your wife, now your house; and he leaves untouched only what he disdains. Let this be a lesson to the smart man. If you covet what the powerful desire, you die. Even the wise are at the mercy of power. Only he remains unscathed who has nothing and who is nothing. Understand what you must and draw your conclusions: Play stupid and survive. Attack from within. Be in the fortress already on the day of judgment, infiltrate with a humble face: as fellow drunkard, as slave, poet, sharecropper. Humble yourself and you breech every wall. Endure ignominy; go devious ways; if the times demand it, bury wild hopes, ardent love, sorrow, grace, humaneness under the hangmen's red cloak.

This is an example of the grand "Wedekind" gesture, for the couplet ends as Akki draws the mask over his face and stands there as the hangman. Again Duerrenmatt has set man's tragic plight in the frame of a fantastic comedy, for the first time with an obvious happy ending, for Nebukadnezar's will is crossed: Kurubi, the grace of God, and her protector Akki are saved. Gulliver seems to be taking a step back, the better to take measure of the giants.

When compared to his other works, *The Visit of the Old Lady* is Duerrenmatt's most conservative play. The idea of absolute justice—

which was earlier personified in the Old Testament concept of a Mississippi—grows to "classic" proportions in the figure of Claire Zachanassian (whom Duerrenmatt himself, in the notes to the play, compares to a Medea). She returns after forty years to exact punishment in kind on the man whom she had loved and loves even now, the man who had caused her deepest humiliation and misery; and conversely, her greatest material triumph and retribution: "The world made a whore out of me, now I am making it into a brothel."

Claire Zachanassian is a figure with a symbolic mission. She is not only the object of human transgression, but she is also the temptation to transgression. Once transgression has been committed, once man has become involved in guilt against her, she gathers her retaliatory strength, a Nemesis meting out punishment by involving those who are the tools of her justice in a guilt which in turn calls for expiation. This eternal escape-proof trap is realized only by two Gülleners: the minister who begs Ill to flee from Güllen lest he tempt his fellow citizens and the teacher who, giving up resistance to material temptations, accepts his full involvement.

Claire Zachanassian symbolically hovers over the play from beginning to end. In the second act she is literally suspended on her balcony over the action below watching the Gülleners change from upright defense of morality to corruption by temptation, patiently observing the progress of the chase until Ill, her black panther, is brought down. She is symbolic of the very corruption which destroys man's moral fiber by letting him first taste the innocent pleasures such as a bit of long-forgotten chocolate or a cigar, whetting his appetite for more, and thus letting him succumb to the corrosive gravity of his own guilt. As Übelohe already knew, man is not wicked, only weak and afraid of the stifled voice within: "Temptation is too great, poverty too bitter." For in the end the now prosperous Gülleners must forever fear the retribution of the Erinyes.

In his "Problems of the Theatre," Duerrenmatt maintains that the old sense of tragic guilt no longer exists—all of us share in it without anyone's being at fault because none of us has willed it, for "it really goes without anybody." But in this play the concept of a community of guilt is broadened so it includes the conscious acceptance of it by all. So Ill insists:

> You must be my judges. I subject myself to your judgment whichever way it may fall. For me it is justice, I don't

know what it is for you. May God grant that you can stand up to your judgment. You can kill me, I shall not complain, I shall not defend myself, but I cannot take your responsibility upon myself.

Here lies the tragic crux as each is placed before the choice of accepting or rejecting evil. Each one of the Gülleners slips into condoning the fact that sooner or later one of them will kill Ill. Duerrenmatt does not allow anyone, including Ill's family, any equivocation. All members of the community must carry out the stern act of justice, having sworn the momentous oath:

> Let him who with a clear conscience wants to see justice done, raise his hand. Claire Zachanassian's foundation is accepted. Unanimously. Not for the sake of money, but for the sake of justice. And for reasons of conscience. For we cannot live if we tolerate a crime amongst us which we must eradicate, lest our souls suffer damage and our worldly possessions.

The very beginning of the play has something of the ominousness of the plague-ridden Thebes of *Oedipus Tyrannus* or of Argos in Sartre's *The Flies*, only that here the mood is covered up by the comedy situation. The name of the place—Güllen—indicates decomposition, for it is identical with "Jauche" or foul-smelling liquid dung. One suspects an ambiguity in the very choice of the name: decay, compost, out of which a new and clean life grows (as the chrysanthemum in *The Dream Play* flowers out of the dirt that surrounds the castle). Our suspicion that we are in the midst of an ancient tragedy is strengthened by the chorus of Gülleners at the railroad station fatalistically watching the trains roll by. In happier days trains used to stop here. The citizens bear their incomprehensible lot with tragicomic resignation as they look forward to a *deus ex machina*, the return of the fabulously wealthy Claire Zachanassian, whose bountiful generosity in adjacent localities has rekindled abandoned hopes in their hearts that perhaps fate may relent. Ill, the town grocer, is the only one who knew her well when as a minx of seventeen she left town. He must talk to her; and his reward is to be the office of mayor. Here the genius of Duerrenmatt posits the dramatic irony: the man who had wronged Claire is expected to be the interlocutor. He accepts in all innocence, for he feels that whatever had happened, could not have been very serious: time and his memory have expunged his wrong.

The *deus ex machina* arrives; the unexpected happens, the Express "Der rasende Roland" that has not stopped in Güllen even in the best days, screeches to a jolting halt to the protestations of the outraged conductor: "One never pulls an emergency brake in this country, not even in an emergency." The comic Greek chorus jumps into action:

THE PAINTER: The express!

THE FIRST MAN: Stops!

THE SECOND MAN: In Güllen!

THE THIRD MAN: In the most impoverished

THE FOURTH MAN: Lousiest

THE FIRST MAN: Most wretched hole on the line Venice-Stockholm.

And so with the accoutrements of a burlesque the play opens. (Although the stage tricks have been largely reduced to flying scenery.) Duerrenmatt's love for comic situations fraught with tragic implications and inviting improvisation on the part of the actor is, if anything, heightened: "You will get the best results if you produce me in the general tone of a folkplay and treat me as a kind of conscious Nestroy." At the same time the tragic tone must be maintained: "it is a wicked play, but for this very reason it must not be played wickedly but in a most humane way, with sadness and with anger, yet with humor. For nothing does more harm to this comedy that ends tragically than beastly earnestness."

In the selfsame notes to the play he outlines the tragic stature of Claire Zachanassian, of Ill, of the citizens of Güllen. Claire is a heroine from the very outset, in spite of a "unique grace" and a "malicious charm." She is immobile, determined, unbending, almost "petrified," and in her tragic progression finally a stone idol carrying off her sacrifice, her beloved. The teacher is aware of her Greek qualities:

It was awful as the old lady disembarked in her black cloth. She reminded me of a Greek goddess of fate. Her name should be Clotho . . . you can believe of her that she spins the threads of life. . . . Uncanny: Risen from Hades. . . . For the first time I feel greatness of antiquity in Güllen.

Duerrenmatt presents Ill at first as a small-townish, almost debonaire person:

> . . . falls at first unsuspectingly prey to her; though guilty he is of the opinion that life had by itself expunged all guilt, an unthinking fellow, a simple man who with fear and horror slowly begins to realize something; something very personal; he experiences justice within himself because he recognizes his guilt and he becomes great by his death. (His death must not lack a certain monumentality.) His death is meaningful and meaningless at the same time. It would be meaningful only in the mythical realm of a *polis* of antiquity. But the story takes place in Güllen.

Duerrenmatt also demands from the actors of the two blinded and castrated false witnesses the same conscious submission to retributory justice, the almost joyous acceptance of punishment. The parts are not to be played realistically: "disgustingly with castrate's voices" but "without reality, softspoken like a fairy tale spook in his plantlike happiness, victims of a total vengeance which is as logical as the ancient lawbooks."

Faithful to his conviction, "comedy alone is suitable for us," Duerrenmatt employs old and new comic devices to spice the tragic action. What could be older than the trick of a comfort station on stage—Claire's father's one and only contribution to the architecture of the town—with the tax collector running for it? A scene of old time vaudeville; yet it serves to highlight the utter impoverishment and degradation of the town of Güllen, where even the contents of the "*Heimatmuseum*" have been sold to America. Was not Güllen the town where once Goethe slept, Brahms had composed a quartet, and Berthold Schwartz had invented gunpowder? And whose fault is it? The Freemasons or the Jews, high finance or international Communism. We even have a parallel to Beckett's *Waiting for Godot* when Claire's husband number seven must start thinking on order, while husband number eight must stop it on order, or the parody on history in the names of the mayor's granddaughter, Hermine and

Adolfine. But the most mordant example of grotesque humor is found in the scene of the town meeting. The saccharine radio announcer —a profession particularly disliked by Duerrenmatt—paints the quaintness of the ancient institution while the solemn oath is taken by the Gülleners. The dreadful weight of it is persiflaged by a short circuit, so that the scene has to be repeated for the benefit of film and radio, the second time, however, without the heartrending outcry of Ill: "Oh Lord." This is interpreted by the huckster as an outcry of joy and is topped after the killing, when the doctor pronounces Ill dead from a heart attack, by the mayor's and the press representative's conclusion: "Death from joy . . . Life itself writes the most beautiful stories."

Finally one must consider the amazing ending of the play. This mixture of musical comedy and Greek tragedy is perhaps a conscious adaptation of the Greek satyr plays. There is a complete change in the appearance of everything and everybody. The station building is gayly bedecked, people are dressed in evening clothes, "the formerly gray world has changed into something shining bright with technology, into prosperity; it culminates in a world-happy-end." The Gülliners, forming two choruses—"approximating Greek tragedy, not by accident but with a designed point of view in the scheme of things, as if a shipwrecked boat far off its course were sending its last signals"—speak in odic verse of their former poverty and the joys of their present prosperity. There follows the grotesque procession of Claire Zachanassian and her entourage with Ill's coffin to the train, and the final choral incantation:

ALL: Let there be preserved for us

PARSON: By a God

ALL: In these times full of pounding and building

MAYOR: Our prosperity

ALL: Let there be preserved for us our most sacred possessions,
Peace and freedom.
May the night stay away
And never again darken our city,
The newly risen, resplendent,
So that we may happily enjoy happiness.

Sartre's Orestes has freed his city of the flies, Ill his of poverty. Have the Gods been appeased?

What in the end is the tragic sense of Duerrenmatt's comedy and who are its heroes, if any? If unmasking is a basic function of comedy, then Duerrenmatt fulfills it in every instance. One basic trait is common to all his characters up to but excluding *The Visit of the Old Lady*, namely immutability. They are what they are, and for better or for worse they remain what they are, unbroken by life or by death. Therein lies also their tragedy, for most of them cannot conceive that their cause may be wrong or selfish or sought in their own image. Their *hubris* is their downfall. They do not pass the *"Bewährunsprobe"* (the test). They do not hesitate, in humility or Promethean vanity, to presume on the will of God or to sit in judgment over their fellow men, be it in the Münster of the Anabaptists, or the Germany of the Thirty Years' War, or dying Rome, or the present age, or Biblical times. They are the self-styled heroes and saviors and martyrs who come back again and again, as the resurrected Saint-Claude and Mississippi sing at the end of their play. As the ancient Bishop in *It Is Written* knows, they try to fly before they learn walking, and their very deeds, whatever their motivation, are the traps of a guilt that they are neither aware of nor understand, but which brings about their punishment.

But then there are also the Jobs of faith like the blind Duke, and the Quixotes like Übelohe. They are not heroes, they are the courageous. And there is Ill, who literally grows as a character as he gradually begins to comprehend his guilt and to accept the necessity of punishment. We witness for the first time in Duerrenmatt's work a tragic transformation from the role of Claire Zachanassian's persuader to a grateful reliance on the incorruptible moral support of his fellow citizens, to his growing suspicion of their betrayal as he realizes that he is the collateral for the new luxuries, including the new church bells, up to a frenzied fear that drives him to attempt an escape by train, only to find himself surrounded by the Gülleners at the station. In the Valency adaptation a new scene is introduced at this juncture. The train has pulled out, the Gülleners have gone. Ill, left alone, collapses with abject animal fear when a truck driver appears offering him a lift to the next town, to freedom. After a moment of hesitation Ill declines and returns home. (The moment of his catharsis, with or without the knowledge of Duerrenmatt, has been made painfully obvious for the Broadway audience.) His Calvary culminates in his self-abandonment, when he refuses to tell his predicament to the representatives of the world press. Though he has now accepted the full weight of expiation he cannot exempt the Gülleners of their share in the guilt by committing suicide. On their acknowledgement of a communal guilt and of their personal responsibility for its universal expiation rests the fervent hope for Divine grace. And thus the tragic comedy of a scapegoat—that bears minute resemblance to the *agnus* —assumes aspects of a religious play.

We have saved for the last that wonderful beggar, Akki. Better than the blind Duke or Übelohe he represents Duerrenmatt's true hero—the nonhero. He is the little fellow, who knows that he cannot win against the mighty and principled. He knows he must survive. For, unless the unheroic Akkis survive, there will be no happiness, no beauty, no poetry, no refuge for Divine grace, only grim pursuit of duty, and sooner or later the great heroes will have finished off each other and the world. This fear of extinction keeps Akki and Kurubi and the world, and us, running:

> I love an earth, which still exists, an earth of the beggars, unique in happiness and unique in danger, wonderful with colorful and wild possibilities, an earth which I conquer ever anew, mad with its beauty, in love with its image, threatened by force, yet undefeated. Go on, girl, move on, child, surrender to death and still be alive, mine for the second time by grace, which now walks with me: Babylon, blind and pale, crumbles with its tower of stone and steel pushing irresistibly upward toward its downfall; and in front of us, behind the storm, through which we hasten pursued by horsemen, shot at by arrows, wading through sand, clinging to slopes, our faces burned; in front of us there lies in the distance a new land, rising out of the dusk, steaming in the silver of light, full of new persecution, full of new promise and full of new songs!

WILLIAM ARROWSMITH

The Comedy of T. S. Eliot

Nobody, I suppose, outside of classical studies, any longer reads
either of A. W. Verrall's delightfully systematic distortions of
Euripides, those two engaging and outrageous books, *Four Plays of
Euripides* and *Euripides the Rationalist*. Yet Verrall as a critic bears
rereading, less for his rationalist hypothesis, which hopelessly trapped
his perceptions, than for the acuteness of those perceptions and his
lucid and suggestive wrongheadedness. Indeed, I sometimes suspect
that the reason classicists, apart from their native dislike of novelty,
have been slow to adopt the techniques of the New Criticism is that
Verrall (along with Samuel Butler) parodied and abused them before
they formally existed, and so put the classicists off for half a century.

I have myself no wish to put anyone off, not even to put the New
Critics off with Verrall. My use here for Verrall is mainly cautionary:
I once had the unhappy but common experience of out-Verralling
Verrall on *The Cocktail Party*, and I have no wish to repeat that
performance, even if I could muster the necessary ingenuity. But I
also wish to discuss Euripides' dramatic structure in relation to Eliot's
comedy in the hope of making the much greater dramatist illustrate
the methods and also (what I take to be) the failure of the lesser.
For, unless I am badly mistaken, Eliot's Christian New Comedy of

Reprinted from *English Institute Essays: English Stage Comedy*, W. K.
Wimsatt, ed., New York, 1954, by permission of the Columbia University
Press.

134

conversion is structurally very close to the movement, though not the meaning, of Euripidean drama. And Verrall, on the crucial point, comes pat to the comparison.

Verrall's theory of Euripidean structure will be immediately intelligible to anyone who has read even a little of recent Melville criticism. It rests entirely on two perceptions, both of which seem to me indisputably accurate. First is what might be called Euripides' quarrel with the gods of Olympos, that transparent rationalism in the tradition of Xenophanes that makes him surround such myths as Leda's egg or Thyestes' feast with a dubious "so men say" or "the story goes"; or, even more strongly, his outright assertion that the *logoi* of the Homeric gods are "the wretched tales of poets." Second, Verrall noticed that in play after play there comes a point where the literal action as dramatized cannot be accepted without gross inconsistency or intolerable paradox; the play appears to say one thing and to dramatize it as real, and then to assert somehow an antithetical reality. Thus in the *Herakles*, for instance, the hero is shown suffering madness as the result of the direct intervention of the goddess Hera's agents, Iris and Madness herself; yet later in the same play Herakles boldly asserts a principle whose apparent consequence is the denial of the reality of the experience out of which the assertion is made in the first place. Herakles, that is, simply denies that the actions of the gods could in fact be such as they have been dramatized to be.

On the basis of these two perceptions, and this suggestion of a double pattern of reality in the plays, Verrall inferred that two simultaneous actions were being presented on two simultaneous "levels": the superficial action was "ostensible" and the profounder action was "real." By an ostensible plot Verrall meant one so constructed as to give no offense to the vulgar and pious when dealing with received religious traditions, an action which presented "things as they are said to be," *as if* they were real, while the real action was a human story entirely divested of the improbable or fabulous. In order to provide this double plot with a double audience, Verrall assumed an elite of *sophoi*, rationalist intellectuals who would see through the ostensible absurdities and enjoy the real play in all its rationalist rigor. The theory was then reapplied to the plays with almost pathological ingenuity, and with atrocious results. Thus Alkestis never really died (for Euripides was too sensible to believe in the nonsense of regeneration), while the great labors of Herakles and his harrowing of Hades were all fictive disguises for the real tragedy of a great man who struggled, not under the lash of a god-driven necessity, but merely with his own megalomania. And so on, with hideous rigor of application, through most of the Euripidean corpus.

Yet for all the visible absurdity of Verrall's conclusions, his theory should command more respect than it does. At least it seems to me both more perceptive and more courageous than most Euripidean criticism with its outraged Aristotelian literalness and its perpetual cry of formal botching and inconsistency. Verrall's own mistake came, I think, not in his double-reality pattern, but in the hypothesis which was meant to mirror what he saw, that division of the play into two continuous levels of action, real and apparent, each autonomous and complete. The worst that can be said of Verrall's theory is that its elaboration was first unnecessary and then untruthful; and in this it appears to me to resemble most critical theories which operate everywhere on the assumption of parallel levels of reality, or of real and apparent meanings. We need, I think, a greater sense of the variety of ways in which reality gets into literature, and I personally wish it were more often possible in contemporary criticism to preserve, for appropriate writers, the notion of reality as apparently fortuitous, and even casual, to keep respect for the simple, formal rightness of luck in things that happen. Verrall certainly had no such respect, and his criticism must pay the cost of a reality so terribly schematized as to be that much less a reality.

It should be obvious by now in what sense Verrall's theory of Euripidean structure is cautionary for Eliot. And perhaps it is too obvious, but in almost all the criticism of Eliot's two comedies with which I am familiar, the crucial difficulty has come in stating precisely just what relationship obtains between the secular framework of the plot and the constant hints of another, and Christian, reality. Are we meant to take the physical cocktail party as the empty vehicle of Christian communion? Do we have two continuous Verrallian "levels," one secular and one Christian? Or is the connection between the doublet reality of the play merely adventitious and momentary, a sudden irruption of the Christian real into the secular terms of the play, illuminating and transfiguring them?

Both Euripides and Eliot present in their plays a double reality, and a Euripidean play no more consists of an "ostensible" action superimposed on a "real" one than an Eliot play consists of one Christian and one secular action. The relation between the two realities is variously systematic and adventitious, and the term I suggest for their connection is that of "conversion"—if, for a moment, I can use the word without its religious connotations. By "conversion" I mean simply the transfiguration of one action or its terms, a conversion or transformation of one reality to another—but not an "epiphany" and not a conversion of "levels."

The commonest form of such conversion in Euripides is that in which a story (i.e., a *logos*) derived from received beliefs—the world of myth and the corpus of "things as they are said to be"—is suddenly, in all of its parts—its terms, its characters, and the values it invokes—"converted," under dramatic pressure, to another phase of reality. What we get is something like a dramatic mutation of conventional or traditional reality, and the leap the play makes between the phases or plateaus of its two realities is meant to correspond, in force and vividness and apparent unpredictability, to mutations in the physical world. It is this violence in the conversion of reality that explains the wrenching dislocation of Euripidean drama from an Aristotelian point of view, and the apparent lack of necessary connection between the parts of the play. The play pivots on two seemingly incompatible realities, and if it insists on the greater reality of what has been dramatically created over what has been traditionally received, it does not do so by denying validity to received reality, but subtly displaces it in the transfiguration of its terms. Euripidean structure mirrors in this way both the artist's intent and his possibilities. Because Euripides is dramatizing the incongruities of a culture—its received values against its actual or ideal values—he must at least allow dignity of reality to the values which the play supersedes. And at least one consequence of such a method is clearly psychological strain for his characters, who have to bear the intolerable burden of the cultural disparity which the play dramatizes. Thus in the *Orestes*, for instance, the matricide is presented in a world in which the institution of civil justice already exists, and, in consequence, Orestes' action exposes his own criminal nature, rather than being, as in the *Oresteia*, a god-driven deed which leads to the creation of civil justice.

In no play is this conversion of reality more sharp than in the *Herakles*. Here two savagely different actions, one conventional and the other set in a world where tradition is dumb and conduct uncharted, are jammed harshly against each other, and the collision of their values is stressed by the most violent peripety of Greek tragedy. The first action is static and conventional melodrama, wholly in-

formed by "things as they are said to be," and rounded off with a
cozy and traditionalized theodicy in which hybris is punished and
virtue rewarded by the benevolent and vindicated gods. Herakles
himself is presented essentially as Pindar had left him: the great
culture-hero of enormous physical strength, self-sufficient and bearing
on his back all the values of aristocratic *aretē*. His civilizing labors
and his harrowing of Hades are accepted as literal truths, and the
ambiguity in tradition which made Herakles the son of two fathers,
Zeus and Amphitryon, is sustained.

Against such a background, the second action breaks with tragic
force and striking transformations, showing first the conquering hero,
the *kallinikos*, reduced to tears, helpless, dependent, and in love,
stripped of that outward strength which until now had exempted him
from normal human necessity, and discovering both his common
ground with men and the internalized courage of the human hero
confronting his condition. And point for point, each of the terms
that was appropriate to the Herakles of tradition is transformed and
displaced. Thus Amphitryon becomes Herakles' "real" father, not by
the fact of conception, but by the fact of love, *philia*, while the literal
descent to Hades is transformed in the refusal to die and the courage
which, under an intolerable necessity, perseveres. The old Hades of
the poets, with its Sisyphos, Cerberos, and torments, is transformed
into the Hades within, here and now, as Herakles himself declares:
"And I am like Ixion, chained forever to a flying wheel." So too the
old labors are replaced by the metaphorical sense of the labors of
human life and the cost of civilization, while the goddess Hera, who
in myth made Herakles mad and the destroyer of his sons, demonstrates her own incredibility as a goddess and passes almost insensibly
into a hovering symbol of all those irrational and random necessities
which the Greeks and the play call *Tukhe*, and which we limply
translate as "Fortune."

All these conversions replace and dislodge, but do not disown, the
first action by transfiguring it at every point. The first action is
neither false nor even unreal, but it is inadequate. Through the force
of contrast with its own transfiguration it comes to seem obsolete,
naive, or even humdrum, much as fresh conviction, formed under
peine forte et dure, insensibly makes the conviction it replaces naive
or jejune in comparison. Under the changed light of experience and
the pattern it imposes, what was once taken for reality comes to
seem illusion at best: true while held as true, but with widened

experience discovered inadequate. And what we see is less the contradiction between the two opposed realities than the counterpointed relation of their development, the way in which, under the blow of experience and insight, one reality is made to yield a further one, each geared to its appropriate experience. We begin with a familiar and conventional world, operating from familiar motives in a field of accepted, though outmoded, values; by the time the play closes, character, motives, and values have all been transfigured and pushed to the very frontiers of reality.

What Verrall saw with great clarity was the defeat of one reality by another in Euripides, and he correctly observed that the victorious reality was essentially a rationalized one. But because he assumed the connection between them was precisely that between false illusion and natural reality, rather than a series of discrete conversions, he stultified the plays and distorted their direction. He observed, that is, the rationalization of the fabulous and the outmoded or barbarous supernatural in Euripides; but he failed to notice that this rationalization was not final, that Euripides more often than not discredits the fabulous only in order to make it good, to re-earn it, on a symbolic or a metaphorical level. Illusion is not merely exposed, but it is first exposed and then transfigured or "converted." Thus Verrall rightly assumed that Euripides believed neither in Hades nor in the physical regeneration of Alkestis, but ignored the moral and metaphorical equivalent of her "death." For the point of the *Alkestis* is surely not, as Verrall thought, that Alkestis neither really died nor went to Hades, but that she had to "die" if Admetos, and hence herself, were ever to be "reborn." But as Eliot saw and put it in *The Cocktail Party*, the crux of the *Alkestis* is, after all, that moral death is the condition of moral rebirth; that Admetos (like Edward) must, even at the risk of apparent weakness, take back his wife from Herakles' hands as a new woman or not at all. But, obsessed by his own rationalist convictions and encouraged by Euripides' clear commitment to *this* world, Verrall imposed upon the plays a crude rationalism foreign to them, and he distorted their structure accordingly.

Between Euripides and Verrall, then, there is some small common ground in an initial rationalism; and while structurally Euripides does possess a doublet-reality, his plays are actually not doublet on two levels but complex conversions. Between Euripides and Eliot, there is, I hope to show, a common technique of transfiguration, though in Eliot the conversion is differently directed. But I should like now to raise the question as to whether Eliot, intending a Christian play along the structural lines of a Euripidean conversion, has not in fact written a Verrallian two-level comedy, and done so under the duress of religious doctrine and poetic theory.

It is essentially a conversion like that of the *Herakles*, though differently oriented and more fortuitous, which I think Eliot's two comedies are intended to exhibit. Both Eliot and Euripides are in some sense dramatizing incongruities, either in a given culture or in their own souls, and both thereby place upon their characters an unnatural strain, a strain which makes Euripides' characters pathological and Eliot's either priggish or negative. And just as in Euripides the unity of the plays depends upon the perception of the conversion, so in Eliot, I think, the perceived convergence of two worlds, the momentary poetic incarnation of Christian reality, is meant to earn that stillness and serene reconciliation which is the mark of Christian "comedy" from Dante on. For to reconcile appearance and reality, the world of men and the world of God, is to make a Christian peace between two intersecting orders at the moment of their intersection.

Thus the Christian component in Eliot's plays is not a profounder "level" but a world of greater reality intended, under the pressure of poetry, to become incarnate in the secular terms of the play. We should be just enough aware of it on the fringes of our emotional field that we may sense or glimpse the transfiguration of the world of the play. Eliot has recently remarked that poetry in the theater should be "a kind of humble shadow or analogy of the Incarnation," and, in saying this, he merely expresses his determination to adapt his technical means to his subject. The more intense moments of the play, the moments when reality breaks upon us, are precisely the moments of poetry: only poetry could bear the intolerable weight of such a reality. Thus the Christian real supervenes in poetry and transforms the play and its persons, who are thereby "renewed, transfigured in another pattern"—to borrow, for a moment, the language of the *Quartets*.

This simple strategy of transfiguration is not, of course, new to Eliot; it runs throughout both his criticism and the late poetry. But it has nonetheless visibly put off critics accustomed to Eliot's tight metaphorical and symbolic allusiveness and his old complexity of reference. For this technique does not "refer" nor is it properly symbolic at all, but opencast, receptive rather than referring, and more like revelation in action than a symbolic *déjà-vue*. Eliot's clearest statement of his intentions is to be found in an old (1934) essay on John Marston, which deserves, I think, being savored:

> It is possible that what distinguishes poetic drama from prosaic drama is a kind of doubleness of action, as if it took place on two planes at once. In this it is different from allegory, in which abstraction is something conceived, not something differently felt, and from symbolism, in which the tangible world is visibly diminished. . . . both symbolism and allegory being operations of the conscious planning mind. In poetic drama, a certain apparent irrelevance may be the symptom of this doubleness; or the drama has an under-pattern, less manifest than the theatrical one. We sometimes feel, in following the words and behavior of some of the characters of Dostoevsky, that they are living at once on the plane that we know and on some other plane of reality from which we are shut out: their behavior does not seem crazy, but rather in conformity with the laws of some other world that we cannot perceive.

How closely that comment on Dostoyevsky parallels the experience of audiences and critics alike with both of Eliot's comedies hardly needs comment, though whether the effect is the same, or the primary realities equal, is a more serious question. More important to observe, I think, is the fact that, besides intending transfiguration, Eliot also intended that transfiguration to be precisely teasing, unanchored, and directly suggestive of the mystery it was meant to record. And for this reason, any attempt to state, rather than to suggest, the quality of conversion and to isolate a particular reference from among the body of invoked possibilities risks the pedantry of naming the unnamable.

Let me therefore risk it. For it seems to me that one of the most damning things about Eliot's comedies is the degree to which these mysteries are structured and the plays sacrificed to them, artificialized in order to make the advent of reality appear fortuitous. We have, that is, the spectacle of verse drama in which cool strategy and an old poetic ontology dictate that the only use of heightened language shall be to trap the Christian reality in the humdrum secular and quasi-prosaic world. Consider Eliot's own words in his essay, *Poetry and Drama:*

> It seems to me that beyond the namable, classifiable emo-
> tions and motives of our conscious life when directed
> towards action—the part of life which prose drama is wholly
> adequate to express—there is a fringe of indefinite extent,
> of feeling which we can only detect, so to speak, out of the
> corner of the eye and can never completely focus; of feeling
> of which we are only aware in a kind of temporary detach-
> ment from action. . . . This peculiar range of sensibility
> can be expressed by dramatic poetry, at its moments of
> greatest intensity.

This fringe on which we can never wholly focus is, in Eliot's practice, almost entirely Christian; and I suppose no focus is possible precisely because it is Christian, a reality beyond the focusing, naming, and referring power of language geared to the lower reality of the world. And if the province of poetry in Eliot's comedies is thus explicitly Christian, the ordinary world and its illusions receive the doubtful benefits of Eliot's humdrum business-verse. Sir Claude Mulhammer says it all apropos of his pots:

> To be among such things,
> If it is an escape, is escape into living,
> Escape from a sordid world into a pure one.
> Sculpture and painting—I have some good things—
> But they haven't this . . . remoteness I have always longed
>   for.
> I want a world where the form is the reality,
> Of which the substantial is only a shadow.

Where ceramics are in question, Sir Claude is almost a pure Platonist, and what he says of his pots is almost identical with what Eliot says elsewhere (*The Aims of Poetic Drama*) of his use of poetry and prose in the theater:

> What I should like to do is this: that the people on the
> stage should seem to the audience so like themselves that
> they would find themselves thinking: "I could talk in poetry
> too!" Then they are not transported into an unaccustomed,

artificial world; but their ordinary, sordid world is suddenly illuminated and transfigured. And if poetry cannot do that for people, it is merely a superfluous decoration.

Poetry in Eliot's two comedies is thus reserved for the contemplation of the Christian idea, as it transfigures the sordid phenomenal reality of the lower half of the Platonic Line, the region of prosaic drama, or prosaic verse.

For Plato, the crucial difficulty with the Theory of Ideas was the difficulty of stating, other than metaphorically, just how the Ideas participated in the particulars they subsumed. And the classic objection against the Theory of Ideas is that, although it began as an attempt to explain the phenomenal world, it ended not in explaining it but simply in duplicating it. For Eliot the problem is altered, not merely because Eliot is a Christian and Christians solved Plato's difficulty by declaring the Incarnation a mystery and so putting it philosophically out of bounds, but because, in dramatic poetry, the only test is really a pragmatic one: is "our ordinary, sordid world" transfigured, or is it not? In asking this question, I do not think we are entitled to object that we are quite content with ordinary reality, or that it is not as sordid as Eliot appears to think. Certainly I have no wish that my own sordid reality should be transfigured as that of the Mulhammers was, but I am anxious that the question of belief in poetry should not be raised here. The questions which I should like to raise are these: First, is it really true that, if poetry does not transfigure ordinary reality, it must be merely "superfluous decoration"? Second, is it possible to transfigure something which, properly speaking, has no figuration in dramatic reality at all? And finally, to what extent is Eliot's all-important assumption, that Christianity is, on the level of dramatic popularity, operative enough to bear this opencast transfiguration and still remain recognizably Christian, a delusion?

Before attempting to answer these questions, let me first try to give particularity to the separate transfigurations as they occur in the plays. Many of them are extremely obvious, perhaps most of them; but, since the play is constructed for them, and is hopelessly diminished if they go unperceived, it is best that they submit to temporary prose impoverishment. As plots, both plays essentially contain a full conversion—and I mean here literal Christian conversion—from the secular to the Christian life. The Christianity of the characters may be fully conscious, as in Eggerson, or conscious but disguised for evangelical purposes as in the Guardians, or effective but inarticulate, as in the Chamberlaynes and Lucasta and Barnabas Kaghan (if I may give him his Christian name), or incipient and transcendent, a gift of the Spirit, as in Celia and Colby. All of the characters suffer their conversion into Christian life as their abilities and their spiritual gifts allow. Further, since each convert dies to be reborn, the coda of each play contains the familiar shadow analogy of the rite of rebirth, the death of the secular self and the putting on of the new Adam in the adoption of God. This conversion, so far as the double reality of the play is concerned, means also reconciliation and convergence: the awful gap between two apparently disparate orders, happily and comically intersecting, closes in the dedication to others which signifies the death of the desiring and worldly self. In the language of the *Quartets* again:

> See, now they vanish,
> The faces and places, with the self which, as it could, loved
> them,
> To become renewed, transfigured, in another pattern.

In this final reconciliation, there is meant to emerge into familiar outline the whole foreshadowed, hinted pattern of the Christian life: church, martyrdom, Easter, *caritas*, the perpetual conspiracy, and the life of Christ informing the lives of men. Thus the Guardians leave Edward and Lavinia as Guardians of Peter, leave for a new "cocktail party" at the Gunnings, and a new communion after a fresh conversion. In *The Confidential Clerk* the conversion is less overt, though more explosive. Eggerson mentions, *en passant*, that his wife gets low-spirited "around this season When we're getting near the anniversary." "The anniversary?" asks Sir Claude, "Of your son's death?" and Eggerson replies, dodging the death of *his* son in order to suggest the Good Friday death of The Son, "Of the day we got the news." And hard on the heels of that death comes of course the Easter of conversion, the birth of Christ in the lives of the *dramatis personae*: enter Athene Guzzard, *dea ex machina*, like a grizzled Easter rabbit, to hand out new lives all around. Down in Joshua Park, the lilies should be in bloom.

This final convergence of the play's double reality is foreshadowed in detail in the isolated transfigurations of the plays. Thus the cocktail party is transformed into the Eucharist, and the conversion is given point in the pure Pentecostal water which the subapostolic Sir Henry drinks—unadulterated with gin—when he is not in his secular disguise. The indefinable aura of divinity and power which attaches to the Guardians finds its source in the divinity of the Christian life itself, which informs their undisclosed conspiracy of conversion. So too, when Colby rejects Sir Claude and Lady Elizabeth he insensibly, and yet, I think, clearly, paraphrases Scripture: we know he is about his "father's business." The play's worldly quest of fathers seeking sons and sons seeking fathers is perfected and transfigured in the adoption of God ("ye have received the spirit of adoption whereby we cry, Abba, Father!"); and the doctrine of Original Sin transfigures Sir Claude's lifelong atonement to a father. Behind the concern with the professions and the vocations lie the greatest Vocation and the gifts of the Spirit, and with the loss of worldly love and ambitions, comes *caritas*, the greatest of the Gifts and the enabling condition of the others. "All that's left is love," says Colby, echoing Paul. He means, of course, worldly love transfigured, "expansion of love beyond desire," the same love that marks the putting on of the new man and the release of the individual and his lesser gifts from the private garden of the self into the service of others and of God. It is with "the drawing of the Love and the voice of this Calling," that conversion can come and Christian reality supervene. Thus the problem of the individual is also the problem of the play: to effect a reconciliation between appearance and reality, to find unity by discovering God and others walking in one's private garden.

"What is the reality of experience between two unreal people?" asks Peter in *The Cocktail Party*, and the answer of both plays is that unreality is at least partly redeemed by the release of the individual into the shared reality of "the body of Christ." "It may be," says Lucasta to Colby, "there's no one so hard to understand As one's brother . . ." and she speaks, of course, of her brother by Adoption: "whosoever shall do the will of God, the same is my brother, and my sister, and mother." Both plays again, without overt consciousness of doctrine, dramatize the famous dualism of the orthodox confession, the life lived according to the Counsels and that according to the Precepts. The Counsels of Perfection are represented in the celibate choices of Celia and Colby, while the Precepts inform the lives of all others, even Eggerson and the Guardians. So Eggerson, and latterly Colby, carry with them, as confidential clerks, Christian *fides*, the substance of things hoped for, the evidence of things unseen. And so on, term for term, throughout both comedies, a series of discrete conversions whose cumulative effect is to bring closer and closer together, in preparation for the final convergence of conversion, the two realities of the plays.

Something like this, with the Christian reality enhanced by being made less explicit and evoked vividly in poetic incarnation, is, I submit, the intent of both comedies. If there is an intent beyond this, it can only be, I think, the conversion (or reconversion) of an audience at least unconsciously Christian—an audience sufficiently at home in the reach-me-down world of Christian habits and terms that the reality of Christian experience can be at least partially restored to them by playing over the fringes of the emotional field, hinting and suggesting, but not evangelizing. Such audience conversion is also the aim of Euripidean drama, but in Euripides, so far as I can judge, the premises on which the conversion rests are better founded on fact and better supported by dramatic genius. That is, the values which Euripides assumes and invokes against received values are clearly operative, even on the popular level of the theater; and further, their effective operation on received material is earned through absolute control of the techniques of persuasion and extraordinary ingenuity in the enlisting and alienation of sympathies.

But with Eliot I am skeptical of the validity of the premises and puzzled in general to know just how he expects any conceivable *popular* modern audience to respond to these transfigurations. For Christian reality looks to me (from the outside) like an extraordinarily complex one, in which understanding of the part is inevitably dependent upon understanding of the whole, or the parts at least mutually illuminate one another. What puzzles me then is to know just how a mystery can be invoked or transfigured, with the richness of its own reality, unless it has the precision of a mystery. There are, after all, mysteries and mysteries: Greek is regrettably a mystery for those who do not know it, but the Incarnation is a mystery even to those who know all there is to know about it. And if my own estimate of the experience of those conventional, unconscious, or merely habitual Christians who saw either of Eliot's comedies is correct, then what they saw was a mystery analogous to the mystery of Greek for the Greekless. They came away in impure puzzlement, aware that something profound, even something Christian, was taking place in the plays, something just outside their ken, teasing and indefinable; but finally, no more interesting than the mysteries of Greek for a practical man. Reality was observed, even felt, and felt, as Eliot wanted, hovering on the fringes of the mind's eye, but for all that utterly unrealized; and so too transfiguration was observed dimly as it broke, but yet there was no transfiguration.

Now, in part, this reaction was what Eliot intended, that the plays should be both teasing and unsettling; but he also intended that they should be evocative and finally satisfying, and in this last he seems to me to have badly miscarried. For what, after all, are the perceptions of the adoption of God or the Incarnation worth unless they are perceived, as mysteries, in the richness of their Christian reality? What can you do with the adoption of God unless you have a belief which illuminates it and a context which can place it? What do the "counsels of perfection" mean to those sub-Christians who live the precepts by force of habit or discipline and have neither knowledge nor tolerance of any other way? What can Colby possibly be, except a prig or a musical eunuch, unless you have the *Ion* to tell you of his musical father, Apollo, and a Christian education to tell you what his Vocation is?

Eliot, that is, appears to me to want it both ways: he wants the precision and richness and reality of Christian doctrine and mystery in order to make his play finally a true comedy of reconciliation, to elicit a genuine order, complete at every point, from the secular disorder with which he begins. But he also wants that evocative power that comes from a mystery comprehended vaguely or not at all, the teasing power of a "plane of reality from which we are shut out." He is, of course, welcome to both, but at least one of the consequences of having them both is that of writing Verrallian double-level comedy: one play, a well-made farce with Christian overtones, and another play, a complete Christian comedy, superimposed, like the *Clementine Homilies*, on a Greek romance and available only to educated Christians or to meddlers like myself. All probability, I think, so far as intent is concerned, opposes the Verrallian interpretation, as do Eliot's own words; and I can only suppose that Eliot has, with good Christian confidence, misjudged the potential Christianity of his popular audience. If he has not misjudged his audience, he has, in good faith, overestimated the power of Christian mysteries to reveal themselves to those who have lost the secrets of their own initiation. For unless the audience feels that the world of the play, and itself with it, has been even momentarily transfigured, and feels it at a profounder depth than that of a mild secular puzzlement, it is hard to see that any transfiguration at all has taken place. Rather, the play will have transfigured "ordinary, sordid" reality only by artificializing it into a rather puzzling, though well-made, wish-fulfillment.

Alternatively, the failure may lie less in doctrine and the strategies of an audience than in the technique of transfiguration itself. Is it, after all, possible to transfigure what has, dramatically, no real figuration of its own? If the relation between father and son, or between lovers, is not, as the world goes and as poetry goes, made real, what happens to the Christian love that is meant to transfigure it? In asking this question, I am trying to suggest that the ontology of Eliot's poetry and his own special version of Christianity is dramatically doomed from the start: the stage, as Plato himself suggested when he destroyed his own tragedies, is no place for Platonists, or for gnostics, or for the theologian of the *Four Quartets*.

For two reasons—his own doctrine of negative transcendence and his gnostic distinction between prose and poetry—Eliot has made a desolation and called it the world. In both of these plays, and even more acutely in *The Confidential Clerk* than in *The Cocktail Party*, the world has been stultified to such a degree that the intended transfiguration is belittled even before it is begun. There is so little here to be transfigured. And just as it is the greatest sinners who make, at least in drama, the most interesting saints, so I should have supposed it was the liveliest illusions that got themselves most firmly transfigured. What we have instead is the spectacle of religious, without dramatic, redemption; of the new man without the old Adam; of transfigured love without the love it was transfigured from. Yet it stands to reason that illumination requires a darkness to dispel, just as Incarnation needs a world of flesh. Here the illusions of the world are allowed almost no dignity whatsoever. How easily, in *The Cocktail Party*, people surrender their selves, their passions, and their identities. How little is required in *The Confidential Clerk* to make a man surrender his illusion of parental love. How little dignity of language these people have in which to report the love and grief we are meant to credit them with. It is exactly because the illusions of this world are left without real dignity that the loss of illusion fails to matter. And yet it is through the loss of their worldly illusions and ambitions that these characters are meant to come upon their Christian reality.

Given Eliot's rather special version of Christianity, this impoverishment of the world was either necessary or natural. You cannot quarrel with a man who makes a desolation of the world as a matter of principle. Yet one reason, I think, why Eliot's two comedies fail where his poetry succeeds is that he has been unable to find the dramatic equivalent of that terrible poetic reality of unreality which is so vivid in the *Quartets*: "Not here, not here, the darkness, in this twittering world." You can't beat a twitter like that for realizing the unreal, but if its dramatic equivalent is Lady Elizabeth's

> Why, I'd no sooner got to Lausanne
> Than whom should I meet but Mildred Deverell.
> She was going to Zurich. So she said "Come to Zurich!
> There's a wonderful doctor who teaches mind control."
> So on I went to Zurich,

or even the fine chatter from the first scene of *The Cocktail Party*, or the pallid suffering of Edward and Lavinia or the incipient passion of Colby and Lucasta, then Eliot is merely mocking, not creating, the terms he intends to transfigure, stripping them of the dignity they need in order to carry their conversion.

A few lines back, I deliberately introduced the phrase "the poetic reality of unreality" to indicate the point at which Platonism in poetry declares itself bankrupt. Ordinarily I dislike such phrases, but I want, even by paradox, to expose what I take to be the misplaced ontology of Eliot's poetic and dramatic practice. As a Christian, Eliot perhaps distinguishes between two worlds in terms of a greater and a lesser reality. But as a poet he makes such a distinction at his peril and also at the peril of his Christian reality. Poetry may, with perfect propriety, be made the servant of Christianity, but to suppose that this privileged service is therefore exclusive of any other seems to me dramatic and poetic suicide. From the fact that Eliot dooms this world to a diminished reality, it hardly follows that the world must also be doomed to diminished poetry. To suppose that it does follow, deprives poetry of all its multifariousness, its disguises, and its very ability to transfigure. For you cannot transform a vacuum except into a purer one; you cannot worthily redeem what is not worth redemption, and so too you cannot make the world declare the glory, or even the greater glory, of God unless you give it some glory to begin with. And what is true of language is true also of men and their illusions of reality in this world. Christianity may, though it need not, suggest that the passage from the world to the spirit is via the way of deprivation, and poetry will guarantee the dignity of that passage by making the experience of deprivation a real one. But to suppose that you get to *caritas* by being only a limp poet in love and thus easily deprived of your small purchase on the world is a strategy whose folly is equaled only by supposing that Christian poetry exhibits its reality best when transfiguring secular prose. The victory is too easy. For a playwright who happens to be both a poet and a Christian, the true test in drama of both faith and poetry would have been, I think, to realize his reality wherever he could, and to have trusted in the greater richness of his Christianity to earn its triumph over the best the world might offer.

In closing, let me briefly set against Eliot's relative failure the example of Euripides, a dramatist who everywhere took the full risks of his convictions and his verse. In play after play occur systematic transfigurations analogous to those intended by Eliot: from a lesser to a greater reality, from a familiar world to an unfamiliar one. But, unlike Eliot, Euripides consistently gives the fullest play of his poetic powers, not to his final transfiguring reality, but to the reality that gets transfigured. Thus in the *Elektra*, a conversion play designed to make the monstrous acquire mercy, everything has been given to the deed—the matricide—which the play is written to execrate, as the new Euripidean imperative of pity dislodges, or perfects, the old Aeschylean ordinance of civil justice. Orestes and Elektra, old heroes become new criminals, are invested with poetry in the full flush of power, with the whole catalogue of heroic myth and the panoply of tradition, with all metaphor and all sympathy. Far from diluting their reality, Euripides intensifies it, and then, setting action against words, he terribly exploits and undoes all the reality he has created. The undoing is, of course, not gratuitous; it is the condition of the conversion and the emergence of pity as the informing law which the play tragically creates. So too in the *Herakles*, the traditional figuration of the hero's greatness is given resonance in a massively powerful dirge which wheels for a hundred lines through the canonical Twelve Labors, earning reality for an image of the hero which the play's second action annuls. For the close of the play is a conversion in which Herakles is reduced, but also raised, to the human condition, and his old heroism transfigured in the perfected humanity of the hero. Or think again of the overwhelming loveliness of language and ecstasy which the *Bakkhai* gives to the chorus, before revealing its hideous depravity; or of the precariously tender sleep scene of the

Orestes, which enhances the hero admired of tradition before the sudden revelation of his terrible brutality.

In all of these plays, reality of poetry or of passion or of situation is the indispensable condition of conversion. What the play will finally disclose as illusion is treated as fully real until the very moment of disclosure. In this way, Euripides, as against Eliot, earns his transfiguration by making his poetry the test of its own truth and the stumbling-block that it imposes on itself; he allows illusion to claim the status and dignity of reality until transfigured and exposed for what it is. Until Mr. Eliot, I think, is willing once more to take the risk of his own gift of tongues and to accept, at least dramatically, the reality of illusion in this world, his own calling cannot be higher than that of a dramatist without compelling Vocation.

JEAN-PAUL SARTRE
The Maids

The most extraordinary example of the whirligig of being and appearance, of the imaginary and the real, is to be found in one of
Genet's plays. It is the element of fake, of sham, of artificiality that
attracts Genet in the theater. He has turned dramatist because the
falsehood of the stage is the most manifest and fascinating of all.
Perhaps nowhere has he lied more brazenly than in *The Maids*.

Two maids both love and hate their mistress. They have de-
nounced her lover to the police by means of anonymous letters.
Upon learning that he is to be released for lack of proof, they realize
that their betrayal will be discovered, and they try to murder
Madame. They fail and want to kill themselves. Finally, one of them
takes her life, and the other, left alone and drunk with glory, tries,
by the pomp of her posturings and language, to be equal to the magnificent destiny that awaits her.

Let us indicate at once a first whirligig. Genet says in *Our Lady of
the Flowers*: "If I were to have a play put on in which women had
roles, I would demand that these roles be performed by adolescent
boys, and I would bring this to the attention of the spectators by
means of a placard which would remain nailed to the right or left of
the sets during the entire performance." [1] One might be tempted
to explain this demand by Genet's taste for young boys. Nevertheless,

Reprinted from *Saint Genet, Actor and Martyr*, translated from the French
by Bernard Frechtman, George Braziller, Inc., New York, 1963, W. H.
Allen and Co., London, 1963. Reprinted by permission of the publishers.

this is not the essential reason. The truth of the matter is that Genet wishes from the very start to *strike at the root of the apparent*. No doubt an actress can play Solange, but the derealizing would not be radical, since there would be no need for her to play at being a woman. The softness of her flesh, the languid grace of her movements and the silvery tone of her voice are natural endowments. They constitute the substance that she would mold as she saw fit, so as to give it the appearance of Solange. Genet wishes this feminine stuff itself to become an appearance, the result of a make-believe. It is not Solange who is to be a theatrical illusion, but rather *the woman Solange*.

In order to achieve this absolute state of artifice, the first thing to do is to eliminate nature. The roughness of a breaking voice, the dry hardness of male muscles and the bluish luster of a budding beard will make the defeminized and spiritualized female appear as an invention of man, as a pale and wasting shadow which cannot sustain itself unaided, as the evanescent result of an extreme and momentary exertion, as the impossible dream of man in a world without women.

Thus, what appears behind the footlights is not so much a woman as Genet himself living out the impossibility of being a woman. We would see before us the effort, at times admirable and at times grotesque, of a youthful male body struggling against its own nature, and, lest the spectator be caught up in the game, he would be warned throughout—in defiance of all the laws of stage perspective —that the actors are trying to deceive him as to their sex. In short, the illusion is prevented from "taking" by a sustained contradiction between the effort of the actor, who measures his talent by his ability to deceive, and the warning of the placard. Thus, Genet *betrays* his actors. He unmasks them, and the performer, seeing his imposture exposed, finds himself in the position of a culprit who has been found out. Illusion, betrayal, failure; all the major categories that govern Genet's dreams are here present. In the same way, he betrays his characters in *Our Lady of the Flowers* and in *Funeral Rites* by warning the reader whenever the latter is about to yield to the illusion of the story: "Watch out. These are creatures of my imagination. They don't exist." The thing to be avoided above all is the spectator's being caught up in the game, like children at the movies who scream, "Don't drink it, it's poison!" or like the naïve public that waited at the stage door for Frédéric Lemaître in order to beat him up.

To seek being through appearance would be to make *proper use* of the latter. For Genet, theatrical procedure is demoniacal. Appearance, which is constantly on the point of passing itself off as reality, must constantly reveal its profound unreality. Everything must be so false that it sets our teeth on edge. But by virtue of being false, the woman acquires a poetic density. Shorn of its texture and purified, femininity becomes a heraldic sign, a cipher. As long as it was natural, the feminine blazon remained embedded in woman. Spiritualized, it becomes a category of the imagination, a device for generating reveries. Anything can be a woman: a flower, an animal, an inkwell.

In *The Child Criminal* Genet has given us the keys of what might be called his algebra of the imagination. He speaks of the director of a home for children who boasts of giving the children tin knives and who adds, "They can't kill anyone with that." Genet makes the following comment: "Was he unaware that by departing from its practical destination the object is transformed, that it becomes a symbol? Its very form sometimes changes. We say that it becomes stylized. It then acts secretly in children's souls. It does more serious damage. Hidden at night in a straw mattress or concealed in the lining of the jacket or, rather, of the trousers—not for greater convenience, but in order to be close to the organ it symbolizes—it is the very sign of the murder that the child will not actually commit but which will feed his reverie and, I hope, will direct it toward the most criminal manifestation. What good does it do to take it away from him? The child will only choose some more harmless-looking object as a sign of murder, and if this also is taken from him, he will guard within him preciously the sharper image of the weapon." As the material grows poorer—steel knife, tin knife, hazel twig—as the distance increases between itself and what it signifies, the symbolic nature of the sign is heightened. The reveries are directed, fed and organized. His maids are fake women, "women of no gynaeceum," who make men dream not of possessing *a* woman but of being lit up by a woman-sun, queen of a feminine heaven, and finally of being themselves the matter for the heraldic symbol of femininity. Genet is trying to present to us femininity without woman.

Such is the initial direction of his derealization: a falsification of femininity. But the shock boomerangs and the performance affects the actor himself. The young murderer, Our Lady of the Flowers, dresses up as a woman one day just for the fun of it. "Our Lady, in his pale blue faille dress, edged with white Valenciennes lace, was more than himself. He was himself and his complement." We know that Genet values above all the labor of derealization. The thing that attracts him in Our Lady of the Flowers is the spectacle of a man being worked upon by femininity. "Our Lady raised his bare arm and—it's astounding—this murderer made the very same gesture, though a trifle more brutal, that Émilienne d'Alençon would certainly have made to rumple her chignon." This hybrid creature, of the race of centaurs and sirens, begins as a male only to go up in smoke as female fireworks. In order to express his superiority both to young men and to all women, Genet invents a wonderful sign: "The chauffeur opened the door. . . . Gorgui, because of his position in the group, ought to have stepped in first, but he moved aside, leaving the opening free for Our Lady. Bear in mind that never does a pimp efface himself before a woman, still less before a fairy. . . . Gorgui must have placed him quite high." The appearance of the imaginary upsets social conventions. Gorgui the Pimp spontaneously adopts bourgeois courtesy. He effaces himself before a glamorous young male who derealizes himself into a young lady whose grace is heightened by the glamor of the murderer. The grace of women is usually despised by roughnecks because it signifies weakness and submission. But here it shimmers at the surface of the great dark force of killers. Hence, they must bow before it. Crime becomes the secret horror of grace: grace becomes the secret softness of crime. Our Lady is the vestal of a bloodthirsty goddess, a great cruel Mother of a homosexual matriarchy.

Thus far we have seen nothing we did not already know. All this is still the reciprocal derealization of matter by form and of form by matter. But now the first whirligig is set going. Genet's poetic themes are, as we know, profoundly homosexual. We know that neither women nor the psychology of women interests him. And if he has chosen to show us maids and their mistress and feminine hatreds, it is only because the necessities of public performance oblige him to disguise his thought. The proof of this is that his second play, *Deathwatch*, the characters of which are all men, deals with exactly the same subject as *The Maids*.

There is the same hierarchy: in one case, Monsieur, in the other, Snowball; the intermediate divinity, Madame and Green Eyes; and the two youngsters who dream of murder but fail to commit it, who love and hate each other and each of whom is the other's bad smell,

Solange and Claire, Maurice and Lefranc. In one case, the play ends with a suicide that the police will take for a murder; in the other, with a fake murder, that is, a real killing which rings false. Lefranc, who is a fake, is a real traitor; Maurice, however, who is too young to kill, is of the race of killers; thus, they too form "the eternal couple of the Criminal and the Saint," as do Divine and Our Lady. This is the same eternal couple that Solange and Claire want to form. And their ambiguous feeling for Madame is discreetly homosexual, as is that of Lefranc and Maurice for Green Eyes. Moreover, Genet himself has known the maids' hatred of Madame. He tells us in *Our Lady of the Flowers* that he himself was once a servant, and in *Funeral Rites* he tells us of another servant, the suffering mother who concealed beneath her skirts "the wiliest of hoodlums." Similarly, it has been said that "Proust's Albertine should have been called Albert." The young actors in *The Maids* are boys playing at being women, but these women in turn are secretly boys. However, these imaginary boys who gleam behind the feminine appearances of Solange and Claire are not to be identified with the real adolescents who embody the characters. They too are dreams, since in the other play they are called Maurice and Lefranc. They are, if you like, on the vanishing line of the appearances, giving them their appearance of depth. But the spectators dimly sense the homosexual drift of the plot, and when the actor raises his bare arm and reveals too much muscle, when he adjusts his bun and makes a gesture "a trifle more brutal" than that of Émilienne d'Alençon, the spectator does not know whether this inordinate muscularity and too evident brutality represent a rebellion of reality or whether they transcend this story about women and symbolize homosexuality. Are the dry and angular gesture and the brusque gait merely the awkwardness of a young male hampered by a woman's dress, or are they not Maurice, who has taken possession of Solange? Are they a return to Being or are they the quintessence of the imaginary? Being changes at this point into appearance and appearance into being. But it may be objected that the homosexual drama is the *truth* of this ancillary fiction. Well and good. But it is an appearance which becomes the truth of another appearance. And then, in another sense, these fake women were the truth of the adolescent boys who embodied them, for Genet, like all homosexuals, is able to discern a secret femininity in the most male of men. As in psychodramas, his actors play what they are. They resemble, feature for feature, the real hoodlum who played the fake-prince-who-is-a-real-hoodlum and who, through the mediation of the prince, was derealized into himself. But if these fake women are the disguise of imaginary men, the young actors are swallowed up by a new absence. As they interpret their own drama, they are the unconscious pawns in a game of chess which Genet is playing against himself.

But we are still at only the first degree of derealization. These fake women who are fake men, these women-men who are men-women, this perpetual challenging of masculinity by a symbolic femininity and of the latter by the secret femininity which is the truth of all masculinity, are only the faked groundwork. Upon this evanescent foundation there appear individual forms: Solange and Claire. We shall see that they too are faked.

The play has four characters, one of whom does not appear, namely, Monsieur, the *man*. Monsieur is Harcamone of *Miracle of the Rose*; he is Snowball of *Deathwatch*. Pilorge is he who *is never there*. His absence represents the eternal abstraction of the handsome Pimps, their indifference. In this bourgeois atmosphere he is the only one who is ennobled by prison. To be sure, he is slanderously accused of a crime which he has not committed, but we know that for Genet guilt comes to the offender from without. It is a collective image, a taboo that settles upon him. Behind this homosexual *Arlésienne* whom everyone talks about and nobody sees is Madame, an ambiguous figure, a mediation, a girl queen in relation to Monsieur and a boy queen in relation to the two maids. To Monsieur she is a faithful dog. Genet ascribes to her his old dream of following a convict to the penal colony. "I wanted to be," he tells us, "the young prostitute who accompanies her lover to Siberia." And Madame says: "I don't think he's guilty either, but if he were, I'd become his accomplice. I'd follow him to Devil's Island, to Siberia." But something warns us—perhaps her volubility or the wild gaiety of her despair—that she is a fraud. Does she love Monsieur? Probably she does. But to what point? There is no way of telling. At all events, she has found, like Ernestine in *Our Lady of the Flowers*, the finest role of her life. It will be noted that Green Eyes, a symmetrical character who is also an intermediary and a "daimon," though he has committed an honest-to-goodness murder, plays, in his state of exaltation, at being a murderer. In Genet's plays every character must play the role of a character who plays a role. In relation to the two maids, Madame represents pitiless indifference.

Not that she despises or mistreats them; she is *kind*. She embodies social Good and Good Conscience, and the servants' ambivalent feelings about her express Genet's feeling about Good. Being kind, Madame can desire only the Good. She feels sorry for them: she gives them dresses; she loves them, but with an icy love, "like her bidet." In like manner, wealthy, cultivated and happy men have, from time to time, "felt sorry" for Genet, have tried to oblige him. Too late. He has blamed them for loving him for the love of Good, *in spite* of his badness and not *for* it. Only an evil individual could love another evil individual for the love of Evil. But evildoers do not love.

As a woman in relationship to Monsieur, Madame has only *relative* being. As the maids' mistress, she retains an absolute being. But the maids are relative to everything and everyone; their being is defined by its absolute relativity. They are *others*. Domestics are pure emanations of their masters and, like criminals, belong to the order of the Other, to the order of Evil. They *love* Madame. This means, in Genet's language, that both of them would like to *become* Madame, in other words, to be integrated into the social order instead of being outcasts. They *hate* Madame. Translate: Genet detests the Society that rejects him and he wishes to annihilate it. These specters are born of the dream of a master; murky to themselves, their feelings come to them from outside. They are born in the sleeping imagination of Madame or Monsieur. Low, hypocritical, disagreeable and mean because their employers dream them that way, they belong to the "pale and motley race that flowers in the minds of decent people." When he presents them before the footlights, Genet merely mirrors the fantasies of the right-minded women in the audience. Every evening five hundred Madames can sing out, "Yes, that's what maids are like," without realizing that they have created them, the way Southerners create Negroes. The only rebellion of these flat creatures is that they dream in turn: they dream within a dream; these dream dwellers, pure reflections of a sleeping consciousness, use the little reality which this consciousness has given them to imagine that they are becoming the Master who imagines them. They flounder about at the intersection of two nightmares and form the "twilight guard" of bourgeois families. They are disturbing only in that they are dreams that dream of swallowing up their dreamer.

Thus, the maids, as Genet conceives them, are *already* fake. Pure

products of artifice, their minds are inside out, and they are always
other than themselves. That there are two of them is a stroke of
genius. Two, exactly the number needed to set up a whirligig. To be
sure, Genet did not invent these criminal sisters out of whole cloth.
The reader has probably recognized Claire and Solange; they are the
Papin sisters.[2] But we already know that Genet has distilled the anecdote, that he has retained only its quintessence and presents it to us
as a "cipher." The *maids* are the mysterious cipher of the pure
imagination and also of Genet himself. There are two of them because Genet is double: himself and the other. Thus, each of the two
maids has no other function than to be the other, to be—for the
other—herself-as-other. Whereas the unity of the mind is constantly
haunted by a phantom duality, the dyad of the maids is, on the
contrary, haunted by a phantom of unity. Each sees in the other only
herself at a distance from herself. Each bears witness to the other
of the impossibility of *being* herself, and, as Querelle says: "their
double statue is reflected in each of their halves." The mainspring of
this new whirligig is the perfect interchangeability of Solange and
Claire, which makes Solange always appear to be elsewhere, *on* Claire
when we look at Solange, and *on* Solange when we look at Claire. To
be sure, this interchangeability does not exclude certain differences.
Solange seems harder; perhaps "she tries to dominate" Claire; perhaps Genet has chosen her to embody the glamorous appearance
and the secret cowardice of the criminal; perhaps he has elected the
gentle and perfidious Claire to symbolize the hidden heroism of the
Saint. In actual fact, Solange's attempts at crime fail: she does not
succeed in killing either Madame or her own sister. Claire also
botches a murder, but, pushing their play-acting to its extreme consequences, she takes her own life. The girl queen has more real courage
than the tough. This means that the fake courage of Solange finds
its truth in the secret courage of Claire, that the fake pusillanimity
of Claire finds its truth in the profound cowardice of Solange.

But Genet does not linger over these familiar themes, which he
develops abundantly elsewhere. Solange and Claire are much less
differentiated than Maurice and Lefranc; their dissimilarities are
dreams which ill conceal a fundamental identity. Both of them are
characterized by the imaginary splendor of their projects and the
radical failure of their undertakings. In reality, Genet has set before
us *a single object*, though a profoundly faked one, neither one nor
two, one when we want to see two, two when we want to see one:

the ancillary couple as a pure crisscross of appearances. And the bond that unites these two reflections is itself a faked relationship. Do the sisters love each other, do they hate each other? They hate each other with love, like all of Genet's characters. Each finds in the other her "bad smell" and one of them proclaims that "filth doesn't love filth." But at the same time, each inwardly clings to the other by a kind of carnal promiscuity which gives to their caresses the tepid pleasure of masturbation. But where is the truth of the ancillary couple? When we see Solange and Claire in the presence of Madame, they do not seem real. Fake submission, fake tenderness, fake respect, fake gratitude. Their entire behavior is a lie. We are led to believe that this falsifying comes from their false relationships with their mistress. When they resume their joint solitude, they put on their true faces again. But when they are alone, they play. Claire plays at being Madame and Solange at being Claire. And we await, despite ourselves, the return of Madame which will cause their masks to fall and which will restore them to their true situation as servants.

Thus, their truth is always elsewhere; in the presence of the Masters, the truth of a domestic is to be a fake domestic and to mask the *man* he is under a guise of servility; but, in their absence, the *man* does not manifest himself either, for the truth of the domestic in solitude is to play at being master. The fact is that when the Master is away on a trip, the valets smoke his cigars, wear his clothes and ape his manners. How could it be otherwise, since the Master convinces the servant that there is no other way to become a man than to be a master. A whirligig of appearances: a valet is sometimes a man who plays at being a man; in other words, a man who dreams with horror that he is becoming a subman or a subman who dreams with hatred that he is becoming a man.

Thus, each of the two maids plays, in turn, at being Madame. When the curtain rises, Claire is standing in front of the dressing table of her mistress. She is experimenting with Madame's gestures and language. For Genet, this is an actual incantation. We shall see later on that, by imitating the gestures of his superior, the domestic treacherously draws him into himself and becomes saturated with him. There is nothing surprising in this, since Madame herself is a fake Madame who plays at distinction and at her passion for Monsieur and who dreams of drawing into herself the soul of a whore who follows her pimp to jail.

Similarly, Genet could, without difficulty, *make himself* Stilitano, because Stilitano himself played at being Stilitano. Madame is no more true in Claire than in Madame herself; Madame is a gesture.

Solange helps her sister put on one of her mistress's dresses, and Claire, playing her role in a state of exaltation, taut and strained, as is Genet himself, insults Solange, as she does every evening, until the latter, driven to extremities, as she is every evening, slaps her. This is, of course, a ceremony, a sacred game which is repeated with the stereotyped monotony of schizophrenic dreams. In short, Genet, whose reveries are themselves often dry and ceremonious and who repeats them day after day until their charm is exhausted, introduces the spectator into the very privacy of his inner life. He allows himself to be overheard in a spell of incantation; he betrays himself; he gives himself away; he hides nothing of the monotony and childishness which spoil his secret festivities and of which he is perfectly aware. And he even invites us to see what he himself will never see because he is unable to get outside himself: the inside and outside, the *reality* (if there is one) and its disguise. As for the role itself, we recognize quite easily Genet's favorite themes: to begin with, the maids *want*, to the point of despair and horror, the servile condition that is imposed upon them; in like manner, Genet wants to be the bastard, the outcast that society has made of him. And this cruel game provides the rigorous demonstration of what we suggested a while ago: one cannot want to be what one is in the imaginary; in order to live their wretchedness to the point of *passion*, to the very dregs, they must make themselves the cause of it. Thus, Solange plays the role of servant. But she would be sticking too close to reality if she remained Solange; there would be no way of deciding whether she takes upon herself her menial condition or whether she *really*, and out of habit, performs her servile tasks. In order to change herself into a maid by her own will, Solange *plays at being* Solange. She cannot *want to be* Solange the servant, because she *is* Solange. She therefore wants to be an imaginary Claire so as to acquire one of the chief characteristics of this Claire, which is to be a servant. A phantom Claire dresses an imaginary Madame. Here a small local whirl is set up: an actor plays the role of a servant who is playing the role of a servant. The falsest of appearances joins the truest being, for to play at being a maid is the truth of the actor and the phantasy of Solange. The result is—and this does not fail to delight Genet—that in order "to be true" the actor must *play false*. The fact is that

Solange, who is not a professional actress, plays her role of maid badly. Thus, the nearer the actor draws to his reality as actor, the further he withdraws from it. Fake jewels, sham pearls, Genet's deceptive loves: an actor plays at being an actor, a maid plays at being a maid; their truth is their lie and their lie is their truth. The same may be said of the actor playing the role of Claire-playing-Madame; Genet confirms it in his stage directions: "Her gestures and tone are exaggeratedly tragic."

The reason for this is that the ceremony has still another meaning: it is a Black Mass. What is played every evening is the murder of Madame, a murder always being interrupted, always uncompleted. It is a case of committing *the worst:* Madame is benevolent, "Madame is kind"; they will kill their benefactress, precisely because she has been Good to them. The act will be imaginary, since Evil is the imagination. But *even in the imaginary* it is faked in advance. The maids know that they will not have time enough to get to the crime.

> SOLANGE: The same thing happens every time. And it's all your fault, you're never ready. I can't finish you off.

> CLAIRE: We waste too much time with the preliminaries.

Thus, the playing of the sacrilege conceals a failure in behavior. It is imaginary to the second degree: Claire and Solange do not even play the fictitious murder; they pretend to play it. They are thereby merely imitating their creator. As I have pointed out elsewhere, Genet prefers imaginary murder to real murder because in the former the will to evil, though remaining entire, pushes the love of nothingness to a point where it reduces itself to impotence. In the last analysis, Solange and Claire are fully satisfied with this *appearance* of crime; what they like about it more than anything else is the taste of nothingness with which it leaves them. But they both pretend, by means of a further lie, that they are disappointed at not having gone through with the thing to the very end. And besides, what would there have been at "the very end"? The true murder of the fake Madame? The fake murder of Claire? Perhaps they don't even know themselves.

The fact remains that in this phantom play-acting, which, even as play-acting, never concludes,[3] the great role this evening is reserved for Claire: it is for her to personify Madame and so to exasperate

Solange that she commits a crime. But Solange personifies Claire. Whence, a new disintegration: the relationships of the fake Madame with the fake Claire have a triple, a quadruple basis. In the first place, Claire makes herself be Madame *because she loves her*; for Genet, to love means to want to be. As Madame, she blossoms out; she escapes from herself. But, in addition, she makes herself be Madame *because she hates her*: resentment derealizes; Madame is merely a passive phantom who is slapped on Claire's cheeks. Besides, the interpretation of Claire is forced; she is not aiming at showing Madame as she is, but at making her hateful. Madame, the sweet and kind Madame, insults her maids, humiliates them, exasperates them. And we do not know whether this distorted caricature tends to reveal the mistress in her true light, to expose the truth of that indifferent good nature which may be concealing a pitiless cruelty, or whether it already wreaks an imaginary vengeance by metamorphosing Madame, by the incantation of the gesture, into a harpy. As psychoanalysis has revealed to us, one of the motives of acts of self-punishment is to force the judge to punish unjustly and thereby to burden him with a guilt which discredits him and makes him unworthy of judging. By means of her performance of Madame's role, Claire transforms her into an unjust judge and rids herself of her. But at the same time, in the guise of Madame, she insults and humiliates Solange, whom she hates, Solange, her bad smell: "Avoid pawing me. You smell like an animal. You've brought those odors from some foul attic where the lackeys visit us at night." But Solange is sheltered: she is playing the role of Claire. First, as we have seen, because it is easier for her as the fake Claire to assume her menial condition; then, because Claire can be Madame only if she seems Madame in her own eyes. Solange's becoming Claire represents the astounding effort of a reflective consciousness turning back on itself and wanting to perceive itself as it appears to others. This attempt is doomed to failure; either the reflective consciousness is real and its object melts into the imaginary (Genet can *see himself* as a thief only poetically), or else the object remains real and it is the reflection that slips into the imaginary (Eric, in *Funeral Rites*, imagines seeing himself with the eyes of the executioner). Solange's play-acting belongs to this second category; it is Claire taking upon herself a reflective view in the imaginary. Claire's audience is the phantom of herself-as-other. It is thus *herself* whom she humiliates; it is to *herself* that she says: "Keep your hands off mine! I can't stand your touching me." Solange, Madame, the intermediate appearances, all vanish. Claire stands alone facing her mirror, in the desert. Thus, the love-hatred she feels for Madame conceals her feeling for Solange and finally her feeling about herself. And each of these feelings has an imaginary side; her hatred of Madame takes on a double aspect; insofar as Claire is the source of it, she derealizes herself and exhausts herself in her caricatural interpretation of this character; but, on the other hand, she passes into Solange, who, as fake Claire, directs upon the fake Madame, on behalf of her sister, a fictive hatred. As for Claire's hatred of Solange, it is completely covered and disguised by the play-acting: it is not, to be sure, fictive, but it finds within reach only fictive instruments and modes of expression; in order to hate Solange, Claire has no other resource but to make herself Madame-hating-Claire. Finally, Claire's hatred of herself makes it necessary that at least one of the two terms of this affective relationship be imaginary: in order to hate and to love, there must be two; hence, Claire can hate only a phantom of herself embodied by Solange. But we again fall upon a whirligig: for *at the same time* the feelings are true; it is true that Claire hates Madame, true that she hates Solange and that, through the mediation of Solange, she tries to hate herself. Once again the false is true and the true can be expressed only by means of the false. And when Claire calls Solange "You slut," when Solange, *in ecstasy*, cries, "Madame's being carried away!" *who* is insulting *whom?* And *who* feels the insult with that masochistic pleasure? Inversely, *who* tempts *whom* to commit murder? And *who* slaps *whom?* This slap is a sacred rite which represents the rape of Genet by the Male. But this whirligig of appearances has made us so dizzy that we do not know whether it is Claire who slaps Madame, Claire who slaps Claire, Solange who slaps Claire or Solange who slaps Solange.[4] It may be objected that the true Solange has never-theless performed a real act and that the true Claire has felt true pain. So they have. But the same holds for this slap as for Genet's thefts. As I have pointed out elsewhere, though these thefts were *really* committed, they were lived in the imaginary. This slap is therefore a poetic act. It melts into a gesture; the very pain that it causes is lived imaginarily. At the same time, it is slurred over, for this true slap which is felt imaginarily is a fake slap that an actor pretends to give another actor.

This extraordinary faking, this mad jumble of appearances, this superimposing of whirligigs which keep sending us back and forth from the true to the false and from the false to the true, is an infernal machine whose mechanism Genet is careful not to reveal to us at the beginning. When the curtain goes up, we see an impatient and nervous young lady who is rebuking her maid. From time to time an unusual word or an inappropriate gesture casts a disturbing light upon this familiar scene. But suddenly an alarm clock goes off: "The two actresses, in a state of agitation, run together. They huddle and listen." Claire, in a changed voice, mutters: "Let's hurry! Madame'll be back." She starts to unfasten her dress. "It's so close this evening"; they are "exhausted and sad"; in order to put their short black skirts on again they need some of that "greatness of soul" that Divine displayed when she put her bridge back into her mouth. However, the spectator, in a dazzling flash, sees through the heart of the darkness to this astounding mechanism of appearances: everything was fake; the familiar scene was a diabolical imitation of everyday life. The entire scene was prepared in order to impose this deception upon us.

The high value of appearance is due, in Genet's eyes, to the fact that, like Evil, of which it is the pure embodiment, it corrodes and does away with itself. Cases of volatilization are rare in ordinary life; the plate breaks and the pieces remain. But appearance offers us a certain being. It gives it to us, hands it over to us, and, if we put out our arm, this being is suddenly reabsorbed. The victim of the three-card trick has not lost sight of the ace of hearts; he *knows* that it is the first card of the third pack; he points to it; the performer turns it up: it's the ace of spades. He then feels a strange and brutal disappointment in his flesh. For a moment he thinks that he has an intuition of nothingness. Yes, the nothing becomes an apparition, nonbeing a richness which fills him; the absence of the ace of hearts is much more virulent, much more immediate, than the presence of the ace of spades. The following instant his perception has regained its fullness, but the instant remains mysterious. The nothingness has disappeared; it allowed itself to be glimpsed and then vanished.

But since nonbeing *is not*, how can it *no longer be*? It is this perverse intuition that Genet prefers to all else: it makes the *nothing* shimmer at the surface of *all*. Where is being? Can it be that something *is*? If the ace of hearts has vanished, why should not the ace of spades disappear as well? And what is nonbeing, if it can suddenly fill me with its emptiness? In *The Maids*, the ambiguous instant of deception, when superimposed illusions collapse like a house of cards, rightly deserves the name of pure instant of the Lie. For when the Saharan mirage vanishes, it reveals true stones. But when the deceptive appearances in the play are dispelled, they reveal in their place *other appearances* (the fake Madame becomes Claire again, the fake maid, the fake woman; the fake Claire becomes Solange again, the fake servant). At this moment the spectator has first the demoniacal intuition of nothingness, that is, being is revealed to be nothing, but, as appearance is usually effaced in the presence of being, the illusions which vanish leave him with the illusion that *it is being* which replaces them. Suddenly the pantomime of a young male who pretends to be a woman *seems to him to be the truth*. It is as if he suddenly understood that the only true thing is play-acting, that the only real women are men, and so on. Being has been revealed as nonbeing and thereupon nonbeing becomes being. This moment in which the lights flicker, when the volatile unity of the being of nonbeing and the nonbeing of being is achieved in semidarkness, this perfect and perverse instant, makes us realize from within the mental attitude of Genet when he dreams: it is the moment of evil. For in order to be sure of never making *proper use* of appearance, Genet wants his fancies, at two or three stages of derealization, to reveal themselves in their nothingness. In this pyramid of fantasies, the ultimate appearance derealizes all the others. Thus, the youngster who plays the role of Claire is derealized into a young man so that the latter may be derealized into a mistress. But, as I have shown, an appearance borrows its being from being: thus, "Claire" borrows her being from the boy who interprets her. But the "fake Madame" is supported in being by *Claire*, who does not exist. And since she thus derives her being from a fantasy, the being of this appearance is only an appearance of being. Whereupon Genet considers himself satisfied; on the one hand, he has achieved pure appearance, the one whose very being is appearance, that is, the one which appears to be appearance through and through, to borrow nothing from being and finally to produce itself, which, as we know, is one of the two contradictory demands of Evil; but, on the other hand, this pyramid of appearances masks the being which supports them all (the true movement, the true words uttered by the young actor in the play, the movement and words which, in actual life, help Genet dream), and as, nevertheless, they *are* in some way, it seems that each borrows its being from the one that immediately precedes it. Thus, as being fades into appearance at all degrees, it seems that the real is something melting, that it is reabsorbed when touched. In these patient fakings, appearance is revealed at the same time as pure nothingness and as cause of itself. And being, without ceasing to set itself up as absolute reality, becomes evanescent. Translated into the language of Evil: Good is only an illusion; Evil is a Nothingness which arises upon the ruins of Good.

NOTES

1. *The Maids* was actually performed by women, but this was a concession which Genet made to Louis Jouvet, who produced the play.
2. The reference is to a famous French murder case—Translator's note.
3. Genet is an old hand at these unfinished ceremonies. He confides to us in *Miracle of the Rose* that he used to caress Bulkaen in thought but would abandon him even before attaining erection.
4. For Solange hates herself in Claire as Claire hates herself in Solange.

JACQUES GUICHARNAUD

Theatre as Proposition: Jean Giraudoux

When novelist Jean Giraudoux's first play, *Siegfried*, was produced by Louis Jouvet at the Comédie des Champs Elysées on May 2, 1928, the then fashionable playwrights suddenly seemed quite definitely second-rate. Giraudoux had created an original universe, corresponding to most of the demands for "true" theatre. Indeed, his was the first coherent and satisfying form of modern theatre presented to a general public. And his plays dominated the French stage all during the thirties and early forties, a time which might be called the Age of Giraudoux.

Although not one of his best plays, *Siegfried* does contain all the indications of what Giraudoux was to become and of the scenic universe he was to create and enrich from play to play. Clearly, he would use simple individual conflicts as metaphors of conflicts between great universal themes: the story of Siegfried, a German political hero who lost his memory during the first World War and discovers that he is in fact Jacques, a French soldier, is but the pretext for an allegorical dialogue between France and Germany, each country being considered in its atmosphere, its culture, its poetry. And clearly, by simplifying the terms of the conflict, Giraudoux would bring out the subtlety of their relations and play freely with the element of surprise

Reprinted by permission from *Modern French Theatre from Giraudoux to Beckett*. Yale University Press, New Haven, 1961.

in unexpected reversals: at the end of the play, Geneviève, having helped bring the French Jacques out from the depths of the German Siegfried, lets herself be charmed by Germany and at the very moment Siegfried has become Jacques, cries out "Siegfried, I love you."

But above all he would "write" his plays. And through the writing itself, on every level of style and composition, both Giraudoux's universe and his true originality are revealed. One of his most apparent devices is the presentation of stylized debates in which the characters embody the great themes in question. One particular scene in *Siegfried* serves as a model or pattern of such precisely defined staging, structure, and composition, that it seems like a beautifully chiselled nail hammered right in the heart of the play, intended to hold down that delicately embroidered stuff, often so light that it would seem to fly off stage: the scene in Act III, in which Siegfried's anguished struggle is exteriorized, represented or acted almost allegorically by Geneviève and Eva, both throwing concrete and opposing arguments into the scale of a balance which is tipped in their favor, until finally the two women throw the conflict back within Siegfried.

Almost all of Giraudoux's works are organized around analogous debates: between war and peace in *la Guerre de Troie*, the love of a young man and the love of an old man in *Cantique des cantiques*, the human and the supernatural in *Ondine* and *Intermezzo*, English morality and natural amorality in *le Supplément du Voyage de Cook*, sensual love and saintliness in *Judith*, man and woman in *Sodome et Gomorrhe*. Each play leads the spectator toward a solution of the conflict by means of great contrasts and sudden reversals, as in *Siegfried*.

Within the debates themselves, Giraudoux would clearly use language to provide the most specific and unexpected images. Often the characters, in explaining themselves, make use of details that are comical in the contrast between their apparent insignificance and the importance of their function. In *Siegfried* Zelten explains that he was unable to bring about his counterrevolution for want of arms, but also and mostly for want of glue to stick up his manifestoes. In a similar way in *Electre*, Clytemnestra explains that much of her hate for Agamemnon stems from the way in which he always, in no matter what circumstances, held his little finger up in the air.

An elaborately wrought language, the reversal of situations, great stylized debates accompanied by the most whimsical and singular details are unchanging in Giraudoux's works, in the masterpieces as well as in his less successful plays. His universe is created more through the fixed elements of his theatrical vision than through the choice and evolution of certain themes and ideas, so often catalogued and analyzed.

Essentially a theatre of language, Giraudoux's works relate to a strong tradition which has characterized the French stage since the Renaissance. From Garnier to Montherlant, French playwrights have been garrulous. Doubtless the reasons for this recourse to language are varied: plays written more to be read than performed, material conditions of staging (in the classical period, for example) reducing physical action to a minimum, the pride of poets. But the fundamental reason would seem to be always the same: a belief in the magic and power of words and combinations of words.

Characters on Giraudoux's stage talk more than they move. The greater part of certain scenes, even of certain plays, can be performed sitting down, for the drama can best be expressed through conversation or verbal debate. The characters reveal their inner struggles through the shock of words and phrases, or, as bearers of contrary truths, they oppose one another like lawyers in court before judges (the gods) and a jury (the spectators). Language, the weapon of poets and diplomats, is the primary instrument of poet-diplomat Jean Giraudoux.

The use of language in Giraudoux's theatre is not merely the result of a particular temperament but also of a deliberate choice. In his article "le Metteur en scène," [1] where he compares German and French theatre, Giraudoux defines French theatre in terms of the sovereignty of language. When the German public, just before the advent of Hitler, was reveling in Max Reinhardt's great spectacles or participating in Piscator's "fire-arms" theatre, the Frenchman remained faithful to his traditions.[2] According to Giraudoux, "the true dramatic effect for him is not the clamor of two hundred extras, but the ironic nuance given to a phrase of the hero or heroine," for the Frenchman believes that the "great debates of the heart" are settled "by conversation":

> He persists in considering dialogue as the supreme form of
> the duel for the creature gifted with words. What he likes

to experience is the power of that dialogue, its effectiveness, its form, hence the purely literary merits of the text. For him, theatrical action consists, not in submitting to a frantic massage of almost physical vision and emotion, from which he leaves exhausted, as from a Turkish bath, but in hanging his worries and the conflicts of his life and personal imagination on a model dialogue which can elucidate them.

A model dialogue: such would seem to be Giraudoux's definition of theatre. Every drama would be one of the spectator's conflicts—conflicts in his life and in his imagination—put into model language. The words that never come, the vital discussions that daily life does not allow, the clarification by category of the soul's and heart's confusion—that is what the spectator would hear on stage. Language would become a prism in which the whitish, monotonous, and imperfect light of life is decomposed into basic and dazzling colors.

It would of course be easy to hold the conception up to ridicule. Do you have a great inexpressible love for peace? Go and see your love take shape in Hector's long speeches in *la Guerre de Troie n'aura pas lieu*. If you can't explain why your husband irritates you and why and how you have been unfaithful to him or killed him, go and listen to Agathe and Clytemnestra in *Electre*. If you are a minor civil servant and are unsuccessful in persuading the romantic young girl you're in love with to marry you, go and hear the Supervisor in *Intermezzo*. Or if you happen to be the young girl, listen to Isabelle in the same play. Yet there is no doubt that the characters' model speeches do more than replace political editorials in the newspapers or the correspondence of Miss Lonelyhearts.

The principle, confirmed by Giraudoux's theoretical writings and immediately apparent as a presupposition of his entire theatre, is that no reality can withstand human language. Giraudoux was a humanist, and doubly so: He not only based his conception of theatre on his knowledge and interpretation of European culture, but he had complete confidence in the human logic of language as a means of accounting for the universe. Language is the spider's web, spun by intelligence, in which reality and sur-reality and the supernatural are caught. The end of *Sodome et Gomorrhe* is the end of the world. But despite God's wrath, the war of the sexes will continue *ad saecula saeculorum*. It was characteristic of Giraudoux to have chosen as an image the voices of man and woman, continuing their discussion all the same:

> THE ARCHANGEL: Are they never going to be quiet! Are they never going to die!
>
> THE ANGEL: They are dead.
>
> THE ARCHANGEL: Who is speaking then?
>
> THE ANGEL: They are. Death was not enough. The scene continues.

Language, even with no support, perseveres in its existence. It lives on independent of the men who use it, just as for a believer the soul survives the body.

Although it does not necessarily create its objects, language does confer a privileged existence upon them, next to which their *unspoken* existence seems less important. In Giraudoux, not only does it give a different reality to the spectator's life ("the style smoothes out wrinkled souls . . ." *l'Impromptu de Paris*), but each character plays with the reality of his own universe by means of words. Ondine makes Hans' love exist by telling it; while another language, that of the Undines, gives a reality to treason in love. In *Judith* the heroine, in her duel with Holophernes, counted not on poison but on words. And through an ironic contrast Lucile's silence in the first act of *Pour Lucrèce* is what brings about the horrible drama that follows. Language does have the power of ordering the universe, either by defining situations in an intelligible manner, or by imposing a direction on the course of events. The importance of its function justifies all the adornments—sentences wrapped in ceremonial robes, as it were—and all the rites. Whence the privileged situation of the long speech in Giraudoux's theatre.

Reintroducing the monologue and the *tirade* was not simply the coquetry of a man of letters who wanted to show his originality through a return to outdated techniques. It is a form of theatricalism, the modern spectator being conscious of the unreality of the *tirade* or monologue. What he hears is not a dialogue of everyday life, but a reorganization of it. Giraudoux insists on such theatricalism by emphasizing the artificiality of the process. Characters and spectators are warned so that they can create suitable attitudes—the spectators within themselves, the others through their positions on stage.

Giraudoux used the monologue time and again. Whether the gardener's *lamento* in *Electre* or Mercury's monologue in the second act of *Amphitryon 38*, the speech is situated somewhat outside the action as an interlude addressed to the spectator, establishing the bridge between the play's universe and his own. It thus creates a higher complicity with the play, making the spectator into a kind of god, while reassuring him as to the humanity of the drama.

The so-called *tirade* is just as literary and artificial. During scenes in which the drama is in full swing, there is suddenly a stop, to give the protagonist of the moment an opportunity to clarify the terms of the conflict he represents. This is true not only of Hector's prayer for the war dead in *la Guerre de Troie*, which is a ceremony in any case, but of long speeches situated in the heart of a debate. And Giraudoux's construction is such that the director is compelled to clear the stage, to arrange the other characters in secondary positions just as the chorus in an opera is grouped around the tenor.

In Corneille the *tirade* is an explanation through reasoning or a justification a posteriori; in Racine it is generally a narrative which results in the actual situation and which, by its very sequence, emphasizes the situation's inevitability; for the Romantics it was a poetic or pseudo-philosophical digression around a situation. In Giraudoux it is neither a digression, nor a minor slackening off of the situation, nor a step ahead. In the flow of the drama, it is a snapshot taken of all the tensions of a particular moment, catching the scenic athlete in mid-air and making it possible for us to examine it with care. It actualizes Lamartine's wish: "O Time, suspend your flight."

The spectator is warned about every stop in the movement by a key word, which carries within itself one of the basic elements of a particular tension. "My language," "my violence!" says Judith at the beginnings of two speeches addressed to Suzanne. "Yes, I hated him!" shouts Clytemnestra in *Electre*. The world "control" is the basis for Armand's speech about the proofs of his wife's fidelity in *Pour Lucrèce*. Giraudoux organized his speeches around a key word, just as in Wallace Stevens' poem *Anecdote of the Jar*, Tennessee takes shape around the jar that was placed upon a hill. In other cases the spectator is warned by a character who catches his breath by saying something like "Understand me," or by beginning with an inadequate response to the preceding line. It is rare for a character, having "answered back," as it were, to give the impression of continuing to speak without having given advance warning as to the length of his inspiration. The characters carry within themselves, in advance, the completed structure of their remarks. And here we are at the antipodes of naturalistic theatre, where language is at the mercy of all stimuli, which determine its successive forms and abundance.

The *tirade* constructed in such a way would seem to imply a conception of reality in which form precedes content. Sartre's article on Giraudoux's Aristotelianism [3] and the discussion taken up by Claude-Edmonde Magny in *Précieux Giraudoux* [4] poses the problem of Giraudoux's philosophy: Is he Aristotelian? Is he Platonic? There is no need here to go into the debate in detail, but it is worth noting that Giraudoux, like the courtly poet or the *précieux*, played on both sides. The characters in the plays and the plays themselves offer a Platonic vision of the world, in which the Idea precedes life. There is an Idea of love, an Idea of Electra, an Idea of Isabelle, an Idea of peace, an Idea of treason, an Idea of the couple situated in the heavens of the drama. The heroes and situations are the closest possible concrete expression of perfection. But the universe itself is not that of the spectator or the poet. For them, Ideas of which they are the imperfect realization do not exist. The poet expresses the Forms toward which our reality would seem to tend through images. The Forms exist only through the extrapolation of intelligence or the imagination. They are posterior to reality and invented by man in order to make his universe intelligible.

Giraudoux's "model dialogue" is the proposition of a poet. It implies a twofold movement in literary creation: the reduction of the real to a diagram, in which the intelligence is capable of establishing the continuity of interrupted lines and introducing symmetries; and the act of bringing concrete content to the perfected diagram. Peacock, in *The Art of Drama*,[5] described it as a "myth-allegory" form; and the process is in fact very close to allegorization. Yet it avoids allegory in that there is no reduction to separate abstract qualities, but to essences, whose totality Giraudoux preserves. The scenes of debate are the most characteristic. Whether domestic quarrels or the disputes of diplomats, they are illusory reconstructions, dreams of the intelligence, a fictional universe in which there is no break between the perceived real and the almost mathematical structure the mind seems to have discovered in it.

A product of the intelligence, Giraudoux's fictional universe is satisfying to the mind because it is made up of all the relations that the mind establishes between the things of the world. Whence the network of so-called *précieux* metaphors which establish its coherence. One of the characteristics of the *précieux* metaphor is the intellectuality of the bond that unites the two terms. Claude-Edmonde Magny points out that it begins with forms very close to the pun and results in a whole complicated reasoning in which contraries are united. It has nothing to do with any analogy imposed by illuminations of the subconscious; it does not spring from an intuition of the real, but gives form to the real from the outside. In Giraudoux it is part of the process of reconstruction. It adds secondary structures to the basic diagram. It contributes to the creation of an imaginary world in which the mind is always satisfied. In *Cantique des cantiques* the President asks Florence, apropos of Jérome:

THE PRESIDENT: Where did you find him?

FLORENCE: We bumped straight into each other on the boulevard. He was running with all his might . . . He hurt me.

THE PRESIDENT: He was coming from far away. He was given a start twenty years ago . . .

FLORENCE: Twenty-one . . . He hurt me . . . I still can't make up my mind whether the exhaustion within me is love or stiffness.

The basic diagram here is formed by a belief in the fatality of a meeting. But Giraudoux also brought in the comic note of a small accident. A purely intellectual liaison establishes a link between the destiny of the lovers and the accident, between what is already an image (the race of life) and Jérome's real race. Then the metaphor is prolonged and the consequences remain an intellectual proposition. The link of the metaphor is expressed by the world "exhaustion," but the two parts remain separate, in the forms of "love" and "stiffness."

Helen of Troy rubbing men against her "like great cakes of soap" to purify herself, Lia reinventing the *carte du Tendre* in her dialogue with the Angel, the Beggar advising Electra to "start from dawn," offer so many suggestive metaphors of a world in which the slightest glance of the mind sees the possibility of creating a web of analogies and correspondences.

Through language, Giraudoux has tried to create a universe which

is not that of just a dream but of a dream of the intelligence.
Claudel's theological universe, Audiberti's poetic universe, Montherlant's ethical universe, Sartre's phenomenological and ideological
universe, Genet's dream-like universe also claim to give concrete
metaphors of the essence of reality, the metaphor being situated very
precisely in a certain beyond, in certain depths of consciousness, or
at a certain level of being. In Giraudoux the essence is *proposed* by
the intelligence. There is no question of discovering the meaning of
God's work, but of actualizing, through art, what the man gifted with
reason would have created had he been God. It means rejecting
Leibnitz's postulate according to which this world is the only possible
world, and showing that with the same materials, a more intelligible
world might be conceived.

Germany and France, war and peace, phantom and Supervisor,
man and woman, virtue and vice, the President and Jérome, England
and the South Sea Islands: Giraudoux's drama is based on simple
conflicts. The conflicts are all the more intense in that Giraudoux, in
his creation of an intelligible universe, starts out with particularly
clear and distinct ideas. Germany is everything that France is not;
the President is everything that Jérome is not; Andromache is everything that Helen is not. The drama somehow springs naturally from
the clarity with which the essences are defined. The major bond between them, the field of conflict, is the hero or heroine—and here
Giraudoux goes back to a classical conception of drama. Hector par-
ticipates in both peace and war; Ondine is caught between man and
the supernatural; Outourou finds himself at the junction between all
the mysteries of Polynesia and Anglo-Saxon ethics, just as Siegfried
carried within himself the definitions of both France and Germany.
In Giraudoux's theatre the hero or protagonist is he who straddles
two essences, he who believes he can participate in two essences at
the same time or who is forced to participate or who is asked to
participate.

Giraudoux's hero is also unique in that he carries his universe
about with him. In Greek tragedy the plague was rampant in Thebes
because of Oedipus' crimes; the series of contaminations, like the
series of murders in Atreus' family, was causal. Giraudoux's hero walks
about with a world that copies his definition or corresponds to it,
just as at the end of *Electre* Aegisthus walks about with an eagle
over his head. The Greek hero provokes events by his acts; Giraudoux's protagonist, like Wallace Stevens' jar, makes the surrounding

world take part in his own being. Giraudoux has been reproached for his color-print landscapes, comparable to the illustrations in primary school textbooks. The France of *Siegfried,* the Bethulia of *Judith,* the Greece of *Amphitryon* or *Electre* are as naïve as pictures in a geography book and at the same time like a modern primitive dream à la Grandma Moses. What is important is the stylization, the structure brought to the landscape by the character's language and its transformation by his very presence. Indeed, the entire universe of the play is transformed: the elements of the landscape change from masculine to feminine, valets begin to speak in verse, villages are seized with poetic delirium, adulterers start to tremble.

The hero or heroine is the agent of a metamorphosis of the world, or an attempted metamorphosis, for the world sometimes resists and may win out. In *Judith* Giraudoux painted a stylized portrait of the Biblical world, with its mythology, its own necessity, and a structure whose evolution is known in advance; in other words, the essence of the Old Testament world as corrected and simplified by Giraudoux. According to its laws, Judith is destined to be the saintly heroine who saves her people by sacrificing herself. But Giraudoux's Judith embodies less the idea of sacrifice than an idea of the young girl. A virgin, she gives herself to Holophernes and then kills him. But she does not kill him to save her people. She kills him because she loves him and wants, through his death, to preserve the perfection of the night she had just spent with him. For Judith's world is not the same as that of the other characters, even in the most concrete details brought out by the dialogue. Her description of the battlefield is quite the contrary of her guardian angel's. Her description of her night with Holophernes is also quite the contrary of her guardian angel's. Were the soldiers on the ground dead or asleep? Did Judith caress Holophernes's body because she loved him or was she disgustedly locating the spot she would strike? Which is the truth? In fact, through language the play presents a kind of double truth: two worlds, or two essences of the world, coexist at the same moment, in the same place—Judith's and that of the angels and the God of the Old Testament. "A question of lighting," says the angel; and what we are asked to accept at the end of the play is the simultaneity of both lightings. The subject of the play is more the hesitation between two truths than the discussion of a problem of religious metaphysics, as André Gide thought.[6]

For Giraudoux's theatre is not a theatre of ideas in Gide's sense of the term. His plays are in the form of debates, but the debates are not really discussions. They are an esthetic equilibrium between contrary definitions. There are no problems concerning political ideas in *la Guerre de Troie*; there is a conflict between a definition of peace and a definition of war. Giraudoux's characters do not reason, they describe. In *Sodome et Gomorrhe* when Jean says that the weather is fine in Sodom, Lia answers that the weather is frightful. What directs the drama toward the victory of one essence or another is the weight of such or such description, of such or such definition. Often a definition or description grows richer by stealing, so to speak, from another, and finishes by conquering it through absorption. In *Intermezzo* Isabelle gives up her phantom, but only because the Supervisor managed to constitute the universe of civil servants as an equivalent of the specter's romantic world.

There are of course irreconcilable definitions, and then the "strongest one" wins: war in *la Guerre de Troie*, the young man's love in *Cantique des cantiques*. But it would be vain to separate Giraudoux's plays into those in which contrary definitions are reconciled through facile satire, a feat of God, or a complicity between gods and men intended to satisfy them both, and those in which the reconciliation never takes place. It would mean putting too great an emphasis on the message or lesson contained in each play (we love peace but war is inevitable; shame on the mean capitalists who destroy the poetry of the French landscape; etc.) and reducing works whose subject is hesitation to some positive thesis. The subject of *la Guerre de Troie* is not the arrival of war, but the hesitation of the world between war and peace; the subject of *Judith* is not the secret formula for making saints (what Gide perhaps wanted to find in it), but the oscillation between the lover and the saint; and it is hardly important, at the end of *Cantique des cantiques*, that Florence chooses Jérome: the subject is the simultaneous presence of two faces of love. What is important in *Sodome et Gomorrhe* is not the weather, and not even knowing whether Jean or Lia is right; nor is it to have the right one win: it is their disagreement; it is the fact that two incompatible universes occupy the same space, that the weather is fine and bad at the same time at the same point in the sky, that there is an essence of man and an essence of woman. Here Giraudoux's desire coincides with that of God: there should be an essence of the couple. Lia and Jean are opposed, and that duality is opposed to a desire for unity. Such is the play of perpendicular tensions underlying the drama.

The drama's intensity is in direct proportion to the range of difference between conflicting definitions. Through his choice of details and images, Giraudoux often increases the intensity to such a point that the spectator has the impression of an absolute impasse. Yet his plays present satisfying solutions. When the curtain goes down, the world is in order.

The denouement is partly determined by Giraudoux's *précieux* attitude. A work characterized as *précieux* generally ends with a usual or well-known solution, or one related to a familiar genre, the final conceit of an intellectual reconstruction of the world. For example, a sonnet of Voiture is resolved by a final conceit of an already known genre (the *concetto* or Petarchian antithesis), and its value lies in the ingenuity of its twists. In the same way, the denouement of a Giraudoux play is one familiar to the spectator, after he has been led to expect almost anything else. Such acrobatics of intelligence and imagination are not a simple game. They represent a challenge. By means of perspective, the writer puts himself on a level with God, thus becoming His rival. He shows that one can arrive at the same result with more clarity, that in accentuating the contrasts and in multiplying the relations of things even the horrors of the universe can satisfy the mind.

The denouements are also determined by the play's genre, somewhat in the manner of the seventeenth century, when every play with more or less ridiculous bourgeois characters had to have a happy ending, every play with noble heroes had to end in a catastrophe or with spectacular acts of high generosity. Giraudoux's genres are personal and varied, but they always evoke a familiar literary horizon. In the historical plays, despite liberties taken with the story itself, the denouement comes from history. In spite of all the contortions, the Trojan War does take place, Hercules will be born, Judith does become a holy figure, Sodom is destroyed. Despite German influences, Giraudoux would have had Joan of Arc die on the stake in Rouen, and not, like Schiller's, on a battlefield. The play's finality comes from the already known denouement. And yet during the plays themselves, we realize that the Trojan War might have been avoided; Judith could have sent Suzanne in her place, her night of love with Holophernes is perhaps just a virgin's first night of love, and although Jupiter did sleep with A¹cmene, it doesn't count. The denouement is faithful to history less because the plot leads to it than because the work must conform to an idea of the legend.

In the plays with invented subjects, it is the tone of the whole, their background of popular anecdote, which leads to suicide, separation, or a victory for the young man. In *Cantique des cantiques* Giraudoux applied his method no longer to Greek myth or to a Biblical or Germanic legend, but to an edifying popular romantic story. Therefore the young man had to win over the old. In *le Supplément au Voyage de Cook* Outourou's last speech is not determined by the play itself, but by anti-Christian eighteenth-century irony, which had originally furnished the idea for the situation. The Ubuesque character of the solution in *la Folle de Chaillot* is a final exaggeration of a secondary aspect of the play, revealing the cultural background of the play's universe: the melodramatic, romantic, and movie world of the mysteries of great cities. The underground chasm into which the pimps disappear is an exaggeration of the sewers in *les Misérables* or the dens of Eugène Sue's characters, just as in the rest of the play, the young lovers, the ragman, and the madwomen are very masked reminders of the fauna in that kind of literature.

In short, Giraudoux did not invent the denouements of the perfect dramas he proposed. Reality and myth or tradition took back their rights. Surprises comparable to the final pistol shots of Salacrou's *Histoire de rire* or of Montherlant's *Brocéliande* are unimaginable in his works. A higher form is superimposed on the drama, a form forged from an idea of tragedy, comedy, melodrama, fairy tale, history, sentimental anecdote, etc. The end of a Giraudoux play is not only the resolution of a conflict proposed during the play by the subject itself; it is also, and sometimes principally, the esthetic resolution of the distance between the subject and the genre to which it belongs.

The characters Giraudoux has put on stage are in full possession of their natures. Their degree of humanity depends largely on just how complex that nature is, and also on their rank in the drama. If the pattern is simple, they seem like puppets or personified entities. When they are neither heroes nor protagonists they are too exceptional for their dramatic situations and seem to be ornaments more than characters. But they all contribute to giving the play's universe its style and specifying its definition. On the whole, we must accept the fact that the world proposed to us by Giraudoux is peopled only by rare creatures. Little girls too intelligent for their ages, café waiter-poets, *précieux* soldiers are exceptional only in relation to the spectator. They are quite naturally in their places within the play's universe. Its form requires such fauna. Yet the play demands that we consider them as metaphors of ordinary humanity, caught of course in a drama played out by heroes. The unreality of the secondary characters predominates, and the spectator's pleasure lies in his recognition of the writer's fantasy, not in the kind of participation or complicity provoked by Greek choruses, the confidants of French classical tragedy, or the sensible characters in Molière's comedy.

We must also accept the very *idea* of Giraudoux's theatre: a play of the reincarnation of perfected essences. Each character is therefore complete in himself and is nothing more than what he says and what Giraudoux tells us. When he expresses himself in clichés and hasty generalizations, he himself is a cliché or a generalization. In more naturalistic theatre, a character can be represented by traits which suggest a whole psychology and behavior, the postulate of such theatre being that each trait is a product, an effect within a whole determined system. For example, a sketchy character is comparable to those studies of certain great painters in which a detailed nose is enough to suggest the rest of the face and reveal a soul. When Giraudoux draws only a nose, it means that the character is nothing more than a nose. Or rather, the sketch of a face by Giraudoux would not consist in the suggestion of it by a study of one of its parts; he would draw a complete circle. Even when individualized to the extreme, Giraudoux's sketchy character will always give the impression of being an archeype—if only of himself—because in fact he is always complete. The same lighting falls on the hero as on the gardener or soldier; the structure of the main character is just more complex. And that is the basis for his hierarchy of characters.

Giraudoux's theatre gives rise therefore to a very special impression, quite the contrary of that ordinarily provoked by ambitious plays: the hero, he who rises above the common mortals, seems more human than the minor characters, who as a rule represent a world nearer to that of the spectator. In the same way that Siegfried, Eva, and Geneviève are more real than the German officers or the custom officials, Judith is more real than the rabbis or Holophernes' officers, Ondine more real than the members of the court, the Madwoman of Chaillot more real than the little people around her. What happens is that we accept the hero as exceptional and find it more normal to hear a hero accumulate metaphors than a soldier or café waiter. Given Giraudoux's method, only through actual excess can life be recreated, or at least an equivalent of the richness, complexity, and struggle of life. While the secondary characters are often prisoners of simple attitudes which completely define them, the hero, through an accumulation of details and retouching, assumes flesh, a personal history, and an illusion of humanity, distinctive of the dramatic character. Everything happens as if the process of adding details and colors to an anatomical diagram of the human body were to give it the quivering equivalent of a particular living human body.

Much of the severe criticism directed at Giraudoux's theatre is based on a judgment of his method, not on the works themselves. For the critic, the method is easily discernible. It implies an essentialist position; and it has been decreed in advance that a work which begins from abstractions (ideas, essences, forms) must necessarily be abstract or, at the very least, will always remain on this side of the illusion of reality. It is *"précieux"* or "formal."

Of course Giraudoux's works *are* those of a man of letters, works in which the writer seems to be both present and outside, in that he always gives the impression of knowing more than his characters. His tragedy, comedy, and criticism were all conceived in the same manner. He knew in advance that after *Phèdre* Racine would not write again; he knew in advance that the Trojan War would take place, that Judith would be a sanctified heroine, that Sodom and Gomorrah would be destroyed, with the result that the spectator may feel like both a god and Micromegas. The mathematical patterns of life, grasped directly in all their complexity, in time and in space, make life seem like a piece of ingenious machinery in which the observer knows everything but "lives" nothing. Yet beyond all the intellectualized movements directing the characters and the plays themselves, there is an *élan* which dominates the whole, creating a movement not only from one form to another or from one level of form to another, but from form to matter.

"Theatre," says little Véra in *l'Impromptu de Paris*, "is being real in the unreal." Giraudoux's ambition is just that elementary and just that unbounded. His universe is deliberately unreal. At the same time what upholds it and makes it vibrate is an intense effort toward reality. Starting from form at its most extreme (an almost medieval conception of the essence), he tried to arrive at the closest approximation of reality: the flesh and blood individual on a dramatic stage. Instead of just remaining the respectful transcriber or explorer of the Creature, Giraudoux tried to repeat the process of Creation, the passage from the plan to the act, and become the rival of that Architect, whose image, as Albérès has shown, constantly recurs in his works.[7]

Yet he always refused to give the illusion of reality by means of trickery which, in his case as in that of any anti-naturalistic playwright, would have consisted in introducing, at a given point, certain traits or remarks "taken from life"—what Anouilh did not hesitate to do, for example, in his *Antigone*. In Giraudoux the Greek hero speaking about his carriage or Judith talking like a fashionable young girl of the thirties is pure burlesque—that is, naturalistic or realistic details are introduced not for themselves or to give everyday reality to the play's universe, but for a pleasant effect of pure literary virtuosity.

An explanation of the life of Giraudoux's universe does not lie in the comic absurdities of its anachronisms. It lies rather in the synthesis, made by the spectator, of all the concrete elements accumulated by the writer. Just as Giraudoux asks the actress in *l'Impromptu de Paris* to recall her own emotions of the day in order to give life to Agnès' line in Molière's *l'Ecole des femmes*, "the little cat is dead," so the spectator feels Giraudoux's characters live through the presence within himself of his own life. His theatre is a theatre of collaboration—a rather different notion from the more fashionable one of participation, but not foreign to it, simply more active. Like reformers such as Jouvet and the Cartel, Giraudoux wanted his audience to be ready for action. He could be accused of illusions or of living in the dream of a world where ideal plays would be applauded by an ideal audience, had he not shown that he was perfectly aware of the sluggishness of his times (*l'Impromptu de Paris*). Like the reformers, he wrote neither for the real public nor for an ideal public but for the potential in the real public.

In the American "living newspaper" of the twenties, actors were mixed in with the audience so that the shouts on either side of a spectator would lead him to recognize the political entities on stage as living symbols of man's destiny on earth. Giraudoux waited for the shout to come spontaneously from within the spectator and assumed that his emotion would give the play its finishing touch: life. At that point, the spectator is truly a god, for he is observer and creator at the same time. There is no great theatre without the spectator's recognition, that last spark in the creation of a play.

At a time when theatre demands no more than immobility from a spectator so that it can painlessly graze him, Giraudoux demands cooperation, the presence of heart and imagination. Hence the "difficulty" of his theatre. His importance in the history of modern French theatre is both to have demanded a very active collaboration on the part of the spectator and to have given back the theatre its function of elucidating the world in fundamental terms. Certain types of theatre may force the spectator to use his mind so as to understand a particularly rare and complex problem. Others may pick up the notions of destiny, death, or love, and feed them to the passive spectator. Giraudoux's theatre is made neither for those in search of intellectual rarities, nor for the passive; it is made for a "normal" audience—the norm being defined as the audience of Greek tragedy, of the Spanish theatre of the *Siglo de Oro*, of Shakespeare, of French Classicism.

> Those who want to understand in the theatre do not understand theatre . . . The theatre is not a theorem, but a spectacle, not a lesson, but a philter. It should enter your imagination and your senses more than your mind. . . .

say the actors in *l'Impromptu de Paris*. Moreover in *Visitations*, Giraudoux wrote that theatre must reveal to the spectator

> . . . these surprising truths: that the living must live, that the living must die, that autumn follows after summer, spring after winter, that there are the four elements, and happiness, and billions of catastrophes, that life is a reality, that it is a dream, that man lives by peace, that man lives by blood, in brief, what they will never know. . . .[8]

Such affirmations may seem in contradiction with the judgment of many critics for whom Giraudoux's theatre consists in works of the mind, their revelations far indeed from the commonplaces of the last quotation. Actually the misunderstanding about Giraudoux that reigned during the thirties can be reduced to the following: his method is complicated and baffling; therefore the idea expressed must itself be difficult to understand. And in fact Giraudoux's theatre offers quite the contrary. It is presented as an initiation to simplicity, in other words a reevaluation of simplicity through the detours that must be made in order to rediscover it. The objective is to exasperate the mind by an accumulation of intellectual subtleties, to the point that an emotional adhesion beyond all comprehension will spring from the network of multiple lines that the intelligence has been following.

Knowledge of a certain order can be acquired only through the delirium of an inferior order. In certain religions the individual must subject his body to the most extreme violations in order to reach mysticism. Giraudoux's postulate seems to be that a manifest truth can be reached and experienced beyond intellection through a paroxysm of the intelligence. Preciosity, burlesque, humanist rationalism, and Aristotelian rationalism are actually so many means of making the mind so dizzy that it bows to the unchallengeable and striking fact of life. The spectator of good faith is expected to relive the adventure of Creation—the very Creation that the writer relived at the time of composition, that also of the director, from the blocking on paper to the performance—from ideas, form, or essences to the synthetic emotion of the human adventure.

In *la Guerre de Troie n'aura pas lieu* peace, represented both mythically and negatively by the title and the first line of the play (immediately challenged by the second, whence the drama):

ANDROMACHE: There will be no Trojan War, Cassandra.

CASSANDRA: I'll take that bet, Andromache.

is specified in the very first scene, then becomes "happiness," then "beauty"—all abstract notions—then the "sun" of that day, then evocative expressions like a "fisherman's house," the "murmur of seashells," and is finally, through a double ambiguity, embodied in a character, Hector. We thus go from what is most abstract in peace (its negative definition: the absence of war) to one man who will take its defense.

The concrete images remain vague enough for each spectator to give peace the face of his choice. The "fisherman's house," the "murmur of seashells," the sun that spreads its "mother of pearl" over the unspecified landscape all indicate a Mediterranean universe without particularizing it, suggesting its essence, from which the spectator can imagine his own fisherman's house, murmur, sun. Owl, station, train, birch tree, cat, silk, fur, hand, armor—Giraudoux's glossary always directs the spectator toward a certain concrete category, concrete feeling, concrete landscape. He never individualizes it; he is satisfied to emphasize its dominant feature. It is up to the spectator to bring about the final individualization. The Germany and France of *Siegfried* are deliberately clichés of the two countries, posters of the French or German railways; the fashionable young girl Judith is hardly more than a literary convention before she takes on the dimension of tragedy; the married life of Clytemnestra and Agamemnon is evoked by a "curly beard" and a raised little finger. There is nothing more concrete than those notations, yet nothing more open to all imaginations. In sparking his text with words that grammarians call concrete but which, in context, are no more than generic terms, Giraudoux launches the spectator out in the direction of a specific, even individual image. But he never actually imposes it; he lets the audience discover its own.

Once again in Giraudoux's works we have the inversion of a habitual approach. Where others impose a particular image from which the spectator is expected to extract generalizations, Giraudoux affirms the general at the beginning and demands not that the spectator imagine an illustration of that generality—the play itself fulfills that function—but that he provide some living correlative. In that respect, Giraudoux's theatre is one of the first complete or total theatres of the French stage. If the playwright devotes himself entirely to his text, the spectator must devote himself to the performance—in other words, his theatre excludes both passive auditors and unimaginative readers. It is not paradoxical to say that Giraudoux's plays are among those that are the most misunderstood when simply read. They are texts composed, "written," like a poem in dialogue, but destined to be spoken, performed, acted—texts which are, and were meant to be, the drama's fundamental means of expression, and consequently incorporates all of its structure, symbols, and ideas. But they become dramas, theatrical works, only when supported by the play of the flesh and blood actor and an appropriate staging. Indeed the most "written" plays are those which are truly grasped only when performed or imagined as performed. And that, Louis Jouvet understood.

Giraudoux claimed to have had two muses: Thalia before, and Jouvet after.[9] His theatre is a theatre of language—but of spoken and acted language. Moreover Jouvet was known as being anything but an unobtrusive director. Although a student of Copeau, and as respectful of the text as he, Jouvet used all the pomp of the scenic spectacle to make it live. A director who at the end of his career would make a special tableau of Sganarelle's last line in *Don Juan* or add the majestic spectacle of a tribunal at the end of *Tartuffe* believed in the importance of scenery and staging for reinforcing and adding life to the text. He did justice to Giraudoux's texts when he called on set designers such as Guillaume Monin (*Electre*), Léon Leyritz (*Intermezzo*), Pavel Tchelitchev (*Ondine*), or Christian Bérard (*la Folle de Chaillot*)—all otherwise designers of ballets or operas. When in his article on the director and in *l'Impromptu de Paris*, Giraudoux himself rose up against "staging," he meant to protest against the systems and theories of pure spectacle in which the text is sacrificed. But in the texts of his plays, he constantly indicated the recourse to stage devices and machines, their power of enchantment, and his belief in the actor and the audience.

Therefore when Clytemnestra delivers her well-known speech on Agamemnon's little finger and curly beard, it must be *heard*. Her dress, the tension of her body, the pillar she leans against, the grouping of the other characters and Electra's isolation must be *seen*. When reading *Intermezzo*, the phantom gives the impression of being merely a voice within Isabelle. When performed, his existence must be believed, for he is really standing up behind Isabelle, draped in his cape, in the semi-darkness of a Limousin evening.

Such is the difference between Giraudoux's plays and other theatres of language—certain dialogues in George Bernard Shaw's political plays, for example, for they are self-sufficient non-dramatic debates that have no need of staging. Actors, scenery, and staging are inseparable in Giraudoux. The text gives the fundamental drama, which is complete only when the three collaborators—the written text, the spectator, and the actual performance—are united. The meeting of all three is necessary to the incarnation of the symbol.

From *Siegfried* to *Pour Lucrèce*, a definite evolution can be seen in Giraudoux's art and thought. It was felt from year to year by drama critics such as Robert Kemp and Pierre Brisson and has been the object of many academic studies. The thematic content of the plays has oscillated from man to the supernatural and from Anglo-Saxon or Germanic culture to Mediterranean culture. After *Siegfried* came *Amphitryon 38*; after the adaptation of *Tessa, la Guerre de Troie*; after *Electre, Ondine*. The oscillation was accompanied by an orientation of the whole, during the course of which Giraudoux discovered tragedy, expressed it through myths and the intervention of various forms of divinity, hesitating all the while between the supernatural and the preternatural, and then let a particular theme invade his works—that of the war of the sexes, last expressed as completely humanized.

But one idea dominates his evolution: the idea that man will never live in peace because he is not alone, that God or the gods, social or psychological forces, the members of the other sex all set definitions before him which are different from his and which attract and repel him at the same time. There is no judgment on the part of Giraudoux; there are merely choices and ambiguities determined by the nature of each play. It is probably exaggerated to say with Jacques Houlet [10] that all Giraudoux's characters "win our sympathy in some way or other." But actually in the combat that takes place on stage between man and the gods, between man and woman, between France and Germany, between Hector and Ulysses, between Lia and Jean, our sympathies are not with either side but with the struggle itself as symbolized by the combat. So that beyond more or less individual definitions or essences, dividing and wrangling over the play's universe, a radically dramatic definition of man's condition is posed. Comedy springs from the triumph of human definitions (and as Georges May pointed out: "Giraudoux's men are expert at beating the gods" [11]); tragedy, from the triumph of forces which refuse man peace.

There has been great emphasis put on the fine formulas scattered throughout his fantasies and plays concerned with God or the gods. For example, Holophernes describes the universe as a place infested by the gods:

> From Greece to India, from North to South, there isn't a country which doesn't swarm with them, each with his vices, his odors . . . The atmosphere of the world for anyone who likes to breathe, is that of a barrack of gods.

Here a pagan is speaking. For Judith and her people, Jehovah and his messengers alone "infest" the universe. Just as each hero carries his universe about with him, so each period, each culture, each genre carries its own gods about—those that can be touched as well as abstractions; in other words, the symbols of that which transcends the individual and attempts to snatch away his privilege of giving order and form to his own world: for a knight of the courtly novel, spirits and enchanters; for the inhabitants of Sodom, a proliferation of angels;

for the French bourgeois of the Second Empire, imperatives of the bourgeoisie's vices and virtues. A secularization of the conflicts does not change the vision of the world and destiny underlying Giraudoux's plays. Metaphors and masks of man's condition vary, but both the situation of man and the poetic vision remain the same.

For in a world expressly constructed to satisfy the mind, there is no break between things and their essences, and the separation between essences leads to the exteriority of things. Worlds can be superimposed on the world, two worlds can occupy the same space at the same time, in the boldest desire of the mind: contradiction. For the individual who is well defined within his own nature, a bearer of his own universe, everything occupying that same space would thus seem supernatural. Woman is a monster for man, man a monster for woman. There is clearly a hierarchy of characters, from the literal-minded, who are willing to see only their own essence and universe, to the "elect," who plainly see the superposition and separation of universes, and accept it so as to be able to combat it, surmount it, or communicate with those other worlds denied or rejected by their fellowmen.

Destiny is the directing force of the election which places such and such character at a junction and gives him the lucidity to see in both directions: Florence between the President and Jérome, Judith between love and sanctity, Isabelle between the phantom and the Supervisor, Ondine between humanity and Nature, Siegfried between France and Germany. Destiny gives the elect just enough freedom to be in agony. Whatever the situation and world in which a man lives, there is always a transcendency—puzzling, repelling, or attractive—and represented by Giraudoux as a concrete and present universe, mixed in with the so-called normal universe but separated from it, like two faces superimposed on a photograph, yet always distinct.

According to Giraudoux,[12] the Frenchman, in a kind of moral and metaphysical Bonapartism, delegates tragedy to tragic heroes and does not identify with it. All of Giraudoux's characters are more or less delegates: his gardeners and soldiers are delegates of our gardeners and soldiers, his waiters, delegates of our waiters. Above them are the great ambassadors, who treat with the supernatural as equals and reveal its dangers, its charms, its grandeurs. Giraudoux's theatre is definitely a diplomatic operation, an open diplomacy, a machine intended to make men conscious of a destiny concerning them and transcending them at the same time, and to rid them of the debate by taking it on in their places.

Giraudoux treats man's condition in the same way as Talleyrand treated Europe: the hand that played with the destiny of nations was the hand of an artist. And if a lesson exists, it is a lesson of artistic perspective. Laurent Lesage [13] interprets the ironic distance established by Giraudoux as an inheritance of German Romantic stoicism. It can also be seen as a lesson for man in how to dominate his own condition, a metaphor of Pascal's thinking reed, of the feeble creature constantly threatened by the supernatural, in danger of being crushed by the universe, but always superior to that universe to the extent that he is capable of "thinking" his own oppression and making it an object of diversion by means of the mind and art. As a result, Giraudoux's theatre has often been reproached with coldness and a lack of pity. Yet through the "delegation" and the perspective furnished by intelligence, Giraudoux succeeded in avoiding that self-pity, so easily confused, in the theatre, with participation.

Despite the value of other methods and other results, Giraudoux has taken a privileged place in the history of the French stage. By avoiding purely psychological identification, too easily and superficially offered by the realistic play, he was the first French playwright to respond to the demands of modern theatre and reach a large public at the same time. He transformed theatre into a feast, comparable to the passing of a Prince, surrounded by his pomp and ceremony, prisoner of his legend, and both separated from his people and bearer of their destiny.

NOTES

1. In Jean Giraudoux, *Littérature*, Grasset, Paris, 1941.
2. During the same period in France, Antonin Artaud was fighting for quite a different conception.
3. Jean-Paul Sartre, *Situations I*, Gallimard, Paris, 1947.
4. Claude-Edmonde Magny, *Précieux Giraudoux*, Paris, Editions du Seuil, 1945.
5. Ronald Peacock, *The Art of Drama*, London, Routledge and Kegan Paul, 1957, p. 205.
6. André Gide, *Journal*, November 12, 1931.
7. R.-M. Albérès, *Esthétique et morale chez Giraudoux*, Paris, Nizet, 1957.

8. Giraudoux, *Visitations*, Ides et Calendes, Neuchâtel and Paris, 1947. Translation by Bert M.-P. Leefmans, *The Kenyon Review*, 1954.

9. Giraudoux, "le Metteur en scène," *Littérature*.

10. Jacques Houlet, *le Théâtre de Jean Giraudoux*, Paris, Pierre Ardent, 1945.

11. Georges May, "Jean Giraudoux: Diplomacy and Dramaturgy, "*Yale French Studies* No. 5, Spring 1950.

12. "la Tragédie et Bellac," *Littérature*.

13. Laurent Lesage, "Jean Giraudoux, Surrealism and the German Romantic Ideal," *Illinois Studies in Language and Literature*, Vol. XXXVI, No. 3, Urbana, University of Illinois Press, 1952.

JAMES E. KERANS

Kindermord and Will in *Little Eyolf*

Underlying this most secretive play,[1] and indeed all of Ibsen's drama,
is a myth of the will. The primary features of this myth have long
been familiar to us: what remains is to draw the lines between them,
to reveal their constellation. Such an undertaking is appropriate less
to an essay than to a book, where there is room for intricate proofs
and qualifications; here we must choose rather to proceed by the
clearest assertions possible in such matters and by limiting ourselves
to one feature and to its place in the whole composition. That feature
is the *Kindermord*[2] motif.

Kindermord is vaguely discernible in Ibsen's early work, but beginning with *Brand* (1865) it unmistakably finds its place in the larger
imaginative order of the play, and in every subsequent play it is
fundamental to the dramatic action. It is subject to so extraordinary
a range of disguise that one cannot but believe that it is forced into
his fictive structures by some irresistible imaginative energy, whether
creative or compelled. It appears now in the dramatic present of a
play, now in its narrative past, now figured through a statue or manuscript, now plainly presented as a child, now done abruptly, now in
two separate stages, now displaced as the "childlessness" of Beata in
Rosmersholm, now as the child that Oswald is in terror of becoming
in *Ghosts*, and so on. Always it preserves certain characteristics in
itself and in its relation to the destiny of the hero, and it is these

characteristics which are to concern us. *Little Eyolf* seems a plausible choice for a paradigm in this study, since it is the one play that takes its title from the child who is to die, and the one most dominated by that event: indeed, we might say that the whole drama consists in the accommodation and transcendence of a *Kindermord*.

The time may well come when we discover that the narrative past of Ibsen's later plays is not simply a body of information cleverly worked in to the conversational stream as a sort of painless exposition, but is rather there to motivate the very process of reflection and revelation which seems to be its by-product. Ibsen would then appear to be interested primarily in the process of recognition, a chemist fascinated more by the transformation of a plate by acids and light than by the faces and backgrounds emerging into the illusory stability of a photograph. However, that is a formal study which must await another occasion. Here we shall be dealing with the events and people of the play as they appear during the extended crisis of their lives which, so to speak, caught Ibsen's imagination, and as they seem to have lived before that crisis. From this point of view, *Little Eyolf* is a relatively economical play, and the past of its characters is conveniently spare.

Both the hero and the moral action involving him derive from the same source: the Allmers family. We learn of this family that it is strikingly—even ominously—ingrown. They all look alike, their names always begin with vowels, they are all poor, they are so turned in upon each other that when Alfred and Asta are orphaned there is evidently no outside source of help or care for them. Even before Asta is born her sex and destiny and personal qualities have been determined by what the family expects and has provided for. That she disappoints them by being a girl (and illegitimate, not an Allmers at all, as we find later) is only one of the ways in which she intrudes into the solidarity of the family an element of the strange and estranging. It is interesting that Ibsen first concerns himself with Alfred Allmers at that point in his life at which he is to be provided with a "Little Eyolf." He comes into existence as the boy-who-is-to-have-a-younger-brother-as-companion, and the play is to trace the transformation of the Alfred/Eyolf relationship [3] from this family fantasy through to the spiritual relationship evoked in the concluding passage.

Despite the persecution of Asta and her mother incurred by Asta's sex and origin, and the ten years difference in age, she is very close to Allmers, and when the parents die the two are drawn even closer, made even more conscious of their need to find protection from the dangers of the "outside world" both in the harmony and peace of their brotherly closeness, and also in cultivating a sense of the value of "human responsibility" in general. From this need derive Asta's attempts to live the role of "little Eyolf" by caring for Alfred and even by dressing as a boy at home, though the pathos of the impersonation is obvious; and from the same need comes Allmers's work on his book dealing with "Human Responsibility." During the time when Allmers is a student he develops his interest in the book, and he realizes that he must find some way to care for Asta financially. His poverty stands in his way on both counts, and he solves the problem by marrying Rita—perhaps for her beauty, but more, as he himself admits, for her wealth, her "gold and green forests." Shortly after their marriage they have a son, Eyolf; and while Eyolf is still an infant he suffers the first, the figurative *Kindermord* in a complex event which should be described with some care.

One day, while Allmers was watching Eyolf as he slept on a table (that is, with his eyes closed),[4] Rita lured Allmers away to make love. While they were together, Allmers told Rita in detail of his relationship to Asta—except for the fact that Asta was illegitimate, which Allmers himself did not know. At the climax of their love-making, Allmers called out the name "Eyolf," meaning, of course, Asta, whom he used to call by that name. While Allmers and Rita were together Eyolf fell from the table, and the result was the injury which has disabled him from full participation in life, and which is symbolized by his crutch. From this event there are two main consequences. The first is the sexual estrangement of Rita and Allmers. Allmers cannot overcome the sense of guilt with which he subsequently associates his sexual relation to Rita and he rejects her (the motives here are complex, but we must defer treating them at present). Rita, on the other hand, recognizes in Eyolf the source of Allmers's sense of guilt, and she rejects Eyolf. Her rejection is so noticeable, in fact, and so effective, that it prompts Asta to step in and take upon herself the emotional care of Eyolf. To these two consequences may be added the shift in the nature of Allmers's concern with the book on human responsibility. The book now absorbs all his attention—not only that which he withdraws from Rita, but that which he would have bestowed upon Eyolf. He cannot bring himself to "see" Eyolf's crutch, which is as much as to say that he cannot, in life, accept precisely the human responsibility he is attempting to write about, and the result is that the book drags on, as crippled—almost exactly, we might hazard—as his son. We may also infer that during the nine-year period of these false relationships Allmers falls back upon Asta as his primary orientation, leaving undeveloped whatever chance his marriage offered him of breaking out of the charmed circle of his family —or what he believes to be left of his family—in the figure of Asta.

Shortly before the action of the play begins, Allmers makes a hiking trip to the mountains, alone. He does this partly out of frustration with his "work," and partly because a doctor advises it for his health. While there he has an encounter with death, in the form of a mysterious "companion," and while we must return in greater detail to this encounter, we may say here that it results in Allmers's decision to "renounce" his book, his work, and to return to his home to put the rest of his life at the service of Eyolf, attempting thereby to enable Eyolf to bring the family destiny to the peak of achievement he had once hoped to attain himself. He returns by foot for the most part, taking the train for the last stage of his trip—a detail which will recur in our treatment.

While Allmers is away, three other developments transpire. Asta had been given by Allmers, on his departure, the task of going through her mother's papers. This she has done, with the result that she discovers the real story of her birth and of her actual relationship to Allmers. Rita, meanwhile, has succumbed to Eyolf's entreaties and bought him a child's uniform, which he is wearing during his only scene in the play. Two other characters make their appearance bringing with them evidence of their activity during this interim. One is Borghejm, an engineer who has been building a road nearby, that is now finished so that he is about to go on to another assignment "up north." His stay in the neighborhood has resulted in his love for Asta, whom he hopes to marry, and whom he has come to the Allmers home to see on the morning the play opens. The second is the Rat-virgin, a witch of sorts, though she is also known as a werewolf. Her task has been to rid the neighboring islands of rats, which she does by luring them into the water with the aid of a "little black dog," her traveling companion, Mopsemand. Exhausted though she is by this task, which has taken her all night (Borghejm, Ibsen stresses, is *not* exhausted), she appears on the morning of the First Act to ask if there is "anything she can do." It may be observed here that these are the only two characters who never meet.

Once the play is under way it is almost impossible to differentiate "events" from the flux and entanglements of recall and regret, which are the real substance of the play. In a sense there is only one event: the drowning of Eyolf. Everything else draws for significance and animation upon this weird actuality that provides a model for the several variations we encounter elsewhere in the play—and, in fact, in Ibsen's drama generally. Reduced to a chronicle, what happens is as follows. Just at that point in the first act at which Eyolf is being made to feel most keenly the discrepancy between his uniform and its implicit pretenses on the one hand, and his crutch, his damaged body and disqualified life on the other, and just as we see Allmers at his most pained and angry—the Rat-virgin arrives and asks if there is anything "gnawing" in the house which she could rid them of. As though to make sure of her prey, she shows Eyolf her horrible but fascinating black dog, and after a flurry of openly sinister *double entendres* she withdraws. During the passage directly following, Ibsen has Rita leave the room, transparently as a way of clearing the stage and counterpointing two statements of the major theme of the play. One statement is the exit of Eyolf, who "steals" out of the room, obviously following the Rat-virgin to his death. The other statement is the apparently innocent exchange in which Allmers notices Asta's briefcase and asks if she has been studying her mother's letters. Asta evades the issue. It is not until later that we learn what the letters contain: the death of Eyolf.

The logic of this episode is not particularly obscure to a reader, but like much in Ibsen's later work it asks a great deal of the concentration and recall of an audience. To spell it out: Asta's destiny, as determined by the Allmers family, was to be a "little Eyolf" to Alfred, a companion. She failed on two counts: first in being a girl, and second in being illegitimate. By renouncing her femininity, as she does by such means as dressing as a boy, acting as a companion to her "nephew," rejecting the proposals of Borghejm, or being, as the confidently feminine Rita somewhat condescendingly says, "clever," she can compensate in part for this error. But the illegitimacy was, so to speak, a "fatal" mistake, for which there is no correction. What is so "wrong" about her, clearly, is that she is sexually eligible for Allmers: as a girl she is not his brother, as illegitimate she is not his sister. The Eyolf in her—the young-brotherly, "constant" companion—has been killed.

One of the thematic currents of the play is the conflict between what Allmers calls "the law of change" and the demand, associated with Allmers's double, Borghejm, that there be "something which does not come to an end." We may put off for the present our treatment of the ironies concealed in Borghejm's position, and glance at the "law of change." Allmers invariably invokes this "law" as a way of accounting for the vagaries of sexual attraction or disinterest. On the other hand, "a brother's and sister's love . . . is the only [relation] that's not subject to the law of change," as he says (*LE*, p. 264). "Eyolf" is a creation exempt from the law of change; more specifically, Eyolf is the name or sign of non-sexual relationships, and when a relationship becomes sexual, or is threatened with sexuality, then Eyolf, as the symbol of that relationship, "goes," and that going is dramatized as *Kindermord*. As we shall see, notions such as non-sexual relationships, or even brother/sister relationships are too vague to account for the peculiar complexities and force of the death of Eyolf or of *Kindermord* in general—they merely screen the fundamental relation of the son to the mother; but at least we are now in a position to see why the image of Eyolf stealing off to his death is an appropriate accompaniment to the conversation about the letters that disclose the real relationship of Asta and Allmers. The relation of the Rat-virgin to Asta, to motherhood, and to sexuality remains to be demonstrated, but in her anecdote about marking "her man" and conjuring him down to the bottom of the sea, and in her compelling lure of Eyolf, we see ample sign of her lethal power, and a hint at least of its sexual content.

What is interesting about the overlap of these two dramatic "statements," from a formal point of view, is that no one could possibly understand the connection at the time it appears on the stage. Properly played, Eyolf's exit must indicate what it is—a surrender to death, to the Rat-virgin's lure. There are roughly two kinds of response to the complex episode of which this is a part. One is to think of the death of Eyolf as screened by the conversation about the letters, thus contributing to our sense, which gathers as the play proceeds, that one of the main determinants of Eyolf's death is his parents' neglect of him. (A small but suggestive detail supports this reading: when the Rat-virgin leaves, Eyolf says, "softly but triumphantly," to Asta, "Just think, Auntie! I've seen the Rat-virgin too!" (*LE*, p. 226.) It is his last line in the play—but no one answers him.) The other is to take the death of Eyolf as a datum coloring the whole scene. By this reading we are given one "certainty," one clear event or image to guide us through the slow and uncertain process of understanding the far more complex relationships for whose elaborate structure this death is the model and complement. This juxtaposition, then, marks a great advance in the definition of Allmers's relation to Asta, and hence to his own nature and destiny. The scene does not yield its effect (unless we suppose that the ominousness of the overlap *is* the full effect Ibsen wanted at that moment) until the significance of the letters, of Asta herself, and so on, begin to come clear.

Immediately after this exchange (Eyolf has by now gone off), there follows its counterpart. Rita returns, still horrified by the atmosphere of death left by the Rat-virgin. This atmosphere colors the talk of Allmers's "transformation," which, we later learn, was in fact determined by association with death as a compelling power which had, also, its aspect of "companionability." Allmers's symbolic death and transformation in the mountains thus draws for point and clarification upon the immediately present dramatic event of Eyolf's being lured by the Rat-virgin. As was the case with the previous scene, the audience has no way of seeing the connection between the compelling power of the Rat-virgin with its odor of death and the death Allmers met in the mountains; and the "precious," "lovely," and above all, "gentle" characteristics of the "companion" figures—Mopsemand, Death, and Asta—have yet to emerge and to make their connections with the destructive forces at work upon Allmers. Not until very nearly the end of the play can we "see," but when we do, it is by the light of the clearly projected, theatrical simplicity of this basic event, the luring of Eyolf into the sea.

The drowning itself, while hazy, is simple. Eyolf seems to have followed the Rat-virgin to the end of the wharf, stared out after her, become dizzy, and fallen. The boys on the beach, "all of whom could swim," simply watched, and when they came to the end of the wharf they looked down into the clear water and saw Eyolf's open eyes looking up at them. Then "something" came and drew him away. Each of these elements finds its place in the reflective passages to be treated later, so we may defer any explications for the moment.

The remainder of the play is a series of conversations in the course of which the destinies of the four leading characters are sorted out and clarified. Allmers, after brooding over the sea and his vague sense of responsibility for Eyolf's death, feels drawn by identification with his son into following him down into the sea physically as well as psychically, and is prevented by Asta's entreaties and his own "earthbound" nature, as well as by the animation supplied by a quarrel with Rita. His drift toward leaving Rita to return to Asta and their "constant" life together is blocked by Asta's disclosure of their real relationship. Asta, after forever rendering up her "Eyolf" nature in the gesture of giving Allmers the water-lilies at the end of the second act, prepares the way for her decision to take Borghejm with her as she leaves. Borghejm, after insisting that Asta, if she is to come with him, must commit herself to him unqualifiedly, the expression of which would be her going with him on the train, unaccountably changes his mind and leaves with her on the "steamer." Allmers and Rita are thus left alone to settle the terms of their life. There is insufficient space to track this process in detail, so our approach must be reductive, and while a play as complex as *Little Eyolf* admits of several possibilities, our concern with the problem of *Kindermord* and will leads us to choose as our fundamental question, What causes the death of Eyolf? and to expect of our answer that it shall clarify in some degree every important relationship in the play.

There is first the question of the "lure." The number of forms taken by this figure is extraordinary. The "charms" of the Rat-virgin, which call to mind the many "bewitching" women in Ibsen's dramas; the compelling power of Mopsemand, of the mountains, of death; the "evil eye" that Allmers accuses Rita of having; the seduction of Allmers by Rita at the time of the first "fall" of Eyolf; Rita's decision to bring up from the shore all the "poor" boys mistreated by their fathers and to put them in Eyolf's place; the undertow which draws Eyolf's body out to sea; the "attractive" power of the little Eyolf in Asta, which is what brings Rita and Allmers together, and eventually draws even the "engineer" Borghejm unexpectedly after her—and there are many others. The perils and decisiveness of these lures are suggested by their association with death or marriage, and their thematic coherence is in turn suggested by the relation of death and marriage as the fundamental alternates open to Allmers. After Eyolf's death, Allmers plans to go back to the mountains, to the "stars," the locale of his companion, death, but finally chooses to remain with Rita in at least a form of marriage. Two generalizations emerge from this welter. One is that, whatever the source of the "draw," it always works upon a male figure; the other is that it seems to fall into three modes, "earth," "sea," and "stars." These are Allmers's terms, but they are given scenic and metaphoric support throughout the play.

By earth is vaguely meant worldly happiness, and it is figured in Rita's "gold and green forests," which is to say the marital satisfaction held out to Allmers by Rita herself and by the home that is the setting of the first act. Allmers's homecoming is a return to earth after his venture into the realm of the stars—of solitude, renunciation, and death, where, as we later learn, it is impossible to live (*LE*, p. 277). It seems also a return to "champagne" and to the sexuality for which that is so obvious a symbol. But Rita's draw upon Allmers is weakened—neutralized, almost—by the guilt which blocks their sexual life, and which seems as strong at the end of the play as ever. His earthly nature is thus unstable, because incapable of fulfillment, and this instability, expressed in various ways, is most vividly projected by his behavior at the end of each act. He rushes in fear out of the "house" and down to the fjord at the end of the first act, goes reluctantly back up at the end of the second, and can promise Rita no relief from the strain and duty of earthbound life, at the end of the play, except that of "looking up" toward the stars.

While Rita may have no very secure power over Allmers at the crucial level of earthly life—the sexual—she can still exercise her influence as a mother in the sense of caring for a child, and she proposes, as she says, to take all the boys on the shore with her up to the house, where she can care for them in place of Eyolf and—significantly—of Allmers himself. Because, as we learn, she proposes to do this only after Allmers shall have left her. In this gesture she reveals the essential motherliness of her nature—and her kinship with Aline Solness, Helen Alving, and certain others of Ibsen's mother-figures. It is interesting, to say the least of it, that Allmers is ready to stay with her, when he learns this, even though he has rejected her sexually.

There is nothing strange about the place in Ibsen's mythology of what Allmers calls "earth": we meet it elsewhere as the "joy of life" or Brand's home in the valley, and so on—though it is not recognized generally, if at all, that the reason the hero's place on this "earth" is so unstable is that its "foundation," a sexually harmonious marriage, is upset by the guilt and dread attending unconscious incest with the mother. It is pertinent to this hypothesis that when Rita suggests to Allmers that he had shared her passion in the early days of their "love," he corrects her and describes his feelings as "dread" (*LE*, p. 261).

The sea is the dominant element of Act II. Allmers's coming down to the shore to brood upon Eyolf's death is the scenic parallel to the drowning itself, and as this meditation deepens into a form of identification with his "son," nearly leading him to suicide, we are prompted to examine the force that draws both hero and child into its figurative element.

What emerges first is its regressive nature. Like Hedvig Ekdal and Ellida Wangel before him, Eyolf faces a crisis—his entry into a world of diminished prospects, in which the awareness of time (of the "law of change," for example), of his own lameness—symbol, clearly, for many forms of inadequacy—of adult expectations, such as Allmers's loading upon him the burden of fulfilling the destiny of the family, all co-operate to expose him as the "wounded little soldier" he really is. He yields to the calm of the sea, to its appearance of soothing constancy; but, like Asta, it is not what it appears to be, and its undertow side, the lethal, vindictive sexuality of the Rat-virgin, is the reality that shocks him into open-eyed death, as had his fall nine years ago. Not for nothing has Ibsen unobtrusively made Asta and the Rat-virgin two sides of the same coin. Each comes and goes by sea, carrying a "little black bag" in which is concealed the death of Eyolf, and while this one association must carry the persuasion of several others, it at least underlines their relation to the sea.

In summary, then, the sea is the temptation of regression, of constancy in one's childish nature, but to commit oneself to that element is to discover too late the incestuous threat concealed beneath the benign surface. In an earlier draft, Ibsen compressed this logic into a scene that is perhaps too clear for the dramatic development he wanted: Eyolf runs out to greet Asta at one point, and instead encounters the Rat-virgin. Allmers's peril is that he will do the same thing, and precisely this accounts for Asta's strange and near-frantic warnings to Allmers not to brood or to approach the fjord, as well as for her decision to tell Allmers "now" about the letters, rather than to wait until some evening when they could talk quietly about them. Allmers survives the danger, but at the price of his own Eyolf nature, and when he has left behind him the earth and the sea he has only the consolation of the stars to look forward to.

The "high crag" of the third act swings us from the fjord, with its atmosphere throbbing with regressive longing, into the vertical "mood." From here we look down upon the "poor boys" on the shore, out over the fjord as the "steamer" withdraws with Borghejm, and up to the "stars" for the restorative vision of the "spirits" of those who have gone. The flag is raised in token, evidently, of the ethical content of some mysterious victory. What has happened? Asta's disclosure, of course; but beyond that is the matter of Allmers's "transformation."

While in the mountains, Allmers came to a lake. There being no way across it, he went around, lost his way, and met with a "traveling companion," death, in the form of his peaceful acceptance of his own death. He walked all day and night with death, and was lifted to the "heights of resolution," after which he came out on the other side of the lake and went directly home to put his life at the service of Eyolf.

What is disturbing about this apparently noble and serene action is, first, its inversion of the drowning. Sinking into the depths becomes a climb along the dizzy precipices; being lost in the timeless constancy of childhood becomes being lost in the spacial wilderness of solitude and a premature acceptance of death (Allmers insists that, like all his family, he will not live long); one action kills Eyolf, the other is to give him life and fulfillment. The other disturbing element is that just as the sea had its "peaceful," Asta surface, and its destructive, Rat-virgin depths, so the death Allmers met as the incarnation of the mountains and solitude and stars had also its "horrifying" side: "My companion came and took [Eyolf]. And then there *was* horror in him" (*LE*, p. 278). What Allmers does not seem to realize is that the *Kindermord* in which his "companion" was involved took place not in the fjord but on the heights, when he renounced his will and his work, which was the embodiment, however failing, of that will. To account fully for this hypothesis we shall have to wait for demonstration that "Eyolf" is in some way identified with Allmers's will. Meanwhile, we might draw attention to a sinister and oblique coincidence. There are two people in the play who offer a prospect, a lure to Eyolf: the Rat-virgin—and Allmers. What the Rat-virgin offers we have seen. Allmers offers Eyolf the task of doing what he himself has been unable to do. Each hides his offer under a riddling phrase, too odd to be inadvertent. When the Rat-virgin sees that Eyolf is "staring fixedly" at Mopsemand, despite his horror, she says, with satisfaction, "Oh, it'll come. It'll come, all right" (*LE*, p. 224). Then she shuts the bag. Earlier, when Allmers had hinted that "someone" would come to do his work better, Eyolf had become very curious (*LE*, p. 219):

> EYOLF: Whoever will that be? Oh, do tell us!

> ALLMERS: Give him time. He'll come all right and declare himself.

> EYOLF: And what will you do then?

> ALLMERS: Then I will go to the hills again . . . up on the heights and the great waste lands.

(Asta and the Rat-virgin go back across their element, the water, but to what other destination we never know.) A moment later, when Eyolf is enthusiastically asking to accompany his father "up to the hills," soon, Asta (so the stage directions say) "changes the subject": i.e., shuts the bag.

There is yet another dissonance in the notion that Allmers's renunciation under the stars is the sign of his arrival at some ethical stability. He returns, he says, "to Eyolf." Not to his marriage. And, in fact, neither his return nor Eyolf's death involves any resumption of his marriage in the essential sense. What decides him to stay with Rita is the possibility of finding meaning in life through aid to the anonymous "boys" or substitute Eyolfs whom Rita is to bring up from the shore. Rita has renounced her marriage in the "earthly" sense of harmonious sexuality—she has become a de-sexualized, "ethical" mother, and in this venture Allmers will join her. It is then that he raises the flag to the top. Behind the lure of the stars lies the renunciation not only of will, but of vitality, leaving only selfless dedication and duty. How do we explain this poverty of alternatives?

The pattern of earth, sea, and sky, together with the forms of "lure" concealed in each, yields itself to a common-sense examination of the phenomenal surface of the play. Beneath this pattern lies another, for the detection of which we need the reductive and hermeneutic techniques proper to psychoanalytic theory. This is the pattern we have called the myth of the will.

Briefly stated, this myth dramatizes certain typical crises in the mother/son relationship. The first crisis is the *Kindermord* itself.

While still an infant, the child's dependence upon the mother for nourishment, warmth, protection, and love is felt not as helplessness, but as security. When this relationship is disturbed by the introduction of a sexual element—which ultimately forces sexual rivalry with the father—the child "feels" that either he must submit to the castration/death that is the penalty for this relationship, or he must give it up. He has no choice but to give it up and withdraw, but he blames his withdrawal upon his mother as well as upon himself or his father, and this withdrawal, this break in the secure relationship to the mother, is dramatized as *Kindermord*. The element in the mother that gives rise to the threat of castration or death is converted in the child's imagination to the frightening, destructive woman whose (fascinating) aim is to drive him to an unequal struggle with the father and thus to death. However, the sexual drive that first attached itself to the mother cannot simply be discarded—it must find an object. For the object to satisfy the unconscious drive toward the mother, it must be radically identical with the mother, but for the drive to be expressible or tolerable at all to the psychic constitution of the child or hero, the object must not be recognizable as a version of the mother—hence the substitute takes the form of a mirror-image or inversion of the original mother, and the relationship between them is now expressed not in the form of sexuality, but as shared participation in the hero's "act of will." If this "will" were not dynamic, not subject, as are all things organic, to the "law of change," this secondary or substitute relationship might persist indefinitely—might, that is, be "constant." But it is threatened from two sides. First and most simply, it strives for ever more complete satisfaction, and thus ultimately discloses its frightening and lethal nature, thus forcing a recapitulation of the first "*Kindermord* or withdrawal of the secondary mother, or both. Second, this relationship with the "mother," through a displacement of sexuality upon will, is crippled, like Eyolf, by a "fall." The fall is that complex moment at which the encouragement of the original mother, her care, was cut off, leaving the child (or hero) hungry, a hunger that ultimately expresses itself in the need for assurance in the form of absolute love, for which the typical words in Ibsen are "sacrifice," "proof," "all," and the like. Thus the hero's will is weakened, and the "ideal project," which is the particularization of that will, is doomed. A simpler way to put this second threat to a continuing or "constant" relationship is that the hero uses up his store of energizing love. When this happens, the hero abandons his "project"—in Allmers's case it is the book on "human responsibility" that he and Asta have been concerned with, but which Rita, of course, quite understandably resents—which is very apt to be tantamount to renouncing not only the "will" or vitality for which the project was the specific mode of expression, but life, with which sexuality is roughly identical, and the result is suicide, as with Rosmer, or an equivalent, such as Allmers's return to the mountains, which he equates with death.

Since we are not concerned here with all the complexities of the myth of the will, but primarily with the *Kindermord* element, we may forego an extended treatment of the myth and outline the relation of the *Kindermord* to the later stages of the hero's development.

The first step is to state the relation of the child to the hero. In a word, they are identical. True, as characters in a drama they are distinct, but as elements in a psychic composition they are only superficially differentiable. The *Kindermord* is really an event in the life of the hero, and that is why every play from *Brand* on contains such an event. If the first *Kindermord* involves only the crippling or disabling of the "child" (Hedvig's approaching blindness, in *The Wild Duck*, the spoiled statue of *When We Dead Awaken*, or the manuscript to be reconstructed from "notes" in *Hedda Gabler* are examples, as well as Eyolf, of course), the hero may play out his project indecisively and unsatisfyingly. But the second *Kindermord*, which more often than not takes place after an interval of about ten years (Eyolf is nine), brings this period of false or inadequate involvement in the project to a close with the abandonment of the project and, not infrequently, of life itself.

Two axioms are essential to this argument: that the hero and child are radically identical; and that the project or act of will through which the hero and the secondary mother are so firmly bound to each other is an inheritance from the tie between the child and the primary mother. This inheritance is already weakened by the fear that forces it into disguise and crippled by its first encounter with sexuality, and it stands always under the threat of the re-emergence of that sexuality. Would this not account for the puzzling truth that Ibsen's heroes are almost invariably sexually estranged from their wives, who inherit, typically, the "providing" characteristics of the primary mother, and yet they cannot, on the other hand, execute their "act of will" with the secondary mother? The second relationship merely recapitulates the first. Cut off, thus, from "earth" and its alternate, what is there to do but "renounce"?

There are no satisfactory tests for the truth of these propositions, but in the view underlying much of our reasoning so far—roughly that of psychoanalytic theory—the affective substructure of an imaginative work may be dealt with as a mimesis of certain forces (by no means all) at work in the imagination of the writer. We then recognize that the figures in Ibsen's drama are not ethically self-determining, nor even in every respect distinct as parts of a composition, but that they are, at a lower level, barely mobilized out of an interior drama whose balance of forces governs the disposition of material at the subtlest verbal and characterological level. A small but startling sign of the self-contained quality of Ibsen's dramatic relationships—in this case, of the radical identity of hero and child—consists in the fact, which may have struck a reader familiar with Ibsen, that the children involved in the *Kindermord* are never singled out of a family. The whole generation dies, whether that generation consists of one child, as is usual, or two, as in *The Master Builder*, or three, as are threatened with the figurative death from Nora's lie in *A Doll's House*. What is even more striking is that it is taken for granted, always, that there are to be no more children. Even in *The Lady from the Sea*, where the prospect would seem clear, the idea is never even mentioned. The reason for this is plain; the child is primarily a function of the psychic past of the hero, and not just another member of the dramatis personae. That the same is true of many of Ibsen's dramatic categories would require separate demonstration, but in the interest of underlining our position thus far, we could at least assert that such is the case, and that the organizing scheme for those categories is the same myth of the will a small feature of which we have been examining.

Full treatment of the problem of will in Ibsen's imaginative work would have to deal with the sociological and philosophical determinants on Ibsen's rational conception of will, the more immediate influences of men like Mill, Kierkegaard, and Hegel, and much more. For two reasons our concern has been only with the structural and psychological determinants. First, we accept as one of the primary tests of value in any essay in dramatic criticism the question, "How does it interest anyone who is to produce or perform in the play?" This question of form and motivation calls for most patient study. Second, and more pertinent to the larger question of response to the plays, is our dissatisfaction with the current attitudes toward Ibsen. Here, as usual, psychoanalytically oriented criticism acts best as a corrective and complicating influence. Criticism of Ibsen badly needs an alternate to the sterile conflict between those who reject symbolic exegesis, preferring to think of Ibsen as a spokesman for permanent, explicit values, such as the striving for freedom, and those who call for a new approach, one that supposes that Ibsen has outlived his age and now qualifies for a bland archtypal reduction or for treatment as a "psychologist"—by which is usually meant that the critic will show that Ibsen saw deeply into the secrets of the human heart, or, worse, will "psychoanalyze" this or that character on the basis of some plausibly revealed syndrome.

The implicit recommendation of our approach is that there is an affective substructure in Ibsen's drama, which influences the development of image, gesture, and crisis, as well as the "behavior" of "characters." However we may speculate upon the determinants of that structure, the first task is to detect and illuminate it—a task, simply, for accurate observation and formal criticism. Anyone who has compared his response to an Ibsen play well performed to the critical raptures about idealism, transcendence, noble sacrifice, wise resignation, and the like must be puzzled at the disparity. That Allmers, or Rosmer, or Solness, or Ibsen himself might talk such language ought not to blind us to the concealed maneuvers that drive toward disastrous cancellations of will, toward despair and death, through which friction is set up against the more assertive and, to be sure, far more interesting maneuvers of the upper or conscious levels of the plays or their attendant responses. In calling attention to and, hopefully, articulating some of the content of the "lower" order we may not be dignifying Ibsen, but we may call it a gain if we are encouraging a more complex response or increased understanding by acknowledging that there is still much more that he can "make us see."

NOTES

1. Henrik Ibsen, *Lille Eyolf*, *Samlede Verker*, Oslo, Gyldendal Norsk, Forlag, 1935, Vol. XII, 175 ff.

    For the reader's convenience all quotations below are from Henrik Ibsen, *The Master Builder and Other Plays*, trans. Una Ellis-Fermor, Penguin, 1958, hereafter referred to as *LE*. Where necessary I have occasionally restored a literal reading from the Norwegian.

2. The term seems preferable, because of its familiarity in critical usage, to the English "child-murder." Either term overstates, as we shall see, the violence or the quality of responsibility involved. "Child-death," on the other hand, is too tame.

3. Note the similarity of the names: it may be pertinent to observe that the drowning of Eyolf is prefigured in a very early draft of *Rosmersholm*, in which Rosmer's son, "little Alfred," is drowned in a lake with his mother.

4. This detail is later inverted into the picture of Eyolf lying dead under the clear water and looking up with his eyes "wide open," having "awakened." The conditions of this awakening cast a darker look over what critics have called Ibsen's transcendental sense of the term in his last play.

FRANCIS FERGUSSON

Don Perlimplín: Lorca's Theater-Poetry

For something like forty years poets in English-speaking countries
have been trying to write poetic drama for the modern stage. This
movement, if something so scattered and diverse may be called a
movement, stems largely from Yeats and Eliot. Their plays are still
the best modern poetic drama we have, and their theories still define
the prevailing conception of poetic drama. But no one is quite satisfied with the results. We still lack a poetic theater-form comparable
to those of more fortunate ages, or to the "unpoetic" convention of
modern realism. Poetic drama in English remains unsure of itself,
highbrow and cultish—unless *Elizabeth the Queen, Venus Observed,*
and *The Cocktail Party*, which are fairly well accepted in the show
shops, are to be called poetic drama.

Federico García Lorca also wrote poetic drama, very much as Yeats
and Eliot have taught us to understand it, yet his plays are neither
cultish nor middle-brow-Ersatz: they are theater-poetry which lives
naturally on the modern stage. Lorca did very little theorizing, but
he found, at a very early age, in pre-Franco Spain, singularly direct
ways to use the stage for the purposes of poetry. It is true that he is
not a creature of the commercial theater. Madrid in his time had a

From *The Human Image in Dramatic Literature*, Doubleday and Co., 1957.
Reprinted by permission of the author. The essay first appeared in *Kenyon
Review* (XVII, Summer, 1955).

theater corresponding to Broadway, but Lorca was always in more or less hidden opposition to it. He was the director of "La Barraca," a group of University players which was subsidized by the government and toured the provincial towns and cities of Spain with a repertory of classics. It is evident that his own plays owe a great deal to this experience. La Barraca found an "off-Broadway" audience in Spain, and since then Lorca's plays have found audiences in France, Switzerland, Germany, Mexico, South America, and college towns all over this country. No one has succeeded in producing him successfully on Broadway, but in being rejected by the timid snobbery of Times Square he is in excellent company. And there is no doubt that he can by-pass the taboos of the market, and reach a wide contemporary audience in free Europe and the Americas.

Lorca's theater-poetry fulfills many of the prescriptions of Yeats and Eliot, but it is strongly marked by his unique genius, his rare combination of talents. And it is nourished by the Spanish tradition, which was showing new vitality just before Franco put out the light. These matters are already clear in his early play, *The Love of Don Perlimplín for Belisa, in His Garden*. *Don Perlimplín* is a romantic farce, slighter and lighter than his most famous pieces, *Blood Wedding* and *The House of Bernarda Alba*, but it is a small masterpiece. When he wrote it he was already in control of his difficult art.

The story is old, lewd and rather savage: that of the old man married to a lusty young wife, one of the standard situations of neoclassic farce. But Lorca, without losing sight of the farce, lifts it to poetry also, and poetry of power and freshness. This he accomplishes in four swift scenes; and to understand his art it is necessary to think over this sequence in some detail.

In the first scene we see Don Perlimplín, a studious type on the dark side of middle age, dressed in a white wig and dressing gown, in his study. His old servant Marcolfa is telling him that it's time he got married, so that when she dies he will have a wife to take care of him. Marriage, says Marcolfa, has great charm, hidden delights; and at that moment we hear Belisa offstage singing a song of shameless childish eroticism. Marcolfa leads Don Perlimplín upstage to the window; we look out with him, and see Belisa on her balcony across the way, very lightly clad. Don Perlimplín gets the point of this vision: Belisa is white inside, like sugar, he says; would she strangle me? Belisa's mother appears, and between her and Marcolfa Don Perlimplín finds himself betrothed to Belisa. The mother is one of those terrible cold-hearted eighteenth-century duennas; she reminds her daughter with speed and clarity that money is the foundation of happiness, and Don Perlimplín has money. The scene ends with Don Perlimplín firmly committed, and trembling with a mixture of terror and delight, like a boy when the possibilities of sex first touch him.

The second scene shows Don Perlimplín's bedroom on the wedding night. In the middle of the stage is a huge ornate bed, and there are six doors, one to the rest of the house, the others giving on to five balconies. First we see Don Perlimplín, magnificently dressed, receiving final instructions from Marcolfa. They disappear and Belisa enters in ruffled negligee, singing to offstage guitar music. After a brief scene between her and Don Perlimplín—who says that she is like a wave of the sea—two sprites draw a gray curtain across the stage, concealing Don Perlimplín, Belisa, and the bed. These sprites giggle and chatter with the inhuman merriment of little girls of twelve or thirteen, say—bright-eyed, heartless, knowing little creatures, as children are when they are full of shrewd curiosity but not yet seasoned by any human experience. Presently they open the curtain and depart. Stage and bed are flooded with bright sunlight coming through the five opened doors to the balconies, the iron church bells of the city are banging for matins, and Don Perlimplín is sitting up in bed beside the sleeping Belisa, with a great pair of horns on his head, decorated with flowers. Belisa, when she lazily wakes, admits nothing, but Don Perlimplín sees five hats under the five balconies which show that five men have visited her during the night. Lorca has thus exaggerated the farcical situation of the old man and his young wife; but the combination of bright light, loud iron bells, and big ornate horns adds pity and terror to the scene. When Belisa wanders off to get dressed, Don Perlimplín is left sitting alone on the edge of the bed, and he sings a beautiful lyric on the theme that love has mortally wounded him.

The third scene shows Don Perlimplín and Marcolfa. Marcolfa is deeply ashamed for her master, and moreover she reports that Belisa has already become infatuated with a sixth man. Don Perlimplín is delighted to hear it. He tells the weeping Marcolfa that she understands nothing, and brusquely sends her away. Belisa enters dreamily, mulling over the new young man, whom she has seen, from whom she has received letters, but whom she has never talked to. Don Perlimplín catches her in this daydreaming, tells her that he understands everything, that (being old) he is beyond mortal life and its

ridiculous customs, and that he will sacrifice himself for her and her
new love.

The final scene is Belisa's rendezvous with the young man, in the
garden, at night. First we see Don Perlimplín and Marcolfa, she .
more grieved than ever, Don Perlimplín more crazily inspired. He
tells Marcolfa that tomorrow she will be free, and that then she will
understand everything; this bit feels like a farewell. When they go
we hear offstage singing, and Belisa enters in her most glamorous
finery. She sings a serenade in alternation with the offstage voices.
Don Perlimplín meets her, and assures himself that she loves the
young man better than she has ever loved before, better than her
own body. He tells her that in order that she may have the young
man forever, he will kill him—and he runs off, drawing his dagger.
Belisa yells for a sword to kill Don Perlimplín: but at that moment
the young man, his head wrapped in a scarlet cape, a dagger in his
breast, staggers in mortally wounded. Belisa pulls off the cape, revealing Don Perlimplín, who dies. He has just time to explain that
this was the triumph of his imagination; he had made Belisa fall in
love with the lover he invented. So he gave her a new and deeper
knowledge of love, made a new woman of her, as Marcolfa explains
at the end: gave a human soul, at last, to the beautiful body. It is
Belisa's initiation into love's mystery, corresponding to Don Perlimplín's initiation in the first scene.

The poetic effect of this sequence is intense and direct, but Lorca
gets it out of a combination of very old and traditional elements.

Thus there is the basic situation of the old man and the young
wife, which in baroque Continental comedy, or on the Restoration
stage in England, is usually treated in the hearty, simple-minded
mode of broad farce. Cervantes wrote a brilliant interlude of this
kind called *The Jealous Old Man*, in which the fun is based on the
disharmonies of human physiology, and the audience is expected to
sympathize solely with the triumphant wife. Lorca expects us to
remember that worldly old theme, and he emphasizes both its theatricality and its ancient, classic quality in the characters, their
language, and their costumes. Don Perlimplín in his white wig and
scholarly dressing gown; Marcolfa in the striped dress of the stage
servant; Belisa's mother with her great wig full of beads and ribbons
and stuffed birds; and Belisa herself, the sharp essence of the amoral
female: this cast of characters is made to seem as old as nightmare,
almost eternal.

But just because the farce and its people seem so ancient, it strikes us as not only farcical but also sinister. Lorca, while keeping the cynical old tale, with its neo-classic stagy glitter, also views it in the perspective of a later, gloomier, and more romantic age; he transposes it to bring out also the love-death theme. That theme also it traditional in European literature, as Denis de Rougemont explained in his book, *Love in the Western World*. He traces the terrible aspiration beyond physical love to some of the Provençal poets, and he thinks that the love-death theme which re-echoes through the nineteenth-century literature obscurely revives the heretical cult of the Cathari. Lorca certainly seems to echo the theme here with a full sense of its deep roots, especially in Don Perlimplín's lyric on the mortal wound of love, and in the final scene in the garden, which has the ceremoniousness of the dark old erotic rite.

It is an extravagant notion to combine farce and *Liebestod*, but Lorca knew that it was extravagant. It is by means of the *style* of the piece that he makes an acceptable fusion of such disparate elements; for a knowing style implies the limitations of mood and viewpoint which the author has accepted in advance, and thus makes them acceptable and comprehensible to the audience. Lorca indicates the style of his play in its subtitle: "An Erotic Alleluya." An alleluya is something like a valentine: a love poem decorated with pictures, gilt cutouts, lace paper, and the like; something heroic, overdone, absurd: an *extravagant* offering to the beloved. All the elements of the production, music, sets, costumes, acting, should obey the requirements of this style. And one must remember that it is a Spanish style, akin perhaps to those drawings and paintings of Goya's—wounded cavaliers, frightening mustachioed old women, greedy young women in discreet mantillas—in which the remains of eighteenth-century elegance are seen in a somber light.

Though this play is so unlike anything in English, it is a species of poetic drama. And it achieves much that Yeats and Eliot sought with only partial success. They were both lyric poets first and dramatists second; and both tended in their early efforts to approach poetic drama as though it were an overgrown type of lyric. Yeats's early plays have the Yeatsian lyric melody, but lack the tensions, the contrasts, and the varied movement of drama. Eliot's *Murder in the Cathedral* and *Family Reunion* sound like his lyrics considerably diluted. Eliot felt that himself, as he has explained; but his usual diagnosis of the trouble is that he has not discovered the right verse form for the stage. He proposes to solve the problem by working out the proper versification. To Eliot's experiments, and to his immense authority, we owe the notion that the problem of poetic drama in our time is simply that of finding a type of verse which will work onstage. And many young poets proceed as though drama could somehow be deduced from the lyric by further exploration of the properties of verse.

Lorca also was a lyric poet before he succeeded on the stage, and his lyric verse shows (like that of Yeats and Eliot) the all-pervasive *symboliste* influence. He is an authentic poet, even by the exigent standards of our masters. But from the first he drew also upon the resources of the old and popular Spanish tradition of balladry: his first collection is entitled *Romancero Gitano*, "Gypsy Balladier." And the ballad is a far more promising clue to drama than the "pure" *symboliste* lyric, precisely because it typically suggests a story: a situation, contrasted characters, a significant event. The *symboliste* lyric, on the other hand, owes its purity to its source in the single feeling of the isolated poet. It is very difficult to derive from it the sense of separate but interacting lives; the movement of real change; the significance of a deed or an event: in short, the objectivity of drama, which is founded (however indirectly) upon sympathy and perception. We must simply recognize, I think, that the inspiration, the poetic point, of the *symboliste* lyric is not dramatic, while that of the ballad is.

It is clear that the whole conception of *Don Perlimplín*—the gentle, absurd, heroic old man; the animal-beauty and her mother; the weepy servant, the struggle with love's cruelty—struck Lorca as poetic. The narrative sequence is itself poetic, like that of the ballads we know. One can conceive a ballad version of *Don Perlimplín*, but not a *symboliste* lyric which would really capture the theme. Thus in trying to get the poetry of the play one must consider not only the passages in verse, beautiful though they are, but the movement of the play as a whole. The poetry is in the characters and their relationships, in the conception of each of the four scenes, and especially in the sharp but quickly resolved contrasts between them. Cocteau's formula applies exactly to *Don Perlimplín*: "The action of my play is in images, while the text is not: I attempt to substitute a 'poetry of the theater' for 'poetry in the theater.' Poetry in the theater is a piece of lace which it is impossible to see at a distance. Poetry of the theater would be coarse lace; a lace of ropes, a ship at sea. . . . The scenes are integrated like the words of a poem." Thus the poetic effect of *Don Perlimplín* strikes us most sharply in the transitions from one scene to another: from Don Perlimplín's study to the glamour and music of the wedding night; from the childish chatter of the sprites to Don Perlimplín's humiliation in the morning. And as soon as we feel the poetry in the whole sequence, Lorca's prose has its poetic effect as well as his music and his visual scheme. Lorca is such a virtuoso of the theater that he can use and control all of its resources to present his poetic vision.

Yeats and Eliot began with verse rather than with the theater, but both of them felt the need of a story and a form which should make the play itself (as distinguished from the language) poetic. And both sought these elements in myth and ritual. Yeats proceeded from Irish myths, to an English version of *Oedipus*, to forms based on the *Noh* play; Eliot experimented with Greek myths and with adaptations of Christian ritual forms. These experiments have proved to be extremely suggestive, and it may well be that they still have much to teach us. But they seem to show, among other things, that it is very difficult to reincarnate a myth in our time. Myths as we read them in learned collections tempt us with their suggestion of deep poetic insights; but the crucial labor of the dramatic poet, faced with the modern stage and the modern crowd, only begins at that point. So many have failed—either relapsing into cultishness or antiquarianism, or reducing the myth to an abstract and pseudo-philosophical scheme—that the very word "myth" has ceased to be respectable. Yet the problem remains; and in its most general form it is probably the heart of our difficulty with poetic drama.

It is this problem which *Don Perlimplín* solves quite naturally and directly. If the story is not strictly a myth, it has the qualities our poets seek in myth: it seems much older and much more generally significant than any history which is literally true; yet Lorca does not seem to have thought it up, but rather to have perceived it, or heard it, in the most intimate chamber of his sensibility. In embodying it on the stage he is careful to preserve this oft-told feeling, like song, or a tale told by a grandmother. This he does with the utmost confidence and simplicity. He is sustained by the knowledge that he is talking about things which other artists have seen before in his Spanish tradition; for Don Perlimplín seems to come from the same world—which we now see is still alive—as Don Quixote and Goya's frightening people.

Because the story has this "mythic" quality, its basic form is quite naturally that of ritual or traditional ceremony. The first scene is a betrothal, and we are made to feel that it has been celebrated count-less times before, and will be endlessly again: it is the first stage of the initiation into love's cruel mystery; for the old man is as virginal as a boy. The second scene (a kind of interlude in the movement of the piece) is not a ritual; but the third scene, a wedding night with all the pomp of music and costume, is conceived as a sinister epitha-lamion, moving with decorum toward its predestined pathos. The final scene in the garden, with its serenade in antiphonal form, its symbolic suicide, its cult of love as death, is the place where Lorca's feeling for the ancient heretical love rites that De Rougemont studies is most unmistakable. It is there that Belisa, in her turn, is "initi-ated." I do not know how consciously Lorca worked all this out; he has the authentic artist's sophistication of feeling combined with philosophical reticence. But I am sure that the ceremonious quality of these scenes (like a duel or a bullfight) must be carefully observed in production, for it is their decorum which gives the underlying passion its cutting edge.

It has been said (notably by Mr. Roberto Sanchez in his valuable book on Lorca) that Lorca is a theatrical rather than a truly dramatic talent. He does not, for example, have Ibsen's moral and intellectual drive, and he rarely deals directly with contemporary scenes or con-temporary issues. He usually finds the clue to a play in painting, or music, or poetry, or even in the theater itself. In all his work (as in *Don Perlimplín*) he relies on stage effects to carry much of the burden. And in these respects his art is akin to that of some modern masters of theatrical style, directors and designers, who do not so much create drama as interpret it in the theater. Mr. Sanchez has a point, but I think he somewhat misinterprets the evidence.

He is thinking of men of the theater like Reinhardt or Copeau, who seem to have had some more or less direct influence upon Lorca. Reinhardt was famous for his allusive and learned experiments with style—doing *Midsummer Night's Dream* as romantic music, playing about with expressionism, or the baroque, or the Commedia dell'Arte. And it is true that each of Lorca's plays is, among other things, a self-conscious period piece. *Doña Rosita* is founded upon the sweet faded conventions of the turn of the century. It is like a delicately tinted family picture in a velvet frame, a provincial keepsake smelling of lavender and Spanish Victorianism. Even *Blood Wedding* and

Yerma, for all their power and violence, owe something to painting
or balladry. This habit of starting with art may seem perilously close
to orchestrating Bach, a substitute for real creation—or even to the
next step: the ads for diamonds or perfume, in which certain tricks
of French painting are used to produce snob appeal. Lorca in fact
does have a fondness for play, self-conscious virtuosity, even chic;
but this does not bother me as much as it does Mr. Sanchez. The
theater, when it has the proper gusto, often feeds upon itself and the
other arts in this way, but without sacrifice of original dramatic
content. Lorca's theater accomplished this, I think. The limitations
which Mr. Sanchez feels in his art are not those of the merely clever,
arty theatrical interpreter, but those of an artist who, in our frag-
mented and polyglot culture, stays within the idioms of one national
culture. When a national culture revives, its art forms seem significant, filled with immediately relevant moral and spiritual content;
and that seems to have occurred in Lorca's Spain. When that happens, the theater, in its play with images from art, may be allusive
without being merely arty.

The House of Bernarda Alba, the play which Mr. Sanchez regards
as the best dramatically, is interesting in this connection. Mr. Sanchez
thinks it a powerful picture of contemporary Spanish provincial life,
with the qualities of the best modern realistic drama. Lorca himself
calls it a photograph; and according to people who know the country,
he has achieved a surface accuracy comparable to Ibsen's or Chekhov's But it would be a mistake to take its realism too straight: the
label "photograph," like the label "alleluya" on *Don Perlimplín,*
indicates the very self-conscious style, which alludes to a whole context of meaning. *Bernarda Alba* is a period piece like the others; it
utilizes the conventions of nineteenth-century realism with the same
kind of sophisticated intention as that with which *Don Perlimplín*
utilizes its more ancient conventions. The blankness of the photograph is part of the composition which includes the severe character
of Bernarda herself, and the deathly white walls within which she
strives to hold her myopic vision steady.

In this problem of Lorca's restaging of Spanish art we must remember the analogies between forms of art and forms of human
life. They are most evident in old countries with whose art and literature we are familiar. One may feel it even on revisiting New England:
the white clapboards, the old ladies, the slender elms still seem to
be "right out of the pages" of Whittier or Hawthorne. The Paris taxi

drivers still argue à la Molière; the hard-bitten concierges in cheap hotels are still imitating Balzac. And the Spanish mark on art and character is one of the deepest. I have never been to Spain, but I have seen Sancho Panza and his burro in northern New Mexico, and the faces of old people reflecting (even at a distance of thousands of miles and many generations) the subtle faces in Spanish painting. Perhaps the natural role of the artist in a living culture is to make these forms, with the changes which time brings, visible and significant again.

But Lorca was unusually fortunate in being able to work with such fertility within his native culture; it is a commentary on our rootless state, in which all the familiar forms of life and art begin to seem vague and irrelevant, that his riches should seem somehow against the rules. It is growing harder and harder in our time for a writer to stay within one traditional culture. Yeats was hardly content with his Irish revival beyond youth. Our own Southern writers hesitate painfully between the South, where their roots are, and the national scene in which they are obliged to live, almost as ill-defined as the rest of us.

The deeply Spanish nature of Lorca's art does not prevent it from speaking to us. His sense of history—"the masquerades which time resumes"—is very modern; in his ability to mingle the most contradictory perspectives in one composition, and to shift with sureness from the pathetic to the farcical-frightening, he is in the class of our favorite poets. And he writes poetry of the theater as our poets would like to do. We cannot use his Spanish language, or the symbolic language of the moral and esthetic forms of his tradition. But we can learn to read it, and to discover thereby an authentic modern poetic drama.

ARTHUR MILLER
The Family in Modern Drama

1

Most people, including the daily theater reviewers, have come to
assume that the forms in which plays are written spring either from
nowhere or from the temperamental choice of the playwrights. I am
not maintaining that the selection of a form is as objective a matter
as the choice of, let us say, a raincoat instead of a linen suit for a
walk on a rainy day; on the contrary, most playwrights, including
myself, reach rather instinctively for that form, that way of telling a
play, which seems inevitably right for the subject at hand. Yet I
wonder whether it is all as accidental, as "free" a choice, as it appears
to be at a superficial glance. I wonder whether there may not be
within the ideas of family on the one hand, and society on the other,
primary pressures which govern our notions of the right form for a
particular kind of subject matter.

It has gradually come to appear to me over the years that the
spectrum of dramatic forms, from Realism over to the Verse Drama,
the Expressionistic techniques, and what we call vaguely the Poetic
Play, consists of forms which express human relationships of a particular kind, each of them suited to express either a primarily familial
relation at one extreme, or a primarily social relation at the other.

When we think of Realism we think of Ibsen—and if we don't we ought to, because in his social plays he not only used the form but pressed it very close to its ultimate limits. What are the main characteristics of this form? We know it by heart, of course, since most of the plays we see are realistic plays. It is written in prose; it makes believe it is taking place independently of an audience which views it through a "fourth wall," the grand objective being to make everything seem true to life in life's most evident and apparent sense. In contrast, think of any play by Aeschylus. You are never under an illusion in his plays that you are watching "life"; you are watching a play, an art work.

Now at the risk of being obvious I must remind you that Realism is a style, an artful convention, and not a piece of reportage. What, after all, is real about having all the furniture in a living room facing the footlights? What is real about people sticking to the same subject for three consecutive hours? Realism is a style, an invention quite as consciously created as Expressionism, Symbolism, or any of the other less familiar forms. In fact, it has held the stage for a shorter period of time than the more poetic forms and styles which dominate the great bulk of the world repertoire, and when it first came into being it was obvious to all as a style, a poet's invention. I say this in order to make clear that Realism is neither more nor less "artistic" than any other form. The only trouble is that it more easily lends itself in our age to hack work, for one thing because more people can write passable prose than verse. In other ages, however, as for instance in the lesser Elizabethan playwrights, hack work could also make of the verse play a pedestrian and uninspired form.

As with any artist, Ibsen was writing not simply to photograph scenes from life. After all, at the time he wrote A Doll's House how many Norwegian or European women had slammed the door upon their hypocritical relations with their husbands? Very few. So there was nothing, really, for him to photograph. What he was doing, however, was projecting through his personal interpretation of common events what he saw as their concealed significance for society. In other words, in a perfectly "realistic" way he did not report so much as project or even prophesy a meaning. Put in playwriting terms, he created a symbol on the stage.

We are not ordinarily accustomed to juxtaposing the idea of a symbol with the idea of Realism. The symbolic action, symbolic speech, have come to be reserved in our minds for the more poetic forms. Yet Realism shares equally with all other ways of telling a play this single mission. It must finally arrive at a meaning symbolic of the underlying action it has set forth. The difference lies in its method of creating its symbol as opposed to the way the poetic forms create theirs.

Now, then, the question arises: Why, if Ibsen and several other playwrights could use Realism so well to make plays about modern life, and if in addition the modern American audience is so quickly at home with the form—why should playwrights over the past thirty years be so impatient with it? Why has it been assaulted from every side? Why do so many people turn their backs on it and revere instead any kind of play which is fanciful or poetic? At the same time, why does Realism always seem to be drawing us all back to its arms? We have not yet created in this country a succinct form to take its place. Yet it seems that Realism has become a familiar bore; and by means of cutout sets, revolving stages, musical backgrounds, new and more imaginative lighting schemes, our stage is striving to break up the old living room. However, the perceiving eye knows that many of these allegedly poetic plays are Realism underneath, tricked up to look otherwise. I am criticizing nobody, only stating that the question of form is a deeper one, perhaps, than we have been willing to admit.

As I have indicated, I have come to wonder whether the force or pressure that makes for Realism, that even requires it, is the magnetic force of the family relationship within the play, and the pressure which evokes in a genuine, unforced way the un-realistic modes is the social relationship within the play. In a generalized way we commonly recognize that forms do have some extratheatrical, common-sense criteria; for instance, one of the prime difficulties in writing modern opera, which after all is lyric drama, is that you cannot rightly sing so many of the common thoughts of common life. A line like "Be sure to take your bath, Gloria," is difficult to musicalize, and impossible to take seriously as a sung concept. But we normally stop short at recognition of the ridiculous in this problem. Clearly, a poetic drama must be built upon a poetic idea, but I wonder if that is the whole problem. It is striking to me, for instance, that Ibsen, the master of Realism, while writing his realistic plays in quite as serious a frame of mind as in his social plays, suddenly burst out of the realistic frame, out of the living room, when he wrote *Peer Gynt*. I think that it is not primarily the living room he left behind, in the sense that this factor had made a poetic play impossible for him, but rather the family context. For Peer Gynt is first of all a man seen alone; equally, he is a man confronting non-familial, openly social relationships and forces.

I warn you not to try to apply this rule too mechanically. A play, like any human relationship, has a predominant quality, but it also contains powerful elements which although secondary may not be overlooked, and may in fact be crucial in the development of that relationship. I offer this concept, therefore, as a possible tool and not as a magic key to the writing or understanding of plays and their forms.

I have used Ibsen as an example because he wrote in several forms; another equally experimental dramatist was O'Neill. It ought to be noted that O'Neill himself described his preoccupation as being not with the relations between man and man, but with those between man and God. What has this remark to do with dramatic form? Everything, I think. It is obvious, to begin with that Ibsen's mission was to create not merely characters, but a context in which they were formed and functioned as people. That context, heavily and often profoundly delineated, was his society. His very idea of fate, for instance, was the inevitability residing in the conflict between the life force of his characters struggling with the hypocrisies, the strangling and abortive effects of society upon them. Thus, if only to create a climax, Ibsen had to draw society in his plays as a realistic force embodied in money, in social mores, in taboos, and so on, as well as an internal, subjective force within his characters.

O'Neill, however, seems to have been seeking for some fate-making power behind the social force itself. He went to ancient Greece for some definition of that force; he reached toward modern religion and toward many other possible sources of the poetic modes. My point here, however, is that so long as the family and family relations are at the center of his plays his form remains—indeed, it is held prisoner by—Realism. When, however, as for instance in *The Hairy Ape* and *Emperor Jones*, he deals with men out in society, away from the family context, his forms become alien to Realism, more openly and self-consciously symbolic, poetic, and finally heroic.

2

Up to this point I have been avoiding any question of content except that of the family relation as opposed to relations out in the world— social relations. Now I should like to make the bald statement that all plays we call great, let alone those we call serious, are ultimately involved with some aspect of a single problem. It is this: How may a man make of the outside world a home? How and in what ways must he struggle, what must he strive to change and overcome within himself and outside himself if he is to find the safety, the surroundings of love, the ease of soul, the sense of identity and honor which, evidently, all men have connected in their memories with the idea of family?

One ought to be suspicious of any attempt to boil down all the great themes to a single sentence, but this one—"How may a man make of the outside world a home?"—does bear watching as a clue to the inner life of the great plays. Its aptness is most evident in the modern repertoire; in fact, where it is not the very principle of the play at hand we do not take the play quite seriously. If, for instance, the struggle in *Death of a Salesman* were simply between father and son for recognition and forgiveness it would diminish in importance. But when it extends itself out of the family circle and into society, it broaches those questions of social status, social honor and recognition, which expand its vision and lift it out of the merely particular toward the fate of the generality of men.

The same is true—although achieved in different ways—of a play like *A Streetcar Named Desire*, which could quite easily have been limited to a study of psychopathology were it not that it is placed clearly within the wider bounds of the question I am discussing. Here Blanche Dubois and the sensitivity she represents has been crushed by her moving out of the shelter of the home and the family into the uncaring, anti-human world outside it. In a word, we begin to partake of the guilt for her destruction, and for Willy's, because the blow struck against them was struck outside the home rather than within it—which is to say that it affects us more because it is a social fact we are witnessing.

The crucial question has an obverse side. If we look at the great plays—at *Hamlet, Oedipus, Lear*—we must be impressed with one fact perhaps above all others. These plays are all examining the concept of loss, of man's deprivation of a once-extant state of bliss unjustly shattered—a bliss, a state of equilibrium, which the hero (and his audience) is attempting to reconstruct or to recreate with new, latter-day life materials. It has been said often that the central theme of the modern repertoire is the alienation of man, but the idea usually halts at the social alienation—he cannot find a satisfying role in society. What I am suggesting here is that while this is true of our plays, the more or less hidden impulse antedating social alienation, the unsaid premise of the very idea of "satisfaction," is the memory of both playwright and audience of an enfolding family and of childhood. It is as though both playwright and audience believed that they had once had an identity, a *being*, somewhere in the past which in the present has lost its completeness, its definitiveness, so that the central force making for pathos in these large and thrusting plays is the paradox which Time bequeaths to us all: we cannot go home again, and the world we live in is an alien place.

One of the forms most clearly in contrast to Realism is Expressionism. I should like now to have a look at its relevancy to the family-social complex.

3

The technical arsenal of Expressionism goes back to Aeschylus. It is a form of play which manifestly seeks to dramatize the conflict of either social, religious, ethical, or moral forces *per se*, and in their own naked roles, rather than to present psychologically realistic human characters in a more or less realistic environment. There is, for instance, no attempt by Aeschylus to create the psychology of a violent "character" in *Prometheus Bound*, or of a powerful one; rather he brings on two figures whose names are Power and Violence, and they behave as the *idea* of Power and the *idea* of Violence ought to behave, according to the laws of Power and Violence. In Germany after the First World War, playwrights sought to dramatize and unveil the social condition of man with similar means. For instance, in *Gas I* and *Gas II* George Kaiser placed the figure of man against an image of industrial society but without the slightest attempt to characterize the man except as a representative of one or the other of the social classes vying for control of the machine. There are, of course, numerous other examples of the same kind of elimination of psychological characterization in favor of what one might call the presentation of forces. In *The Great God Brown*, for instance, as well as in *The Hairy Ape*, O'Neill reached toward this very ancient means of dramatization without psychology—without, one might say, behavior as we normally know it. *Everyman* is another work in that long line.

In passing, I must ask you to note that expressionist plays—which is to say plays preoccupied with the open confrontation of moral, ethical, or social forces—seem inevitably to cast a particular kind of shadow. The moment realistic behavior and psychology disappear from the play all the other appurtenances of Realism vanish too. The stage is stripped of knickknacks; instead it reveals symbolic *designs* which function as overt pointers toward the moral to be drawn from the action. We are no longer under quite the illusion of watching through a transparent fourth wall. Instead we are constantly reminded, in effect, that we are watching a theater piece. In short, we are not bidden to lose our consciousness of time and place, the consciousness of ourselves, but are appealed to through our intelligence, our faculties of knowing rather than of feeling.

This difference in the area of appeal is the difference between our familial emotions and our social emotions. The two forms not only spring from different sectors of human experience but end up by appealing to different areas of receptivity within the audience. Nor is this phenomenon confined to the play.

When one is speaking to one's family, for example, one uses a certain level of speech, a certain plain diction perhaps, a tone of voice, an inflection, suited to the intimacy of the occasion. But when one faces an audience of strangers, as a politician does, for instance—and he is the most social of men—it seems right and proper for him to reach for the well-turned phrase, even the poetic word, the aphorism, the metaphor. And his gestures, his stance, his tone of voice, all become larger than life; moreover, his character is not what gives him these prerogatives, but his role. In other words, a confrontation with society permits us, or even enforces upon us, a certain reliance upon ritual. Similarly with the play.

The implications of this natural wedding of form with inner relationships are many, and some of them are complex. It is true to say, I think, that the language of the family is the language of the private life—prose. The language of society, the language of the public life, is verse. According to the degree to which the play partakes of either relationship, it achieves the right to move closer or further away from either pole. I repeat that this "right" is given by some common consent which in turn is based upon our common experience in life.

It is interesting to look at a couple of modern plays from this viewpoint and to see whether critical sense can be made of them. T. S. Eliot's *The Cocktail Party*, for instance, drew from most intelligent auditors, a puzzled admiration. In general, one was aware of a struggle going on between the apparencies of the behavior of the people and what evidently was the preoccupation of the playwright. There were a Husband and a Wife whom we were evidently expected to accept in that commonly known relationship, especially since the setting and the mode of speech and much of its diction were perfectly real if inordinately cultivated for a plebeian American audience. Even the theme of the play was, or should have been, of importance to most of us. Here we were faced with the alternative ways of giving meaning to domestic existence, one of them being through the cultivation of self, partly by means of the psychoanalytic ritual; the other and victorious method being the martyrization of the self, not for the sake of another, or as a rebuke to another, as martyrdom is usually indulged in in family life, but for the sake of martyrdom, of the disinterested action whose ultimate model was, according to the author, Jesus Christ. The heroine is celebrated for having been eaten alive by ants while on a missionary work among savages, and the very point is that there was no point—she converted nobody at all. Thus she gained her self by losing self or giving it away. Beyond the Meaningless she found Meaning at last.

To say the least, Eliot is manifestly an apt writer of verse. The inability of this play to achieve a genuine poetic level cannot therefore be laid to the usual cause—the unpoetic nature of the playwright's talent. Indeed, *Murder in the Cathedral* is a genuine poetic play, so he had already proved that he could achieve a wholeness of poetic form. I believe that the puzzlement created by *The Cocktail Party*, the sense of its being drawn in two opposite directions, is the result of the natural unwillingness of our minds to give to the Husband-Wife relation—a family relation—the prerogatives of the poetic mode, especially when the relationship is originally broached, as it is in this play, through any means approaching Realism.

Whether consciously or not, Eliot himself was aware of this dichotomy and wrote, and has said that he wrote, a kind of line which would not seem obtrusively formal and poetic to the listening ear. The injunction to keep it somehow unpoetic was issued by the central family situation, in my opinion. There was no need to mask his poetry at all in *Murder in the Cathedral*, because the situation is social, the conflict of a human being with the world. That earlier play had the unquestioned right to the poetic because it dealt with man as a public figure and could use the public man's style and diction.

4

We recognize now that a play can be poetic without verse, and it is in this middle area that the complexities of tracing the influence of the family and social elements upon the form become more troublesome. *Our Town* by Thornton Wilder is such a play, and it is important not only for itself but because it is the progenitor of many other works.

This is a family play which deals with the traditional family figures, the father, mother, brother, sister. At the same time it uses this particular family as a prism through which is reflected the author's basic idea, his informing principle—which can be stated as the indestructibility, the everlastingness, of the family and the community, its rhythm of life, its rootedness in the essentially safe cosmos despite troubles, wracks, and seemingly disastrous, but essentially temporary, dislocations.

Technically it is not arbitrary in any detail. Instead of a family living room or a house, we are shown a bare stage on which actors set chairs, a table, a ladder to represent a staircase or an upper floor, and so on. A narrator is kept in the foreground as though to remind us that this is not so much "real life" as an abstraction of it—in other words, a stage. It is clearly a poetic rather than a realistic play. What makes it that? Well, let us first imagine what would make it more realistic.

Would a real set make it realistic? Not likely. A real set would only discomfit us by drawing attention to what would then appear to be a slightly unearthly quality about the characterizations. We should probably say, "People don't really act like that." In addition, the characterization of the whole town could not be accomplished with anything like its present vividness if the narrator were removed, as he would have to be from a realistic set, and if the entrances and exits of the environmental people, the townspeople, had to be justified with the usual motives and machinery of Realism.

The preoccupation of the entire play is quite what the title implies —the town, the society, and not primarily this particular family— and every stylistic means used is to the end that the family foreground be kept in its place, merely as a foreground for the larger context behind and around it. In my opinion, it is this larger context, the town and its enlarging, widening significance, that is the bridge to the poetic for this play. Cut out the town and you will cut out the poetry.

The play is worth examining further against the Ibsen form of Realism to which it is inevitably related if only in contrast. Unlike Ibsen, Wilder sees his characters in this play not primarily as personalities, as individuals, but as forces, and he individualizes them only enough to carry the freight, so to speak, of their roles as forces. I do not believe, for instance, that we can think of the brother in this play, or the sister or the mother, as having names other than Brother, Sister, Mother. They are not given that kind of particularity or interior life. They are characterized rather as social factors, in their roles of Brother, Sister, Mother, in Our Town. They are drawn, in other words, as forces to enliven and illuminate the author's symbolic vision and his theme, which is that of the family as a timeless, stable quantity which has not only survived all the turmoil of time but is, in addition, beyond the possibility of genuine destruction.

The play is important to any discussion of form because it has achieved a largeness of meaning and an abstraction of style that created that meaning, while at the same time it has moved its audiences subjectively—it has made them laugh and weep as abstract plays rarely if ever do. But it would seem to contradict my contention here. If it is true that the presentation of the family on the stage inevitably forces Realism upon the play, how did this family play manage to transcend Realism to achieve its symbolistic style?

Every form, every style, pays its price for its special advantages. The price paid by *Our Town* is psychological characterization forfeited in the cause of the symbol. I do not believe, as I have said, that the characters are identifiable in a psychological way, but only as figures in the family and social constellation, and this is not meant in criticism, but as a statement of the limits of this form. I would go further and say that it is not *necessary* for every kind of play to do every kind of thing. But if we are after ultimate reality we must make ultimate demands.

I think that had Wilder drawn his characters with a deeper configuration of detail and with a more remorseless quest for private motive and self-interest, for instance, the story as it stands now would have appeared oversentimental and even sweet. I think that if the play tested its own theme more remorselessly, the world it creates of a timeless family and a rhythm of existence beyond the disturbance of social wracks would not remain unshaken. The fact is that the juvenile delinquent is quite directly traced to the breakup of family life and, indeed, to the break in that ongoing, steady rhythm of community life which the play celebrates as indestructible.

I think, further, that the close contact which the play established with its audience was the result of its coincidence with the deep longing of the audience for such stability, a stability which in daylight out on the street does not truly exist. The great plays pursue the idea of loss and deprivation of an earlier state of bliss which the characters feel compelled to return to or to re-create. I think this play forgoes the loss and suffers thereby in its quest for reality, but that the audience supplies the sense of deprivation in its own life experience as it faces what in effect is an idyl of the past. To me, therefore, the play falls short of a form that will press into reality to the limits of reality, if only because it could not plumb the psychological interior lives of its characters and still keep its present form. It is a triumph in that it does open a way toward the dramatization of the larger truths of existence while using the common materials of life. It is a truly poetic play.

5

Were there space, I should like to go into certain contemporary works with a view to the application in them of the forces of society and family—works by Clifford Odets, Tennessee Williams, Lillian Hellman, William Saroyan, and others. But I will jump to the final question I have in mind. If there is any truth in the idea of a natural union of the family and Realism as opposed to society and the poetic, what are the reasons for it?

First, let us remind ourselves of an obvious situation, but one which is often overlooked. The man or woman who sits down to write a play, or who enters a theater to watch one, brings with him in each case a common life experience which is not suspended merely because he has turned writer or become part of an audience. We—all of us—have a role anteceding all others: we are first sons, daughters, sisters, brothers. No play can possibly alter this given role.

The concepts of Father, Mother, and so on were received by us unawares before the time we were conscious of ourselves as selves. In contrast, the concepts of Friend, Teacher, Employee, Boss, Colleague, Supervisor, and the many other social relations came to us long after we gained consciousness of ourselves, and are therefore outside ourselves. They are thus in an objective rather than a subjective category. In any case, what we feel is always more "real" to us than what we know, and we feel the family relation while we only know the social one. Thus the former is the very apotheosis of the real and has an inevitability and a foundation indisputably actual, while the social relation is always relatively mutable, accidental, and consequently of a profoundly arbitrary nature to us.

Today the difficulty in creating a form that will unite both elements in a full rather than partial onslaught on reality is the reflection of the deep split between the private life of man and his social life. Nor is this the first time in history that such a separation has occurred. Many critics have remarked upon it, for instance, as a probable reason for the onset of Realism in the later Greek plays, for it is like a rule of society that, as its time of troubles arrives, its citizens revert to a kind of privacy of life that excludes society, as though man at such times would like to banish society from his mind. When this happens, man excludes poetry too.

All of which, while it may provide a solution, or at least indicate the mansion where the solution lives, only serves to point to the ultimate problem more succinctly. Obviously, the playwright cannot create a society, let alone one so unified as to allow him to portray man in art as a monolithic creature. The playwright is not a reporter, but in a serious work of art he cannot set up an image of man's condition so distant from reality as to violate the common sense of what reality is. But a serious work, to say nothing of a tragic one, cannot hope to achieve truly high excellence short of an investigation into the whole gamut of causation of which society is a manifest and crucial part. Thus it is that the common Realism of the past forty or fifty years has been assaulted—because it could not, with ease and beauty, bridge the widening gap between the private life and the social life. Thus it is that the problem was left unsolved by Expressionism, which evaded it by forgoing psychological realism altogether and leaping over to a portrayal of social forces alone. Thus it is that there is now a certain decadence about many of our plays; in the past ten years they have come more and more to dwell solely upon psychology, with little or no attempt to locate and dramatize the social roles and conflicts of their characters. For it is proper to ascribe decay to that which turns its back upon society when, as is obvious to any intelligence, the fate of mankind is social.

6

Finally, I should say that the current quest after the poetic is fruitless. It is the attempt to make apples without growing trees. It is seeking poetry precisely where poetry is not: in the private life viewed entirely within the bounds of the subjective, the area of sensation, or the bizarre and the erotic. From these areas of the private life have sprung the mood plays, the plotless plays for which there is much admiration as there is much relief when one turns from a problem to a ramble in the woods. I do not ask you to disdain such plays, for they are within the realm of art; I say only that the high work, the tragic work, cannot be forged waywardly, while playing by ear. There is a charm in improvisation, in letting one chord suggest the other and ending when the moment wanes. But the high order of art to which drama is fated will come only when it seeks to account for the total condition of man, and this cannot be improvised.

Whatever is said to describe a mood play, one point must be made: such plays all have in common an air of self-effacement—which is to say that they wish to seem as though they had not only no plot but no writer. They would convince us that they "just happen," that no directing hand has arranged matters—contrary to the Ibsen plays, for instance, or, for that matter, the Shakespearean play or the Greek.

Furthermore, the entire operation is most moody when the characters involved have the least consciousness of their own existence. The mood play is a play in hiding. A true plot is an assertion of meaning. The mood play is not, as it has been mistaken for, a rebellion of any kind against the so-called well-made play, especially when Ibsen is widely held to be a writer of well-made plays. For there is as much subjectivity and inner poetry in *Hedda Gabler*—I daresay a lot more—as in any of these mood plays. What is really repulsive in Ibsen to one kind of contemporary mind is not openly mentioned: it is his persistent search for an organizing principle behind the "moods" of existence and not the absence of mood in his work.

An art form, like a person, can achieve greatness only as it accepts great challenges. Over the past few decades the American theater, in its best movements, has moved courageously and often beautifully into the interior life of man, an area that had most often been neglected in the past. But now, I think, we are in danger of settling for tears, as it were—for any play that "moves" us, quite as though the ultimate criterion of the art were lachrymosity. For myself, I find that there is an increasing reliance upon what pass for realistic, even tough, analytical picturizations of existence, which are really quite sentimental underneath; and the sentiment is getting thicker, I think, and an end in itself. Sentimentalism is perfectly all right, but it is nowhere near a great challenge, and to pursue it, even under the guide of the exotic atmosphere and the celebration of the sensuous, is not going to bring us closer to the fated mission of the drama.

What, after all, is that mission? I may as well end with such a question because it underlies and informs every word I have written. I think of it so: Man has created so many specialized means of unveiling the truth of the world around him and the world within him—the physical sciences, the psychological sciences, the disciplines of economic and historical research and theory. In effect, each of these attacks on the truth is partial. It is within the rightful sphere of the drama—it is, so to speak, its truly just employment and its ultimate design—to embrace the many-sidedness of man. It is as close to being a total art as the race has invented. It can tell, like science, what is—but more, it can tell what ought to be. It can depict, like painting, in designs and portraits, in the colors of the day or night; like the novel it can spread out its arms and tell the story of a life, or a city, in a few hours—but more, it is dynamic, it is always on the move as life is, and it is perceived like life through the motions, the gestures, the tones of voice, and the gait and nuance of living people. It is the singer's art and the painter's art and the dancer's art, yet it may hew to fact no less tenaciously than does the economist or the physician. In a word, there lies within the dramatic form the ultimate possibility of raising the truth-consciousness of mankind to a level of such intensity as to transform those who observe it.

The problem, therefore, is not simply an aesthetic one. As people, as a society, we thirst for clues to the past and the future; least of all, perhaps, do we know about the present, about what *is*. It is the present that is always most evasive and slippery, for the present always threatens most directly our defenses against seeing what we are, and it is the present, always the present, to which the dramatic form must apply or it is without interest and a dead thing, and forms do die when they lose their capacity to open up the present. So it is its very nature to bring us closer to ourselves if only it can grow and change with the changing world.

In the deepest sense, I think, to sophisticated and unsophisticated alike, nothing is quite so real to us, so extant, as that which has been made real by art. Nor is this ironical and comic. For the fact is that art is a function of the civilizing act quite as much as is the building of the water supply. American civilization is only recently coming to a conscious awareness of art not as a luxury but as a necessity of life. Without the right dramatic form a genuine onslaught upon the veils that cloak the present is not possible. In the profoundest sense I cannot create that form unless, somewhere in you, there is a wish to know the present and a demand upon me that I give it to you.

For at bottom what is that form? It is the everlastingly sought balance between order and the need of our souls for freedom; the relatedness between our vaguest longings, our inner questions, and private lives and the life of the generality of men which is our society and our world. How may man make for himself a home in that vastness of strangers and how may he transform that vastness into a home? This, as I have repeated, is the question a form must solve anew in every age. This, I may say, is the problem before you too.

JOHN HENRY RALEIGH

O'Neill's *Long Day's Journey into Night* and New England Irish-Catholicism

Eugene O'Neill's *Long Day's Journey into Night* has been rightly praised as his finest play (and tragedy) as well as perhaps the finest play (and tragedy) ever written on this continent. It does not have much competition, to be sure, but whatever competition it may have —*Winterset, Death of a Salesman*, O'Neill's own early tragedies, and the like—is so completely outdistanced that there is no point in making comparisons and contrasts. *Long Day's Journey* stands by itself. All the power in characterization and the compassion for humanity that everyone knew O'Neill always had and which always showed itself, even if fitfully under such lugubrious surfaces as *Lazarus Laughed*, comes out clearly, cleanly, and unambiguously in *Long Day's Journey*. And the considerable talent for humor that manifested itself in *Ah, Wilderness!* is here joined to a somber plot; so that we have the final paradox that this darkest of tragedies is continually breaking out into wild comedy.

O'Neill's severest critics have never denied him, in a word— "Power"; and this is his most "powerful" play. In all his other "powerful" plays, there are always touches or stretches of staginess and awkwardness. But *Long Day's Journey* is clean, almost pure, one might say.

The first question to be asked is where does this clean power come

Reprinted by permission from *Partisan Review* (XXVI, 4).

from? It comes, first of all, from the autobiographical sources, as he tells us in the preface, the "old sorrow, written in tears and blood," and the final strength and courage "to face my dead at last and write this play." After biblical and Greek–Civil War descents into past history (*Lazarus Laughed* and *Mourning Becomes Electra*), after travels in the Orient (*Marco Millions*), after primitivism (*The Emperor Jones* and *The Hairy Ape*), after racial imbroglios (*All God's Chillun Got Wings*), after nineteenth-century New England (*Desire Under the Elms*), after the sea, after Greek masks, after dynamos, after all kinds of themes and devices and bizarre subjects, he finally returned home to New London, Connecticut, to his family, and to himself. As Stephen Dedalus says in *Ulysses*:

> *If Socrates leaves his home today he will find the sage seated on his doorsteps. If Judas goes forth tonight it is to Judas his steps will tend.* Every life is many days, day after day. We walk through ourselves, meeting robbers, ghosts, giants, old men, young men, wives, widows, brothers-in-love. But always meeting ourselves.

For certainly even a most superficial knowledge of the O'Neill family and of the facts of Eugene O'Neill's early life show that the play is very close to being straight autobiography (no matter what discrepancies may ultimately be pointed out). In another sense it does not matter how close to, or how far from, are the facts of O'Neill's life to the facts of the play, for *Long Day's Journey* is more impressive as a cultural document than it is as an autobiographical document. Furthermore, its distinctive qualities are given, not so much by family, as by culture, or by family-culture, since the two cannot be separated. The culture is, of course, New England Irish Catholicism, and it is this that provides the folkways and mores, the character types, the interrelationships between characters, the whole attitude toward life that informs *Long Day's Journey* and gives it its meaning. As such, *Long Day's Journey* is the great cultural expression of American Irish-Catholicism; it puts permanently into the shade all the "stage-Irish–St. Patrick's Day–'Going My Way'–'Mother Mc-Cree'" type of sentimentality that has encircled the image of the Irish in America. Just as effectively does it underline the shallowness of the higher-level sentimentality of Edwin O'Connor's *The Last Hurrah*, a whimsical account of the farcical and shoddy character and career of Boston's James Michael Curley. The only other American

Irish-Catholic document that even approaches O'Neill's in power and truth is the *Studs Lonigan* trilogy of James T. Farrell, but Farrell's novel is tendentious and therefore "dates," and it lacks both the compassion and the humor of O'Neill's picture. Farrell's novel was written in anger—well justified, it should be added—but O'Neill's play was written out of sorrow, forgiveness, and, strangely enough, a kind of joy. Its world therefore exists on a higher level, humanely speaking, than does that of Farrell. In Farrell's novel there are all kinds of things to blame for the vulgarity and pettiness of the characters' lives. In O'Neill there is no pettiness, no real vulgarity, and nothing is to blame except everybody. Social forces, as such, do not exist and, as in Greek tragedy, we are face to face with guilty-innocent humanity on the purely personal level. All the terrible things that members of a family—in this case an Irish family—will do to one another, often in innocence, and always without reference to outside people or events, are presented in a relentless and yet compassionate honesty. (It should be added, although it will not concern me here, that the finest primarily comic expression of the same culture is O'Neill's *Ah, Wilderness!*).

1

When Yeats and Shaw founded the Irish Academy of Letters, they invited O'Neill to become an associate member, which he did, although he was an American by birth. For it would be no exaggeration to say that an American of Irish-Catholic parentage born in New England in the late nineteenth or early twentieth century was really not American but Irish.[1] This distinctive, closely knit culture, which is in our day relaxing, produced a whole gallery of "un-American" types. Here is how O'Neill describes one of them in *A Moon for the Misbegotten:* he is Mike Hogan.

> He has a common Irish face, its expression sullen, or slyly cunning, or primly self-righteous. He never forgets that he is a good Catholic, faithful to all the observances, and so is one of the élite of Almighty God in a world of damned sinners composed of Protestants and bad Catholics. In brief, MIKE is a New England Irish Catholic Puritan, Grade B, and an extremely irritating youth to have around.

But it also produced Eugene O'Neill and the four haunted Tyrones of *Long Day's Journey*, end-products, you might say, of the Irish famine of the late 1840's, which set off the vast migrations to America. James O'Neill himself was born in County Kilkenny in Ireland, in the year 1849 and came to this country at the age of five, bringing with him the penuriousness and the land-hunger that obsess James Tyrone, the father of *Long Day's Journey*. More important, he was a member of a vast group of immigrants who did not so much leave Ireland as bring Ireland to America. In New England, in particular, partly because of their intense clannishness, partly because they were "outsiders," partly because they found themselves "ruled" by a Protestant Anglophile culture—it was Ireland all over again with the hostile "strangers" in control—the Irish remained "Irish" and did not get assimiliated for several generations, sometimes for a half century or more; they were not merged in one or two generations, as were other foreign groups, particularly Northern European ones, in other parts of the country. James Tyrone, of course, was born in Ireland and is a professional patriot who thinks that Shakespeare and the Duke of Wellington were dyed-in-the-wool Irish Catholics. But even his two sons, who are in rebellion and who scorn this patriotic nonsense, are still—hopelessly for them—"Irish," their whole characters being dominated by the passionate tribal and familial customs and resultant character typology in which their souls were forged.

How extraordinarily profound and pervasive were these characteristics can be only fully appreciated when one becomes aware of the fact that historical accounts of the Irish national character, even in medieval and antemedieval times, sound remarkably like a description of the Tyrone family. It would be no exaggeration to say that a straight line can be drawn from the primitive forests of antique Ireland to the haunted New London, Connecticut, residence of the Tyrone family in the twentieth century.

In the first place there were no clans in ancient Ireland, with the family being the basic unit although the family was not a one generation affair. According to Sean O'Faolain in his *The Irish—A Character Study*, the basic family unit was symbolized by the hand: "The limits of the sacred nexus were symbolized by the hand. The palm was the common ancestor; the joints of the finger were his descendents into his grand-children; the finger-nails were his great grand-children." These families, moreover, were not inclined toward communal enterprises, such as the founding of cities, and it was the Normans, Danes, and Tudors who first constructed every Irish town of any consequence that exists. To these observations by O'Faolain should be added two more by Shane Leslie from his book *The Irish Tangle*. First, there is the immemorial Irish cult of chastity which was, evidently, a pre-Christian phenomenon (although some modern students of Irish culture claim that the ancient "chastity" is really a projection imposed upon the past by modern historians). There was the legend that an Irish girl could travel unmolested throughout the whole of Ireland, carrying a gold ring as a wand; a legendary Irish king was supposed to have drowned nine daughters at Doon in Keery because one had a lover and he could not determine which one it was. Second, and at the opposite moral pole, there is the constant turbulence and recourse to drink. These national habits are best underlined by the anecdote concerning the Cromwellian who bequeathed to an Irish community a supply of dirks and whisky, hoping they would all get drunk and kill one another.

Four more observations should be made. First, as Robin Flower points out in *The Irish Tradition*, medieval Irish love poetry was dominated by two diametrically opposed impulses: delicate sentiment and beauty, on the one hand, and the most astringent kind of irony, on the other. Second—and this scarcely needs documentation— there is the national concern with betrayal, the "Judas-complex" that dominates Irish life and literature. For centuries the "informer" was a constant political fact of the most bitter importance, and in a literary document like *Ulysses* one can see it as a constant leitmotif of Dublin life; as Mr. Deasy says to Stephen: "Helen, the runaway wife of Menelaus, ten years the Greeks made war on Troy. A faithless wife brought the strangers to our shore here . . . a woman too brought Parnell low." Joyce himself was deeply possessed by the national Judas-complex and was always talking of those who "betrayed" him. (He even used the word "crucified" at times.) Third, again requiring no documentation, there is the national commitment to Roman Catholicism, which produced both the most extravagant devotion and the most deeply felt blasphemy, as in *Ulysses*, for example. Fourth and finally, there is the national preoccupation with rhetoric and the national eloquence.

Excessively familial; noncommunal; sexually chaste; turbulent; drunken; alternately and simultaneously sentimental and ironical about love; pathologically obsessed with betrayal; religious-blasphemous; loquacious: these are some of the historical attributes of the Irish character. To these nine characteristics should be added a tenth, which was an emergent, post-famine phenomenon, namely, a tendency toward less and later marriage on the part of the young men and a tendency, therefore, for these young men to remain at home with their father and mother. In short, here is an abstract picture of the Tyrone family, and it is on these generic lines that the characters, and the interrelationships, in *Long Day's Journey* are formed.

There is a further historical complication in the play, which makes the whole situation much more concrete and which cuts across the generic abstractions outlined above, in that *Long Day's Journey into Night* also shows the Irish in the process of assimilation, or, rather —for none of these characters can properly be called assimilated—in the process of breaking away from the culture of the "Old Country." There are at least four levels of this process represented in *Long Day's Journey*. There is first of all—never seen on the stage but talked about by the Tyrones—an authentic, unregenerate Irish peasant-farmer—a tenant of the Tyrones—named Shaughnessy, cunning, crafty, powerful, and possessed of a "terrible tongue." The Tyrones pretend to be shocked but are secretly delighted when they learn that Shaughnessy, just by use of this "terrible tongue," has run a Standard Oil man named Harker off his property although he was quite guilty of what Harker had come to accuse him. This incident, which must have been based on fact, amused O'Neill immensely, and he presented it directly and fully in *A Moon for the Misbegotten*, where he changes "Shaughnessy" to "Hogan" and "Harker" to "Harder." Hogan's verbal assault on Harder is a masterpiece and one of the high points of O'Neill's humor, and Irish mock-eloquence. (What had happened was that Hogan had let his pigs—of course, he keeps pigs—wallow in a pond on Harder's property.) Hogan's peroration is worth quoting; he has accused Harder of giving his pigs pneumonia:

> All prize pigs, too! I was offered two hundred dollars apiece for them. Twenty pigs at two hundred, that's four thousand. And a thousand to cure the sick and cover funeral expenses for the dead. Call it four thousand you owe me. (*Furiously*) And you'll pay for it, or I'll sue you, so help me Christ! I'll drag you in every court in the land! I'll paste your ugly mug on the front page of every newspaper as a pig-murdering tyrant! Before I'm through with you, you'll think you're the King of England at an Irish

wake! (*With a quick change of pace to a wheedling confidential tone.*) Tell me now, if it isn't a secret, whatever
made you take such a savage grudge against pigs? Sure, it
isn't reasonable for a Standard Oil Man to hate hogs.

There is too on stage in *Long Day's Journey* Cathleen the serving
girl, ignorant, cheerful, bumptious.

A cut above Shaughnessy-Hogan and Cathleen is James Tyrone
himself, who, according to O'Neill, is in fact still a peasant: nerve-
less, full of vitality, physically powerful, penurious. Still less of the
earth is Mary Tyrone, neurotic, idealistic, dope-addicted, religious;
further up still are the nihilistic sons, drunken, cynical, libidinous,
spouting *fin de siècle* estheticism and pessimism (Swinburne and
Nietzsche are the favorites). Nevertheless, the generic outline still
stands, despite this historical progression. One is not Irish, it seems,
with impunity and even in rebellion, the norms are still there.

2

I shall proceed through my catalogue of attributes, in reverse order,
beginning with the tendency for late marriages and subsequent prolonged adolescence.[2] Jamie, 33, and Edmund, 23, are still, from, say,
the contemporary American point of view and practice—which
seems to be steadily pushing the normal age for marriage back into
late childhood—in adolescence, living at home with the father who
grudgingly doles out "allowance" money to them. It is true that
Jamie is a wastrel and that Edmund is tuberculous; it is true too that
both have left home, at one time or another, but like Willie and Biff
Loman, they really *cannot* leave home, and they always return. This
feeling goes so deep that it is not even explained or discussed by the
play; it is a fact, like the weather, the "given" of a situation.

Loquacity, like drink, is one of the national addictions, and this
should not be confused with eloquence, which is the property of the
French. Irish "eloquence" is highly overrated, as any critical examination of Irish literature will show. Wilde once said to Yeats: "We
Irish are too poetical to be poets; we are a nation of brilliant failures,
but we are the greatest talkers since the Greeks." Wilde's own
"elegance," O'Casey's meanderings, Joyce's purple passages ("his
soul swooned slowly"), Synge's "keening," Shaw's attempt to be
poetical with Marchbanks, George Moore's sentences ("squeezed"
out of a tooth paste tube, as Yeats said), O'Neill's attempts at

"poetry": all these—Yeats alone excepted—show a singular poverty of genuine and organic eloquence. The real forte of the Irish is just in talking, and talking in a special way, histrionically: striking a comic pose and exaggerating it into a burlesque. The funniest parts of *Ulysses*—"Cyclops" or "Nausicaa"—consist of just this. And O'Neill is only at ease, rhetorically speaking, in similar situations, as, witness, the Hogan episode quoted above, or the performance of Jamie Tyrone which will be quoted below. Loquacity, besides humorous exaggeration, implies repetition. Critics have complained that *Long Day's Journey* is too long; it all could have been said in shorter compass and could have been, therefore, of greater artistic impact. I don't agree with this criticism from an esthetic point of view, and from the point of view I am adopting—the play as cultural artifact —this criticism is completely off the point. For the motto of the Irish, especially the drinking Irish, is that a thing is not said unless it has been repeated almost *ad infinitum*. This verbal repetitiousness, this insistent urge to exaggerate and repeat, colors Irish literature as well. O'Casey's autobiographical volumes are filled with it: "But the O'Briens, the Dillons, and the Healy's, mudmen, madmen, badmen, bedmen, deadmen, spedmen, spudmen, dudmen, . . ."; or, a description of Hell-Fire ". . . in a sea of fire, surgin', singin', scourgin', scorchin', scarifyin', skimmin', waves o'fire . . ." As O'Casey himself says in *Drums Under the Windows*:

> Keltic blood is usually accompanied by excited brains and a reckless temperament, and is always an excuse for exaggeration. When not whining or wheedling, the Kelt is usually in a state of bluff, or funk, and can always wind up to the kind of rhetoric no housemaid can resist.

In the words of the immortal washerwoman in *Finnegan's Wake*: "Wash quit and don't be dabbling. Tuck up your sleeves and loosen your talk-tapes." Or in the words of an Irish medieval monk in a verse concerning a cat:

> Hunting mice is his delight
> Hunting words I sit all night

The dualism of religion-blasphemy likewise runs through the Tyrone family. The father—and this is often true of Irish families— is conventionally pious, without any deep commitment to the Old Faith. He uses his religion in a purely conventional fashion, to blame,

for example, the worldly failures of his two sons on the fact that they
have both become apostates: "You've both flouted the faith you
were born and brought up in—the one true faith of the Catholic
Church—and your denial has brought nothing but self-destruction!"
The mother, on the other hand, is deeply, neurotically, but still
honestly, pious. Like Claudius, she cannot lie to God, He being so
real to her. Rather in her case, as might be expected, it is the Virgin
Mary who, in effect, usurps the Trinity and becomes "God," for the
Virgin is the symbol of female purity and is thus inevitably the patron
saint of Irish Roman Catholic convent girls. As such, the Virgin
signifies innocence and childhood, the shelter of the convent, the
benign smile of the Mother Superior, the loving earthly father at
home—in short, the happy times before she married the hard-drink-
ing, rather crude, though kindly, James Tyrone, and had encountered
the rude male world of tobacco, alcohol, cronies, and sweat, the
agonies of childbirth, the failure of children, the black abyss of dope
addiction. Yet she cannot pray, although she would like to, for God
or the Virgin sees all:

> *Longingly.*
>
> If I could only find the faith I lost, so I could pray again!
>
> *She pauses—then begins to recite the Hail Mary in a flat,
> empty tone.*
>
> "Hail, Mary, full of grace! The Lord is with Thee; blessed
> art Thou among women."
>
> *Sneeringly.*
>
> You expect the Blessed Virgin to be fooled by a lying dope
> fiend reciting words! You can't hide from her!

The morphine is a road back to that virginal childhood and her
"Long Day's Journey into Night" is a psychological regress to her
convent days.

The sons are militantly atheistical. Edmund's favorite author is
Nietzsche, whom he quotes: " 'God is dead: of His pity for man
hath God died.' " The blasphemous reaction is not emphasized in
Long Day's Journey, but it is in *Moon for the Misbegotten* where
Jamie Tyrone, now in his early forties, plays a leading role. Here he
tells of his blasphemous conduct after his mother's death. He had

been abstemious for two years, but on the news of his mother's death
an intolerable desire for desecration overcame him. He gets drunk,
almost breaks out into a diatribe at the wake, and when escorting
the coffin, in the baggage car of the train, to the East from Los
Angeles, he continues his drinking and has a nightly assignation with
a fat, blonde, fifty-dollar whore. In his drunken revels with the
blonde he sings the last two lines of a "tear-jerker" song that he
knew as a child:

> And the baby's cries can't waken her
> In the baggage car ahead.

The idea of betrayal, the "turncoat" psychology, permeates all the
Tyrones. Everybody has betrayed everybody else. The father betrayed
the mother because of his stinginess: when she was in pain once, he
hired a cheap doctor, who unscrupulously started her on morphine;
and the father will also probably betray Edmund by sending him to
a cheap sanatorium. The mother betrayed Edmund just by bearing
him, by bringing him into his painful existence. Jamie, in effect,
had killed the son Eugene, who died in infancy, after having been
visited by the contagious Jamie (who had been told to stay away).
Edmund and Jamie fail their parents by their wasted lives, and Jamie
betrays Edmund by trying to corrupt him. (They all are always
honest enough to admit all these enormities.) The mother betrays
them all by beginning to take dope on the day of the "long journey."
Culturally, psychologically, they "know" that nobody is to be de-
pended upon, father, mother, sibling. Whatever the weakness is, it
will be given in to. The dope addict mother can't be cured—they all
know this, and expect it. In fact, they would be disappointed in a
deep, obscure sense if she broke off, and they were all to be happy
and secure. They don't expect to be happy, for life is not like that.
Always there is the fierce, primitive suspicion that no one is to be
trusted. The promises to the parents and the relatives, the "pledge"
to the priest, the "bargain" with God, about "the drink" (or dope)
—all these go out the window, in a moment, when the implacable
imagination, the seizure of the nerves, the impossible desire for a
nirvana that lies at the bottom of a bottle of whiskey, comes over
the Irishman. Then there is the constant chorus: "You drink!" "You
failed!" "You'd like to see me dead!" "You take dope!" "Where's
the hophead?" says Jamie of his mother.

The combination of sentiment and irony in matters of love is likewise a Tyrone characteristic, and most cogently illustrated by the mother in her relationship to her "loved ones." For she does love them all, deeply, and is quite sentimental about them. In her most sentimental moments she is capable of misty-eyed dreams of the future happiness of the family. Edmund, the gifted son, is an especial love. Yet she is capable of the most searing and corrosive statements to all of them. To Edmund, her beloved, she can say:

> *Turns on Edmund with a hard, accusing antagonism—almost a revengeful enmity.*
>
> I never knew what rheumatism was before you were born! Ask your father!

Throughout the play we find her alternately sentimental and corrosive. As Edmund says of her:

> Deliberately, that's the hell of it! You know something in her does it deliberately—to get beyond our reach, to be rid of us, to forget we're alive! It's as if, in spite of loving us, she hated us.

Love for all of the Tyrones is ambiguous, unresolved tension between tenderness and hate, sentimentality and irony.

It is impossible to estimate accurately the cosmic import of the "bottle" in the lives of the Tyrones (the only reason that the mother does not take to it is because she possesses something stronger). In a way the Irish addiction to drink is a simplifying element in their lives, for this is how all problems are met—to reach for the bottle. When the mother takes to dope on the morning of the "long day," she knows, as a matter of course, that her men will all be drunk by nightfall. "The Bottle" is at the center of the room, and in many ways is the most important object in the room. If not using it, they talk about it. It enters into their very characters; the father's penuriousness is most neatly summed up by the fact that he keeps his liquor under lock and key and has an eagle eye for the exact level of the whiskey in the bottle he has grudgingly set forth. By the same token, the measure of the sons' rebellion is how much liquor they can "sneak." It is doubtful if the phrase and the action of "sneaking a drink" have in any other cultural group the immense significance that they have with the Irish. Allied to this peculiarly Irish custom are the concomitant phrase and action: "watering the whiskey," that is, filling the bottle with water to the level where it was before you "sneaked your drink." (The pathology of this custom is very curious, for obviously you fool nobody since the next person who uses the bottle instantly knows it has been "watered." And it doesn't take much imagination—since you know the habits of your family—to guess who has been doing the "watering." Thus James Tyrone knows that Jamie "waters" his whiskey, and Jamies knows that his father knows. Yet he will continue to do so: a rite that signifies a fictitious secrecy.) In some Irish households whole quarts of whiskey, indeed whole cases of whiskey, would slowly evolve into a watery, brown liquid, without the bottles having ever been set forth socially, so to speak. This act—the lonely, surreptitious, rapid gulp of whiskey— is the national rite, and probably deserves a sculptural embodiment, like Rodin's "The Thinker."

The "turbulence" of the Tyrone family hardly needs to be re-marked upon. The play is, in part, psychologically speaking, a "free-for-all," with everybody's hand against everybody else. Yet it is not this simple, for their love for one another is equally overpowering. No relationship has any stability and, sometimes, second by second, it alternates between love and hate. Here, for example, is an inter-change between James Tyrone and Edmund (they are both drunk, of course); the father speaks first:

> You'll obey me and put out that light or, big as you are, I'll give you a thrashing that'll teach you—!
>
> *Suddenly he remembers Edmund's illness and instantly be-comes guilty and shamefaced.*
>
> Forgive me, lad, I forgot— You shouldn't goad me into losing my temper.
>
> EDMUND: *Ashamed himself now.*
>
> Forget it, Papa, I apologize, too. I had no right being nasty about nothing. I am a bit soused, I guess. I'll put out the damned light.
>
> *He starts to get up.*
>
> TYRONE: No, stay where you are. Let it burn.
>
> *He stands up abruptly—and a bit drunkenly—and begins*

turning on the three bulbs in the chandelier, with a childish, bitterly dramatic self-pity.

We'll have them all on! Let them burn! To hell with them! The poorhouse is the end of the road, and it might as well be sooner as later!

He finishes turning on the lights.

EDMUND: *Has watched this proceeding with an awakened sense of humor—now he grins, teasing affectionately.*

That's a grand curtain.

He laughs.

You're a wonder, Papa.

TYRONE: *Sits down sheepishly—grumbles pathetically.*

That's right, laugh at the old fool! The poor old ham! But the final curtain will be in the poorhouse just the same, and that's not comedy!

Then as Edmund is still grinning, he changes the subject.

For the Irish are just what the popular legend about them says: mercurial. As another American Irishman, F. Scott Fitzgerald, once said of himself: "I was always saving or being saved—in a single morning I would go through the emotions ascribed to Wellington at Waterloo. I lived in a world of inscrutable hostiles and inalienable friends and supporters."

The sexual chastity of the Irish is likewise a motivating force in the play. In the mother's preoccupation with the Virgin we can see its feminine manifestation. For while it is never said in so many words, we can see that one of the mother's basic difficulties lies in that initial rude shock of the male assault and that the morphine addiction is an effect, not a cause. For the dope is her way back to her virginal childhood. Tyrone himself explains that she was not quite the nun-like, little girl that she now pictures herself. On the contrary, she was attractive, flirtatious, almost hoydenish, and she fell immediately and irrevocably in love with the handsome and charming young actor that was James Tyrone. Yet the hard facts of the marriage were too much for her, too little prepared for by the sweet, misty existence of the convent. It is after marriage that she learns that Tyrone had had a mistress, that he drinks, that he will go out with cronies and get drunk, while she remains alone in a "cheap" (as she keeps repeating) hotel room. Always in her mind is the terrible discrepancy between her life as a girl, or her metaphor for it, and her life as an adult married woman.

The sons, especially Jamie, represent the obverse side of the sexual chastity of the Irish. For while they are anything but chaste, they yet cannot partake of normal sexual relations and connect sex with love. For them it must always be a desecration, consecrated by drink and debauchery. The mother laments the fact that they never have anything to do with "nice" girls. Precisely, because they in their way are devotees of the Virgin too. Yeats said of Dowson: "Sober, he looked on no woman; drunk, he picked the cheapest whore. 'He did not even want them clean,' said a friend. 'I have been faithful to thee, Cynara, in my fashion.'" Jamie Tyrone will have only whores, and only fat ones, and to them he recites, of course, Dowson. As Edmund describes it:

> It's a good likeness of Jamie, don't you think, hunted by himself and whiskey, hiding in a Broadway hotel room with some fat tart—he likes them fat—reciting Dowson's "Cynara" to her.

> *He recites derisively, but with deep feeling.*

> "All night upon mine heart I felt her warm heart beat,
> Night-long within mine arms in love and sleep she lay;
> Surely the kisses of her bought red mouth were sweet;
> But I was desolate and sick of an old passion,
> When I awoke and found the dawn was gray:
> I have been faithful to thee, Cynara! in my fashion."

> *Jeeringly.*

> And the poor fat burlesque queen doesn't get a word of it, but suspects she's being insulted!

Fat, blonde, whores: that is the reaction of some Irish males to the sexual prohibitions that his culture imposes on him. This is the Saturday night dream of young Studs Lonigan: going to bed with a buxom blonde. For it is generally buxom women, with marmoreal thighs and full breasts, as if size alone could make up for the imposed frustrations and inhibitions. Abbie in *Desire Under the Elms* is "buxom, full of vitality. Her round face is pretty but marred by its rather gross sensuality." Nina in *Strange Interlude* is "tall with broad square shoulders, slim strong hips and long beautifully developed legs— . . ." But the O'Neill-Irish sexual fantasy receives its proper apotheosis in *Moon for the Misbegotten* in Josie Hogan who is

> five feet eleven in her stockings and weighs around one hundred and eighty. Her sloping shoulders are broad, her chest deep with large, firm breasts, her waist wide but slender by contrast with her hips and thighs. She has long smooth arms, immensely strong, although no muscles show. The same is true of her legs. . . . She is all woman.

Jamie himself says: " 'I like them tall and strong and voluptuous, now, with beautiful big breasts.' " And looking at Josie, this monument of female flesh (which is available to him, if he so desires, but which he has classified as "nice girl"), he murmurs—he is drunk— "You have a beautiful strong body, too, Josie—and beautiful eyes and hair, and a beautiful smile and beautiful warm breasts." It would seem that only a gigantic female breast, cosmic in scope, can make up to the Irish male for his frustrations. And, characteristically, Jamie Tyrone spends the last hours of his fictional existence (the last scene in *A Moon for the Misbegotten*) with his head resting on the bosom of Josie Hogan. Characteristically too, since he has (wrongly) classified her as a "nice girl," like his mother, a devotee of the Virgin, so to speak, he keeps the relationship scrupulously filial. So too when Joyce came to create his woman of the earth, Molly Bloom, she must be monumental in proportions. The first glimpse that we have of her is through the voyeuristic eyes of Mr. Bloom, at eight o'clock in the morning in the bedroom at 7 Eccles Street (this is the first description in the book of Molly): "He looked calmly down on her bulk and between her large soft bubs, sloping within her nightdress like a she goat's udder."

A secondary creation of the male rebellion against the Puritan aspects of his culture is the "ne'er-do-well." Any large Irish family used to produce at least one of these. (He's usually your "uncle.") He tends to be, of course, unmarried; he is usually good-looking; he has more than his share of the Irish charm; he has a fine sense of humor; and everybody likes him. He is also completely irresponsible, can never hold a job; and devotes himself to liquor and women, although the liquor is usually more important to him. In short, he is Jamie Tyrone. Very often—since he represents in the Irish national drama the Prince of Darkness—he is positively "Mephisthophelean," which is the word used to describe Jamie Tyrone. Lest we think this is an artistic stroke of O'Neill's imagination, we may remember that, according to Frank Budgen, Joyce, who was in his own inimitable way an Irish "ne'er-do-well," was called by the chorus girls in the Stadt theater in Zurich "Herr Satan" and that Budgen's landlady was actually afraid of this satanic gentleman, with his long thin face, thick glasses, high forehead, and jaunty demeanor.

The Tyrones, like their ancient ancestors, are, to a man, non-communal. Save for the reference to the Standard Oil Company and a trip to the drugstore, modern American society does not exist for them and certainly it plays no role in the play. But it is not only a question of society; other people have no existence for the Tyrones. The father, it is true, has his drunken cronies, but the family has no social life at all, and the two sons and the mother are lone wolves. The mother in particular feels and laments their isolation and loneliness:

> If there was only some place I could go to get away for a day, or even an afternoon, some woman friend I could talk to—not about anything serious, simply laugh and gossip and forget for a while—someone besides the servants—that stupid Cathleen!

Now it is true too that the Irish are indefatigably gregarious—witness the people in *Ulysses*. Yet they are capable, especially in an alien environment, of great isolation and loneliness, as *Long Day's Journey* evidences.

For they are most profoundly and primarily committed—to get to my last point—to the family. Everything pales beside the fact of the *family*, which is the macro-microcosm that blots out the universe and takes the place of Hardy's Cosmic Forces, or Marx's march of history, or Shaw's evolutionary powers, or Sinclair Lewis's middle class, or Arthur Miller's "changing America." They are always swarming all over one another, simultaneously loving and torturing each other. They can't leave one another alone, either in love or hate, yet each assault—"you wish I were dead!"—is punctuated by an un-abashed sentiment and humorous affection.

It should be said too that the family swarm produced a violently negative reaction as well (not dealt with by O'Neill in *Long Day's Journey*), just as the religious intensity generated the blasphemy. As in the case of the blasphemous reaction, it was the male who rebelled against the dominion of petticoats and the responsibilities of fatherhood that home and offspring imposed. Some of the violence of this reaction can be gauged from a fact of history, rather than poetry, namely, Stanislaus Joyce's account in *My Brother's Keeper* of his own father's successful flight to freedom and ultimate irresponsibility. When Mrs. Joyce lay dying of cancer, John Joyce blurted at her: "I'm finished. I can't do any more. If you can't get well, die. Die and be damned to you!" And within two years after the mother's death, the family was scattered. "I'll get rid of you all," he would say, "and go back to Cork. But I will break your hearts before I go. Oh yes, by God! See if I don't. I'll break your hearts, but I'll break your stomachs first." He succeeded in divesting himself of his "fleas," as he called them in more jocular moments, and had for himself twenty-six or twenty-seven years of freedom be-fore he died and during which time he frequently complained about his being deserted by his unnatural family. For the pressures of the Irish family seem to lead either to total intimacy or to total estrange-ment.

The peculiarly intimate relationships of the Irish family were given, I think, by two conditions. First of all, it is a democracy in a wild sort of way. These are not parents and children, each with their appropriate range of personality and behavior. They are all *equal*, and can condemn one another openly, irrespective of age or rank. The children are not children but little adults. The adults are not adults but big children. The second factor is that they have no *prohibitory conventions*: that is, there are no agreed-upon prohibi-tions, either in the realm of action or the realm of subject matter. There are no certain things that everybody mutually agrees to keep silent about; there is no norm of conduct beyond which one does not venture. Above all, there is no reticence. Everybody says just what he or she thinks; so that one enormity after another is uttered. Yet so deeply are they involved with and committed to one another that these enormities in reality mean nothing. They pass like the

air that gave them voice. For while the Irish may know that life is
a tragedy—"We begin to live," said Yeats, "when we have conceived life as a tragedy"—they have a deep suspicion that it may
well be—for all they know—a farcical comedy. And against Yeats's
observation we must place the perhaps better known one of George
Bernard Shaw:

> An Irishman's imagination never lets him alone, never
> convinces him, never satisfies him; but it makes him that
> he can't face reality nor deal with it nor handle it nor con-
> quer it: he can only sneer at those that do . . . and imagi-
> nation's such a torture that you can't bear it without
> whiskey. . . . And all the while there goes on a horrible,
> senseless, mischievous laughter.

These two observations, of Yeats and of Shaw, define precisely
the unique quality of the atmosphere in which the Tyrones live,
and O'Neill himself puts both observations in the mouths of the two
characters in the play, the mother and Edmund, who are the most
perceptive and intelligent of the Tyrones. A pessimistic version of
Yeats's observation is put, most appropriately, by the mother:

> None of us can help the things life has done to us. They're
> done before you realize it, and once they're done they make
> you do other things until at last everything comes between
> you and what you'd like to be, and you've lost your true self
> forever.

But Edmund, in the middle of a serious conversation with his father,
makes Shaw's point. The father has just turned out a light bulb, and
Edmund suddenly realizes the humor of the father's stinginess, which
has also caused tragedy:

> *Edmund suddenly cannot hold back a burst of strained,
> ironical laughter. Tyrone is hurt.*

> What the devil are you laughing at?

> EDMUND: Not at you, Papa. At life. It's so damned crazy.

And his own philosophy, which verges upon the old-style O'Neillian
bathos and pseudo-poetry—"I dissolved in the sea, became white sails

and flying spray, became beauty and rhythm . . ."—is saved by irony and humor:

> He grins wryly.

> It was a great mistake, my being born a man, I would have been much more successful as a sea gull or a fish.

And later on he says of himself: "Stammering is the native eloquence of us fog people."

Constantly—except for the mother—they see the wild humor of the tragic or grotesque things that they do. Thus Jamie on the night of the "long day's journey" behaves characteristically; he gets drunk and goes to Mamie Burns's whorehouse, where he picks "Fat Violet," whom Mamie has threatened to fire because she is bad for business; Jamie takes her upstairs and starts reciting "Cynara."

> She stood it for a while. Then she got good and sore. Got the idea I took her upstairs for a joke. Gave me a grand bawling out. Said she was better than a drunken bum who recited poetry. Then she began to cry. So I had to say I loved her because she was fat, and she wanted to believe that, and I stayed with her to prove it, and that cheered her up, and she kissed me when I left, and said she'd fallen hard for me, and we both cried a little more in the hallway, and everything was fine, except Mamie Burns thought I'd gone bughouse.

Jamie continues:

> This night has opened my eyes to a great career in store for me, my boy! I shall give the art of acting back to the performing seals, which are its most perfect expression. By applying my natural God-given talents in their proper sphere, I shall attain the pinnacle of success! I'll be the lover of the fat woman in Barnum and Bailey's circus!

For they are all animated by a tremendous zest for this life that is so terrible for them, whiskey and all. What they fear is madness and death, and what they fear most of all is suicide (both Edmund and the mother had once made attempts). Drink then is a form of suicide, a day-by-day one, a suicide from which one can awake in the morning. Like gambling, it is suicide without death: and it drowns out that senseless, mischievous laughter always going on high in the background.

3

> The peoples of "the Celtic Fringe," with the Atlantic at their backs and a host of formidable aggressors ever bearing down upon them from the Continent, were naturally inspired to seek imaginative relief from the pressure of an adverse human environment by dreaming of an Elysium hidden in the bosom of the Ocean . . .

Thus Toynbee in A *Study of History* on the Celts: the perpetual imaginative escape from the intolerable situation. And it is obvious that most of the characteristics that I, and others, have ascribed to the Irish are the result of a passionate people being imprisoned by an endless stasis: historical, political, religious, cultural, sexual, and personal, with the resulting ambiguity of a people and a culture that is at one and the same time violently rebellious and anarchic and inhumanly passive and acquiescent, given, culturally, to musing over past glories in a dull and tedious present, as in the "Cyclops" episode of *Ulysses,* or given, personally, to mulling over the personal past, its motivations, its mistakes, its total determinism over the present, as do characters of *Long Day's Journey.* This peculiarly retrospective mood under which the past is both a lost and glorious paradise and an unyielding tyrant who has fixed his inflexible and murderous hold upon the present (the mood of Mary Tyrone, in short) can be described in two ways: either it can be called an absence of the sense of time (time means nothing to the Tyrones), or an overly acute sense of the past, which makes *it* the living and the present. Both methods of description have been employed, appropriately enough, by Sean O'Faolain in his two books on Irish character and culture. The lack of a time sense is precisely the feeling that O'Faolain in *The Irish—A Character Study* attributes to the ancient Celt's idea of Paradise: "His [the Celt's] idea of Heaven is free of Time but it is rooted in place." But a stranger entering modern Dublin may think of this sense, as O'Faolain describes it in *The Story of Ireland,* as that of living in the past:

> He [the traveler] soon realizes that there are two clocks in Dublin. Some might say—of this world and the next; it is going far enough to say—of today and a very far-off yester-

day. He will soon come up against an attitude to life that he will call either traditional or antiquated; venerable or primitive, according to his philosophy.

History, collective and individual, is a "nightmare," in Joyce's words, from which nobody can awake.

NOTES

1. Obviously things have changed, as the smiling face of Senator Kennedy on the cover of *Life* or *Time* attests. [This essay was written in 1958.]
2. Since writing this, I have read Agnes Boulton's *Part of a Long Story*, and have learned that Edmund (Eugene) had married and divorced before he married her and before the year in which *Long Day's Journey* takes place. As she says: "Who, having seen *Long Day's Journey into Night*, would ever realize that Edmund, the younger son, had been married and divorced and was the father of a child nearly three years old on that August evening in 1912?" (p. 206). But I think my point still stands.

HUBERT C. HEFFNER

Pirandello and the Nature of Man

The students and critics of Pirandello are almost unanimous in their
assertions that a chief, if not the chief, contribution of his dramatic
works lies in his reevaluation of the nature of man and his reassess-
ment of conceptions of reality. Joseph Wood Krutch, for example,
in his Messenger Lectures delivered at Cornell University in October
of 1952 and later published under the title *"Modernism" in the
Modern Drama*,[1] places Pirandello among the chief four or five
modern dramatists and among the foremost contributors to modernism chiefly because his plays are centrally concerned with the "dissolution of the ego" and hence sets Pirandello centrally in that main
stream of modern thought about the nature of man represented
likewise by the novels of Proust and James Joyce, among others. In
his perceptive analysis he finds Pirandello the most nihilistic of all
the vociferous deniers in modern drama because his plays contain
"the most inclusive denial of all, namely, the denial that the persistent and more or less consistent character or personality which we
attribute to each individual human being, and especially to ourselves,
exists at all." [2] Such a "dissolution of the ego" Krutch points out,
following Pirandello, undermines all moral systems, all attempts to
deal systematically with human life, and, of course, all individual

A lecture delivered at Carleton College, 29 November, 1956. Reprinted from
the *Tulane Drama Review* (I, 3), by permission of the author and the
publisher.

responsibility. Pirandello's conception of the nature of man, or, to be more precise and a bit more inclusive, Pirandello's characterization is important not merely for an understanding of his plays, but also for the contributions of this conception to modern thought and modern literature. The way in which man conceives himself in any age is a determinate of the kind of personality he will develop and the kind of actions he will perform. Pirandello can aid us to an understanding of what modern man thinks himself to be.

We can define all drama as a rendering of a human action by human agents; hence drama is an exploration of the potentialities of human action and an exploration of human character. Drama is the chief art concerned with the relationship of human character to human action, though it shares this consideration of relationship with other literary arts. In drama, however, the characters must stand alone, so to speak, uninterrupted by the comments and interpretations of their author, unanalyzed and unexplained, except only in so far as they are self-explanatory. Drama is, then, the art purely of character in action. As such it is a most significant instrument for understanding the conceptions of the nature of man in each age and each period of our civilization from the ancient Greeks to the present day. I hasten to say that I would not have you think that I am arguing that playwrights alone create these conceptions. While the view of man prevalent in the works of any dramatist is in a certain sense the product of his individual vision, on the other hand he in his characterizations distills, summarizes, and epitomizes the prevalent conceptions of his age arrived at through a variety of sources and influences. Later I shall attempt to show some of the sources and influences operative upon Pirandello in the shaping of his characters.

My purpose in this paper is to examine the nature of character (or, perhaps somewhat more specifically, characterization) in drama in a summary way, to point out some of the differences between dramatic and fictional characters and living personalities, and to account for some of the changes which have occurred in the portrayal of man in modern drama which will aid us in understanding Pirandello's contributions.[3] By way of conclusion I will have some specific statements to make about Pirandello's conception of man.

What is character in drama, or, for that matter, in fiction, such as the short story and the novel? Each of these presents or renders an action by means of human agents. Character is the differentiation of one agent from another agent in the action. This differentiation is accomplished by means of ascribing traits of different kinds to the agents. Any differentiation of agent from agent is therefore characterizing. Man-agent versus woman-agent, which we may call a biological differentiation, is characterizing. The degree of differentiation, hence the degree of characterization, in this instance depends upon the culture in which it occurs.[4] Man-agent versus woman-agent in the United States today—where men and women grow up together, are educated together in the same schools and in the same disciplines, and enter the same professions—is by no means as differentiating as it was in early nineteenth-century America. Nor is it as differentiating with us today as it is in, say, an oriental culture such as that of India. Nevertheless for purposes of the dramatic and fictional rendering of action man-agent versus woman-agent is still with us a character differentiation. This biological difference has been an age-old device out of which comic actions have been contrived. It is an important aspect of serious action in *Antony and Cleopatra* and in *A Doll's House*, to mention only two plays from different ages and dramatists. One of the well-known and ancient devices of comedy, that of dressing a boy in girl's attire or a girl in boy's, hinges upon it. But there is not time now for examining at length the manifold ramifications in drama of this device of characterization. My point here is merely to show that man-agent versus woman-agent, the biological differentiation, represents a category of character traits, a way of characterizing agents in drama. We may say that in terms of the hierarchy of levels of characterization it is a low, but often basic, level of devices.

Another category of character traits on approximately the same level as the biological is the physical. Tall-skinny-man-agent versus short-fat-man-agent is characterizing. Think of the innumerable times that this device of characterization has been employed on the vaudeville stage for comic purposes. Down through the ages obesity has been considered comic and the fat man or fat woman an object of laughter. We need merely recall Falstaff to have a fitting example. In somewhat the same way, though not to the same degree, the thin man has at various times been considered sinister, discontented, dangerous. Do you recall Cassius with the lean and hungry look? The ancient Greeks, a dark-haired Mediterranean people, considered red hair, perhaps associated with ludicrous northern barbarians, funny and passed on to the Romans the red wig as the badge of

the comic slave. The Elizabethans inherited and employed this differentiating device for similar comic purposes and to this day the
red wig, especially in our "Toby shows," is a badge of the comic.
Blond-woman-agent versus brunette-woman-agent has had various
connotations through the history of drama. In the nineteenth century
the blond wig was often the badge of the floozy or the madame. In
the modern age, especially after Anita Loos told us that gentlemen
prefer blonds, the blond has been rehabilitated. Some writers even
speak of a blond or brunette disposition, seeing the physical trait as
a sign of the psychological nature of human beings. You will recall
the hunchback of Richard III, an example of the formerly widely
accepted idea that outward physical deformity was a clear sign of an
inner twisted soul. You may see how important physical traits are
in popular drama if you will note the time and attention that Holly-
wood pays to ideal measurements of the human figure, especially the
female figure. Physical traits include all of the visual aspects of a
character—size, height, coloring, mannerisms of movement, facial
features, costume, and even by extension the quality and tone of the
voice. Some of these physical traits, you will see, are thought of as
permanent traits of the character, others, such as dress, are acquired
traits. All of them, however, when employed by an author or an
actor, are characterizing. Their uses through the ages are so numerous
and varied in drama that I cannot here attempt even to catalogue
them.[5]

The third category of character traits is even more complex and
varied. It is the category of bent or disposition. We often say of a
human being "he was born mean," or "he was born with a happy
disposition." Actually, so modern psychologists assure us, human
bent or disposition is largely acquired in infancy and childhood.
Nevertheless, we consider it a composite of basic distinguishing
qualities inherent in the individual from birth. Iago was born evil;
Falstaff was born with a humorous disposition; Hamlet was born
introspective—if we may speak in this metaphorical manner of
characters in a play who have no actual birth, no actual coming into
this world, as human beings have. It can readily be seen that traits
of bent or disposition are basic qualifications in the separations of
sympathetic and unsympathetic, good and evil characters. Sometimes, and very frequently in popular literature, bent or disposition
is attenuated to mere attitude. This attenuation is frequently all
that is needed for a comic character. Recall the perennial old maid,

the absent-minded professor, the braggart soldier, the miser, the
conventional depiction of the grasping capitalist, the equally conventional picture of the exploited worker, and you will easily recognize bent or disposition attenuated to attitude in their depictions.
Sometimes it is further attenuated to acquired attitude conditioned
by status or profession, of which some in the list already given are
examples. Bent or disposition may be further attenuated to a mere
attribute of luckiness or unluckiness, and the like. Often in detective
stories it is an attribute of a certain kind of skill. These examples
will have to suffice and will serve to show that characterization on
this level is a kind of characterization by classification. Though the
range of possible classifications is potentially very wide, in each age
a relatively few conventional classifications attain popularity and
hold the stage. When these become outmoded and are replaced by
newer classifications, the resulting characters seem quite modern and
original.[6]

A yet more complex and more highly formal category of character
results from characterization by traits of feeling, emotion, passion.
This is a more highly formal level because emotion can result
directly in action. We readily recognize feelings and emotions as
driving forces in human action and equally readily recognize the
emotional makeup or emotional pattern as a distinctive attribute of
a human being's personality. Sometimes in a human being and in a
fictional character as well the emotional needs and drives of the
character may be epitomized as his desires, what he wants most,
what he is by his feelings forced to try to get. Traits of emotion
and passion may serve to render serious or comic characterizations.
Not all characters in drama are characterized in terms of intense
passion; nor is it necessary that they should be. In some characters
the traits of passion enter hardly or not at all; in others it is attenuated to mere vague feeling or slight reactions to other characters.
Passion has its moral valuation, though the valuation may change
from culture to culture. A desire for revenge, for example, among
the Elizabethans was viewed differently from our present attitude.
Sexual passion as a device in characterization has undergone considerable change along with our changing conceptions of the relationships of men and women. With the Greek dramatists it was
dominantly a ludicrous passion; with Shakespeare and especially with
Racine we see it utilized in serious characterizations.

Passion epitomized as desire may, if not immediately gratified, lead to deliberation, the fifth category of character traits. Deliberation may take either one or both of two forms: It may be expedient deliberation about ways and means, or it may be ethical deliberation, about right and wrong. The latter kind, ethical deliberation, occurs only in serious drama, for when the ethical aspect of a desire or a potential action is considered the character making such a deliberation thereby becomes serious. On the other hand, a wide variety of expedient deliberations may be found in comedy and comic characterizations. Even pseudo-ethical deliberations may be used in comedy. Witness Falstaff's famous deliberation on honor. Significant ethical deliberation represents a very high level of characterization found only in great tragedy. Its employment as a device of characterization renders man in one of the highest aspects of human character, the intellectual, an aspect that distinguishes him from all other animals.

Deliberation leads to decision, to choice, the highest level of characterization and the final category of character traits. Decision is the highest level, for it is that point at which all of the qualifications, the qualifying traits, of character become, as it were, action. In a good characterization an exercise of the will is conditioned and motivated by all of the lesser character traits. These traits of bent or attitude, emotion, and deliberation determine the kinds of choices the character will make; and choice is the most highly characterizing, the most completely differentiating of all of the aspects of character. Like deliberation, choice may be either expedient or ethical or both. Ethical choice makes the resultant action serious; hence is found only in serious drama. Expedient choice is found in both serious and comic drama. Choice may eventuate in change of attitude, in words, or in physical deeds. It may eventuate in all of these. Frequently only that eventuation in physical deeds is called action; but this is wrong. In drama any exercise of the will, however it eventuates, is action. And this exercise of the will, this deliberate choice or failure to choose is the most complete differentiation of agent from agent that a dramatist can employ.

This quick summary of the hierarchy of character traits should serve to reveal that character in drama is a deliberately made thing, an artificial thing made through the artifice of the playwright and the actor. It is not the same as personality in life, though both playwright and actor often strive deliberately to make character in drama seem exactly like personality in life. Herein lies an important aspect of Pirandello's representation of man. Through modern science, especially psychology and anthropology, through modern philosophies, such as the philosophy of Bergson, and especially through the modern naturalistic theory of art Pirandello came to see that man in life represents a variety of roles, including the role of himself as he sees himself and the roles that his fellow men thrust upon him. Moreover, he had come to see that human personality, made up of these various roles, is in a constant state of change. It will help us better to understand Pirandello's point of view and to grasp one of his constant concerns in characterization if we contrast character in drama with personality in life. Allow me in this contrast to restrict the term character to drama and fiction, to the made thing, and the term personality to living man. We sometimes use the word character to apply to living human beings much as we use it in drama as, for example, when we say of some eccentric fellow "that man is a character." When we say, on the other hand, he is a man of high character, we are using the word character to evaluate personality.

The term *persona*, from which we derive personality, is a Greek word employed originally to mean a mask, such as was used in the Etruscan farces. Apparently this mask had in its mouthpiece a kind of megaphone through which the actor wearing the mask spoke, hence the derivation of the term "persona" from "personare," which means literally to sound through. By metonymic change "persona" referred, almost from its origin, not entirely to the vocal aspect but rather more fully to the visual aspect of the mask. In transition the word changed in reference to the sounding voice, to designate the appearance of the mask worn, and finally to a general term which signified the character portrayed.

Though some philologists object to this derivation of the term, we are on surer grounds when we come to the Latin usage by such writers as Cicero. In his writing the term is employed with four slightly different but connected meanings. In his usage *Persona* means, first, as one appears to others but not as one really is. Secondly, it means the part some one, a philosopher or statesman, plays in life. Third, it was used to designate an assemblage of personal qualities which fitted a man for his particular work in life. Fourth, it designated a certain distinction and dignity, as, for example, a style in writing. The church Fathers borrowed the Latin usage and employed in certain of their writings the term to designate the

Trinity. By the third century the term had become widely used in the plural to designate the three persons in the Trinity. Long speculations and discussion over the question whether God would have to abandon two roles in assuming a third role of the Trinity led to the identification of *persona* with substance rather than with appearance. Therein lies the modern basis of our usage to designate the inner reality of a human being by the term personality. On the basis of this theological usage Boethius could thus define *persona*: "Persona est substantia individua rationalis naturae." Thus Boethius takes the substantial nature of person for granted and distinguishes it with the attribute of rationality. He was followed by a long line of later philosophers. Thus John Locke, coming after the great changes in scientific thinking, still defines a person as follows:

> a thinking, intelligent being, that has reason and reflection and can consider self as itself.

Though Locke here emphasizes intelligence, he even more than Leibnitz stressed the element of self consciousness as the central attribute of personality.[7] Time will not permit us to follow the ramifications of changing meaning in the term which led to the idealization of the conception of personality found in Romanticism and the romantic philosophy. Thus Kant could say in his *Critique of Practical Reason:*

> Everything in creation, except one thing, is subject to the power of man, and can be used by man as a means to an end; but man himself, man the rational creature, is an end in himself. He is the subject of moral law and is sacred by virtue of the autonomy of his individual freedom.

This idealization of personality accounts for the emphasis placed upon character by romantic critics, such as Goethe, Coleridge, and their host of later followers. You have but to recall the approach to Shakespeare and the emphasis of romantic critics from Coleridge to Bradley to see the way in which this conception of personality with its attendant stress upon character in drama underlies the modern misconception that character and not plot is the chief part of drama.

Against this romantic conception of a sacred and ego-centered rational personality the naturalists of the late nineteenth century rebelled. The naturalistic conception of man and the naturalistic philosophy of art are both directly derived from the naturalists' reliance upon the new discoveries and hypotheses of biological science, represented by Darwin and his followers. The hypotheses of biological science, and especially the hypothesis that the physical nature of animate species is rigidly determined by a process of mutation strictly controlled by heredity and environment, an hypothesis seemingly irrefutably confirmed by Darwin, was applied to sociological phenomena. Out of this application arose modern sociology, modern psychology, the deterministic philosophy, and naturalism in art. Taine and Zola in France were, as you know, among the first to apply the new scientific principles to art and literature. It was Zola who gave the name naturalism to this new aesthetics. According to this naturalistic aesthetic and its underlying deterministic philosophy man and his personality are as rigidly determined by heredity and environment as are the physical structures of animate material objects. The romantic conception of a sacred personality, ego-centered, with a self-originating will is, according to the naturalist, a delusion; hence man's independent choices are likewise delusions. Man in all the aspects of his personality is rigidly determined by his genes and by his environment. In the strict sense therefore man cannot be held morally accountable for his actions. Basically he is merely a higher animal more complexly conditioned with a more complexly developed nervous system than those of other animals. We shall return to naturalism, its influence upon drama and its effects upon Pirandello presently. Let us now proceed with the brief contrast of personality and character.

A personality is an indefinite quantum of traits which is subject to constant flux, change, and growth from the birth of the individual in the world to his death. A character, on the other hand is a fixed and definite quantum of traits which, though it may be interpreted with slight differences from age to age and actor to actor, is nevertheless in its essentials forever fixed. In so far as character is fixed and definite, its actions can be determined in a way that is not strictly true of a personality. A character is shaped and determined towards a given end; that is, the character is what it is because of its function in a specific kind of action. A playwright assigns qualities and traits to a character in a play in order to make probable the actions which he must perform in the play and the words which he must say. The function of the character in the whole action determines the traits and characteristics which he must have. No human being is so teleologically determined. In the beginning of a human personality the totality of his life cannot be known in the way in which a playwright knows the totality of action which a character must perform in a play. In life personality precedes and determines actions; whereas in drama action, as it were, precedes and determines the form of the character. As an illustration of this, let us assume that when Shakespeare sat down to revise the old Kydian *Hamlet* he had said to himself: "This is old-fashioned, outdated drama. I can't really make a tragedy that will appeal to contemporary audiences out of it. I know what I'll do. I'll write a comic burlesque of the whole revenge tragedy type." What would have happened to the characterization of Prince Hamlet in such a rendering?

Characters in drama are limited in yet another way that is not usually true of human personalities. They have only a single age and a brief moment upon the stage. Hamlet has no youth (except for the one brief moment in the Graveyard when he recalls riding upon the back of Yorick) and no old age. Lear has no youth and no middle-age, only old age. Macbeth has no youth and no old age, only middle-age. Othello has maturity but hardly any youth and no old age. A full, human personality changes from infancy to old age.

A human personality changes in yet another way. Assume that two close friends with compatible personalities were conversing intimately together. Now assume that a third individual with a personality antagonistic of each of these two enters. You can readily imagine various adjustments that occur within the personalities of the three individuals in such situations. A human personality has the power of constantly changing adjustments to other personalities; hence we can say that, chameleon like, it changes coloring with each personality with whom it comes into contact. The personality response of a character to other characters is, however, forever fixed. The reactions of Hamlet to Polonius cannot change.

Human personalities subtly shift and adjust according to the roles an individual is called upon to assume. A man as husband and father in a household exhibits a somewhat different personality than that which he assumes as the head of a big business, or as a good club member among congenial club mates, or as a leading citizen participating in an important town meeting. Moreover, the per-

sonality of father as each of the children sees him differs from the
personality of husband as the wife sees him. If he begins to play
the role of big-business leader to his wife and children in the intimacy of his home, he becomes ludicrous and if he persists in such
an incongruous confusion of his roles, he may well end upon a psychiatrist's couch or even in an institution. Sanity consists in being
able to discriminate among the various roles we are called upon to
play and in playing them properly at the appropriate times.[8] There
is really no such complexity of roles required of any character in
drama, though Pirandello and other modern dramatists, cognizant
of this complexity in life, have tried to give a slight similarity to
certain of their characters. In drama, however, a character is more
restricted in both feeling and in function than is a personality.
Usually a character is mde up of one or a few dominant emotions
or passions and has a singleness of purpose not allowed to man.

These differences between character and personality are usually
unknown to audiences. Indeed, the aim of the playwright and the
actor is often to obscure or hide them altogether. Likewise they
are frequently obscured in critical writings because of the assumption that art and nature, art and life are essentially the same.
Naturalism reiterated this ancient fallacy, holding that a play should
be a mere *tranche de vie*, a mere slice of life scientifically observed
and objectively set down. Plot, usually thought of in the late nineteenth century as the contrivances of the well-made play, must be
dispensed with and in its place a mere chronological ordering of
the incidents must be subordinated to the chief thing, character.[9]
A play should be neither a comedy nor a tragedy but, like life, a
mingling of both. Other concomitant ideas of naturalistic art, resulting from the more or less general acceptance of deterministic
philosophy, included an emphasis upon meticulous observation and
faithful rendering of objective details of environment, a preference
for characters from humble life and even from degraded social
status, a consequent deep concern about social conditions and social
problems and a tendency to embrace the kindred Marxian doctrine
of social determinism and dialectical materialism, and, to end this
catalogue, a preference for common speech, idiomatic, and even
dialectical expression. Much as naturalism owed to romanticism,
the naturalists were nevertheless often violently anti-romantic and
staunchly anti-theatrical. They were especially opposed to the theatrical conventions, patterns, and devices exemplified in the Scribean

well-made plays, that whole complex of dramatic conventions which Shaw called "Sardoodledom."

Pirandello began his career as a writer in the Italian school of naturalism known as "Verism," which, though it differed somewhat from northern naturalism owed its essential tenets to much the same cluster of scientific and philosophic ideas. But even in his naturalistic period he was attracted away from complete preoccupation with the external and objective aspects of reality towards the inner nature of man. As early as 1904, in his novel, *Mattia Pascal*, in which an unhappy husband pretends to drown himself and assumes a new personality only to find that the new personality eventually becomes as burdensome as the old, this concern with the inner nature of personality manifests itself. Under the impetus of this interest he finally became identified with the new school of the "Grotesque," initiated by Chiarelli and allied to French "symbolism" and German "Expressionism." Perhaps, as Domenico Vittorini says in his *The Drama of Luigi Pirandello*, his first play unmistakably to show the influence of the grotesque is *Cap and Bells*, which appeared in 1915.[10] In that play a ludicrously ugly old man is completely adjusted to marriage with a pretty young woman who is deceiving him with his wealthy and influential employer. So long as this situation is not generally known, the ugly Ciampa can continue to play his role and wear his mask of husband before the public. But the jealous wife of the employer, Donna Beatrice, insists upon exposing it by having her husband arrested in the home of his mistress and thereby brings near ruin to both husbands. In the end Ciampa insists that the only way to save the situation and allow him to resume his mask and former role in society is for the wife to pretend insanity and enter an institution. Though this play is still strongly naturalistic, in it is the familiar Pirandello concern with personality as the role or roles, which human beings play in life and also the idea that insanity itself may be merely another kind of role.

Such an idea appears even more prominently in his famous play, *Henry IV* (1922), in which a young man on his way to a masquerade ball suffers an injury at the hands of a jealous rival that renders him temporarily unbalanced. In his unbalanced condition he imagines that he is Henry IV, Emperor of Germany, humiliated by Pope Gregory VII. His family humor his illusion and hire attendants to play the roles of confidential friends and retainers. Henry's sister, suspecting his ruse, on her death bed exacts a promise from her son to have his uncle examined by an alienist. With the alienist come the rival, the woman whom Henry loved, and her daughter to Henry's "castle," dressed in a manner to befit his mad illusion. The alienist plans to shock Henry into a realization of the passage of time by confronting him with both mother and daughter at the propitious moment. In that moment Henry stabs his old rival and as a consequence, though he has been entirely sane for some time, must now go on to the end of his life pretending insanity. This situation gives Pirandello opportunities to present dramatically some favorite ideas about the nature of sanity and insanity, about the enigma of personality, about the nature of reality, and about time. The ideas of personality and the illusion of reality likewise appear in two other plays that belong to the year 1922; namely, in *Right You Are if You Think You Are* and in *Naked*, but are by no means restricted to these plays.

Perhaps Pirandello's most famous play and best known representation of these ideas is *Six Characters in Search of An Author*, produced in 1921. Actually among the characters there are seven, including six members of a family and Madame Pace, the brothel keeper. The paradoxically ludicrous situation of these six discarded characters interrupting a rehearsal and demanding to be heard and the grotesquely sordid but fragmentary story of their lives which they insist upon telling would be entirely comic if Pirandello did not with considerable artistry and skill make us glimpse in the telling the sufferings of these characters in their complicated relationships. That this inextricable mingling of the grotesque and the sad, the humorous and the tragic, was an important part of Pirandello's vision of life we know not only from his plays but also from his impressive treatise entitled *Humor* (*Umorismo*) published in 1908.

Let us briefly review some of the comic aspects of the play. To begin, the paradoxical idea that characters have an independent existence apart from the author who conceives them, can come upon a stage of their own volition, interrupt a rehearsal, demand to act out their fragmentary story, and argue with live human beings the nature of personality and existence is a magnificently comic paradox akin in degree to, say, the comic paradox of Aristophanes in *Lysistrata* that sex starvation may make men stop fighting and end a war. But Pirandello was not an Aristophanes nor a Molière. Even the characters in their traits are from one aspect comic. The over-intellectual husband whose warped sense of integrity perhaps partially motivated his handing over of his meek and peasant-like wife to a supposedly more congenial soul mate, the husband's secretary, but who afterwards could not make a clean break away but hovers over the new family like a mother-hen over a brood of goslings, is certainly in large part comic. With all of his assumed dignity, sensitivity, and constant philosophizing, this intellectual, forced by the common call of lower animal nature, must resort to a brothel. The elder son of the mother and the first husband is surely in his absurd and supercilious disdain of the mother and her second family entirely comic, even absurd. The elder daughter, with all of her loathing of the actions that fate has thrust upon her, is nevertheless absurdly shrill in her desires to tell her story and to bring remorse to the father. Even the mother, pathetic as she is made, has a large admixture of absurdity in her character, especially in her relations to the elder son. The perplexities and exasperations of the Manager and his constant frustrations by the "Characters" are wholly ludicrous, entirely laughable, though they give rise to serious arguments about such things as personality and the nature of reality. In the same way, the contrasts between stage conventions and the real, such as is represented, for example, in the scene in which the actors attempt to portray the "Characters," is also fully comic, though again it is a loaded device whereby Pirandello comments upon the differences between art and reality and takes satiric thrusts at the romantic concoctions seemingly preferred by audiences. Even the absurd deaths of the two children among the Characters is lacking in the genuine seriousness of death and seem largely incidents contrived to give the Characters something to talk and be sad about. Certainly they could not have been genuine deaths as we know death, for here these children are again, ready to re-enact their stories. The very device that Pirandello uses of having the Manager constantly question the Characters' assertions that they are characters serves to give a comic twist to the whole. Madame Pace and her dialect are, in the original Italian especially, wholly comic. Time does not permit a fuller catalogue of the comic elements and devices scattered throughout this play. We must now turn to some of the ideas in it, ideas which are frequently in themselves paradoxically absurd, yet significant in relation to Pirandello's conceptions of reality and personality.

I have already mentioned the idea of characters created by an author having an independent existence and a life apart from the imagination that gave them shape. That there is an element of truth in this contention will be recognized if we reflect for a moment upon the existence and persistence of a Hamlet, a Falstaff, a Romeo, a Medea, and a Clytemnestra. The Father asserts that a character such as he is has more reality in that he has definiteness and permanence than has a living personality which is constantly changing. As the Father says:

> THE FATHER (with dignity, but not offended): A character, sir, may always ask a man who he is. Because a character has really a life of his own, marked with especial characteristics; for which reason he is always "somebody." But a man —I'm not speaking of you now—may very well be "nobody."

> THE MANAGER: Yes, but you are asking these questions of me, the boss, the manager! Do you understand?

> THE FATHER: But only in order to know if you, as you really are now, see yourself as you once were with all the illusions that were yours then, with all the things both inside and outside of you as they seemed to you—as they were then indeed for you. Well, sir, if you think of all those illusions that mean nothing to you now, all of those things that don't even *seem* to you to exist any more, while once they *were* for you, don't you feel that . . . the very earth under your feet is sinking away from you when you reflect that this *you* as you feel it today—all this present reality of yours—is fated to seem a mere illusion to you tomorrow?

I have quoted this passage from the third act in its entirety because I think you will recognize the semantic shifts in words so characteristic of Pirandello in his enigmatic treatments of personality and reality. A character is further a "somebody" in the Father's terms because it is the embodiment and epitome of one supreme passion. Yet the Father recognizes the multiplicity in character when he insists that his whole being must not be judged in terms of that one aspect of his character uppermost in his conduct in the brothel. He recognizes that there is himself as he sees himself and himself as the daughter sees him. Through this and a variety of other characters in other plays Pirandello advanced the idea of complex and changing character and raised the question of the centrality of the ego amidst such constant flux.

Yet another important idea is the conception of reality and illusion, to which is related also some of the statements in this play about art and drama. The conception that reality as we perceive it is a kind of illusion is certainly as old as Plato's famous metaphorical symbol of the cave in his *Phaedrus*. It was reinforced in the Lockean philosophy of the late seventeenth century. On the basis of the science of Galileo and Newton, Locke posited a material universe of solid objects existing in mathematical space and time. These objects in their essential essence, however, were not perceivable to the sense organs of man. We may, for purpose of understanding, analogize that conception of matter as motion to our conception of matter as composed of atoms not directly perceptible to our sight, touch, taste, smell, or hearing. When any of the objects of the irrefutable material universe impinged upon the consciousness of man, according to Locke and other philosophers of his age, we then saw or apprehended through one of the senses that object not as it actually is within mathematical space and time, but as illusion. Our sense perception of the material universe is, then, according to Locke and other philosophers, an illusion of the actual reality that makes up this material universe. Thus the ancient doctrine of reality as an illusion is brought once again centrally within man's conception and this time is based upon seemingly irrefutable scientific evidence. Pirandello through his training in philosophy at the University of Bonn was well aware of this philosophic doctrine of reality, and especially conversant with its later development and extension in the idealistic philosophy of Kant and Hegel. You can readily understand, as did Pirandello, that in our world of illusion the nature and characteristics of what we understand as reality hinge upon the nature of the perceiver; hence Pirandello examines in play after play the ancient question: "What is Man?"

I have attempted by my previous discussion to throw some light upon the answers which Pirandello tried to give to this question. Though the answers are repeated and reiterated in play after play, they did grow and develop as Pirandello's thinking changed. We have no time here to examine that development but in conclusion I will state certain prominent aspects of Pirandello's conception of man. Man is born into this world as man, rather than as a plant or a beast, by mere chance. His conscious will has no power over his coming hither or his going hence. With plant and beast he shares the essential characteristic of instinct but the very nature of his instinct gives rise to the development of intellect. Intellect will not let man live in joyous abandonment to instinct such as it allows plants and animals. But instinct continuously asserts itself in man's passions and intellect causes man to feel a sense of guilt in yielding to passions. Man has of himself a painfully limited knowledge, which in most men extends only or largely to their material aspects, their bodies, their worldly possessions, their social relations. The personality of man is not only "immobilized" in his self conception, it is also immobilized in the conception of him which each of his friends and acquaintances has of him. Man as personality is therefore complex and is subject to constant changes. In like manner his emotions and feelings become set and conventionalized in molds that tragically dwarf human sentiment. Deep within man there are desires, needs, and emotions that he hardly dares express to himself and when these become evident, a consequent sense of guilt inevitably follows. Though we grow up with a belief that we are one and individual, life proves to the intellectual man that this belief is not true. Nevertheless, closed within our subjectivism, we interpret the acts of others in our own terms and our own words. This subjective isolation leaves us no direct contact with the consciousness of others. This creature of instinct and intellect cannot live in harmony with a serene nature, for nature is neither serene nor always friendly. It is all too often "red in tooth and claw," man's destroyer as well as man's nurturer. Even man's modern civilization built by a compulsive drive is merely a device by which he attempts to escape his torment of intellect. Man as instinct attempting through intellect to transcend bodily wants and emotional demands reminds us of Plato's psychology of the soul, but for Plato man could attain salvation through intellect reigning supreme over will. But for Pirandello the drama often begins when instinct has lost its youthful and impetuous drive under the cold, dissecting analysis of intellect; hence in many of his characters only reason, such as it is, dominates. In character after character this reason is rendered as a perplexed state of mind, which, as in the case of Hamlet, corrodes the will. Yet will there is in these characters, limited as it may be, otherwise they could not act. Through intellect and will man sometimes attains a vision of lofty reality. As one of the characters says in *Each in His Own Way*: "We have all seen, in certain moments, appear and kindle within us a light that seems to emanate from the skies—which permits us to gaze into the most profound depths of our souls and gives us the infinite joy of feeling ourselves lost in a moment of eternity—eternal without it." Somewhere deep within man, then, there is a soul capable of visioning higher reality. It is this vision that in large measure tempers the pessimism of Pirandello. We might well call him, as Vittorini does, a disillusioned idealist.

That "dissolution of the ego," which Krutch, Adriano Tilgher, and others find the distinctive contribution of Pirandello to modern drama is, then, on closer inspection, somewhat like reality to certain Pirandellean characters, something of an illusion. The ego does not disappear in Pirandello's characters; it grows more complex, taking on some of the aspects of change which we find in human personality. In that change the character is constantly asking who am I but he is always sure there is an I, different as the I of today is from the previous I's which he has known. Moreover, the I in various characters has bent or attitude, passion and desire, deliberation, and expedient decision; hence Pirandello's characters act, suffer, and react.

Yet, despite their suffering and their pathos, Pirandello refuses to make his characters tragic protagonists or outright comic figures. As a result, his plays are neither genuine comedies nor complete tragedies; they are, rather, a mingling of the two forms. This sadness in mirth and mirth in sadness was, Pirandello believed, the condition of life itself. The ancient fallacy that held art and nature, art and life, to be the same thing, reinforced by modern naturalism, accounts for this failure in no small measure, a failure which Pirandello shares with other modern dramatists. But the failure goes deeper than a mere confusion of art and nature and is, I believe, ultimately based upon Pirandello's conception of man. That conception, as I have tried to indicate, is ambivalent. Pirandello could not see man as consistently significant or noble enough for sustained tragedy, nor ludicrous enough for pure comedy. Man is for him indeed common man, all too common. We might conclude by saying that man for Pirandello is a human animal with a proletarian soul.

NOTES

1. (Ithaca, New York: Cornell University Press, c. 1953.) Krutch's book is, as he himself indicates in his "Foreword," an argument to a thesis. He is concerned with defining "modernism" by exploring and exposing

an aspect, the nihilism or denying spirit, which characterizes it most specifically in the author's opinion. In a sense these lectures are a continuation of Krutch's earlier *The Modern Temper*, first published in 1929 by Harcourt, Brace and Company, and recently reissued in their paperback "Harvest Books" series. Since Krutch is propounding only one specific interpretation of "Modernism" in his discussion of modern playwrights, it is not surprising that other aspects, sometimes contradictory aspects, of their works should not appear in his discussion.

2. P. 77. Krutch's argument that Pirandello represents in drama ". . . the denial that the persistent and more or less consistent character or personality which we attribute to each individual human being, and especially to ourselves, exists at all" must not be construed as Pirandello's total contribution to the depiction of the nature of man. That this "dissolution of the ego" is to be found in many Pirandello plays is unquestionable; yet what a paradox Pirandello, who delights in paradoxes, made of this! Take as an example the play to be produced, *Six Characters in Search of an Author*, of which this lecture is a kind of prologue. In that play seven, not six, characters of their own volition come upon a stage and insist upon acting out their life stories. There is in all drama no more complete exhibition of the centrality of ego as will. If by ego is meant (1) the consciousness of one's self as an entity, (2) "the self-assertive and self-preserving tendency, as distinguished from the *libido*, and (3) volition or will as the highest manifestation of ego, how could a dramatist more forcefully and more powerfully demonstrate the supremacy and persistence of ego than by having characters, so to speak, generate themselves? In this play the seven characters quite independently of the author who originally conceived them, bring themselves into being and argue with "living" human beings not in the context of their original lives nor in the context of their original organic actions. They are capable of conducting an argument and getting the better of that argument about matters for which they were not initially conceived. In this play, then, Pirandello is presenting an argument for the persistence of personality which Krutch in his concentration upon the "dissolution of the ego" overlooks or rather does not find pertinent to the thesis which he is expounding. It must, therefore, be inferred that Pirandello's contributions to a conception of the nature of man goes beyond the nihilism represented in this one aspect of his characterization.

3. What is here said of character and characterization is taken from a chapter of an extended study, "Character in Drama," upon which I have been engaged for a number of years. Some parts of that work have been issued to former students in mimeographed form.

4. The six categories of character traits enumerated in the following discussion are hierarchical. In the construction of character they have a matter-form relationship; hence they have a material and a formal

causal relation. They correspond roughly to the six parts (plot, character, thought, diction, music, spectacle) of a play as a whole but only roughly. For example, the biological and the physical traits are rendered in spectacle; attitude, emotion, and deliberation require diction and thought; decision is rendered in action.

5. In the extended study, "Character in Drama," I have collected and analyzed a far wider range of physical traits, as well as traits belonging to other categories. In this discussion I am concerned with a distinction between personality and character and have therefore limited the illustration of characterization to the briefest possible summary. The distinction between character as a made thing and personality in a living human being is necessary to understand what Pirandello was attempting to do in his characterizations and to clarify his contributions to a conception of man.

6. Dr. Willard Welsh in his unpublished doctoral dissertation on the characterization of the protagonist in serious American drama from approximately 1870 to 1920, presented at Stanford University, has shown that even in depicting serious characters American dramatists have relied chiefly on traits that belong to the biological, physical, and attitude or bent categories; that such deliberation as does occur in these plays tends usually to be merely expedient deliberation; and that truly moral deliberation and choice are largely absent. It is not surprising, therefore, that the majority of these plays tend towards melodrama in form.

7. A more extended, though still concise, summary of the use of the term personality may be found in Gordon W. Allport, *Personality: A Psychological Interpretation* (New York: Henry Holt and Company, c1937). See also Adolf Trendelenburg, *Contributions to the History of the Word Persona* (Chicago: Open Court Publishing Company, 1910); Alfred E. Briggs, *The Concept of Personality* (Los Angeles: University of Southern California Press, 1935), primarily concerned with the term in the legal sense; Ralph Linton, *The Cultural Background of Personality* (New York: Appleton-Century-Crofts, Inc., c1945), an anthropological interpretation; Clyde Kluckhorn and Henry A. Murray, *Personality in Nature, Society, and Culture* (New York: Alfred A. Knopf, 1948). There is, of course, a very extensive literature in the fields of psychology, sociology, and cultural anthropology dealing with personality. So far as I am aware no previous attempt has been made to differentiate clearly between character and personality. Most literary studies tacitly assume the terms to be synonymous, thereby introducing a considerable confusion into the discussion of character. In the case of Shakespearean criticism this confusion has been noted by Levin L. Schücking and E. E. Stoll in their various studies.

8. See Ralph Linton, *The Cultural Background of Personality*, for a fuller

analysis of the roles which a culture and a society impose upon an individual.

9. For an admirable setting forth in English of the naturalistic theory of drama see John Galsworthy, "Some Platitudes Concerning the Drama," published in his *The Inn of Tranquility and Other Essays.*

10. I am under considerable indebtedness to Vittorini's excellent study, published by the University of Pennsylvania Press in 1935.

FREDERIC JAMESON

The Problem of Acts

No Exit is without what is ordinarily called action: the characters
are no longer able to do anything, they have done it all before the
curtain rises, and they are obliged to spend the time of the play
simply thinking about what has already been done once and for all,
without being able to add to it. This is why, in a kind of gross common sense distinction based on an entertainment aesthetic, such
plays have been described as "idea-plays." Yet the "ideas" of this
philosopher's play are wholly different in quality from the thoughts
developed in the philosophical works. There also acts are analyzed,
are raised to a meaning; but this phenomenological analysis is ex-
pansive, centrifugal: it attempts to enlarge itself with more and more
detail until the act has been shown to be the mere central complex
of a large and intrinsically intelligible unity, and its isolation to be
illusory. The characters of this play think about their pasts in the
other direction: they want to reduce the things they have done to
mere examples of qualities, to be able to fix names and adjectives
to them; the meanings they are looking for have a solid and indispensable core of language. The source of these meanings is popular
everyday value judgment: bravery, cowardice, goodness, evil, mutually exclusive alternates; so that a character like Garcin is imprisoned
in his very thought about himself and his life. He faces a kind of

From *Sartre: The Origins of a Style*, Yale University Press, New Haven,
1961. Reprinted by permission.

schoolbook proposition about himself: that he is a coward; and the only choice he seems to have is to affirm it or deny it. The level on which such problems are posed is in appearance much more primitive than the kinds of consciousness registered by earlier modern writers; and the only possible expression of such a dilemma seems to be talk, the posing of the various alternatives or the settling for one or the other of them.

The image around which the play is organized, the notion of a hell or limbo of this kind, suggests another possible relationship to the past at the same time that it eliminates it as a real issue: Garcin is painfully aware that if he had lived, he would have been able to do something different, he would have had at least the possibility of setting an act of a new quality against the repetitive examples of his past weakness. This act would in no sense have changed the facts of his life, would not even have permitted us to "forget" about them. It would have merely rearranged them, organized them in a new way, and the weight of the new act would have gradually swung these older facts out of the pattern of simple cowardice and lent them the value of mere passing errors, accidents, corrected failings. This suggests that the past can be described in two different ways: it is that which can no longer be changed, which has passed out of reach, still felt as ourselves but fixed forever; and yet at the same time it is constantly subject to change and renewal at our hands: its meaning is as fluid as our freedom and every new thing we do threatens to revalue it from top to bottom. The aspect of the past which is changeless is what Sartre calls our "facticity," but it is only one way in which facticity manifests itself, along with the genetic structure of our bodies and the necessity for us to exist at a given moment of history in a given society, although there is no reason why it should be this one rather than that, any more than there is any reason why our unique consciousness should "inhabit" a body of this particular shape and be born of these particular parents. Facticity is that core of being which resists any reduction to thought, to reasons; it is the necessity for every phenomenon, no matter how intelligible it may be, to be at the same time absolutely unique; it is the necessity for us to be always "in situation," without its making any difference what that situation may be, for us to always have a past no matter what its contents are. Garcin recognizes his past as *his* through the anxiety it causes him, but it is not his to alter any more than he can rearrange the bones of his face by thinking about it. We will come to see later just how heavy with consequences such an idea is for the work of art.

Yet although the meaning of these brute irrevocable facts might be somehow altered by a new act, although no failure is enough to definitively rule out the possibility of change but merely pushes it further into the future, there is no future in terms of the situation of the play and Garcin is dead. He is thus reduced to a purely contemplative attitude toward his own life, he is passive before it, he can only think about it; and in some ways the secret theme of the play is a kind of symbolic playing out of the opposition between a philosophy of knowledge and a philosophy of consciousness or action, between an impressionistic and an expressionistic aesthetic. Garcin is left with nothing but "psychological analyses" of himself: he cannot act, he cannot change the facts, the only area of uncertainty accessible to him, where he might find something to help him resolve his problems one way or the other, is that of his "motives":

> ESTELLE: But you ought to remember; you must have had reasons for doing what you did.
>
> GARCIN: Yes.
>
> ESTELLE: Well?
>
> GARCIN: Are they the real reasons?
>
> ESTELLE: *(annoyed)* How complicated you are.
>
> GARCIN: I wanted to set an example . . . I had given it a lot of thought . . . Are those the real reasons? [1]

This importance of the motive is part of a dialectic of good and bad intentions that goes back at least as far as medieval Christian thought; but in it the act is so thoroughly separated from its motive (which can be of another quality) that there is no way back from the motive to the act: the "reason," or all the different possible ones, come loose from the act, fall into subjectivity while the act remains resisting and impenetrable. Any of the motives seems to fit because there is nothing in the act itself that can stand in a privileged relationship to this one rather than that. The world of motivations becomes autonomous, a kind of self-sufficient mirage reflecting the solid world of facts upside down, and in this unreal psychological world, against the perspective of a past out of the reach of change, subjective decisions suddenly seem to enjoy far more authority than they did in "real life":

> GARCIN: Estelle, am I a coward?

> ESTELLE: How would I know, my love, I'm not in your skin. You have to decide for yourself.

> GARCIN: *(with a gesture of weariness)* That's just what I don't manage to do.[2]

This suggestion of the possibility of a fiat, of a purely intellectual decision settling the problem once and for all, is an optical illusion brought on by the terms in which the problem has been posed. Not only is change impossible in the purely contemplative conditions of this limbo, but the very judgments themselves: bravery, cowardice, will not work from the inside. They are in their very nature the judgments of other people, fixed to the outside of the individual consciousness with the verb to be. They suggest a convenient reduction of consciousness to a set of qualities or attributes, conveniences for the purpose of predicting behavior, parts of the describable nature of these things which are other people for us. But such "qualities" are impossible to feel from the inside because consciousness never "is" anything, but is always action. Only when we gaze back at the feared similarity of all the things we have done with each other does the impression of a kind of "quality" arise; but we do not feel it directly, we deduce its presence just as if we were looking at the acts of someone else. Yet the alienation of these characters is so complete that the judgments have been passionately interiorized, raised to absolutes before which in vain they try to justify themselves. Their lives after death are the most intense image of lives surrendered wholly into other people's hands—the hands of the living; and no single corner of their minds is safe from these autonomous categories of "objective" social values. It is at this point that the possibility of abandoning such worn-out categories suggests itself, that the possibility of a kind of "authenticity" arises; and it is at this point also that most of Sartre's works stop—with the emergence of freedom at the end of *The Flies*, of the social solidarity of *Lucifer and the Lord*, with the promise of a theory of values at the end of *Being and Not-Being*. For here the problem of individual life can no longer be isolated from the society in which it is to be lived, and is suddenly subordinate to history and the problem of social change.

The play consists therefore of a language in a void, of sentences that can never cross the distance that separates them from the acts they attempt to describe, of thinking turning around and around in a sealed past without the oxygen of a real present or future. It certainly has a didactic purpose but in another sense it reflects the condition of a society without a visible future, a society dazzled by the massive permanence of its own institutions in which no change seems possible and the idea of progress is dead. But this distance between people and their own acts is not merely a function of the specialized situation of *No Exit*, where the intolerable conversation never manages to dent the solidity of the finished lives. It is visible also in those moments when, at the other end of time, characters who have not yet acted are about to do so: in a play like *Dirty Hands*, where a drama which is in a sense that of all action is concealed behind a grosser, more melodramatic category that bears the same name (just as the notion of freedom is simplified, "vulgarized," when it makes its appearance in the novels as a special kind of condition rather than as the essence of all human reality). In this play the desire of Hugo to *act* is to be understood not only against the background of his past, that middle-class existence to which he wants to oppose an existence of a wholly different quality, but also in terms of that malaise of continental intellectuals with their own specialized work which prevents it from ever seeming real work, real action; so that in the midst of the clandestine journalism which is just as much an act or an engagement in its own terms, Hugo has the nostalgia of what seems to him to be its opposite: terror, violence, an activity close to death and to which death seems to lend a kind of gravity.

Yet what is essential in this new kind of action that Hugo wishes for himself is not so much its violence but the quality of its time, not a cumulative everyday action which is lived as a routine and which little by little conceals from the actor the fact that he is engaged in a project, but a single moment, something to be reached across a waiting, through a period of preparation and fear, something that happens all at once, something which can be *anticipated*, as in this moment where Hugo sees another terrorist succeed:

> OLGA: He did it. . . .
>
> HUGO: He did it. Before the week is up, the two of you will be here, on a night just like this, and you'll be waiting to hear something; and you'll worry and you'll talk about me,

and for once I'll amount to something in your eyes. And you'll ask each other: what's he *doing?* And then there'll be a phone call, or a knock at the door, and you'll be smiling the way you are right now, and you'll say: "He did it." [3]

The future act, the totally new, already exists in an ill-formed manner in the present: parts of it are being slowly born in Hugo's mind, the easiest parts and those most familiar to him. The room he is standing in, the people he is looking at and listening to, are ready-made material which can be turned into future by making only the slightest of changes. But these words through which the act comes to its first still fragmentary existence are more than a momentary awakening of the imagination inside Hugo's head: they are a way of preparing himself, of making himself believe in something of which there are as yet no traces, no hints, in the real world. They help him weigh the unforeseeable future down with a kind of seriousness, so that it does not float with the lightness of a dream but is stiffened with the expectations of others.

This is very different from a purely "intellectual" awareness that something is going to happen. It is a kind of belief, a sudden intuition of the impending act which is so vivid, that absent as it is, the characters are already able to see its effect on things. This is what happens when Hugo's wife suddenly *knows* that Hoederer will be killed. Her drama is a repetition of Hugo's on another level: the same feeling of counting for nothing in the midst of a serious, solid world, the survival of a child's relationship to grown-ups and their things and activities, the frigidity in terms of which the sexual act becomes a kind of crude symbol of human action in general. All of this prevents her from taking Hugo's act any more seriously than he does himself; so that the moment of belief, when it happens, has to change the whole world to make a place for itself:

JESSICA: You're going to kill a man.

HUGO: Do I even know myself what I'm going to do?

JESSICA: Let me see the gun.

HUGO: What for?

JESSICA: I want to see how it looks.

HUGO: You carried it around with you all afternoon.

JESSICA: Then it was nothing but a toy.

HUGO: (*handing it to her*) Be careful.

JESSICA: Yes. (*Examining it*) It's funny.

HUGO: What is?

JESSICA: I'm afraid of it now. Take it back. (*Pause*) You're going to kill a man.[4]

Nothing is changed: the gun is exactly what it was, her husband remains a predictable being, with familiar mannerisms, a familiar face, nothing in the room and its silence has been tampered with; only suddenly a mysterious depth has opened up in all of these things; clear and easily covered with a glance, each of them suddenly possesses a "beyond" that escapes her, gives onto a real change in everything. The cold dead object, the easily handled revolver, has turned without warning into an instrument that will be used, and handling it suddenly becomes a tempting of fate. In a sense this transformation of things into what they will be has been caused: the bomb unsettled the world that Jessica had been playing in, made her see it in a new way before she knew what she was doing. From a purely intellectual point of view it showed her how dead serious the plot on Hoederer's life is:

> It's not my fault. I only believe what I can see. Just this morning I wouldn't have ben able to imagine him dying. (*Pause*) I went into the office a little while ago, there was that man bleeding and you were all corpses. Hoederer was a corpse; I saw it on his face! If you don't kill him, they'll send somebody else.[5]

Yet the essential part of this new belief is not a new piece of information that makes her revise her estimate of the situation; it is the concrete, material fact of seeing the future in front of her. Her own imagination is too weak to have any effect on the outside; she lives it as pure fantasy, as that which in the very nature of things will not take place. But here the world itself horribly begins to do the work of her imagining for her. All she has to do is look, the future is inscribed in the things themselves, in these pale astonished faces which are already frozen into waxy masks.

We can understand the need for this complicity on the part of the world itself through the objective relationship of these people to the world they live in. Unproductive, they have never acted on things or changed them, they have grown up surrounded by objects that seemed as unhistorical as trees, immutable parts of a city landscape divorced from human activity and therefore impregnable to it; nothing in their own experience gives them any confidence in the power of their own subjectivity to leave any traces on this massive wall of things: only the things themselves can announce their impending dissolution. Yet this dizziness of the subjectivity before a silent unresponsive world outside of it is in another sense a moment of all action: Goetz feels it, in *Lucifer and the Lord*, as he gazes at the city he is about to destroy and is astounded that he will be able to have any effect at all on the self-sufficient cluster of roofs and routines and traditions that he can see with his own eyes before him and beside the visual evidence of which the future he plans seems to lack all substance, as weak as a mere wish. For consciousness *is* nothing in comparison to the ponderous being of things, and even in the moment in which it turns on them to leave its presence inscribed in their resisting surfaces, it senses its own lack of being and the presumptuousness of the assault it is about to make.

These moments, in which the future act seems to draw near and to pull the present out of shape under the force of its approach, remain "subjective": the world changes in them, without really changing at all. In contrast to the act itself, the gunshot sound, the floor with a body suddenly lying on it, they have to be told and not seen—and even the scenery that the characters see change has to be described because its changes are not visible for us. Only in the moment of the act itself can something be said to happen really: this moment without past or future, a place of silence and of total freedom, in which Hoederer turns his back and Hugo is left alone with a single wholly new gesture to perform, a trigger to squeeze in a vast transparent lucidity with nothing to help him do it and no way to make it happen painlessly and gradually, bit by bit—this is a kind of symbolic representation of the purest execution of an act, that which permits the freedom of the actor to express itself the most painfully and accessibly to him and to those who contemplate his drama. We know that Hugo misses his chance, and that he finally shoots under other circumstances, in a moment so jammed with emotions and suddenness that he is able to do it almost without knowing what he is doing, or why. But in any case the instant of the act, once it is over, rushes wordlessly into the past, separates itself automatically from the subjectivity that accomplished it, and the world of things, altered, closes up again in front of the consciousness that a moment before had come into decisive contact with it.

It is at this point that we rejoin the drama of Garcin, that struggle against something which has already happened, except that Hugo is in the privileged position of being still alive. In his prison he relives the introspective situation of No Exit, the perpetual and circular analysis of his motives, and this experience is long enough to make him realize that the only way for him to possess the fact of the now distant past is to add to it a new act that will give it new value. This possibility, which as we have seen Garcin himself was obsessed with even after it was too late, is what Sartre calls the "assumption" of a past, of a facticity. And once more the intrigue of the play provides a kind of imperfect and striking symbol, in the mode of the unique gesture, of something which the philosophical works show to be part of the permanent structure of all human experience. For we can have no direct experience of our own facticity. In a kind of rough parallel to the earlier philosophy of knowledge in which the things-in-themselves are always out of reach, and necessarily apprehended through the organs of perception that transform them immediately into things-for-us, we necessarily humanize, we *assume* everything we come into contact with, and the basic facticity of the things around us and of our own bodies and lives is felt only as a limit, the most stubbornly inhuman becomes human through the fact of our awareness of it. Thus the steepness of the hill we are climbing is an objective fact, but an abstract one; and each of us lives it in a different way and decides when to stop because it is "too hard." So also our facial structures and our bodies are inherited, but they are not simple static facts that we have to cope with, but are constantly assumed and mediated through expression (and repose is of course a human expression like any other): it is the body in movement which is the concrete phenomenon, and except insofar as they are the result of a historical process, its measurements are abstract. This is why it is impossible to give content to the idea of facticity: any approach to it is already an assumption, all "facts" are human, and in attempting to experience facticity directly we immediately draw it into the human world, and the brute, meaningless core of being which the

word stands for retreats further out of our grasp. This is why also
the past always is assumed: we are not free to have no attitude toward
it. It cannot be changed; but we always lend the changeless facts a
meaning in terms of the lives we lead and even the forgetting of
them, as Freud showed, is a relationship to them.

But in the play, this *perpetual* necessity of ours to assume our
facticity takes the form of a single, an exemplary choice. The brute
fact is the death of Hoederer, with its any number of motives:
jealousy, political expediency, etc. But when Hugo is asked to forget
his old name, and the past that went with it, to enter into a relationship with this act of his which will be no more privileged than a
stranger's connection with someone else's life, to work for the party
again as if it were the "first time," the intrigue of the play suddenly
brings an opposite of assumption into existence, and the oblivion
which in philosophical terms was merely one mode of assumption
among others becomes, in the distorting mirror of the thought-world
of the play, a possibility of total renunciation of the past. This renunciation is at first only tentative: "If I renounced my act, he would
become an anonymous corpse, just another one of the party's waste
products. Killed by accident. Killed for a woman." [6] The language
is still more or less innocuous: the colorless verb "become" hardly
imposes any materialization on the abstract sentence that describes
a possible meaning of the death of Hoederer; and the renunciation
remains here a kind of assumption. But this vocabulary tends to
develop on its own, once set in motion; and as the possibility of a
real renunciation of the act emerges, the assumption of it is transformed into a striking, solitary gesture far different in quality from
what assumption was when it named the process of humanization
which is our daily life.

What is involved is apparently only a way of talking about
things; yet the gesture that will turn the silent fact of Hoederer's
death into a meaning will be itself another wordless event: the death
of Hugo himself, the closing of the door on his own assassination
as the curtain closes. And its very absence from the play indicates
that it has to take place somehow first for us in words, just as the
first murder began to emerge verbally long before it really happened.

The inadequacy of mere action, of a self-supporting intrigue the
dialogue of which has no autonomy, which constitutes mere gestures
among gestures of another order, no more privileged than physical
movements, can be sensed if we reflect on the "improbability" of the

play's story. The atmosphere of the stage sets, of the play's conventions, of its everyday language, invites us to imagine ourselves witnessing something more or less naturalistic: the stylization is not blatant, it is out of sight and detected only at a certain angle, where we least expect it. Something in the play prevents us, while it is going on, from being aware of just how "philosophical," how uncommon and even unlikely is this spectacle of a man getting himself killed for an interpretation of history.

Undoubtedly Hugo's relationship to Hoederer permits us to think of this act in terms of personal devotion. But it is above all the presence of death that transforms the merely abstract quality of the act, that returns against the exemplary decision to confer a new reality on it. Since Hugo *has* given his life, it is the problem of "meaning," of historical value, that is suddenly changed, that suddenly becomes an idea crucial enough to die for. Only the extremest act of assumption is enough to make the assumption "credible" at all: the only realism possible in this situation is its most violent outer limit, and without the "extreme situation" everything dissolves into abstractions and mere discussed problems.

The presence of death is also that which permits the language to reach its most figurative limits without becoming decoration: "I haven't killed Hoederer yet, Olga. Not yet. I'm going to kill him right now, and myself along with him." [7] The possibility of a renunciation has become real at the same time: it is no longer a mere figure of speech to say that Hoederer has not yet been killed—the act, in the past, did not manage to take place completely, it still remains to be done, it can still go unfinished, drift into the past and simply vanish; and if it is the death of Hugo himself that gives him the right to this language, it is at the same time this language, this image of an act which has happened and yet not happened, that makes the death speak, that lets the new fact, taking place outside the dialogue, confirm the solidity of the dialogue that it finally seals.

What does subject matter like this imply for the work of art? The act is always at a distance from the person who commits it, to whom it "belongs"; it is not self-sufficient, has no ready-made meaning of its own, but has to be constantly assumed and reassumed. It never really happens objectively: it has to be anticipated beforehand; when it takes place it immediately alienates itself, and afterwards it has to be made to happen again for it to have happened at all.

This unsubstantial, alienated nature of human action is a category imposed on our attention by plays; and it is the stage itself that is partly responsible for the terms in which we have had to think the problem. For the theater is a kind of mixture of language on the one hand, and the merely seen, sets and gestures, on the other. Things can take place before our eyes, and then be discussed as well and enter a purely verbal mode of existence. It is thus possible for a play to have its area of facticity: the brute visual facts, the moments of pure happening; and its area of assumption: the speeches in which these events are taken up into the language. And once an aesthetic of the theatre is established on the basis of this opposition, the events themselves begin to come loose from the play and slide out of it: dialogue establishes itself on the stage before us and the off-stage bcomes the place in which things "really" happen. Or in another sense it is in the language that things are really taking place, and the events themselves, off-stage or on, become merely necessary and not sufficient. This seems a curious description of a theater so full of violence, so little "poetic" in the bad sense, as Sartre's; but it is precisely the violence, the most exaggerated kind of facticity, that ensures the meaning of its opposite, and without it the language would weaken and become gratuitous embroidery, a sterile poetry. So that along with the naturalism and the melodrama, there is another perspective in which all these violent events turn out to be illusion and only the language really happens: the plays are strange examples of an inherited melodramatic form which has been subverted into literature, into occasions for the elaboration of a new language.

In prose however the opposition between dialogue and stage action no longer exists: the gestures and the settings are themselves described, and dialogue is no longer the only way to show the relationship of characters to the things they have done. The subject matter is moreover greatly expanded; the novel is not limited by the nature of its medium to human beings and the things they do; as in the movies things and landscapes can become active participants in the drama, and the larger form, in which everything is now language, transcends the category of human acts and opens onto events in general. It is certain that if this structure of acts which we have examined is the way in which Sartre's world has to express itself in the play form, it corresponds to something in that world that will find its way into the novels; but it is certain also that within the new form it will appear in a wholly different way.

NOTES

1. *Théâtre*, p. 158.

   ESTELLE: Enfin tu dois bien te rappeler; tu devais avoir des raisons pour agir comme tu l'as fait.

   GARCIN: Oui.

   ESTELLE: Eh bien?

   GARCIN: Est-ce que ce sont les vraies raisons?

   ESTELLE: *dépitée.*—Comme tu es compliqué.

   GARCIN: Je voulais témoigner, je . . . j'avais longuement réfléchi . . . Est-ce que ce sont les vraies raisons?

2. Ibid., p. 158.

   GARCIN: Estelle, est-ce que je suis un lâche?

   ESTELLE: Mais je n'en sais rien, mon amour, je ne suis pas dans ta peau. C'est à toi de décider.

   GARCIN: *avec un geste las.*—Je ne décide pas.

3. *Les Mains sales*, pp. 55–6.

   OLGA: Il a réussi. . . .

   HUGO: Il a réussi. Avant la fin de la semaine, vous serez ici, tous les deux, par une nuit pareille, et vous attendrez les nouvelles; et vous serez inquiets et vous parlerez de moi et je compterai pour vous. Et vous vous demanderez: qu'est ce qu'il fait? Et puis il y aura un coup de téléphone ou bien quelqu'un frappera à la porte et vous vous sourirez comme vous faites à présent et vous vous direz: "Il a réussi."

4. Ibid., pp. 184–5.

   JESSICA: Toi, tu vas tuer un homme.

   HUGO: Est-ce que je sais ce que je vais faire?

   JESSICA: Montre-moi le revolver.

   HUGO: Pourquoi?

   JESSICA: Je veux voir comment c'est fait.

   HUGO: Tu l'as promené sur toi tout l'après-midi.

   JESSICA: A ce moment-là, ce n'était qu'un jouet.

   HUGO: *el lui tendant.*—Fais attention.

JESSICA: Oui. (*Elle le regarde.*) C'est drôle.

HUGO: Qu'est-ce qui est drôle?

JESSICA: Il me fait peur à présent. Reprends-le. (*Un temps.*) Tu vas tuer un homme.

5. Ibid., p. 185.

"Ce n'est pas ma faute: je ne crois que ce que je vois. Ce matin encore, je ne pouvais même pas imaginer qu'il meure. (*un temps.*) Je suis entrée dans le bureau tout à l'heure, il y avait le type qui saignait et vous étiez tous des morts. Hoederer, c'était un mort; je l'ai vu sur son visage! Si ce n'est pas toi qui le tue, ils enverront quelqu'un d'autre."

6. Ibid., p.259.

"Si je reniais mon acte, il deviendrait un cadavre anonyme, un déchet du parti. Tué par hasard. Tué pour une femme."

7. Ibid., p. 259.

"Je n'ai pas encore tué Hoederer, Olga. Pas encore. C'est à présent que je vais le tuer et moi avec."

ERIC BENTLEY

The Making of a Dramatist (1892–1903)

It was clear from the start that Bernard Shaw was a man of ideas. Later it turned out that he was a fabulous entertainer. But few have granted that the two Shaws were one. The old tendency was to grant that he was a publicist, a critic, an essayist, even a philosopher, but to add: "not, of course, a dramatist." The later tendency was to concede that he was a great showman but to discount his thoughtful side. As Egon Friedell said, you could suck the theatrical sugar from the pill of propaganda, and put the pill itself back on the plate.

Neither in the old days, then, nor in the later ones was Shaw considered a dramatist, for even the later generations have only thought him a master of the theatrical occasion, a man with a theatrical line of talk and a theatrical bag of tricks, a highly histrionic jokester—a comedian, certainly, but hardly a writer of serious comedy. The fact is that the shock of that long career in the theater has still not been absorbed. Shaw has not yet been seen in perspective.

In these circumstances, it is interesting to go back and look at what happened in the eighteen nineties. In 1891, Bernard Shaw had still not written a play, though he was thirty-five years old. A dozen years later, though he could describe himself as "an unperformed playwright in London," he had written *Widowers' Houses* (1892), *The Philanderer* (1893), *Mrs. Warren's Profession* (1893–94),

This essay is the Foreword to *Plays by Bernard Shaw*, New American Library, New York, 1963. Reprinted by permission of the author.

Arms and the Man (1894), *Candida* (1894–95), *The Man of Destiny* (1895), *You Never Can Tell* (1895–96), *The Devil's Disciple* (1896–97), *Caesar and Cleopatra* (1898), *Captain Brassbound's Conversion* (1899), *The Admirable Bashville* (1901), and *Man and Superman* (1901–03).

Let us take for granted that these plays are full of ideas and jokes, and ask if they do not also meet the demands of dramatic criticism as such. The drama, everyone agrees, presents character in action. Human actions become "an action" in the drama when they are arranged effectively—when, that is, they are given what we can recognize as a proper and praiseworthy structure. Of character dramatic critics have required many different things. One of them is emotional substance.

Let us ask, then, how Shaw, when he set about playwriting, tackled the problem of structure; and let us ask if he gave his characters' existence the requisite emotional substance.

STRUCTURE

How did Shaw put a play together? To think of questions about Shaw is to think also of the answers he invariably provided to them. In this case, he said: "I avoid plots like the plague. . . . My procedure is to imagine characters and let them rip. . . ." The quotation is from his *Table-talk* but (again, as usual) he said the same thing on many other occasions. One always has to ask not what he means (which may be clear) but what he is getting at. All Shaw's critical prose is polemical, as he freely admitted, and his writing on the theater is devoted to the destruction of some kinds of drama and their replacement by some others (or one other). Here the enemy is the kind of play which had been dominant throughout the latter half of the nineteenth century—"the well-made play," as perfected by Eugène Scribe. In this dramaturgy, the Aristotelian doctrine of the primacy of plot had been driven to an improper extreme. The plot was now not *primus inter pares*, but all that mattered. It lost its originally organic relation to character and theme. So it became anathema to the apostles of the New Drama at the century's close. As late as 1946, when Allardyce Nicoll declared that Shaw was himself influenced by the well-made play, the old playwright went into print to deny it.

If the well-made play is defined as having no serious content, if it is defined by the relation (or lack of relation) of its plot to character

and theme, then obviously Shaw did not write well-made plays. Yet,
Professor Nicoll had a point, and a strong one, which was that, for
all the disclaimers, Shaw's plays did have plots and, furthermore,
that these plots tended to be old acquaintances for those who knew
their well-made play. Actually, the playwright had no need to be
scandalized, for no dramatist had been more influenced by the well-
made play than his own idol of those days, Henrik Ibsen. The Norwegian had begun his theatrical career by directing a large number of
these plays: he made an exact imitation of them in his own *Lady
Inger of Ötrât*; and he had continued to the end to use many of their
characteristic devices. Hence, it would have been quite possible for
a writer in 1890 to denounce Scribe and Sardou and simultaneously
to steal their bag of tricks—from Ibsen. It is doubtful, though, if
Bernard Shaw needed to deceive himself in this way. It seems more
likely that he took the main situation in *Arms and the Man* from one
of Scribe's most successful plays, *Bataille de dames*.

A situation is not, of course, a plot, and the plot of *Arms and
the Man* is not simply lifted from Scribe, even though parts of it
may have been. Plagiarism is not the point. The point is that even
when Shaw's story diverges from Scribe, it remains Scribean. The
play *Arms and the Man* is hung, as it were, on the cunningly told
tale of the lost coat with the photograph in its pocket. The reader
need only go through the text and mark the hints, incidents, accidents, and contretemps of this tale and he will be finding the layout,
the plan—yes, the plot—of this play. Or at any rate, the plot of
what could have been a first draft of the play. Shaw, one gathers,
did not write such first drafts but, supposing he had, what would
be the difference between the first draft and the final one? In the
answer to this question lies the secret of Shavian dramaturgy.

A corollary of the view that "plot is all" is this proposition: the
cause of any incident is another incident. It is known that Scribe
used to chart out a configuration of incidents and then write his
play. This is to go far beyond Aristotle. It is to set no store at all
by human initiative and assign to events themselves a kind of
fatality: they are a network in which mankind is caught. Granted
that the conception might in certain hands have its awesomeness; in
Scribe's hands it had only triviality, because he manipulated the
events till the issue was a pleasant one. It is curious how often that
manipulation had to be arbitrary and drastic. Do events, when given
their head, rush downward to disaster? To guarantee a happy ending,

the well-making playwrights often needed their emergency weapon: sheer accident. Hence the Shavian complaint that well-made plays were badly made, after all.

Hence also Bernard Shaw's first drama, which is an adaptation of an adaptation of a well-made play. The subject is one that Scribe and the younger Dumas brought to the nineteenth-century theater: marrying, or refusing to marry, money. The immediate source is an unfinished play of William Archer's, *Rhinegold*. Archer's source is *La Ceinture dorée*, by Emile Augier. When a young man discovers that his young lady's inherited money was acquired by her father in an immoral way, what does he do? William Archer's answer was: he pitches it into the Rhine. One presumes that Archer's action would have been set on a convenient balcony beside that river. Augier's hero is not so privileged. To preserve his honor, he would simply have to forgo the pleasure of marrying the lady, if the author did not provide him and the play with a convenient accident (or money *ex machina*). The whole French economy has to meet with a crisis (war breaks out) so that our heroine's father may be reduced to poverty; it is now honorable for our hero to propose to our heroine. In the well-made play, one incident leads to another with a logic that is inescapable—except when the author decides to escape it. Perhaps Shaw's objection was less to the inescapability than to the egregious, last-minute escapes.

His first play, *Widowers' Houses*, may not be great art but it is a great reversal of custom. Shaw's key decision was to refuse to accept Augier's ending, to refuse to have accident (masquerading as fate or otherwise) intervene. Such a refusal leads a man—leads a born playwright, at least—back and back into the earlier stages of a story and he ends up writing an utterly different play—an utterly different *kind* of play.

Not one but two conceptions of Augier's were being rejected: not just the solution-by-sheer-accident (which condemns a play to meaninglessness) but also the autonomy-of-incidents—something, by the way, which was no part of Augier's conscious philosophy but was imposed on him by the Scribean design. Dramatists are committed to the doctrine of free will. They can say they don't believe in it, but they have to write their plays as if they did. (In this they resemble human beings in general, for your most ardent determinist acts on the assumption that determinism is false.) People in plays have got to be able to make decisions, and these decisions have got to be both real and influential: they have to affect events. I see no reason to object to Aristotle's declaration that plot is the soul of the drama, but Aristotle would have objected to Scribe's attempt to cut the soul off from the body—that is, from character.

What *does* a young man do when he finds that his bride's dowry comes from a tainted source? There are two ways for a writer to arrive at an answer. He can say: "I can think of several answers— on the basis of several different possibilities of 'theater.' Answer A will give you Big Scene X; Answer B will give you Ending Y; and so on." Or he can say: "I cannot give you any answer at all until the terms of the proposition are defined, including the term 'tainted.' Above all, I need to know who these people are: what bride? what young man?" The first way to arrive at an answer would commonly be thought the playwright's way: the reasoning is "craftsmanlike" and "of the theater," and would earn a man commendation on Broadway in 1960. The second way is only the human way. That makes it the way of the real dramatist and so of Bernard Shaw.

It could be said that we have this perfectly functioning machine of the well-made play and that a Bernard Shaw is throwing a monkey wrench into it—the monkey wrench of character. That is how it must seem from the Scribean viewpoint. From the viewpoint of dramatic art, however, one would say that this particular engine had been revolving all too fast and uselessly; only when a Shaw slips in the clutch can the gear engage and the vehicle prove itself a vehicle by moving.

"My procedure is to imagine characters and let them rip. . . ." The pertinence of this remark may by now be clearer: if the young man has been "imagined," the dramatist can find the decision he would make as to the young lady's money. But at this point, we realize that Shaw's words leave out of account the fact that the situation confronting the young man had been established in ad- vance of the imagining of his character. It had been established by Augier and Archer and by Shaw's own decision to use their work. Hence, Shaw's own interpretation is both helpful and misleading— or, perhaps, is helpful only if those who are helped do a lot of work on their own.

Shaw put *Widowers' Houses* together—how? He took from cer- tain predecessors not only a situation but a story, and not only a story but that clever, orderly, and theatrical arrangement of a story which we call a plot. Then he changed the plot—or as he would

have said, let the characters change it for him. Now, had he retained
Augier's characters, they could only have caused him to break off
the action one scene earlier than Augier did: instead of the happy
ending created by a national emergency, we would get the unhappy
ending which the emergency reversed.

Characters in a well-made play are "conventional"—that is, they
behave, not according to laws of psychology but according to the
expectations of an audience in a theater. A type of drama in which
the plot is given a free hand cannot afford any less passive or more
obtrusive *personae*. Conversely, if a playwright abandons the plot-
determined play, he will have to be more inventive as to character.
To assume the initiative, his characters will have to be capable of it.
So Shaw's first contribution to the drama was: more active characters. They were more active, first of all, in the most obvious
fashion: they were violent. More important, they made decisions
which affected the course of events, and they made them on the
basis of their own nature, not of the spectator's. And so these characters were surprising. For a number of years, they were too surprising to be acceptable. Like all surprising art, Shaw's dramaturgy
was damned as non-art. The critics' formula was: Not a Play.

Augier's hero could not consider being the husband of a woman
with a tainted dowry. Shaw creates a hero who has the effrontery
to ask the heroine to throw up her dowry for his sake. But the
Shavian joke—the Shavian reversal—is already what it would characteristically be in the future: a double one. To this demanding hero he
adds an even more demanding heroine: she simply refuses to be
poor to preserve her innocence. That is the nub of the first Shaw
comedy. Then Shaw works his way out of the apparent deadlock,
not by having the heroine weaken (that is, "improve"), but by
having the hero renew his strength (that is, "deteriorate"). This
the latter does by way of recovering from a shock. The shock comes
from without and might be called an accident (like Augier's outbreak of war), except that it belongs to the logic of the situation.
It turns out that the source of the hero's own unearned income is
the same as that of his girl's father. End of Act Two. In the third
and last act, our hero comes around and gets the girl by accepting
the nature of capitalism. Socialist propaganda? Precisely. Shaw
boasted of it. But he boasted with equal reason that he was writing
comedy in the most traditional sense.

"Take what would be done by Scribe, Sardou, Dumas *fils*, or

Augier and do the opposite." Is that the Shavian formula? It is certain that Shavian comedy is parodistic in a way, or to an extent, that Plautus, Jonson, and Molière were not. These others, one would judge, took a convention they respected and brought it to the realization of its best possibilities. Shaw took conventions in which he saw no possibilities—except insofar as he would expose their bankruptcy. The injunction "Do the opposite" was not whimsical. Shaw decided to "do the opposite" of Scribe in much the way Marx decided to do the opposite of Hegel—not to stand everything on its head (Hegel, he held, had done this) but to set everything back on its feet again. That was revolutionary thinking, and Shaw's art, for all the polite and charming trappings, was revolutionary art. The usual relations were reversed.

Such reversals as we see in the ending of *Widowers' Houses* are relatively simple. Shaw's weakest plays are those in which he has done little more than turn the ending around: the price you pay for the brilliant ending of *The Devil's Disciple* is that of a rather dull, and decidedly conventional, first act. His best plays are those in which the principle of reversal has pervaded the whole. Such a play is *Arms and the Man*.

The idea of taking two couples and causing them to exchange partners is hardly novel and, as I have said, the little tale of the coat and the portrait is Scribean in pattern. But Shaw can justifiably plead that this is no well-made play because the artifices of the plot are not what ultimately achieve the result. Here is one of the decisive turns in the action:

> BLUNTSCHLI: When you get into that noble attitude and speak in that thrilling voice, I admire you; but I find it impossible to believe a single word you say.
>
> RAINA: Captain Bluntschli!
>
> BLUNTSCHLI: Yes?
>
> RAINA: Do you mean what you said just now? Do you *know* what you said just now?
>
> BLUNTSCHLI: I do.
>
> RAINA: I! I!!! How did you find me out?

With this last query, Raina passes over forever from Sergius's

world to Bluntschli's: as a result of nothing in the Scribean arrangement of incidents, but of words, words, words. It is here that, to
many, the Shavian drama seems vulnerable. In drama, actions are
supposed to speak louder than words. Writers on the subject invariably know their etymology—"drama" derives from a Greek verb
meaning "to do"—and use it as a cudgel. Their error is a vulgar
one: action need not be external. It can often be carried by words
alone. Shaw used to remark that his plays were all words just as
Raphael's paintings were all paint.

There is a degree of legerdemain in that remark, for Scribe, too,
put down his plays in words. What was confusing to Shaw's readers
and spectators half a century ago was that after indicating unmistakably that he was playing Scribe's game, Shaw proceeded to break
the rules. The fact that Bluntschli conquers by words gains its
peculiar force from a context in which the opposite was to be expected. To look over *Arms and the Man* with an eye to technique
would be to conclude that what we have here is Scribe most subtly
interwoven with Shaw. Yet this formulation is inadequate, for who
did the interweaving? There was a Scribe in Shaw, and there was a
counter-Scribe in Shaw; what makes his works dramatic is the interaction of the two.

The passion and preoccupation of Scribe was the idea of climax:
to the Big Scene at the end—or, rather, a little before the end—all
his arts are dedicated. In Bernard Shaw there was almost as great
a predilection for anticlimax. It is the Shavian "effect" par excellence; no other playwright has come near finding so many possibilities in it. The bit I have quoted from Bluntschli and Raina is an
apt example. *Arms and the Man* contains a corresponding scene
between Sergius and Louka. Where, in a well-made play, Bluntschli
and Louka would have to soar to the heights of Raina and Sergius,
in the Shaw play Raina and Sergius drop with a bump to the level
of Bluntschli and Louka. Such is resolution by anticlimax. It is
dramaturgically effective, and it enforces the author's theme. But
this is not all of Shaw: it is only the counter-Scribe.

The dual anticlimaxes do not round off *Arms and the Man*. What
does? Not the disenchantment of Raina and Sergius but the discovery that Bluntschli the realist is actually an enchanted soul whom
nothing will disenchant. He has destroyed their romanticism but is
himself "incurably romantic." This is another point that is made
in "mere words"—"mere words stuck on at the end," if you wish—

and yet stuck on very well, for they are firmly attached to that little
tale of the coat and the photograph which gives the work its continuity and shape:

> BLUNTSCHLI: Yes: that's the coat I mean. . . . Do you
> suppose I am the sort of fellow a young girl falls in love
> with? Why, look at our ages! I'm thirty-four: I don't suppose
> the young lady is much over seventeen. All that adventure
> which was life or death to me was only a schoolgirl's game
> to her . . . would a woman who took the affair seriously
> have sent me this and written on it: "Raina, to her choco-
> late cream soldier—a souvenir"?
>
> PETKOFF: That's what I was looking for. How the deuce
> did it get there?
>
> BLUNTSCHLI: I have put everything right, I hope, gracious
> young lady.
>
> RAINA: I quite agree with your account of yourself. You are
> a romantic idiot. Next time I hope you will know the differ-
> ence between a schoolgirl of seventeen and a woman of
> twenty-three.

In this scene, plot and theme reach completion together, and the
play of thesis and antithesis ends in synthesis.

The supreme triumph of Shaw's dramaturgical dialectics is to be
found in *Man and Superman*, and, for all the blarney in the preface
about the medieval *Everyman* and the eighteenth-century *Don Gio-
vanni*, the method is the conversion of old materials into nineteenth-
century terms, both thematic and technical. Shaw's claim to be
returning to a pristine Don Juan is valid to the extent that the theme
had originally been less of psychological than of philosophical, indeed theological, interest. It is also true that Don Juan had run away
from his women. However, he had run away from them only after
possessing them. In Shaw's play, he runs away to prevent *them* from
possessing *him*. It is a comic parody of the old motif, embodying
Shaw's standard new motif: the courting of the man by the woman.
And where the old dramatists and librettists had used the old,
"open" type of plot (or nonplot), Shaw substitutes an utterly
Scribean "closed" structure.

This very "modern" and "twentieth-century" play is made up of narrative materials familiar to every Victorian theatergoer. We have a hero who spends the entire evening hotly pursued by his foes; a clandestine marriage celebrated in defiance of a hostile father; a lovelorn hero who sacrifices himself so that the girl will go to his rival; a villain whose function is to constitute for a while the barrier to denouement and happy ending. The subplot about the Malone family rests upon two separate uses of the "secret skillfully withheld," then skillfully released. Traditional farcical coincidence binds together Straker and Mendoza. The play bears every sign of careful workmanship—all of it School of Scribe.

But as with *Arms and the Man*, as soon as we examine particulars, we find, interwoven with the Scribean elements, those typically Shavian verbal exchanges which constitute further action. Violet's marriage could have been made a secret of in any Scribe play, and Scribe could have been relied on to choose an effective moment for the release of the secret. In Shaw, what creates both the fun and the point of the news release is not the organization of the incidents but their relation to theme:

> TANNER: I know, and the whole world really knows, though it dare not say so, that you were right to follow your instinct; that vitality and bravery are the greatest qualities a woman can have, and motherhood her solemn initiation into womanhood; and that the fact of your not being legally married matters not one scrap either to your own worth or to our real regard for you.
>
> VIOLET: Oh! You think me a wicked woman, like the rest. . . . I won't bear such a horrible insult as to be complimented by Jack on being one of the wretches of whom he approves. I have kept my marriage a secret for my husband's sake.

An incident which Tanner wishes to use to illustrate his "modern" philosophy thus comes to illustrate a contrasting thesis: that Violet lives by a nonmodern philosophy.

Simple? Yes, but closely linked to a point that is unsimple enough to have generally been missed: Tanner is a windbag. Indeed, the mere fact of the woman courting the man would probably not yield comedy at all were it not for a further and more dynamic reversal: the woman, who makes no great claims for herself, has all the shrewdness, the real *Lebensweisheit*, while the man, who knows everything and can discourse like Bernard Shaw, is—a fool. Tanner is, in fact, like Molière's Alceste, the traditional fool of comedy in highly sophisticated intellectual disguise. Ann Whitefield, into whose trap Tanner falls, is the knave—in skirts.

While Don Juan Tenorio is Superman—or is on the road to him—John Tanner, M.I.R.C., is merely Man, and as such belongs to The World As It Is. Of dramaturgical interest is that the kind of plot Shaw evidently considers capable of giving an image of The World As It Is should be the kind that is generally considered (by himself, for instance) artificial, unreal, arbitrary, inane. Shaw the critic championed the new Naturalism, and among French dramatists especially favored Brieux, who produced dully literal theatrical documentaries. Yet, when Shaw wrote an essay entitled "A Dramatic Realist to His Critics," the example of "realism" he gave from his own work was *Arms and the Man*—on the grounds that the characters respond naturally even if the situations aren't natural. We are entitled, then, to insist on his choice of "unnatural" situations. He must intuitively have understood something which, as a critic, he failed to grasp: that plot does not merely reproduce external reality. The violence and intrigue in Shakespeare, which Shaw the critic declared extraneous, provides the objective correlative of Shakespeare's feelings about life, and the "idiocies" of the plot of *Man and Superman* provide an objective correlative for Shaw's sense of modern life. The very fact that Shaw despised Scribe helps to explain the particular use he made of him.

The Don Juan episode in Act Three is neither a well-made play nor a portion of a well-made play. It stands apart as something appropriately more austere and august. It is not a traditional work of any kind, not even a Platonic dialogue, the relation between Socrates and his interlocutors being quite different. It is not even a debate, for two of the speakers, the Commander and Ana, hardly present arguments at all: they simply represent a point of view. Do even the Devil and Don Juan *discuss* anything? A devil is scarcely a being one can convert to a Cause, and if the Don is busy convincing anyone it is himself. Certainly it is the philosophy of Bernard Shaw that he is given to speak, but is persuasion exercised—even on the audience? Rather, the contributions of the four presences come together as a vision of life—and an intimation of superlife.

Man—and Superman. The comedy of John Tanner—and the

vision of Don Juan Tenorio. Shaw—and counter-Shaw. Thesis and
antithesis are, to be sure, of separate interest, and yet, as usual, the
great Shavian achievement is to have related one to the other. Tanner
seems a wise man and proves a fool. Don Juan passes for a philanderer but proves an explorer and a missionary of the truth. In our
trivial, tawdry, clever, Scribean world, intellect is futile and ever at
the mercy of instinct. Take away the episode in hell, and Shaw
has written an anti-intellectual comedy. The episode assigns to intellect the highest role. No longer, therefore, is Ann the center and
source of things—only a possible mother for Superman. Here Don
Juan dominates. Here (or rather, in heaven) intellect is at home,
and the Don is cured of that occupational disease of Shavian heroes
—homelessness. He "comes to a good end"—only it is not an end,
it is an episode, and from these celestial-infernal heights we must
descend to earth with the shock of Shavian anticlimax, to earth and
to Tanner, from Superman back to Man. One section of the play
gets an electric charge from the other.

Of Shaw's "playmaking" one must conclude that he knew how
to put together a Scribean plot; that he knew how to subordinate
such a plot to his own purposes; and that, in *Man and Superman*,
he knew how to take the resultant Shavian comedy and combine it
dynamically with a disquisition on (and by) Don Juan.

EMOTIONAL SUBSTANCE

If Shaw's plays are, or begin by being, a parody of the more conventional drama of his time, that parody is by no means confined
to the form. We have already seen that the themes, too, tend to get
turned around: these compositions not only do the opposite, as it
were, but say the opposite.

What of the emotions? Whatever the ultimate purpose of drama,
its immediate impact is a strongly emotional one, and one cannot
conceive of a story having an emotional effect upon an audience
unless it is an emotional story and has a certain emotional structure.
I may be forgiven for stating so rudimentary a principle because the
Shavian drama presents us with a paradox: it has flooded a thousand
theaters with emotion and yet has often been held to be emotionless.

Of course, this common opinion is absurd, bolstered though it
can be with remarks of Shaw's own about being a mere "work
machine" and the like. What we confront here is originality. Shaw
may not have been an original thinker; he tried, rather, to make a

synthesis of what certain others had thought. But he was an original person. What fitted him so well for the role of the enemy of convention was that his natural responses were not those of other people but all his own. His emotional constitution was a peculiar one, and that peculiarity is reflected in his plays.

Sex is, without doubt, the crucial issue. Comedy remains fertility worship, however sublimated, and it is fair enough to ask what Bernard Shaw made of the old sexual rigmarole—courtship and the barriers thereto. It is even fair to use any facts about Shaw himself that are a matter of public record.

On the other hand, one is not honor-bound to side with "modern" opinion against "Victorian" as to what is good and bad. The very "modern" Dr. Kinsey implied that human vitality could be measured in statistics on orgasms. Our subject Bernard Shaw will not pass into any Kinseyite paradise. Though he lived to be ninety-four, he seems to have experienced sexual intercourse only between the ages of twenty-nine and forty-three. "I lived a continent virgin . . . until I was 29. . . . During the fourteen years years before my marriage at 43 there was always some lady in the case. . . . As man and wife we found a new relation in which sex had no part. It ended the old gallantries, flirtations, and philanderings for both of us." This quotation is from a letter to Frank Harris, who, as a Kinseyite before Kinsey, wrote: "Compare his [Shaw's] private life with Shakespeare's. While Mary Fitton was banished from London Shakespeare could write nothing but tragedies. That went on for five years. When the Queen died and Shakespeare's Dark Lady returned, he wrote *Antony and Cleopatra*, his greatest love story. As nothing like that happened in Shaw's life we can only get a textbooky, sexless type of play." A remarkable blend of ignorance, invention, and arbitrary assumption! For, actually, Shaw concealed from Harris most of his private life; nothing whatever is known about Shakespeare's feelings for any woman; and no critic or psychologist of repute has even argued that a man's writing has to be "textbooky" and "sexless" unless he is carrying on an adulterous romance; a more familiar argument would be that precisely the abstinent man's imagination might well be crammed with sex. But there is no settling the question a priori.

William Archer declared that Shaw's plays reeked with sex. It is a more suggestive declaration than Harris's. It reminds us that Shaw was able to re-create the sexual charm of both men and women to a degree unequaled by any English dramatist except Shakespeare. To be sure, he doesn't need bedroom scenes to do this. Morell only has to talk and we understand "Prossy's complaint." Undershaft only has to talk and we understand why he is a problem to his daughter. To say nothing of the long line of sirens from Candida to Orinthia! Few of the "sexy" ladies of Restoration comedy, by contrast, have any sex appeal at all. One thing Archer is sure to have had in mind is that the women in Shaw pursue a sexual purpose in a way absolutely unknown to Victorian literature. Of all the reversals in Shavian drama, this is inevitably the most famous: the reversal in the roles of the sexes. Shaw once committed himself to the view that all superior women are masculine and all superior men are feminine. In his comedies, most often, the woman is active, the man passive. Perhaps by 1960 the theme has been restated *ad nauseam*; to Archer it was startling—as was Shaw's determination to rub the sore places of the sexual morality of his time. *Mrs. Warren's Profession* was for many years too "raw" a play for production in London, and it created a memorable scandal when it was produced in New Haven and New York in 1905. Like most of the major modern dramatists and novelists, Shaw mentioned the unmentionable. He even claimed to have "put the physical act of sexual intercourse on the stage" (in *Overruled*). Archer evidently felt that Shaw could not give the subject of sex a rest: he may not always have been at the center of it but he was forever touching its fringes.

Here Frank Harris would have interjected: "He was always *avoiding* the center of it." And the interjection is called for. The impression that a man is unemotional in general and sexless in particular does not come from nowhere. Nor are the kinds of sex I have been noting what the average spectator is looking for if he demands a "sexy" show. *Overruled* does not really "put the physical act of sexual intercourse on the stage," and, even if it did, it would do so comically—depriving the act of precisely that element which people miss in Shaw, which is not sex in general but the torridity of sexual romance. At that, if this element were simply absent, Shaw might very well have got away with the omission. But it is explicitly rejected. It is not that a Shavian couple cannot consider intercourse but that they are likely to consider it and decide not to. If the characteristic act of the French drama of the period was the plunge into bed, that of the Shavian drama is the precipitate retreat from the bedroom door.

Harris would be right in reminding us that such was Bernard Shaw's emotional constitution. What other writer has ever created all the normal expectations in a scene between a king and his mistress (*The Apple Cart*), only to reveal later that their relationship is purely platonic? *Captain Brassbound's Conversion* shows the Shavian pattern to perfection. Is there sexual feeling in the play? There is. The process by which Brassbound and Lady Cicely are brought closer and closer is positively titillating. After which, what happens? They are parted. The play has a superb final curtain. "How glorious!" says Lady Cicely, "how glorious!" Then with one of those quick changes of tone that mark the Shavian dialogue: "And what an escape!" Is this unemotional? No. But the emotion is not erotic —rather, it is relief at a release from the erotic. Such is the emotional content of this particular Shavian anticlimax.

As far as conscious intention goes, all Shaw's plays might bear the title he gave to three of them—Plays for Puritans—for that intention is to show romance transcended by a higher-than-erotic purpose. It is a classic intention—an application, really, of the traditional conflict of love and honor, with honor winning hands down, as it did in Corneille and even in one masterpiece of Racine's *Bérénice*. We are concerned here not with philosophic intention but psychological substance. Where the philosopher insists that Shaw does not cross the threshold of the bedroom, the psychologist asks: why does he hover at the bedroom door?

We know from the correspondence with Mrs. Pat Campbell that Shaw liked to play with fire. Even the correspondence with Ellen Terry entailed a playfulness not quite devoid of "danger." The boy Shaw had been witness to an odd household arrangement whereby his mother's music teacher contrived to be (it would seem) almost but not quite her lover. A slightly older Shaw has recently been portrayed as the intruder into a friend's marriage, like his own Eugene Marchbanks: this is speculation. Let us look at the play *Candida*, which is a fact.

It has a notable Big Scene at the end, which is characterized by an equally notable improbability. A comfortable, sensible parson's wife doesn't let herself get jockeyed into "choosing" between her husband and an almost total stranger. People—such people at least —don't do such things. A respectable woman's choice was made before the banns were read.

Perhaps Candida is not really respectable? That is the line of interpretation taken by Beatrice Webb, who declared her a prostitute. Will the play, taken as a play, bear this interpretation out? A dramatist's license to have the truth turn out different from the impression given to the audience is very limited, for it is to a large extent by giving impressions that he creates characters. Shaw has given the impression that Candida is *not* a prostitute.

Against this it can be urged that Shaw himself took Beatrice Webb's side and attacked Candida—in remarks he made about her in letters to James Huneker, Richard Burton, and others. True, but was that legitimate? He himself admitted that he had no more right to say what his plays meant than any other critic. One might add that he may have had less, for when an author intervenes to correct our impressions of his work, he is often intervening to change or misinterpret that work.

Outside the play, Shaw is against Candida. Inside it, he is both for and against her, but he is for her effectually, and against her ineffectually, because the direct impression is favorable, while it is only by throwing logic back into the story when it is over that you can reach an unfavorable judgment. This means, I should think, that though Shaw's intellect is against Candida, his emotions are for her.

What is it that this play has always projected in the theater, and can always be counted on to project again? The charm of Candida. This is a reality so immediate and all-pervasive that it is hard for any other element in the play to make headway against it. Leading actresses know this, and hearing their director speak of Candida's essential badness, can afford to smile a Candida smile, strong in the knowledge that there is nothing a director can do about this badness, once that smile has been displayed on stage as well as off.

I would say that it is a confused play but that the confusion goes unnoticed because of Candida's charm and may even be the cause of a degree of emotional tension unusual in a Shaw play. Candida is made out of a Shavian ambivalence: he would like to reject this kind of woman, but actually he dotes on her. One quickly senses that he *is* Marchbanks. One also finds he protests (too much) that he is *not* Marchbanks. "I had in mind De Quincey's account of his adolescence in his Confessions," he wrote. "I certainly never thought of myself as a model." From the empty pretense of being De Quincey, no doubt, comes the prodigious unreality of many of the lines. As a character, Marchbanks must be reckoned a failure. Shaw was hiding. What better image to hide behind than that of the kind of writer he himself was not—a romantic poet? Especially if De Quincey would do the job for him?

It didn't work, of course, except as pure histrionics. (Marchbanks, though a poorly drawn character, is always an effective stage role, and still seems to correspond to the actor's idea of a poet.) But if no one in the play can reject Candida, there is a noteworthy niche in it for the man whom she will reject. This niche Marchbanks can fill nobly, and has his dramatic moment as he marches into it: his final exit is a magnificent piece of action. Possibly everything before that (in this role) is just an improvisation. Shaw could not make us believe in the poet's poetry, but he does make us believe in his pain and his nobility, for at these points he could identify himself with Eugene completely without having to "think of himself as a model."

Dramatists usually speak of their characters individually, and that could be regarded as strange, because the drama, all through the centuries, has done much less with separate persons than with relationships. The traditional characters are, if you will, simplified to the point of crudity. What is not crude, as treated by the old dramatists, is the interaction of these characters: the dynamics of human relations are fully rendered. If what you do not get is detailed psychological biography, what you do get is the essence of such relations as parent and child, boy and girl, man and wife.

Now, modern playwrights, happily, have not departed from the classic patterns as much as they are supposed to have, and what rings true, emotionally, in *Candida* corresponds to Shaw's ability to find and re-create some of these elemental relationships. An inner obstacle, one would judge, hampered him when he tried to "do" the Marchbanks-Candida relationship, but the Morell-Candida relation is both clear and challenging. It is, as Shaw himself said, the relationship of Nora and Torvald Helmer turned around: in Shaw's play the man is the doll. But where Ibsen tells the story of a doll who finally comes to life, Shaw tells the story of a seemingly living person who turns out to have been a doll all along. (In other words, the relation of Shaw to Ibsen, instead of being as direct as it might seem, is an inverse one, exactly like the relation of Shaw to other nineteenth-century drama.) Into Morell Shaw can put that part of himself (a child) which finds Candida irresistible, just as into Candida he can put that part of Woman which he finds irresistible

—the mother in her. One would have to be as naïve a psychologist as Frank Harris to consider the mother-and-child relation less emotional than that of lovers.

Or less dramatic. Relationships become dramatic not in the degree of their eroticism but to the extent that they contain conflict. Pure love would not be a dramatic subject at all. Love becomes dramatic when it is impure—when the loving element is submerged in a struggle for power. The axis about which *Candida* revolves is that of strength and weakness, not love and hate. And if one knows Shaw's views on the topic of the "weaker sex" in general, the conclusion of *Candida* follows naturally: instead of the little woman reaching up toward the arms of the strong man, we have the strong woman reaching down to pick up her child. It is remarkable how far Shaw's thought is from the standard "advanced thinking" of his generation, with its prattle of equality and comradeship. He is closer to Nietzsche.

Of the ending of A *Doll's House* it has been said: perhaps Nora has walked out in a mere tantrum and will be back in the morning. How much more savage is the ending of *Candida!* Only Strindberg could have written a sequel to it. The cruelty of the heroine—merely implicit in the present play—would have to come to the surface in any continuation of the story. Candida has chosen to let her husband discover his shame: she, as well as he, will have to take the consequences. Let the stage manager hold razors and strait jackets in readiness!

One reason why Shaw got so little credit for his treatment of the emotions is that the emotions he treats are not the ones people expect. The very fact that his favorite device is anticlimax should tell us that what he most insistently feels is "letdown." It may be retorted that on the contrary, Bernard Shaw was the most buoyant and vivacious of men. That is also true. The axis "strength-weakness" is not more important to Shaw's content than the axis "elation-depression" is to his form. The dialogue ripples gaily along; then comes the sudden letdown. The circus has familiarized us with the pattern: it is the light of heart who take the pratfall. Even as the fool pops up in Shavian comedy in the highly intellectualized shape of a Jack Tanner, so the pratfall is transmuted into an anticlimax that has a positively climactic force. It has been customary to take these anticlimaxes as expressions of an idea—the idea of disenchantment. It is *the* idea of modern literature, and it is inseparable from an emotion far commoner and far more influential than romantic excitement. There seems to be no name for this emotion—and that, too, is significant. Let us call it desolation.

You cannot be disenchanted without having been enchanted. One is sometimes tempted to believe that our human desolation might have been avoided if only we had not started out so undesolate. It is not the fact that we don't have things that worries us, but that we have lost them—or rather, been deprived of them. Desolation is the feeling of having been driven from paradise.

A friend of Bernard Shaw's said that when he saw *The Wild Duck*, the bottom dropped out of the universe. One difference between Ibsen and Shaw is that the former produced this effect on the audience, whereas the latter produced it on the characters in a play. Just as a character in a melodrama loses a fortune, so a character in a Shaw play loses a universe. The experience may be given a playful treatment, as with Raina and Sergius. In the case of Morell, the treatment is only partly playful. It gets more serious as the play *Candida* proceeds. Morell finally loses his image of his wife and of himself. The curtain has to be rung down to save us from the Strindberg play that would have to follow.

What of *Mrs. Warren's Profession?* The starting point was a treatment by Maupassant of the theme of a girl finding out that her mother is a courtesan. In an early version of the tale, Maupassant had the girl kill herself. In the later and better-known text (*Yvette*), he saves her life to engineer for himself an ironic-poignant ending: she becomes a kept woman like her mother before her. Curtain! That is the kind of inversion of a suicidal ending which Shaw did *not* go in for. Or not any more. If Shaw had shown a "surrender to the system" (in comical fashion) in the ending to *Widowers' Houses*, he was now intent on showing a rejection of the system. In the first instance, Vivie Warren's revolt represents Shaw's rational rejection of capitalism, but the play culminates in a scene that has no necessary connection with economics—a scene of family crisis, a scene in which a daughter rejects her mother. Which, after all, is archetypal Shaw: instead of the emotions of lover and mistress, he renders the emotions of parents and children, and particularly the emotion of the child rejecting the parent. *Major Barbara* is perhaps the grandest example of this archetype. The great last act of *Pygmalion* is the same thing in disguise, for Henry Higgins is the progenitor of the new Eliza, and that is why she must break free of him. Shaw's Joan has a father, too—in heaven—and she comes at times almost to the point of breaking with Him. That she does not quite do so is the upshot of a play which, while it shows Joan's isolation from men, ends with a stretching of arms toward the heavenly Father. Vivie Warren is already a Saint Joan in that the experience Shaw gives her is that of being desolated. It is the experience he felt most deeply—presumably because it was the experience he had most deeply experienced. In any event, the two long scenes between Vivie and Mrs. Warren are emotional playwriting such as England had not seen for a couple of centuries.

The background, however, is blurred. A Scribean climax is arranged to provide *élan* for the announcement that Vivie's romance is incestuous:

> CROFTS: Allow me, Mister Frank, to introduce you to your half-sister, the eldest daughter of the Reverend Samuel Gardner. Miss Vivie: your half-brother. Good morning.
>
> FRANK: [. . . *raising the rifle*.] You'll testify before the coroner that it's an accident, Viv. [*He takes aim at the retreating figure of Crofts. Vivie seizes the muzzle and pulls it round against her breast.*]
>
> VIVIE: Fire now. You may.

Direct climax (as against anticlimax) was not really in Shaw's line, and in failing to parody Scribe here, Shaw has himself tumbled into the ridiculous. Perhaps the following act was bound to be an anticlimax in a way not intended—a mere disappointment. Yet, it is hard to believe that the particular disappointments it brings are simply the result of a technical ineptitude. Rather, they involve hesitations about the subject. After so strongly creating the impression of incest, Shaw shuffles the notion off in the next act in a surprisingly ambiguous way. It would be easy enough, from a technical viewpoint, to make clear that no incest had been committed. Why did Shaw leave the situation doubtful? So that Vivie could dismiss the issue as irrelevant? In that case, what is relevant? Why is she giving Frank up? One can think of possible reasons, but what reason is one *supposed* to think of?

Unclarity in the work of so careful a craftsman, a writer, moreover, who has more than once been accused of excessive clarity, surely bears witness to inner uncertainty and conflict. To think of

Mrs. Warren's Profession in this personal way is to realize what powerful aggressions it embodies. Shaw combined the themes of prostitution and incest in order to make quite a rational point: our mad society draws back in horror from incest, which is certainly not a pressing menace and perhaps not even a bad thing, while it encourages prostitution, which is a virulent social pestilence. But both themes have a resonance far beyond the bounds of intellect. It is as if they proved more than Shaw had bargained for. The incest theme is sounded—all too boldly. Then the young dramatist has no idea what to do with it. He takes it back. Only, it is too late. So he half takes it back. After all, what is troubling Vivie does go beyond the rationally established causes. Deep water! And Shaw flounders in it. Which has some interest for the student of the emotions. Even where Shaw's plays are faulty, they are not unemotional. On the contrary, it is because of a certain emotional involvement in the material, not because of incapacity for such involvement, that Shaw was not able to resolve certain problems and truly finish certain plays. *Candida* and *Mrs. Warren's Profession* could be cited in evidence. There is material in both which was not successfully "worked through."

Is there similar material in Shaw's collected plays which *was* worked through? To my mind, a good answer would be: yes, *Pygmalion*. This play might well have proved just as ambiguous as the others, for it might have seemed that Eliza must love Higgins, and therefore that her leaving him is but an overrational afterthought of the author's, like his afterthoughts on Candida. Some people, including the author of *My Fair Lady*, think that is just what the Shavian ending is. I, on the other hand, feel—and it is feeling that is in question—that Eliza's rebellion grows organically out of what preceded. She is Higgins' creation: she cannot *be* at all unless she become independent of her creator. If he has "sex appeal," that makes the break more difficult but not less necessary. A girl's father quite normally has sex appeal for her. That is not to justify incest. Here Shaw does cope with incest, and in the best way—by avoiding it.

The ending of *Pygmalion* is the classic Shavian situation: someone is clamorously refusing to enter the bedroom. The friends of Frank Harris are thereby disgusted. That is their right. But there is a point to be made about Shaw's rendering of emotion. Refusal is emotional. There is more turbulence in conflict between Eliza and

Higgins as conceived by Shaw than in romance between them as in *My Fair Lady*.

Man and Superman, on the other hand, might seem to be without emotional substance. The attempt made at a straightforward emotional climax is certainly rather unsuccessful:

> TANNER: I love you. The Life Force enchants me. I have the whole world in my arms when I clasp you. But I am fighting for my freedom, for my honor, for my self, one and undivisible.

> ANN: Your happiness will be worth them all.

> TANNER: You would sell freedom and honor and self for happiness?

> ANN: It would not be all happiness for me. Perhaps death.

> TANNER: [*groaning*] Oh, that clutch holds and hurts. What have you grasped in me? Is there a father's heart as well as a mother's?

If there is capital here, it is the kind that yields no dramatic return, and indeed a criticism of this false climax would lead us to complain of the introduction of the "Life Force" in the first place. There seems no such organic relation between Tanner and Ann as there is between Vivie and her mother, Eliza and Higgins, Candida and Morell. The pair are sometimes compared to Benedick and Beatrice. The comparison is not apt. Shakespeare shows the erotically "dangerous" element in the hostility of his couple. But Tanner and Ann draw no sparks from each other. A cynic might say: here there can be no love since there is no hate. There is really no relationship at all, except that she insists on having him and he cannot evade her successfully because the author won't let him. In this case, we have either to conclude that Frank Harris's kind of criticism applies— or that this is "drama of ideas" and we must not ask it to be otherwise.

Emotional substance? The farce of Tanner and Ann, taken in isolation, has very little, but oddly enough, the episode in hell has a good deal, and this spreads itself over the work as a whole. Even here, though, there is a discrepancy between intention and achievement. The final effect of the Don Juan scene is not that we find the positive message inspiring. We find it at best important, at

worst gallant—a brave effort to make sense of things that cannot
be made sense of. It is all rather like a speech made in wartime,
saying that our side is bound to win because we are right. Perhaps.
Perhaps. But the words that burn with irrefutability are all words
expressing not aspiration toward a better future, but recognition of
a bad present. Don Juan himself is at his best when denouncing
people. The speech that steals the show ("And is Man any the less
destroying himself . . .") is made by the Devil. Which is because
it is not only a very reasonable speech but a very emotional one,
a speech that springs from the very desolation which Shaw's best
people experience.

This note of personal poignancy is not heard very often after
Saint Joan (1923). So much the worse, perhaps, for the later plays.
They have considerable merit, yet they often lack urgency even
when the author makes Urgent Statements in them. And it is interesting that they lack not only dynamic and turbulent personal
relationships but also close structure. There had been a connection
between the emotional and the dramaturgic construction of the
earlier plays; and when one went, so did the other.

I am not proposing a complete theory of the Shavian drama. Nor
am I asking my reader to assume that all drama is dominated by
the emotional conflicts of its author, much less that it ought to be.
For that matter, I have had to remark that unresolved conflict sometimes resulted in unresolved art. What I am affirming is, first, that
some Shaw plays communicate personal feeling of great intensity
and, second, that even some Shaw plays which are less overtly emotional do embody powerful feelings, though not of the kind that is
usually expected.

ROBERT BRUSTEIN

Male and Female in August Strindberg

To all appearances, August Strindberg would seem to be the most revolutionary spirit in the theatre of revolt. Actually, that distinction must go to Ibsen, but Strindberg is certainly the most restless and experimental. Perpetually dissatisfied, perpetually reaching after shifting truths, he seems like a latter-day Faust with the unconscious as his laboratory—seeking the miracle of transmutation in the crucible of his tormented intellect. The metaphor is precise, for transmutation—the conversion of existing material into something higher—is the goal of all his activity, whether he works in science, turning base metals into gold, or religious philosophy, turning matter into spirit, or in drama, turning literature into music. His entire career, in fact, is a search for the philosopher's stone of ultimate truth through the testing of varied commitments. In his theatre, where each work is almost a new departure, he experiments with Byronic poetic plays, Naturalistic tragedies, Boulevard comedies, Maeterlinckian fairy plays, Shakespearean chronicles, Expressionistic dream plays, and chamber works in sonata form. In his religious and political attitudes, he covers the entire spectrum of belief and unbelief, skirting positivism, atheism, socialism, Pietism, Catholicism, Hinduism, Buddhism, and Swedenborgian mysticism. In his

Reprinted from *The Theater of Revolt* by Robert Brustein, by permission of Little, Brown and Co.–Atlantic Monthly Press. Copyright © 1962 in Robert Brustein.

scientific studies, he ranges from Darwin to the occult, from naturalism to supernaturalism, from physics to metaphysics, from chemistry
to alchemy. His literary work is really one long autobiography,
whether it takes the form of confessional novels, misogynistic short
stories, revolutionary verses, anguished letters, scientific treatises,
theatrical manifestoes, or short plays, full length works, double
dramas, and trilogies. More than any dramatist who ever lived,
Strindberg writes *himself*, and the Self he continually exposes is
that of alienated modern man, crawling between heaven and earth,
desperately trying to pluck some absolutes from a forsaken universe.

Because of his restless Romanticism, and particularly because he
initiated an alternative "anti-realistic" theatre in opposition to Ibsenist
"realism," Strindberg has generally been regarded as Ibsen's anti-
mask, the non-conformist Bohemian in contrast with the stolid practical bourgeois. At first sight, indeed, the two Scandinavians do seem
separated by a much wider gulf than the boundary that divides their
two countries. Compare *Pillars of Society* with *A Dream Play*. The
one, tightly structured and carefully detailed, proceeds from the daylight world of domestic problems, casual discourse, and social awareness; the other, shadowy in outline and fluid in form, emerges out of
a chimerical world of fantasy, delusion, and nightmare. Yet, these
two plays are extreme examples of each man's art; and the contrast
between the two playwrights, while unquestionably strong, has been
somewhat overemphasized at the expense of their similarities. As a
matter of fact, both are part of the same dramatic movement, sharing
certain general traits which have rarely been explored.

Undoubtedly, Strindberg himself is largely to blame for this unfair
emphasis, since he had a tendency to define himself *against* Ibsen,
and spent most of his career directly or indirectly attacking what he
thought to be the older man's themes and forms. His hostility is
understandable. When Strindberg came to artistic maturity, Ibsen
was considered the master dramatist of Europe—and like all figures
of authority to Strindberg, he was therefore ripe for attack. Yet,
Strindberg never understood Ibsen very well, and his antagonism
often seems to be based on rather willful misconstructions of the
Norwegian's work. It is clear, for example, that while Strindberg was
obsessed with the conflict between the sexes, this subject hardly
interested Ibsen, except as a metaphor for a wider conflict between
man and society. But since Strindberg had come to regard art (like
life) as a battleground in which there was no room for subtlety or

neutrality, he became convinced that Ibsen was the fervent champion of his hated enemy, the emancipated woman.

The play that convinced him was, of course, A *Doll's House*. For in spite of the fact that, in early years, Strindberg had identified deeply with Ibsen's Brand, he always preferred to couple Ibsen with this more domesticated work, which he called "sick like its author." Here he found the seedbed for that "Nora-cult" of feminism which he saw infecting Scandinavia like a loathsome pestilence; and ignoring the complexity, ambiguity, and essentially non-sexual character of A *Doll's House*, he simply concluded that Ibsen was the leader of the other side, fomenting plots to undermine masculine domination. As a result of this initial misunderstanding, he mistakenly interpreted *Ghosts* as a treacherous attack on Captain Alving, a dead man no longer able to defend himself against character defamation;[1] he assumed that *The Wild Duck* was a libel on his family life, thinking that Ekdal's doubtful paternity of Hedwig was meant to suggest that he, Strindberg, was not the father of his own child; and he found in *Hedda Gabler* and *The Master Builder* (two plays which did not support his convictions about Ibsen's feminism) conclusive evidence that Ibsen had fallen under his spell and changed his views. Throughout his life, Strindberg was subject to severe paranoiac symptoms, in which fears of persecution alternated with delusions of grandeur; and while his ability to transform these symptoms into art constitutes one of the most thrilling triumphs of modern drama, his paranoiac tendencies hardly qualify him for objective evaluations of other people's work and motives. Yet, it is Strindberg's view of Ibsen's subject matter, coupled with that tiresome characterization of Ibsen as a mouthpiece for social problems in realistic form, which dominates most comparisons of the two dramatists.[2]

If these assumptions are correct, and Ibsen is merely the champion of bourgeois realism and the emancipated woman, then the gap between the two men is unbreachable. Since the assumptions are quite wrong, let us attempt to close the gap a little. Where do Ibsen and Strindberg join hands in the theatre of revolt? Quite clearly, in this basic artistic attack. Both are essential autobiographical writers, exorcising their furies by dramatizing their spiritual conflicts; both are subject to a powerful dualism which determines the changing direction of their themes and forms; and both are attracted to the more elemental aspects of human nature. But above all, both are Romantic rebels whose art is the unrelieved expression of their revolt.

In the beginning of his career, in fact, Strindberg's point of departure is almost indistinguishable from Ibsen's. "I am Jean-Jacques' *intime* when it comes to a return to nature," he writes to a friend in 1880. "I should like to join him and turn everything upside down to see what lies at bottom; I think we are so much entangled, so terribly much regulated that things can't be put right, but must be burnt up, blasted, and then begun afresh." Two years later, at the age of 33, Strindberg puts these sentiments into verse form. In a poem called "Esplanadsystemet" (The Building Program), he envisions the young razing everything to the ground, while a respectable pillar of society looks on with disapproval:

"What! This is the spirit of the times! Demolishing houses!
Dreadful! Dreadful! What about constructive activity?"
"We're tearing down to let in light and air;
Don't you think that constructive enough!" [3]

Even as late as 1898, in *To Damascus*, Part II, Strindberg—through the mouth of the Stranger—is still expressing his determination to "paralyze the present order, to disrupt it," envisioning himself as "the destroyer, the dissolver, the world incendiary."

In these images of demolition, the destructive fantasies of a total revolutionist, Strindberg joins Ibsen in his uncompromising revolt against modern life. Finding common roots in Rousseau and the Romantics, each hopes to redeem mankind from spiritual emptiness through desperate remedies: Strindberg by clearing away rotten buildings, Ibsen by torpedoing the Ark—both by unremitting warfare on all existing social, political, and religious institutions. The negative, individualistic, and essentially anti-social quality of these attacks exposes their metaphysical sources. Both playwrights begin as Messianic rebels, animated by strong religious needs, and determined to war on the God of the old while advancing towards something new. Strindberg's early plays—works like *The Freethinker*, *The Outlaw*, and *Master Olof*—are often strongly reminiscent of Ibsen's *Brand* and *Emperor and Galilean* in their rebellion against God, sometimes even embodying open attacks on God as the author of madness and the father of evil. In the epilogue to *Master Olof*, for example, it is God who maliciously introduces misery into the world ("The creatures who live [on Earth]," He declares, "will believe themselves gods like ourselves, and it will be our pleasure to watch their struggles and vanities"), while it is Lucifer, the rebellious son who, Prometheus-like, tries to bring good to man, and is outlawed for his pains.

Strindberg's identification with Lucifer, rebelling against a mad, merciless, mechanical will, is quite clear throughout the first phase of his career. In his opposition to established authority, Strindberg also identifies with related figures like Cain, Prometheus, and Ishmael—all rebels against God—willingly, and sometimes rather theatrically, embracing their pain and torment as well. Like Ibsen voluntarily exiled from his native land, Strindberg wandered over Europe, alienated from the world of men even when most honored there. In fact, he often describes himself as a pariah—"a beggar, a marked man, an outcast from society" (*Inferno*)—outlawed from paradise, his brow marked with the sign of the rebellious son. Strindberg's admiration for religious rebels presses him well beyond the usual revolutionary postures to an embrace of Satanism, under the spell of which he practices black arts, worships the occult, and studies the transmigration of souls, considering himself dangerous and diabolical. As the Confessor says, in *To Damascus*: "This man is a demon, who must be kept confined. He belongs to the dangerous race of rebels; he'd misuse his gifts, if he could, to do evil." Strindberg's flair for self-dramatization leads him to exaggerate his demonic activities, for they were really harmful to nobody but himself (he suffered severely from sulphur burns). But there is no doubt that he thought himself pledged to Lucifer by a kind of Mephistophelian pact.

This seems like a much more radical form of rebellion than anything found in Ibsen. But as Strindberg implies in *Inferno* ("From childhood onwards," he writes, "I have sought for God and found the devil"), his revolt against authority is really the reverse of his desire for authority, just as his Satanism is actually a blasphemous form of Christianity. In consequence of this shaky posture, Strindberg's revolt is always a little nervous and uncertain, rather like the act of a man in constant dread of retribution. For if Ibsen's Messianicism is based on his conviction that God is dead, Strindberg's is generally tempered by his fears of divine revenge from an omnipotent power. And even when he considers himself a freethinking atheist, these fears are never far from the surface. He became an unbeliever, as he declares in *Inferno*, because "the unknown powers have left the world to itself without giving any sign of themselves." But when these "unknown powers" do begin to appear to him in the Nineties, his Messianicism becomes less and less defiant, until he finally becomes convinced that the powers are personally guiding his destiny, and revealing themselves to him in every material object.

Even then, however, vestiges of his Messianic defiance remain. He wishes to do the will of these nameless authorities, but even in his moments of submission, he "feels rebellious and challenges heaven with doubts." Reflecting on the wayward history of his beliefs, he even begins to blame the Powers for his own spiritual uncertainty:

> You have guided my destiny ill; you have made me and commissioned me to chastise, to overthrow idols, to stir up revolt, and then you withdraw your protection from me and disown me in an absurd way, telling me to creep to the cross and repent! . . . When young I was sincerely pious, and you have made me a free-thinker. Out of the free-thinker you have made me an atheist, and out of the atheist a religious man. Inspired by humanitarian ideas, I have been a herald of socialism. Five years later, you have shown me the absurdity of socialism; you have made all my prophecies futile. And supposing I again become religious, I am sure that in another ten years, you will reduce religion to an absurdity.
>
> Ah, what a game the gods play with us poor mortals.
>
> (*Inferno*)

These tones reveal the equivocal nature of his surrender. He would like to be obedient; yet he cannot entirely suppress the suspicion that the Powers are malevolent humorists who kill men for their sport. Thus, even when Strindberg seems to have repudiated his revolt, he is still rebelling against the authorities he both hates and fears.

On the other hand, his surrender has made him modify the *form* of his revolt. For just as Ibsen, trying to discipline the Messianic tendencies of *Brand*, disguises his rebellion in the objective social mode of *Ghosts*, so Strindberg adapts his Messianic rebellion later in his career to conform with his new desire to submit. The cry of pain one hears in the above passage, in fact, is to become Strindberg's most characteristic tone in later plays like *Easter*, *A Dream Play*, and *The Ghost Sonata*—for there his revolt is Existential, directed against the meaninglessness and contradictions of human existence. Thus, while Strindberg and Ibsen both begin at the same point of departure, they soon develop in different directions. Ibsen, continuing to believe in the importance of the will, begins to measure his rebellious ideals against the social reality: he seeks a spiritual and moral revolution which will transform the soul of man. Strindberg, coming to believe in a strict determinism (the Higher Powers), loses faith in his rebellious ideals: he seeks deeper spiritual insights in order to resolve his own painful dilemmas. Ibsen continues to reject God; Strindberg wavers between affirmation and negation, finally giving way to a melancholy fatalism which one never finds in Ibsen. For while Ibsen works through to a Greek tragic *form*, his rebellion remains strong and constant. Strindberg finally works through to a Greek tragic *mood*, his rebellion partially dissipated by his effort to accept and understand.

On the other hand, while Ibsen is the more faithful rebel, Strindberg is the more faithful Romantic, for he will make fewer concessions to the world beyond his imagination. It is here, in the comparative degree of their involvement in the world of others, that the essential difference between the two playwrights is exposed, for Ibsen offers a superficial deference to external reality which Strindberg totally refuses. This is not to say that one is objective and the other subjective —both are essentially subjective writers, insofar as each makes his own internal conflicts the subject of his art. But since Ibsen's resistance to the demands of his unconscious is stronger than Strindberg's, and more disciplined by the real world, he is willing to disguise his spiritual autobiography in the conflicts of semi-objectified characters, while Strindberg remains the unashamed hero of his work, endorsing his psychic, marital, and religious attitudes through the medium of his art. Consequently, while Ibsen will measure the consequences of rebellion on the happiness of others, Strindberg concentrates almost exclusively on the conflicts in the rebel's own soul.

In other words, Classicism is a mode totally alien to Strindberg, even when he seems to be exploiting it. For even the techniques of "Naturalism" are, for him, a springboard for his unabashed Romanticism. Unlike Ibsen, he is unable to test his subjective responses on the objective world because, also unlike Ibsen, he doesn't much believe in the objective world. Anticipating Pirandello, Strindberg works on the assumption that the world beyond his imagination has no fixed form or truth. It becomes "real" only when observed through the subjective eyes of the beholder, and (here he differs from Pirandello) especially "real" when the beholder has poetic, clair-voyant, or visionary powers. Strindberg's subjective relativism explains why his art always turns inexorably in on himself and his own responses; in a world of elusive truth, only the Self has any real validity. Thus, if Ibsen is primarily concerned with self-realization—or blasting avenues of personal freedom through the cramped quarters of modern society—Strindberg is primarily concerned with *self-expression*—or justifying the superiority of the poet's vision in a world without meaning or coherence. Both are Romantic goals and closely allied. But since Strindberg lacks even Ibsen's grudging respect for external reality, he is by far the more self-involved Romantic, one who worships the "culture of the Ego," (as he puts it in *Inferno*), as "the highest and ultimate aim of existence." In his personal life, this Ego-worship often takes the form of severe psychotic delusions in which Strindberg loses his grip on reality altogether; and it robs his art of such Ibsenist virtues as self-discipline, detachment, and dialectical power. But it provides Strindberg with a Dionysian vitality which carries us along in spurts of ecstasy, lyricism, irrationality, cruelty, and despair—and a dramatic technique which, in his early plays, is almost totally free from the need for balance or moderation, and, in his later ones, has almost totally burst the bonds of restraining rules.

Because of his commitment to a subjective art, it is impossible to analyze Strindberg's work without some reference to his life, especially to that dualism which, like Ibsen's, plagued him throughout his career. In Strindberg's case, this dualism was psychological rather than philosophical, and began at the moment of his birth. The child of a tailor's daughter who had seen domestic service and a *déclassé* shipping agent who claimed to have noble blood, Strindberg was inclined to regard these circumstances as the source of all his later troubles, interpreting them in a manner which is always psychologically revealing, if not always psychologically accurate. In *The Son of a Servant* and elsewhere, for example, Strindberg expressed his conviction that—since he was conceived against his parents' will (i.e., illegitimately)—he was born without a will (i.e., essentially passive and feminine). And since he identified his father and mother with the highest and lowest classes of society, he concluded that this inheritance accounted for his vacillation between peasant servility and aristocratic arrogance.

On top of this, Strindberg's childhood followed an almost classical Oedipal pattern. He adored his mother with a passion he was later to call (with astonishing pre-Freudian frankness) "an incest of the soul," and he hated his father as a powerful and threatening rival. Like Strindberg's feelings throughout his life, however, these early emotions were confused and contradictory. Since his mother had rejected him in favor of his brother, Axel, he sometimes detested her as well—feeling, at times, that she was the dearest creature on earth, at other times, that she was depriving him of love and nourishment.[4] And since he generally measured his own weakness by his father's strength, he tempered his hatred of the older man with a kind of cringing fear and respect.

The consequences of Strindberg's ambivalence towards his father were later to be realized in his ambivalence towards all male authority, notably in his alternating rebellion against and submission to the Higher Powers. His ambivalence towards his mother had a different effect, determining the shape of his love life and his general attitudes towards women. Like those Romantics described by Mario Praz in *The Romantic Agony*, Strindberg had split his mother in two—the chaste Madonna and the erotic Belle Dame Sans Merci—and unconsciously recapitulating his early feelings later in life, he vacillated between an intense worship of the female and an even more intense misogyny. Strindberg was himself aware, in more lucid moments, that his misogyny was "only the reverse side of my fearful attraction towards the other sex" (in his early years he had even been a partisan of free love, companionate marriages, and feminism!). Yet caught in a thoroughly entrenched neurotic web, he was never able to transcend his ambivalence, and alternated between regarding women as evil vampires, sucking out his manhood, and virtuous maternal types who gave him the comfort he so sorely craved.

Sometimes, he revealed this ambivalence by dividing women into two distinct classes: 1) the "third sex"—composed of emancipated females—whom he detested for their masculinity, infidelity, competitiveness, and unmaternal attitudes, and 2) older, more motherly women (generally sexless)—such as Mamma Uhl, his mother-in-law, and the Mother Superior of the hospital of St. Louis [5]—whom he adored for their kindness and compassion. More often he tried to combine the two types in one person—and when he succeeded, he usually married her. For he was always attracted to women he could love for their maternal qualities and hate for their masculinity, reacting to them with bewildering changeability.[6] Consider his violent feelings towards his first wife, Siri Von Essen, as described by Strind-

berg in *Confessions of a Fool*. As long as she was married to another
man, and their union remained "spiritual," Strindberg worshiped
her as a superior being—idealizing her aristocratic bearing, "white
skin," and ethereal purity ("frigidity," according to her unromantic
first husband, Baron Wrangel). It was Strindberg, too, who encouraged her to go on the stage, but as soon as they were married, he
began to accuse her of careerism and competitiveness, not to mention
lesbianism, infidelity, drunkenness, coquetry, uncleanliness, bearing
him another man's child, doubting his sanity, trying to dominate
him, and not keeping the accounts! In his next two marriages—to
Frida Uhl, an ambitious journalist, and Harriet Bosse, a lovely young
actress almost thirty years his junior—the pattern repeated itself,
though with diminishing intensity, as Strindberg gradually realized
that his ambivalent feelings stemmed from his own psychic disorder.

Strindberg's tendency to find a comforting mother and an evil
wanton in every woman he loved accounts for his curious attitude
towards erotic relations. He expects to have his spirit elevated through
Romantic love, only to find he has been dragged down into the mud:

> In woman I sought an angel, who could lend me wings,
> and I fell into the arms of an earth-spirit, who
> suffocated me under mattresses stuffed with feathers
> of wings! I sought an Ariel and I found a Caliban;
> when I wanted to rise she dragged me down; and con-
> tinually reminded me of the fall. . . .
>
> (*To Damascus*, Part III)

What he is describing here is the sexual experience; and what he
implies is a profound distaste for the sexual act. This distaste—
accompanied throughout his life by a pronounced revulsion to all
physical functions and secret fears for his virility—provides some clue
to Strindberg's vacillating feelings. For his hatred of the flesh was
probably the consequence of his nostalgia for the spiritual purity he
enjoyed during childhood, when he was permitted to love his mother
with a love beyond the body. When he matured, however, and
began seeking his mother in the women he married, he had to deal
not only with the divided love-hate feelings he inherited from that
early relationship, but also with the incest taboo. It was this taboo
that caused him to transform the mother-woman into a spider-woman
—he had to justify his attraction to her—and when this transformation failed, he became impotent as an unconscious defense against

his own guilt.[7] As for his obsession with female domination, Strindberg's desire for a mother reduced him to a weak and passive dependent, while his intellect rebelled against this childlike state. In short, Strindberg wished to have the purity and passivity of the child and the masculine aggressiveness of the adult. Desiring to dominate and be dominated, seeking *eros* and *agapé* in this same woman, he was the victim of contradictory needs which left him in perpetual turmoil and confusion.

I must apologize for this bare Freudian treatment of Strindberg's dualism; but so much of it has been established, or at least suggested, by Strindberg himself [8] that the analysis is essential, especially since the roots of Strindberg's art are so clearly sexual and pathological. In Strindberg's dualism, moreover, we will be able to see the nucleus not only of his sexual problems, but of his various artistic, scientific, religious, and philosophical attitudes as well. For the struggle in Strindberg's mind between the male and the female, the father and the mother, the aristocrat and the servant, spirit and matter, aggressiveness and passivity, is the conflict which determines the direction of his career. If we project Strindberg's dualism onto the whole of his drama, we shall be able to understand his development from Naturalism to Expressionism, from scientific materialism to religion and the supernatural, from a convinced misogynist to a resigned Stoic with compassion for all living things. We shall also understand the changing nature of Strindberg's revolt, for his conversion from Messianic prophet to an Existential visionary is directly connected with the resolution of Strindberg's conflicts after years of horrible suffering.

The mature writings of Strindberg fall into two well-defined periods, separated by the Inferno crisis—a dark night of the soul lasting five or six years, during which Strindberg wrote no dramatic works at all. To his first period (1884–1892) belong works like *The Father, Miss Julie, Creditors, Comrades,* and about nine one-act plays, in which the recurring subject—treated further in the essays, stories, and autobiographical novels written during this period—is the battle between men and women. Almost all of these works are conceived in a Naturalistic style, which is contradicted in execution by a number of non-naturalistic elements—especially the author's undisguised partisanship of the male character and the masculine position. Strindberg's control of the Naturalistic method is further weakened by his tendency to strip away all extraneous surface details, and sometimes even to sacrifice character consistency and logical action, for the sake of his concentration on the sex war.[9] Still, there is no doubt that Strindberg thinks of himself as a Naturalist during this period—not only in his approach to playwriting but in his approach to science and metaphysics as well. Having abandoned the religion of his youth, he is now a freethinker, with inclinations towards atheism; and having been converted to Darwinism, he tends to conceive of characters in terms of the survival of the fittest, natural selection, heredity, and environment. Buckle's relativistic approach to history has taught him to doubt all absolute truths; and his interest in materialistic science has encouraged him not only to experiment with the chemical qualities of matter, but even to regard human beings as objects of scientific curiosity, to be examined without pity or sentiment.

Strindberg's conception of the war between the sexes was undoubtedly influenced primarily by the emotional crisis he was experiencing with Siri Von Essen; but his convictions about sexual relations were supported by certain philosophical sources as well, which Strindberg (like the Captain in *The Father*) consulted in order to find support for his attitudes. It is highly probable, for example, that Strindberg read Schopenhauer's *Metaphysics of the Love of the Sexes*, which affirms that sexual attraction is a diabolical invention for the propagation of the race by the "will of the species . . . ready relentlessly to destroy personal happiness in order to carry out its ends"—and that the satisfaction of this will leaves the love with "a detested companion for life." Strindberg's readings in Nietzsche must also have confirmed him in his sexual attitudes, for the philosopher shared many of Strindberg's prejudices—not only against Ibsen (whom Nietzsche called "that typical old maid") but against the emancipated woman ("Thou goest to women?" Zarathustra asks. "Do not forget thy whip!"). When Strindberg sent *The Father* to Nietzsche, in fact, the German philosopher replied that he was highly pleased to see "my own conception of love—with war as its means and the deathly hate of the sexes as its fundamental law . . . expressed in such a splendid fashion."

In the next few years, Nietzsche probably observed a good many more of his ideas in Strindberg's work, for he becomes the single most important influence on Strindberg in this period. Under this influence (which lasted until the philosopher went mad, and sent Strindberg a letter signed *Nietzsche Caesar!*), Strindberg continues to develop a rigorously masculine program, which consists in despising weakness, worshipping the superhuman, and regarding life as a war to the death between master and slave, strong and weak, possessed and dispossessed. Strindberg also shares with Nietzsche an over-whelming contempt for Christianity, a religion he declares is fit only for "women, eunuchs, children, and savages." And declaring Christianity to be a weak and female religion, he begins to reject the softer Christian virtues—like compassion, sympathy, pity, and tenderness—as also suitable only for women.

In their place, Strindberg exalts the hard masculine virtues. The most admirable quality for Strindberg, at this time, is strength—strength of will, strength of intellect, strength of body. Thus, his male characters are often conceived as Nietzschean Supermen, endowed with the courage to live beyond the pale and commonplace bourgeois morality. For Strindberg professes to find a grim pleasure in the tragic quality of human existence and the tough, predatory character of human nature. It is this Nietzschean ecstasy, in fact, that Strindberg opposes to Ibsen's tamer *livsglaede* when, in the preface to *Miss Julie*, he declares: "I myself find the joy of life in its strong and cruel struggles." In his discipleship of Nietzsche, as in his discipleship of Darwin, Strindberg sometimes vulgarizes, exaggerates, or distorts the master's ideas. Nevertheless, his attraction to Nietzsche is unusually strong—so strong, in fact, that he describes the philosopher's influence on him in the imagery of marriage: "My spirit has received in its uterus a tremendous outpouring of seed from Frederick Nietzsche, so that I feel as full as a pregnant bitch. He was my husband." [10]

We would not pause to find any significance in such metaphors were it not that Strindberg's life and work also suggest his feminine passivity. For there is abundant evidence that Strindberg's defiant masculinity is more an impersonation than an actuality, designed to conceal the weaker, more womanish aspects of his nature. Strindberg was sometimes perfectly conscious of this—he often expressed the thought that he should have been born a woman—but, at this time at least, he is at great pains to hide it. It is clear, however, from his fears for his virility and his fears of being dominated, that even when he seems to be blustering most, his masculine identification is highly uncertain. As for the Strindberg hero, he may look like a Nietzschean strong man, but he is quite often in danger of being symbolically castrated. For while the author, in his paranoiac fantasies, will identify with the robust heroes of antiquity, his artistic honesty makes him put these fantasies in perspective: his Hercules is often robbed of his club and set to do women's tasks at the distaff.

Strindberg himself is aware of the ambiguous manliness of his male characters, though not of the reasons for it. In discussing the hero of *The Father* with Lundergard, he writes: "To me personally, he represents a masculinity which people have tried to undervalue, deprive us of, and transfer to a third sex. It is only in front of women that he appears unmanly, because she wants him to, and the laws of the game compel a man to play the part that his lady commands." We may safely question whether "the laws of the game" are responsible for the Captain's passivity; but *something* unmans him, as it unmans almost every male character Strindberg creates in this period. For the typical development of his "Naturalist" hero is from a position of aggressiveness to a position of helplessness: in *The Father*, the Captain ends up in a strait jacket; in *Creditors*, Adolf collapses into an epileptic fit; and even in *Miss Julie*, where the male triumphs, Jean becomes a sniveling coward at the end, shivering at the sound of the Count's bell.[11]

In all of these plays, the antagonist is a woman—more accurately, an emancipated woman—an Omphale who will not rest until she has reversed roles with her Hercules, and assumed his position of authority. The conflict of these plays, therefore, is provided by the opposition of male and female, and the issue is not resolved until one of them has conquered. As a member of the "third sex," the typical Strindberg heroine (Laura, Miss Julie, Berta, Tekla) has a strong masculine streak in her nature too—sometimes even stronger than the man's, for while he occasionally expresses a childlike desire for tenderness, she remains adamant until she feels herself invulnerable. The paradox of this struggle, therefore, is that while the male is physically, and often intellectually, superior to the woman, he frequently falls victim to her "treacherous weakness;" for, in all plays but *Miss Julie*, the heroine lacks honor and decency, pursuing her ends by subtle, invidious, and generally "unconscious" means. Yet, even when Strindberg permits the woman her victory, he feels compelled to demonstrate her basic inferiority. When she competes with the man in a worldly career, as in *Comrades* and *Creditors*, it is only through his help that she succeeds at all; and the man must be brought to realize, as Strindberg was brought to realize, that the sexes cannot co-exist on equal terms.

The Father (1887), though by far the most aggressive work

Strindberg ever wrote, is typical of the plays of this period. The work has a contemporary domestic setting, and contains a few hints about the importance of heredity and environment, so Strindberg sent it to Zola as an example of the New Naturalism. (Zola admired it, but criticized its obscure social milieu and its incomplete characterization.) Yet, it is incredible that *The Father* could ever have been taken for a Naturalistic document. It is more like a feverish and violent nightmare—so irrational, illogical, and one-sided that it seems to have been dredged up, uncensored, from the depths of the author's unconscious. Furthermore, Strindberg's identification with his central character is so explicit that it is sometimes difficult to determine whether the author or the character is speaking; and Laura is such a highly colored portrait of Siri Von Essen that the character is almost totally malevolent—and sometimes quite incomprehensible without some understanding of Strindberg's confused attitudes towards his marriage. Strindberg himself was perfectly conscious, at the time he wrote it, of the subjective nature of his play: "I don't know if *The Father* is an invention or if my life has been so," he wrote to Lundegard, "but I feel that at a given moment, not far off, this will be revealed to me, and I shall crash into insanity from agony of conscience or suicide." Strindberg was actually to do neither, though for a long while he was very close to both. But in *The Father*, he was clearly "acting a poem of desperation," hoping to placate his furies by giving his personal history full dramatic expression.

He was also endeavoring to pay off an old score. For Strindberg partially designed *The Father* as a reply to Ibsen's *A Doll's House*, using Laura as a diabolical contrast to Nora Helmer. One might say that both plays attack conventional sexual attitudes, Ibsen dramatizing the woman's revolt against the tyrannizing male, and Strindberg the male's revolt against the tyrannical woman. But despite the superficial neatness of the parallel, it is not very accurate. For while Strindberg had a personal stake in the "woman question," Ibsen was completely indifferent to it except as a metaphor for individual freedom. Nora's real antagonist is not Torvald, but society itself, insofar as it restricts her desire (shared by most of Ibsen's heroes) for self-realization. The Captain's antagonist, however, is Woman, and he is opposed only by those social conventions which grow from a misunderstanding of the venomous female nature. With the issue reduced to a struggle between the sexes rather than a conflict of ideas, Strindberg's work differs from Ibsen's even in its use of props. In A

Doll's House, for example, the lamp is an instrument of enlightenment, underscoring significant revelations—but in *The Father*, it is
purely an instrument of aggression: the Captain throws it at his wife
after a particularly trying interview.

For while *A Doll's House* uses the techniques of the well-made
play, hinging on tortuous twists of plot and reversals of character,
The Father has a positively relentless power which carries it through,
without psychological complexity or manipulated action, to a violent
and furious conclusion. Compare Ibsen's elaborate stage directions
with Strindberg's peremptory notes. The setting of *A Doll's House* is
so carefully documented that the Helmer household is as tangible
and solid as the real world, but the walls of the Captain's house seem
flimsy and penetrable, as if incapable of containing the explosive
forces within. Actually, the setting of *The Father* is less a bourgeois
household than an African jungle where two wild animals, eyeing
each other's jugular, mercilessly claw at each other until one of them
falls. It is not to Zola's Naturalism that we must turn for precedents,
but to works like Kleist's *Penthesilea* and Shakespeare's *Othello*—
and to Aeschylean tragedy, for like Agamemnon and Clytemnestra,
the Captain and Laura are monolithic figures hewn out of granite,
and stripped of all character details extraneous to their warring
natures.[12]

Because of the intensely subjective nature of the play, it is somewhat difficult to separate Strindberg's conscious artistic design from
the distortions unconsciously introduced by his sense of personal
grievance. On the basis of its bare plot, *The Father* seems to have
been conceived as the tragedy of a freethinker. The Captain, a vigor-
ous cavalry officer,[13] who combines a military career with scientific
work, has lost his belief in God and the afterlife. Consequently, he
must—somewhat like D'Amville in Tourneur's Jacobean play, *The
Atheist's Tragedy*—seek his immortality almost exclusively through
his child, Bertha. He therefore attempts to educate her mind and
mold her will in strict accordance with his own views, so as to leave
a piece of himself on earth after his mortal remains have decayed.
This brings him in conflict with his wife. For while the Captain
wishes to raise Bertha as a freethinker, preparing her to be a teacher
and eventually a wife, Laura wants her to have religious training,
and to follow an artistic career. In order to achieve ascendancy,
Laura proceeds to destroy her husband. Having learned from the
Captain's adjudication of a paternity suit against a subordinate that

no man can be sure he is the father of a child, she proceeds to pour the henbane of doubt in his ear about the true paternity of Bertha. His growing jealousy and suspicions, aggravated by his wife's success in frustrating his career, eventually goad him to acts of violence for which he is declared insane. At the end, when he is immobilized and impotent, Laura proclaims her victory and seizes the prize: "*My child! My own child!*" (Emphasis mine.)

But Strindberg, who had a deeper intention than this in mind, proceeds to universalize the action. When the Captain, writhing in a strait jacket, turns to the audience and cries, "Wake, Hercules, before they take away your club," his words ring with all the activistic force of Marx's call to the workers to shake off their chains. Clearly, *The Father* is designed as a kind of allegory, with the Captain as Everyman and Laura as Everywoman, an object lesson to sanguine husbands, urging them to revolt against their domineering wives. The play, then, is really about a struggle for power which began long before the dispute over Bertha's education. Considered thus, it is not only the tragedy of a Freethinker but the tragedy of a Romantic as well, for it is meant to mirror the strife which rages beneath the surface of all modern romantic marriages.

In this sphere of action, the Captain is portrayed as a clumsy giant who, having learned too late the true nature of women, is brought to suffer the consequences of his early innocence. When he first married Laura, he had worshiped her as a superior being, attempting like most Romantics to find salvation through his love. But, like most Romantics, he had failed to reconcile his desire for a mistress with his need for a mother. The two desires were, in fact, irreconcilable, for as Laura tells him: "The mother was your friend, you see, but the woman was your enemy." Yet, it is to the mother in Laura that the Captain turns in his moment of greatest suffering, even though it was the woman in Laura who is the cause of it: "Can't you see I'm helpless as a child? Can't you hear my crying to my mother that I'm hurt? Forget I'm a man, a soldier whose word men—and even beasts—obey. I am nothing but a sick creature in need of pity." If the Captain were willing to remain in a state of childlike dependency, there would be no strife, for Laura can accept him as a child; but since the Captain feels compelled to assert his masculine power, she hates him "as a man." [14] The two faces that Laura shows the Captain lead him to act with alternating tenderness and hostility towards her, an ambivalence reflected in the mood of the play where the energy of battle is occasionally broken by nostalgic interludes, during which the two antagonists pause to reflect, in tones of gentle poetic melancholy, on the mother-child relationship which was their only ground for mutual affection.

It is in these contemplative scenes that the origin of the struggle is revealed. When his Romantic expectations of marriage had failed, the Captain—resenting his slavery to a woman he had offered himself to as a slave—began to sublimate through intellectual activity; and his life with Laura turned into "seventeen years of penal servitude," presided over by a ruthless, competitive warder. For Laura, who could respond to her husband only when he came to her as a helpless child, was repelled by his sexual embraces ("The mother became the mistress—horrible"), and determined to revenge herself by dominating the marriage. Though Strindberg only faintly suggests this, it is likely—considering his filial relation to Laura—that the Captain shared her revulsion for physical contact. But his recurring doubts about his manhood made him misconstrue her reaction and become even more aggressively ardent: "I thought you despised my lack of virility, so I tried to win you as a woman by proving myself as a man." This fatal mistake resulted in total warfare between them, to which the dispute over Bertha provides only the catalystic climax.

The struggle is the substance of the play, and it turns the entire household into an armed camp. Its outcome, however, is fore-ordained, since the house is crawling with women, and most of the men in the area are too conventional or too gentlemanly to accept the Captain's interpretation of the female character. As the Captain looks desperately about him for allies, determining who is "in league against me" or "going over to the enemy," the sides divide; and Strindberg's personal stake in this war leads him to divide his characters as well, judging them wholly on the basis of their attitude towards the Captain's position. *The Father* includes, among its *dramatis personae*, an Ibsenist Doctor and Pastor, but they are judged by quite different standards than Ibsen uses. Doctor Ostermark, for example, acceptable enough when Strindberg sees him as a humanist, a scientist, and a male, is condemned when he becomes a muddleheaded tool of Laura; and the Pastor, while occasionally satirized for his religious beliefs, is tolerated because of his masculine sympathy for the Captain.

As for the women, Strindberg marks the deck by identifying all his female characters—those onstage and off—with some form of quackery. And since he associates women, at this time, with religion and superstition, their quackery invariably takes a supernatural form. As the Captain notes:

> The house is full of women, all trying to mould this child of mine. My mother-in-law wants her to turn into a spiritualist; Laura wants her to be an artist; the governess would have her a Methodist, old Margaret a Baptist, and the servant girls a Salvation Army lass.

Bertha herself believes in ghosts, and practices automatic writing upstairs with Laura's mother; and even the Captain's old nurse, Margaret—the most sympathetic woman in the play, since she is the most maternal—is called hard and hateful in her religious convictions. It is Margaret, too, who deals the Captain his death blow by tricking him into the strait jacket (she pretends that she is the mother and he the child, and she is fitting on his woolen tunic). For sweet as she may be, her female nature instinctively aligns her with the Captain's enemies. Since the Captain, like Strindberg at this time, is a rationalist, a materialist, and a misogynist, the lines are drawn between intellectual freethinking men and irrational, superstitious, and malevolent women. And on this sexual battlefield, almost everybody seems to act in rather mechanical conformity with his or her unconscious alliance.

This sounds dangerously like paranoia; and it is certain that the Captain's persecution complex is one of the major factors in his mental breakdown. But since Strindberg shares his hero's paranoiac distemper, he is clearly undecided about the state of the Captain's mental health. We are as befuddled as the Doctor, for example, over whether the Captain's acts of violence are to be construed as "an outbreak of temper or insanity." Is he a healthy man driven insane by Laura's poisonous insinuations or are the seeds of madness present in his mind before the play begins? Strindberg hedges. On the other hand, he sees the Captain as a relatively stable man on the verge of an important scientific discovery [15] who, infuriated by the false rumors his wife has spread about his mental condition, the frustrations she has put in his way, and, most of all, the doubts she has sown about the paternity of his child, is goaded into madness ("All steam-boilers explode when the pressure-gauge reaches the limit"). In this view, the Captain's sense of persecution is perfectly understandable since he *is* being persecuted—not only by Laura but by

every woman in the house. On the other hand, Strindberg suggests
that the Captain's will has been diseased since birth, that he feared
for his sanity before the action begins, and that Laura's stratagem
merely exacerbates a dangerous existing condition: it is in cases of
instability, as the Doctor tells Laura, that "ideas can sometimes take
hold and grow into an obsession—or even monomania." Thus we
have a character who fears for his reason, yet believes his reason to be
"unaffected"; who declares himself, by turns, both weak and strong
of will; who is subject to persecution mania, yet actually being persecuted. In short, Strindberg, unable to objectify his own difficulties,
hesitates between writing a balanced play about a paranoiac character
and a paranoiac play about a balanced character—illogically introducing elements of both.[16] Before ambiguity of this kind, we must
simply fold our hands, admitting the futility of trying to extract any
logical consistency from this intensely subjective nightmare.

Yet, like a nightmare, *The Father* does possess a kind of internal
logic, which makes all its external contradictions seem rather minor;
and it maintains this dream-like logic right up to its shattering
climax. For it assumes total warfare between men and women, in
which unconscious thoughts are as blameworthy as explicit actions,
and every woman in the world is either adulterous or treacherous,
and, therefore, the natural enemy of man:

> My mother did not want me to come into the world because
> my birth would give her pain. She was my enemy. She
> robbed my embryo of nourishment, so I was born incom-
> plete. My sister was my enemy when she made me knuckle
> under to her. The first woman I took in my arms was my
> enemy. She gave me ten years of sickness in return for the
> love I gave her. When my daughter had to choose between
> you and me, she became my enemy. And you, you, my wife,
> have been my mortal enemy, for you have not let go until
> there is no life left in me.

In the weird logic of the play, the Captain's conclusions are perfectly
accurate, for just as he was defeated by the evil Laura, so he is
finally led into the trap by the maternal Margaret. Caught in a net
like Agamemnon, roaring like a wounded warrior, he can shout that
"rude strength has fallen before treacherous weakness." But though
he remains defiant, it is perfectly clear that it is his own weakness
which has betrayed him—for over the strait jacket lies the soft,

vanilla-scented shawl of the mother. Even at the last moment, in fact, his fatal ambivalence is clear, for after spitting his curses on the whole female sex, he lays his head upon Margaret's lap, declaring: "Oh how sweet it is to sleep upon a woman's breast, be she mother or mistress! But sweetest of all a mother's." And blessing Margaret, he falls into a paralytic swoon. But though the Captain has ceased to struggle, Strindberg's revolt against women continues to the end. For the "blessed" Margaret has betrayed this freethinker once again —falsely claiming that "with his last breath he prayed to God."

Slanderous, prejudiced, one-sided, these are certainly accurate descriptions of the play. Having dramatized the hostility which accompanies all romantic love, and having discovered some of the psychological reasons for it, Strindberg would seem to have invalidated all his insights through his exaggerated misogyny; yet these very exaggerations provide the play with its impact, and the very unfairness with which it is executed provides its momentum. Fourteen years later, in *The Dance of Death*, Strindberg will take up similar characters in a similar situation, treating them with much greater balance, detachment, and cogency; but the tortured, consuming, inflammatory power of this play is something he will never equal again.

In *Miss Julie*, written a year later (1888), Strindberg seems to have gained a good deal more control over himself and his material. The play is a decided advance in objectivity, generally free from the author's paranoiac symptoms. And while the subject of the work is still the mortal conflict of the sexes, it is, significantly, the male who conquers here, and the female who goes down to destruction. The victory of Jean, the valet, is assured by the fact that he has nothing feminine in his nature at all. Compared with the hero of *The Father*, in fact, he seems to be pure brute, for he shares neither the Captain's sense of honor, nor his need for motherly comfort, nor his lacerating doubts about his manhood. As Strindberg describes Jean, he possesses "both the coarseness of the slave and the toughmindedness of the born ruler, he can look at blood without fainting, shake off bad luck like water, and take calamity by the horns." Strindberg, attracted as usual to masculine strength, identifies deeply with Jean in many ways, and is exhilarated by his brutishness, though he is too fastidious to make a complete identification with this ambitious servant. Nevertheless, as his conception of his hero suggests, Strindberg is feeling much more security in his own masculinity at this time. And the

play embodies, in abundance, those qualities which Strindberg associates exclusively with the male: discipline, control, self-sufficiency,
cruelty, independence, and strength.

In the fine preface he has appended to the work—obviously composed in a mood of brashness, confidence, and high spirits—
Strindberg documents his achievement, giving these male virtues
their aesthetic and philosophical equivalents. For here he expounds
his theory of Naturalism. Beginning by ridiculing the debased ideas
found in the commercial theatre, Strindberg goes on to repudiate, as
well, all drama with an ethical motive, where the spectator is induced
to take sides or pass judgments. We do not know if he would include
The Father in that category, though it certainly belongs there. But
Miss Julie, at least, is offered as a work without tendency, moralizing,
or subjective prejudices: a simple scientific demonstration of the
survival of the fittest. Strindberg concedes that the fall of his heroine
may arouse pity, but he attributes this response to the spectator's
"weakness," and looks forward to a time when, through the progress
of science, audiences will be strong enough to view such things with
indifference, having dispensed with those "inferior and unreliable
instruments of thought called feelings." Echoes like these of Darwin
and Nietzsche, Strindberg's scientific and philosophical authorities
during his "male" period, resound throughout the preface, and so
do echoes of Zola, Strindberg's masculine dramatic theoretician. For
Miss Julie is undoubtedly the closest thing to a Naturalist drama
that Strindberg is ever to write. The hero and heroine—"char-
acterless" like real people—have been provided with an elaborate
social-psychological history, and are determined by heredity and
environment; the action is loose, natural, and compact without being
plotty; the dialogue has the aimlessness of real speech; and the acting
style, makeup, costumes, settings, and lights have all been designed
for a minimum of artificiality.

Yet, despite all these unusual concessions to the "real," *Miss Julie*
is not, strictly speaking, a Naturalistic work—partly because of the
ballet, mime, and musical interlude Strindberg introduces into the
work in the middle, but mostly because the author is constitutionally
incapable of Naturalist impartiality.[17] It is true that Julie is much
more objectively conceived than Laura and that Jean is a much more
complicated character than the Captain. But if the play has an
appearance of detachment, this is because an entirely new element
has been introduced which balances Strindberg's sympathies. For if,

formerly, Strindberg was mainly concerned with the sexual war between men and women, he is now examining a social conflict as well,
between a servant and an aristocrat. And while he is still identifying
with the male as a Hercules in combat with Omphale, he is also
identifying with the female as a Don Quixote in conflict with an
unscrupulous thrall. In short, Strindberg has not suspended his
partialities, he has merely *divided* them. Both Jean and Julie are
projections of the splits in the author's nature—the male versus the
female, and the aristocrat versus the servant—and, in each case, he
is defending himself against the side that he fears the most.

Strindberg's split sympathies can be detected even in the preface,
though in disguised form. Despite his pretense at scientific impartiality, for example, his misogyny is still perfectly clear, for he
characterizes Julie as a "man-hating woman," a type that "forces
itself on others, selling itself for power, medals, recognition, diplomas,
as formerly, it sold itself for money." [18] Similarly, though he affects
a Darwinistic indifference to the supersession of the "old warrior
nobility" by the "new nobility of nerve and brain," he admits that
the aristocrat's code of honor was "a very beautiful thing," and that
the new man rises in the world only through base and ignoble tactics.
Strindberg's admiration for the sexual aristocracy of Jean, in fact, is
qualified by his sense of the servant's inherent vulgarity: "He is
polished on the outside, but coarse underneath. He wears his frock
coat with elegance but gives no assurance that he keeps his body
clean." Jean's lack of cleanliness is not something designed to endear
him to Strindberg who, throughout his life, had an intense revulsion
to dirt; and it signifies that if Jean is the sexual aristocrat, he is the
social slave, just as Julie is the sexual slave and the social aristocrat.
In each case, Strindberg's sympathies, despite his protestations, are
enlisted firmly on the side of the aristocracy.

The dramatic design of *Miss Julie* is like two intersecting lines
going in opposite directions: Jean reaches up and Julie falls down,
both meeting on equal grounds only at the moment of seduction, in
the arms of the great democratizer, Sex. Both are motivated by strong
internal (in Julie's case, almost unconscious) forces which propel
them towards their fate—underscored by social-sexual images of
rising and falling, cleanliness and dirt, life and death. These images
inform the entire play but are unified in two contrasting poetic
metaphors: the recurring dreams of Jean and Julie. In Julie's dream,
she is looking down from the height of a great pillar, anxious to fall

to the dirt beneath, yet aware that the fall would mean her death; in Jean's, he is lying on the ground beneath a great tree, anxious to pull himself up from the dirt to a golden nest above.

The crossover is the crux of the action: Jean seduces Julie during the Midsummer Eve festivities, and then induces her to cut her throat in fear that their impossible liaison will be discovered. Julie's descent, therefore, is a movement from spirit to flesh, motivated by her attraction to dirt and death. She unconsciously desires to degrade herself, to be soiled and trampled on, and when she falls, she ruins her entire house. Born, like Strindberg, of an aristocratic father and a common woman (her mother is associated with dirt through her fondness for the kitchen, the stables, and the cowsheds), Julie finds in her parentage the source of her problems. Her father's weakness has taught her to despise men, and the influence of her mother, an emancipated woman, has encouraged her to dominate and victimize them. Jean has seen her with her weakling fiancé, forcing him to jump over her riding crop like a trained dog; and in the torrent of abuse which pours from her after she has been seduced, her hatred of men is further underlined. On the other hand, neither her class arrogance nor her sex-hatred is total. Her fiancé has filled her with egalitarian ideas, so that she tempers her aristocratic impudence with democratic condescension ("Tonight we're all just happy people at a party," she says to Jean. "There's no question of rank.") And her natural sexuality, heightened by suggestions of masochism, weakens her masculine resolve ("But when that weakness comes, oh . . . the shame!") Like Diana, her wayward bitch, therefore, she is a thoroughbred who consorts with the local mongrels, since her unconscious impulses lead her, against her will, to roll herself in dirt.

By contrast, Jean's ascent is associated with cleanliness and life, and is a movement from the flesh to the spirit. He wishes to be proprietor of a Swiss hotel; and his highest ambition is to be a Rumanian count. Like Julie, he is trying to escape the conditioning of his childhood—a childhood in which filth, muck, and excrement played a large part. As we learn from his story of the Turkish outhouse, in fact, his strongest childhood memory is of himself on the ground yearning towards cleanliness. Having escaped from the Turkish pavilion through its sewer, he looked up at Julie in "a pink dress and a pair of white stockings" from the vantage point of weeds, thistles, and "wet dirt that stank to high heaven." At that time, he went home to wash himself all over with soap and warm water. Now he is still washing himself, in a metaphorical sense, by trying to rise above his lowly position and aping the fastidious manners of the aristocracy. For just as Julie is attracted to his class, so is he impelled towards her. He has become a lower-class snob through his association with his betters, wavering between an aristocratic affectation of French manners and tastes, and a slavish servility amidst the Count's boots.

The contrast between the two characters is further emphasized by their conflicting views of the sexual act and the concept of "honor." Despite her mother's influence, Julie believes rather strongly in Romantic love and Platonic ideals, while Jean, despite his rather pronounced prudishness, regards love merely as an honorific term for a purely animal act—as Iago would put it, as "a lust of the blood and a permission of the will." Jean, in fact, is the Elizabethan Naturalist come to life in the modern world, though, unlike the Elizabethans, Strindberg does not make him a villain. Jean is superstitious, and pays lip service to God (a sign, Strindberg tell us, of his "slave mentality"), but, in effect, he is a complete materialist, for whom Platonic ideals have no real meaning whatsoever. Though he admires Julie's honor, he knows it is only a breath; truth, like honesty, is wholly at the service of his ambition, for he will lie, cheat, and steal to advance himself; and as for conscience, he might say, had he Richard III's eloquence, "It is a word that cowards use." It is because of his pragmatic materialism that Jean so values reputation, while Julie, the idealist, seems to scorn it. For like the Elizabethan Machiavel, he knows that it is external appearances rather than personal integrity that determines one's success in the world. Strindberg undoubtedly views Jean as a link in the evolution of the Superman. And though he secretly disapproves of all his values, he is willing to countenance Jean, in spite of his baseness, because of his effective masculine power.

Jean, therefore, differs from the Captain in his toughness, self-sufficiency, and total lack of scruples; but Strindberg has apparently decided that Iago's ruthlessness, rather than Othello's Romantic gullibility, is the necessary element in achieving victory over the female. Yet, if Jean is no Othello, then Julie is no Desdemona either; and just as Julie learns that Jean is not a shoe-kissing cavalier, so Jean is disillusioned in his expectations of Julie. Jean's disenchantment is signified by his growing realization that the aristocracy is also tainted. For, in getting a close look at Julie, he sees that she, too,

has "dirt on your face," and that the inaccessible golden nest is
not what he had hoped:

> I can't deny that, in one way, it was good to find out that
> what I saw glittering above was only fool's gold . . . and
> that there could be dirt under the manicured nails, that the
> handkerchief was soiled even though it smelled of perfume.
> But, in another way, it hurt me to find that everything I
> was striving for wasn't very high above me after all, wasn't
> even real. It hurts me to see you sink far lower than your
> own cook. Hurts, like seeing the last flowers cut to pieces by
> the autumn rains and turned to muck.

Julie, in short, has achieved her unconscious desire. She has turned
to muck, and been cut to pieces by the rain. And now there is
nothing left for her but to die.

In this act of expiation, Jean serves as Julie's judge and executioner;
but it is in her death that she proves her social superiority to Jean,
even though she has been sexually defeated by him. In the most
obvious sense, of course, her suicide signifies his victory; just as he
chopped off the head of Julie's pet canary, so he must chop off hers,
lest she decapitate him (the sermon in church that morning, significantly, concerned the beheading of John the Baptist). But if
Jean triumphs as a male, he is defeated as a servant, for her honorable
suicide, a gesture he is incapable of, makes his survival look base.[19]
Strindberg dramatizes Jean's ignobility by his servile cringing at the
sound of the Count's bell. Slobbering with uncontrollable fear, he
hypnotizes Julie into going into the barn with his razor. But despite
this display of will, it is Julie, not Jean, who is finally redeemed.
Hitherto convinced of her own damnation because of the Biblical
injunction that the last shall be first and the first last, Julie discovers
that she has unwittingly attained a place in paradise through her fall.
While still an aristocrat, she learns that "I'm among the last. I *am*
the last"—not only because she is last on the ladder of human
degradation, but because she is also the last of her doomed and
blighted house. As she walks resolutely to her death, and Jean shakes
near the Count's boots, the doubleness of the play is clarified in the
conclusion. She has remained an aristocrat and died; Jean has remained a servant and lived; and Strindberg—dramatizing for the first
time his own ambiguities about nobility and baseness, spirit and

matter, masculine and feminine, purity and dirt—has remained with them both to the very end.

The Father and *Miss Julie*, twin prayers in Strindberg's worship of the masculine and the finest works of his first phase, are followed within a few years by a profound spiritual crisis, during which Strindberg's last resistance to the feminine and religious aspects of his nature is broken, and after which his art undergoes an emphatic change. Strindberg's harrowing diary of this crisis, *Inferno*—along with *To Damascus*, an autobiographical trilogy written after the crisis is over—documents the history of his artistic, sexual, and religious "conversion." Strindberg, after divorcing Siri in 1892, has separated from Frida Uhl in 1894, a year after their marriage. Living like a derelict in Paris, he has repudiated the drama and given himself over entirely to scientific experiments; his literary output during a five-year period consists of only three treatises on chemistry. Despite his apparent dedication to science, however, Strindberg is becoming increasingly interested in the supernatural, as he grows more and more convinced that there are unknown powers guiding his destiny. Actually, Strindberg is already preparing to renounce what he calls the "antiquated, degenerate science" of the nineteenth century as limited and unimaginative. "Dedicated from my childhood to the natural sciences," he writes in 1895, "and later on a disciple of Darwin, I had discovered how unsatisfactory the scientific method is, which accepts the mechanism of the universe without presupposing a Mechanician." Strindberg's quest for a "Mechanician" is a sign of his growing need for a religious view of life—a need he first expresses, invertedly, by his Luciferian worship of evil, his Satanic appearance (he has adopted, at this time a Mephistophelian cape and beard), and his occult experimentation. Nevertheless, Strindberg's revolt continues unabated. Even when he later gives up his Satanism, he still remains too rebellious to commit himself to any creed or institution for long. Sometimes he is attracted to Catholicism, primarily because of its mother-worship in the cult of Mary; sometimes to Buddhism, because "I am, like Buddha and his three great disciples, a woman hater, just as I hate the earth which binds my spirit because I love it." These short-lived commitments, themselves so ambivalent, indicate Strindberg's continuing dualism. Searching for absolutes, he is perpetually pressed back into relatives, still too proud to bend his spirit to any higher authority.

It is this "devilish spirit of rebellion," as Strindberg calls it in *To Damascus*, that "must be broken like a reed." And it is partially broken, too, after a prolonged period of unrelieved physical and spiritual torment. For Strindberg, his persecution mania growing, feels convinced during this period that he is being hounded by invisible enemies who are discharging poisonous gases into his room and trying to electrocute him by means of an infernal electrical apparatus. Fearing for his sanity, he flees from Paris to consult a number of baffled doctors, only to be afflicted with electrical shocks in every European city he visits. In the home of Mamma Uhl, his mother-in-law and a Swedenborgian Catholic, however, he does find some relief—through her consoling influence, Strindberg begins to relax like an unhappy child awakening from a dreadful nightmare. Yet, even with her, Strindberg's old ambivalence manifests itself. Believing that the Feminists have laid a morbid plot against his life, he even begins to suspect his mother-in-law of complicity: "I had forgotten that a female saint is still a woman, *i.e.*, man's enemy."

Under the sway of this maternal woman, though, Strindberg continues his readings in Swedenborg, in whose mystical visionary writings he finally discovers what he thinks to be the explanation for his months of agony. He has been suffering from a religious state called *Devestatio*—God has been seeking him, and he has been too proud to let himself be found. Freed from his torment after this insight, Strindberg determines to live a life of repentance. And, indeed, he does give up his occult and scientific studies, begins to wear a penitential habit of monkish cut, and even considers entering a monastery after the publication of *Inferno*. As for his philosophical position, this, as we learn from a crucial passage in *To Damascus*, Part III, has evolved from a pitiless one-sidedness to a compassionate doubleness through Strindberg's acceptance of life's contradictions:

> Thesis: affirmation; Antithesis: negation; Synthesis: comprehension! . . . You began life by accepting everything, and then went on to denying everything on principle. Now end your life by comprehending everything. Be exclusive no longer. Do not say: either—or, but: not only—but also! In a word, or two words, rather, Humanity and Resignation.

Humanity, Resignation, and the melancholy understanding of two conflicting positions—these are to be the tones struck in Strindberg's drama from this point until the end of his career.

For Strindberg, at last accepting the ambivalence which has been in him since birth, has finally permitted himself to accept those elements in his nature which he always feared the most and fought the hardest. Freudians might say that, after a long period of trying to identify with his father, he is now permitting himself to identify with his mother as well; theologians might say that he has finally found his way to God after a long period of resisting Him. Strindberg himself is inclined to interpret his experience religiously, identifying with Paul of Tarsus, claimed by the Lord on the road to Damascus. But whatever interpretation one chooses, it is certain that Strindberg is now confirming those attitudes and accepting those influences which he used to reject as too passive, weak, or feminine. His new interest in the unconscious, for example, is evidence of his change— in the past, it was only women who pleaded its claims. And his endorsement of religion, including Christianity (fit for "women, eunuchs, children, and savages"), shows that he is no longer afraid of female spirituality. Instead of masculine mentors like Darwin, Nietzsche, and Zola—those theoreticians of a tough, ruthless view of life—Strindberg is seeking out more compassionate teachers, generally those with a spiritual or supernatural vision. Swedenborg is a crucial influence at this time, along with Buddhist theologians and Hindu philosophers; and Symbolist writers like Maeterlinck, formerly too ethereal for Strindberg, are now his primary literary models. No longer defying the universe or trying to become God, Strindberg is now yielding to the unknown and seeking to do its will, having replaced his former naturalism and atheism with a new concern for the supernal forces behind material things.

The effect of Strindberg's conversion is, of course, especially evident in his plays, where in this second phase of his career (1898–1909) it has profoundly influenced his conception of theme, subject matter, character, and form. Strindberg is still inclined to view the relations between the sexes as strife; but he is much more willing now to regard this struggle from the woman's point of view. For, influenced by Balzac's *Seraphita*—"he-she . . . *l'époux et l'épouse de l'humanité*"—Strindberg has at last determined to affirm the male-female split in himself. As a result, women begin to play a much more central and sympathetic role in his plays: The Lady in *To Damascus*, Jeanne in *Crimes and Crimes*, Eleanora in *Easter*, the title character in *Swanwhite*, Indra's Daughter in *A Dream Play*, the Hyacinth Girl in *The Ghost Sonata*—some of these are surrogates for the author,

and all have that maternal quality which Strindberg so admired
without any of the wantonness which used to accompany it. In addition, the religious piety of these women, formerly a stimulus for
Strindberg's scorn, is now a sign of tenderness, warmth, and virtue.
In his new veneration of the religious life, Strindberg is anxious to
exalt the worshiper—as he is anxious to exalt the priest (compare the
sympathetic Abbé in *Crimes and Crimes* with the rather simple-
minded Pastor in *The Father*). The frequent subject of his satire
now, in fact, is his old impious self—the rationalistic, blasphemous
male with aspirations towards the superhuman, like Maurice in
Crimes and Crimes. For, in this second phase of his career, many of
Strindberg's plays are designed as acts of penance, in which he tries
to expiate his sense of guilt and scourge his desire for worldly vanities.

As for Strindberg's dramatic techniques, the change in these can
also be attributed to his conversion. In repudiating philosophical
Naturalism, Strindberg repudiated dramatic Naturalism as well,
scornfully classifying this genre as a sympton of "the contemporary
materialistic striving after faithfulness to reality" (*Notes to the Intimate Theatre*). Gone is the compact form and psychological detail
of *Miss Julie*. In their place has come a flowing, formless, fluid series
of episodes—so feminine in their feeling of flux—in which Strindberg
imaginatively uses lights, music, visual symbols, and atmospheric
effects to cut through the materiality of life to the spiritual truths
beneath. The chamber play, a short episodic work in which Strindberg tries to approximate the condition of music, becomes an important experimental mode at this time, but even when his plays are
longer, they tend to assume a musical form. Many of these works
belong to that genre which we now call Expressionism. The term is
apt only in suggesting that they are expressions of Strindberg's unconscious. Plays like *To Damascus*, *A Dream Play*, *The Ghost Sonata*,
and *The Great Highway* are more accurately described by Strindberg's
own phrase, as "dream plays." For they are alike in their use of free
form, so close to the form of a dream, and in their languid abstract-
ness: locations are vague; space is relative; chronological time is
broken; and characters possess names like the Stranger, the Student,
the Poet, the Hunter, and the Dreamer. The dream plays are, of
course, only a sampling of the works that Strindberg wrote during
his second phase. Yet, even in his Shakespearean chronicle plays
(*Gustavus Vasa*, *Eric XIV*), and his more realistic chamber plays
(*The Pelican*, *The Storm*), we are never too far from the author's

unconscious where the supernatural dominates and subjective fantasies are given full play.

On the other hand, it is important to realize that the change in Strindberg is just a question of emphasis: the qualities he is now openly admitting into his drama were always there, though forcibly suppressed. The unconscious source of his inspiration was perfectly clear, for example, in *The Father*, and so was the essentially passive nature of his sexual, emotional, and intellectual responses. In this later period, Strindberg, understanding his dualistic conflicts better, is no longer resisting them so vigorously. Yet, he has still not been able to resolve them. His short-lived marriage to his third wife, Harriet Bosse, for example, indicates that his sexual problems have remained fairly constant. And while the tone of his plays is more saintly and forgiving, his thematic concerns have also remained essentially the same. Even his new religious humility is modified by traces of the old skeptical arrogance; in *Crimes and Crimes*, Maurice agrees to go to the Abbé's church to repent, but he will go to the theatre the next evening; and in *To Damascus*, the Stranger—brought to the door of the Church in Part I—is still afflicted with doubts at the end of Part III, even though he is being initiated into a monastery. Like these characters, Strindberg remains in a state of suspension. If he is no longer fighting God, he is still questioning Him, for he is still a rebel, raging against the awful limitations of his humanity. He has tried to escape from life into a realm of pure spirit, but he cannot resist the pulls of the body which drag him back into the filth, muck, and flesh of the material world.

Strindberg, in fact, is becoming more and more obsessed with human grossness at this time. In *Black Banners* (1904), he writes of his nausea at the sound of men sucking their soup (eating was always a source of repugnance to him), at sweating and stinking human bodies, and at garbage heaps, toilets, and spittoons. Strindberg's revulsion at dirt was inferentially suggested in *Miss Julie*; in his later works, his disgust is even more openly expressed. In *The Ghost Sonata*, for example, it is the task of "keeping the dirt of life at a distance" which weighs down the characters, for there Strindberg even seems to be revolted by such simple household chores as cleaning ink off the fingers and fixing a smoking chimney. The "dirt of life" is, of course, life itself, and especially the life of the flesh. For Strindberg's hatred of dirt is intimately bound up with his life-long disgust at the physical functions of man, especially the physical expression of love which he sees as a base animal act degrading a lofty spiritual feeling.

In the light of his attitude towards the body, Strindberg's commitment to a life of spirit becomes a little clearer, for he tends to regard the physical world, to borrow John Marston's imagery, as "the very muckhill on which the sublunarie orbes cast their excrement." It was Freud who observed that to attempt to rise above the body is to treat the body as an excremental object; and there is no question that Strindberg possesses what Norman O. Brown has called the "excremental vision": [20] he equates the human body with dung. Lesser writers with similar feelings (Maeterlinck is one) generally respond to their hatred of the flesh by turning away from reality altogether, creating a never-never land of airy fantasy. But the superior genius of Strindberg lies in his ability to confront his feelings courageously. It is, in fact, the inescapable interdependence of body and spirit, lust and love, dirt and flowers, which forms the major theme of these later plays, where he tries to explore, in dramatic terms, the melancholy Yeatsian paradox: "Love has pitched his mansion in the place of excrement." He cannot affirm this paradox; he will no longer try to deny it. He will only, in accordance with the Hegelian synthesis he has adopted, try to understand it. But in this desperate effort at understanding, where Strindberg projects his tortured dualism onto the whole of life, his existential rebellion finds its greatest expression.

Of all the works that Strindberg wrote during this period, A *Dream Play* is probably the most typical and the most powerful. To judge from the parallel dreams of Jean and Julie, Strindberg always believed in the significance of the dream-life; but here he has converted this conviction into a stunning dramatic technique. Though the "dream play," as a genre, is probably not Strindberg's invention—Calderón, and possibly even Shakespeare in *The Tempest*, anticipated his notion that "life is a dream," while Maeterlinck certainly stimulated his interest in the vague, spiritual forces "behind" life—the form is certainly his own, in which time and space dissolve at the author's bidding and plot is almost totally subordinate to theme. The Dreamer, whose "single consciousness holds sway" over the split, doubled, and multiplied characters is, of course, Strindberg himself, who is also present as the Officer, the Lawyer, and the Poet, and, possibly, as Indra's Daughter. As he describes the Dreamer in his preface, "For him there are no secrets, no incongruities, no scruples and no law. He neither condemns nor acquits, but only relates, and since on the whole, there is more pain than pleasure in the dream, a tone of melancholy, and of compassion of all living things, runs through the swaying narrative."

Because of the absence of "secrets," A *Dream Play* is even more self-exploratory than *The Father*; but although a direct revelation of Strindberg's unconscious, it is almost entirely free from any personal grievance. For Strindberg, the drama is no longer an act of revenge, but rather a medium for expressing "compassion for all living things." In A *Dream Play* the world is a pestilent congregation of vapors; the miseries of mankind far exceed its pleasures; but, for these very reasons, humans must be pitied and forgiven. The prevailing mood of woe in the work stems from the author's sense of the contradictions of life, some of which are suggested by the Poet in the Fingal's Cave section. After chancing upon the sunken wrecks of ships called "Justice, Friendship, Golden Peace, and Hope," this poet offers a petition to God in the form of anguished questions:

> Why are we born like animals?
> We who stem from God and man,
> whose souls are longing to be clothed
> in other than this blood and filth.
> Must God's image cut its teeth?

Indra's Daughter quickly silences this rebellious questioning—"No more. The work may not condemn the master! Life's riddle still remains unsolved"—but it is the unraveling of this painful enigma of existence which is the purpose of the play. Consequently, the work is structured on similar contrasts, conflicts, and contradictions: Body versus Spirit, Fairhaven versus Foulstrand, Winter versus Summer, North versus South, Beauty versus Ugliness, Fortune versus Misfortune, Love versus Hate. Even the sounds of the play communicate Strindberg's sense of the dissonance of life: a Bach tocatta in 4/4 is played concurrently with a waltz in 3/4, a bell buoy peals in chords of fourths and fifths. For in this work, life itself is no more than a disordered and chaotic struggle between opposites, and the movement of the play is towards explaining the cause of these divisions.

Like *Faust*, the play begins with a prologue in Heaven, a celestial colloquy over the lot of mortals. The God Indra explains to his Daughter that the earth is both fair and heavy because "revolt followed by crime" destroyed its almost perfect beauty. Listening to the wail of human voices rising from below, he determines to send the

Daughter through the foul vapors to determine if human lamentation is justified. Indra's Daughter, descending, becomes the central character of the play. Indicating how far Strindberg has come from his old misogyny, she is—like Eleanora in *Easter*—a "female Christ," expressing the author's sympathy for the fate of humanity and his readiness to redeem man by sharing in his sufferings. She is also Strindberg's Eternal Feminine; each man finds in her sweet, forgiving nature the realization of his own particular Ideal. To the Officer, the first of Strindberg's dream surrogates, the Daughter is Agnes, "a child of heaven," and in her encounter with this embittered character, the Daughter is already beginning to see some motive for human complaint. He is imprisoned in a Castle which grows, throughout the action, out of manure and stable-muck. Likened to the flowers (they "don't like dirt, so they shoot up fast as they can into the light—to blossom and to die"), the Castle is an image of Life itself: the human spirit, trying to escape from the excremental body, aspires upwards towards the heaven, but is always rooted in filth.[21]

Against this paradox of life, the Officer strongly protests, striking his sword on the table in his "quarrel with God." For despite his urge to aspire, he, too, is mired in filth. Like the Captain in *The Father*, he is another Hercules, doomed to an unpleasant labor: he must "groom horses, clean stables, and have the muck removed." Imprisoned in eternal adolescence, he is being punished for a childhood sin, for he once permitted his brother to be blamed for the theft of a book which he himself had torn to pieces and hidden in a cupboard. When the Daughter offers to set him free from the Castle (i.e., from his neurotic fears and guilts), he is, however, equally dubious: "Either way I'll suffer!" And when time and space dissolve back to the Officer's childhood, we see why adulthood is just as painful as adolescence. In this scene, the Officer's father has given his mother a silk shawl—still a symbol of maternal compassion for Strindberg. But she gives it away to a needy servant, and the father feels insulted. In this life of shifting sands, what seems a generous act to one is an evil act to another; all of existence is suffering; and, as the Daughter is now to observe throughout the play, "Humankind is to be pitied."

But the Daughter, still believing in worldly redemption, exclaims, "Love conquers all"; and the scene dissolves again for the first demonstration that she is wrong. The setting is a stage door, much like the place where Strindberg used to wait for Harriet to finish at the theatre, and the motif of the scene is—waiting. Waiting for Victoria, his heart's desire, with a bunch of flowers is the Officer, now freed from the Castle. But Victoria never comes. Time passes, with an accelerated whirring of lights; the Officer grows older and shabbier; the roses wither. The Daughter sits with the Doorkeeper, having taken from her the shawl (once the mother's), now grown gray from its absorption of human misery. For nobody is contented except a Billsticker who, after fifty years of waiting, has attained *his* heart's desire: a net and a green fishbox. Yet, even he grows unhappy after a time: the net was "not quite what I had in mind," the fishbox not quite as green as he had expected. Suffering the twin tragedies of getting and not getting what they want, everybody in the world is afflicted with unhappiness. But behind a cloverleaf door (the Officer, poking at it, has an *intermittence du coeur*, recalling the guilty cupboard of his youth) lies the explanation of human misery and the secret of life. Yet, the Law forbids the opening of it.

The scene dissolves once again to the Lawyer's office, where the Daughter and the Officer hope to get the door opened. Everyone there has grown ugly from "unspeakable suffering." And the Lawyer's face, like the Mother's shawl, is marred by the absorption of human crime and evil. The second of Strindberg's dream surrogates, the Lawyer shares with the Daughter some of the qualities of Christ. Like Jesus, he has taken on himself all the sins of the world; and like Jesus, he is in conflict with the righteous, who condemn him for defending the poor and easing the burdens of the guilty. When he is denied his Law degree during an academic procession, the Daughter's shawl turns white, and she fits him with a crown of thorns. But since he too is a rebel, quarreling with God, she must explain to him the reasons for injustice: Life is a phantasm, an illusion, an upside-down copy of the original. And the four Faculties (Theology, Philosophy, Medicine, and Law) are merely voices in the madhouse, each claiming wisdom only for itself while scourging the sane and the virtuous.

Determined to put her theory of redemption through love to the test, the Daughter marries the Lawyer. But it is in this familiar Strindberg domestic scene that the irreconcilable conflicts of life are most agonizingly dramatized. While Kristin, the maid, pastes all the air out of the apartment, the couple engage in sharp quarrels over their conflicting tastes in food, furnishings, and religious beliefs. Neither is right or wrong. It is simply a condition of life that one's sympathies are the other's antipathies, "one's pleasure is the other's pain." [22] The Daughter, stifling in the house, tied to her husband by their child, and revolted by the dirty surroundings, feels herself "dying in this air." And when the Officer—now at the top of the seesaw of fortune—enters seeking his Agnes, the Daughter and the Lawyer decide to part. The Lawyer dissolves their marriage through the paradox of the hairpin. Like a hairpin, a married couple remain one, no matter how they are bent—until they are broken in two.

The Officer has decided to take the Daughter to Fairhaven, the land of youthful summer love, but through some miscalculation, they land in Foulstrand, an ugly, burnt-out hell, dominated by a Quarantine Station. In this land, where life itself is a form of prolonged quarantine, young people are robbed of their color, hopes, and ideals; fortune turns to misfortune, youth becomes age. Strindberg's third dream surrogate enters, a visionary Poet who embodies the theme of opposition. Alternating between ecstasy and cynicism, he carries a pail of mud in which he bathes. The Quarantine Officer explains that "he lives so much in the higher spheres he gets homesick for the mud," leading the Officer to comment "What a strange world of contradictions." Yet, even in Fairhaven, the heavenly paradise, contradictions mar the holiday atmosphere. The pleasure of the rich is attained only through the suffering of the poor; the fulfilled love of beautiful Alice leaves the passions of Ugly Edith unrequited; the "most envied mortal in the place" is blind. Even in this place, in short, happiness is fleeting and ephemeral; and the only way to sustain pleasure is to die at the moment of achieving it, as a newly wed couple proceed to do, drowning themselves in the sea.

It is, to be sure, a grim vision that informs this work, combining the woeful sense of vanity in Ecclesiastes with the Sophoclean plaint that it is best never to have been born. Despite his conviction that life is universal suffering, however, Strindberg seems to have exonerated human beings from responsibility for it. It is not mankind but the system which is evil—not human character but the immutable conditions of existence. For, as we learn in the Schoolmaster scene, where the Officer, once again imprisoned in adolescence, is forced to learn his lessons over and over like a child, life takes the form of an eternal recurrence, a cycle of return which defeats all efforts at progress, change or development. "The worst thing of all," as the Lawyer tells the Daughter, is "repetitions, reiterations. Going back. Doing one's lessons again." Caught in his own repetition compulsion, locked in the pattern of his neurosis, Strindberg has found in his own personal torment the universal agony of mankind, where one is forced to repeat mistakes, despite the consciousness of error. Thus, when the cloverleaf door is finally opened, the secret of life is discovered to be —nothing. The area behind the door is a vast emptiness.

Condemned by the righteous for bringing man the truth, the Daughter has had enough. She has suffered with all humanity—more extremely than others because of her sensitive nature—and now she knows that human complaint *is* justified. Shuffling off her earthly bonds, as her companions cast their sorrows into the purifying flames, the Daughter prepares to leave the world behind. But first she must provide the answer to the Poet's riddle, explaining the origin of the conflicts she has seen. Her interpretations, expressed in images of Buddhist and Hindu philosophy, is the perfect symbolization of Strindberg's dualism. In the dawn of time, she says, when Brahma, the "divine primal force," let himself be seduced by Maya, the "world Mother," the issue was the world—compounded ever since of elements both spiritual and fleshly, male and female, sacred and profane. Trying to escape from female matter, the descendants of Brahma sought "renunciation and suffering," but this, in turn, conflicted with their need for sexual love. Torn in two directions at once, groping towards heaven and dragged down to earth, man became the victim of "conflict, discord, and uncertainty"—the "human heart is split in two"—and that is why the immortal soul is clothed in "blood and filth." Having given her answer, the Daughter blesses the Poet for his prophetic wisdom, and ascends to Indra, as the Castle blossoms into a giant chrysanthemum. It is the end of the dream, for the Dreamer has awakened; it is the orgiastic vision of the Poet, his mind dressed in its visionary Sunday clothes; but it is also the continual aspiration of the soul after the body has died. In death only, Strindberg seems to be saying, is there redemption—for only in death are contradictions resolved, and the fleshy recoil finally stilled.

It was only through death, too, that Strindberg was able to resolve his own contradictions. When he succumbed to cancer in 1912, hugging a Bible to his breast and muttering, "Everything is atoned for," he had at last found his way to that peace which, half in love with death, he had been seeking all his waking life. The conflicts within him had almost torn him in two; but his art is witness to the fact that he had never surrendered to his own despair. Always ashamed of being human, Strindberg rejected the external world so completely that he often bordered on insanity. But except for his most disordered years, he was usually able to convert pathology into a penetrating, powerful, and profound drama. This transformation was perhaps his most impressive achievement, for his art was in a constant state of flux, always yielding to the pressures from his unconscious. When, in later years, he learned to control his misogyny and soften his resistance to the female principle, he faced life with the detachment of a Buddhist saint, sacrificing his defiant masculinity to the need for waiting, patience, ordeals, and expiation. But though his mood had changed and his spirit was chastened, his quarrel with God was never far from the surface. His rebellious discontent, expressed through a drama of perpetual opposition, had simply found its way into a dissatisfaction with the essence of life itself. Strindberg left instructions before he died, that his tomb be inscribed with the motto of *Crimes and Crimes:* AVE CRUX SPES UNICA. But considering his life-long unrest and uncertainty, and his inability to commit himself to any particular creed, a more appropriate epitaph might have been the final lines from his last play, *The Great Highway:*

> Here Ishmael rests, the son of Hagar
> whose name was once called Israel,
> because he fought a fight with God,
> and did not cease to fight until laid low,
> defeated by His almighty goodness
> ....
> Bless me, whose deepest suffering,
> deepest of human suffering was this—
> I could not be the one I longed to be.

With his work in our hands, it is perfectly clear that this rebel's eternal struggle with God is the key to his greatness. And it is the glory of his art that despite his perpetual dissatisfaction with himself, few could wish him to be anything other than what he was.

NOTES

1. See *The Father*, Act I, where the Doctor says: "And I should like you to know, Captain, that when I heard Mrs. Alving blackening her late husband's memory, I thought what a damned shame it was that the fellow should be dead." Either the Doctor or Strindberg has not read

Ghosts very carefully, because, before the end of the play, Captain Alving's blackened memory has been partially whitened again.

2. Pär Lagerkvist's comments are typical. In order to praise Strindberg, Lagerkvist has to attack Ibsen, employing all the rusty artillery of anti-Ibsenist criticism: "Ibsen, who was long the modern writer *par préférence* because he exhaustively plodded through all the social, sexual, and mental-hygienic ideas and ideals which happened to come up for discussion, merely weighs us down with his perfectly consummated and fixed form, impossible of further development. . . ." ("Modern Theatre: Points of View and Attack," *Tulane Drama Review*, Winter 1961, p. 22). At this point it should hardly by necessary to repeat that Ibsen's forms are far from fixed and his basic subject matter has very little to do with social, sexual, or mental-hygienic ideas.

3. I am indebted to Evert Sprinchorn for calling my attention to this untranslated poem. The translations I have used in this essay are those of Elizabeth Sprigge, except for that of *Miss Julie* which is by Professor Sprinchorn.

4. Love and nourishment, in fact, are always rather closely related in Strindberg's mind. His striking image of the Vampire cook in *The Ghost Sonata*—who "boils the nourishment out of the meat and gives us fibre and water, while she drinks the stock herself"—probably stems from his childhood feelings of love-starvation; the Milkmaid, on the other hand—reflecting the other side of Strindberg's ambivalence—is a symbol of female generosity and mammary abundance. The miserly Mother in Strindberg's chamber play, *The Pelican* (1907), who starves the household of food and love—thus murdering her husband and weakening her children—is another example of the ungiving maternal Vampire.

5. Elizabeth Sprigge, in her sensitive biography, *The Strange Life of August Strindberg*, has called attention to the soothing influence this gentle and maternal woman exercised on the ailing dramatist. She called him "my child" and Strindberg called her "Mother." As he writes to Frida Uhl, "The mere presence of this *mère* comforts and soothes me. *La douce chaleur du sein maternel*, as Baudelaire calls it (I think it was he), does me good." Needless to say, I am deeply indebted to Miss Sprigge's voluminous researches throughout this essay.

6. All his wives remarked upon Strindberg's continual alterations in feeling. Harriet Bosse, more sympathetic than the other two, puts it this way: "I have a feeling that Strindberg revelled in meeting with opposition. One moment his wife had to be an angel. The next the very opposite. He was as changeable as a chameleon." (*Letters of Strindberg to Harriet Bosse*, ed. and trans. by Arvid Paulson, p. 87.)

7. Strindberg's uncertain virility is clear not only in his work but in his letters; one of his greatest fears is that he will not be considered an

adequate lover. Writing to Harriet, he says: "The day after we were wed, you declared that I was not a man. A week later you were eager to let the world know that you were not yet the wife of August Strindberg, and that your sisters considered you 'unmarried.' . . . We did have a child together, didn't we?" (*Letters to Harriet*, pp. 52–8.) Strindberg had the conviction, also, that "where sensual pleasure is sought, there will be no children." Considering his need to keep the sex act pure, it is remarkable he was able to have relations at all.

8. Strindberg eventually grew quite lucid about the pathological origins of his feelings towards women; and though he could never cure himself of his neurosis, he knew himself to be imprisoned in a cycle of eternal repetition, dating from his childhood.

9. Strindberg's concept of Naturalism is far from conventional, for he rejects the typical Naturalist play as mere "photography," offering a special form of conflict in its stead: "This is the misunderstood naturalism which holds that art merely consists of drawing a piece of nature in a natural way; it is not the great naturalism which seeks out the points where the great battles are fought, which loves to see what you do not see every day, which delights in the struggle between natural forces, whether these forces are called love or hate, rebellious or social instincts, which finds the beautiful or ugly unimportant if only it is great." ("On Modern Drama and Modern Theatre," 1889.)

10. Strindberg is very fond of this image. He uses it again, after reading *Hedda Gabler*, to describe his imagined influence on Ibsen—though now, significantly, the husband-wife roles are reversed: "See now how my seed has fallen in Ibsen's brain-pan—and germinated. Now he carries my semen and is my uterus. This is *Wille zur Macht* and my desire to set others' brains in molecular motion."

11. It should be noted that in two of these plays, the male figure is reduced to impotency by the connivance, direct or indirect, of an older man who is related to the female antagonist: Julie's father, the Count, in *Miss Julie*; Tekla's first husband, Gustav, in *Creditors*. In a Freudian analysis, this older man would be seen as a father-figure, punishing the son—through a symbolic emasculation—for his incestuous relations with the mother. This hidden theme—as Denis de Rougemont has pointed out in *Love in the Western World*—is very common to European love literature: its literary source is the Tristan myth, but its psychological source is the family romance. Strindberg's unconscious dramatization of the family romance is especially clear in *Creditors*, a play which evokes Strindberg's feelings towards Siri and her first husband, Baron Wrangel —both unconsciously identified with her own parents. Here Gustav (Wrangel) revenges himself on Adolf (Strindberg) for stealing away his wife, Tekla (Siri). Thus, Adolf's fit of epilepsy at the end of that play is really a symbolic castration.

12. If *The Father* is a reënactment of Aeschylus' *Agamemnon*, *The Pelican* in a modern version of *The Choephori*. Frederick and Gerda, the two dispossessed children, are like Orestes and Electra swearing vengeance on their mother for the "murder" of their father. The Aegisthus of the piece is Axel, the mother's second husband and co-conspirator.

13. It is interesting to note that Strindberg—determined to give his hero a masculine profession—provides him with the calling of Baron Wrangel who was also a Captain in the Guards. Strindberg regarded Siri's first husband, like he regarded his father, as a figure of superior virility, and often tried to supplement his own weakness by identifying with Wrangel's strength. Even in *Creditors*, this partial identification is clear —for if Gustav is the father revenging himself on the son, he is also Strindberg revenging himself on Siri.

14. Considering the Captain's willingness to act the passive infant, in fact, he seems rather obtuse when he asks, in Act I, "Why do you women treat a grown man as if he were a child?"

15. The ability to function as a scientist is always a proof of balance for Strindberg, though it would make little impression on a psychiatrist. In Act I, the Doctor shows astonishment that the Captain's mind might be affected, because "his learned treatise on mineralogy . . . shows a clear and powerful intellect." In *Inferno*, Strindberg also refers to his scientific experiments to convince himself that he could not be insane.

16. Strindberg's hesitation is also evident in his conception of Laura's character. Is she consciously evil, like Iago—a predatory animal who fights with everybody who thwarts her will? Or is she merely *unconsciously* wicked, having unthinkingly perpetrated, as the Pastor calls it, "a little innocent murder that the law cannot touch. An unconscious crime." Just as the Captain waivers between his love of the mother and his hatred of the wife, so Strindberg wavers between these two interpretations of Laura. When there is no longer any need to lie, Laura tells her husband: "I didn't mean this to happen. I never really thought it out. I must have had some vague desire to get rid of you— you were in my way—and perhaps, if you see some plan in my actions, there was one, but I was unconscious of it." The Captain answers, "Very plausible"—but the plausibility of Laura's defense is hardly supported by her other speeches to her husband, by her cunning insinuations to the Doctor, and by her obvious decision to proceed with her plan right after she has been informed that an insane man loses his family and civil rights.

17. It is doubtful if such a thing as Naturalist impartiality can ever be absolute, since the need for some principle of selection ultimately invalidates the fiction of pure detachment. Yet, even a casual comparison of *Miss Julie* with the work of Chekhov, for example, will show how far short Strindberg falls of objectivity. Actually, Strindberg's

animus against emancipated women, his attraction to aristocratic supermen, and his revulsion to dirt are all qualities which testify to his
essential alienation from the Naturalist vision—which is often democratic, egalitarian, "advanced" on such social questions as female
rights, and rather obsessively rooted in sordid details.

18. Actually, Julie—with her white skin, aristocratic bearing, and emancipated opinions—is another, more lucidly executed portrait of Siri. And
so there may be a touch of self-contempt in Strindberg's remark that
"degenerate men unconsciously select their mates from among these
half-women."

19. Martin Lamm reports that, in Strindberg's original conception, Julie
was to snatch the razor from Jean's hand with the taunt, "You see,
servant, you cannot die."

20. See Brown's fascinating book, *Life Against Death*. The excrementalist
is appalled by the sexual act because it is consummated so near the
excretory organs. Jonathan Swift, a writer obsessed by this fact, writes:
"Should I the Queen of Love refuse/ Because she rose from stinking
ooze?" In writing to Siri, Strindberg uses much the same imagery:
"You're walking in filth—you, the queen with the sunlit forehead."
Even the act of writing often seems excremental to Strindberg. To Siri,
he says, "I can get poetry out of filth if I must," and he tells Harriet,
"To put things into words is to degrade—to turn poetry into prose!"
After a while, Strindberg came to believe that the very act of living was
filthy, and the only thing clean and pure was death.

21. In *The Ghost Sonata*, Strindberg uses the image of the Hyacinth in
the same way. The bulb is the earth; the stalk is the axis of the world;
and the six-pointed flowers are the stars. Buddha is waiting for the
Earth to become Heaven: i.e., for the Hyacinth to blossom, aspiring
beyond its mired roots.

22. This, like everything else in the play, is a perception which Strindberg
reached through personal suffering. As he writes in *Inferno*: "Earth,
earth is hell—the dungeon appointed by a superior power, in which I
cannot move without injuring the happiness of others, in which others
cannot remain happy without hurting me."

TRAVIS BOGARD

The Comedy of Thornton Wilder

The theater is the natural home of the cliché. Stereotypes of character, situation, and belief which a novelist would be embarrassed to
conceive, much less develop, come to their particular fulfillment in
the theater. Only at the theater is one treated so frequently to innocent adulteries and guilt-ridden matrimonial triangles, to psycho-
pathic villains terrorizing the incipiently courageous, to drifters
questing for mothers who have betrayed them, to homespun philosophers crackling with rural wisdom, to melodramatized conflicts between dark and light, right and left, vice and virtue. Only at the
theater is experience formulated in terms of repetitious stylizations
of human behavior and accepted with so little effective question.

At its worst, the theatrical cliché beggars insight, heating the
theater with false passion, with concepts empty of thought, and with
attitudes that have been assumed for the occasion without reference
to morality or to psychology. The bulk of drama, prefabricated from
this rotten timber, crumbles, and what survives is so jerry-built, so
patched and misshapen that it can command no real respect from
those to whom art is more than a plaything. The phenomenon of
antidrama, Ionesco's *The Bald Soprano*, for instance, indicates the
degree of revulsion and contempt which even dramatists themselves
feel for a genre which, in large part, is so essentially mindless.

The drama may indeed be dismissed as the subliterary toy of the director and actor who have power to divert audiences in spite of the cliché-ridden script. Yet even the greatest drama is not proof against the cliché. In many instances, major playwrights appear to find solid timber in the rubble of stereotypical theatrical patterns. The tedious, routine story of the revenger told repeatedly in the late Elizabethan theater peaked in Shakespeare's treatment to *Hamlet*; the sophisticated and cynical man-of-the-world who unexpectedly falls in love—such staple fare of the comedy of the Restoration— becomes Congreve's Mirabel; the wife's choice of a lover or husband —the dusty furniture of so many plays by Arthur Wing Pinero and Henry Arthur Jones—becomes, when Shaw develops it, *Candida*; and the mother-questing hero—that common coin of the American dramatist—becomes in O'Neill's work Eben Cabot and Edmund Tyrone.

The great dramatist uses, rather than avoids, the cliché, turning it into a source of strength for his purposes. He is not dominantly an innovator in his themes or his methods. His novelties are in his atti- tudes, as with Shaw, his finesse, as with Congreve, his intensity, as with Shakespeare and O'Neill. In an art form partaking of ritual and ceremony, the chief strength lies not in novelty, but in the symbolic patterns which involve playwright, performers and audience in a kind of communion. Cliché, carefully developed, can serve as myth serves, to establish a basis of belief.

A dramatist must do more than give new names to old situations. He must not merely accept them, but must search them for their human roots. He must fit them into a larger concept of his action so that they do more than thrill cheaply the emotions of the spectator. The best balance sets character as both individual and symbol, ex- ploring in a given situation the dilemmas of the individual man and the meaning he has in a larger scheme of implication. In establishing both the immediate and the general, the cliché character and situa- tion are often serviceable as connecting points, for they base them- selves on possible human actions; at the same time, because they have been used in so many dramas, they suggest an archetypical possibility through which the largest significance of the action may be developed.

Thornton Wilder has been highly praised as an innovator, a man who, along with O'Neill, freed the American theater from its tradi- tional forms through his experiments in *Our Town* and *The Skin of*

Our Teeth. Quite properly, he may be placed in parallel with Bertolt Brecht as a dramatist who uses the technique of alienation to develop an anti-illusory, openly theatrical theater. In *The Skin of Our Teeth* and many of the short plays which preceded it, there are anticipations of such a seemingly new theatrical style as that developed by Tennessee Williams in *Camino Real.* At some moments, he seems to be writing anti-drama in a manner anticipatory of Ionesco. Yet, at the center of all his dramatic work—indeed almost as its major structural element—lies the cliché.

Compared with his drama, Wilder's novels seem fresh-minted, new conceptions whose effects are not repeated. In his novel *The Woman of Andros* (1930), he describes the return of a dead hero from the underworld to relive an ordinary day in his fifteenth year. "Suddenly, the hero saw that the living too are dead and that we can only be said to be alive in those moments when our hearts are conscious of our treasures; for our hearts are not strong enough to love every moment. And not an hour had gone by before the hero who was both watching life and living it called on Zeus to release him from so terrible a dream. The gods heard him, but before he left he fell upon the ground and kissed the soil of the world that is too dear to be realized."

Wilder developed the same suggestion for the climactic moment of *Our Town,* but in the play when Emily returns from the dead to relive a day when she was totally happy, there is instantly summoned to mind dozens of sentimental dramatic romances such as *The Return of Peter Grimm, Smiling Through,* and J. M. Barrie's *Mary Rose.* In the drama the quality of the novel's situation is altered. What was new becomes stereotyped; and yet, with a paradox that can only be resolved by a consideration of the difference between novel and drama, it is Emily who is remembered, just as it is through his dramas, rather than his novels, that Wilder's reputation has become international.

Wilder's earliest dramatic work was published in 1928, following the success of his novel, *The Bridge of San Luis Rey.* In a volume entitled *The Angel that Troubled the Waters,* he collected sixteen one-act plays, some so brief as to be scarcely visible. Many are less than scenes of five minutes' duration. Were it not that each centers firmly on a moral conflict, the plays would more properly be called "Imaginary Conversations" than drama. Yet, although brief and experimental, they are not trivial.

The scope of their conception is astonishing. The *dramatis personae* of the volume include Christ, Satan, Judas and Gabriel; a French dancer and her tubercular husband; Mary, Joseph and Hepzibah, the talkative donkey bearing the Holy Family into Egypt; St. Francis; a great actress and her lover; a mermaid; Ibsen, Shelley, Mozart and Childe Roland. Scenically, were a designer to take Wilder's stage directions literally, each play would require a setting of staggering expense: heaven, hell, the bottom of the sea, a pool in an oriental mosque. A five-page play called *And the Sea Shall Give Up Its Dead* opens with this stage direction:

> The clangor of Judgment Day's last trumpet dies away in the remotest pocket of space, and time comes to an end like a frayed ribbon. In the nave of creation the diaphanous amphitheater is already building for the trial of all flesh. Several miles below the surface of the North Atlantic, the spirits of the drowned rise through the water like bubbles in a neglected wine glass.

In no way, except in their essential conflict, are the majority of these plays fit for, or intended for, the theater. They are exercises of unusual kinds, which Wilder, as he makes clear in his preface, constructed for his amusement to satisfy his curiosity in matters of literature and humanity. Yet they are the beginning, and their quality should be marked.

Their elaborate production schemes, so disproportionate to their length, reflect an unconcern for the routine practices and limitations of the realistic theater. Stripped of embellishments they reduce to very simple elements: to the "three boards and a passion" called for as a prime dramatic essential by older dramatists. In essence they are most like the dramas of the cyclical medieval religious dramas, uncomplicated in their psychology, deceptively naive, and permitting, though not requiring, elaborate production schemes.

They are not especially concerned with characterization as that term, post-Freud, has called for intricate exploration of psychological motivation. They center, instead, on situation and the emotion emerging from the conflict it engenders. The externals of character are sufficiently revealed to provide human habitation for emotion and no more. Man is viewed at a distance, *sub species aeternitatis*, and in this long view much particularizing detail drops from him.

None of these short works is cheap or sentimental. A conversation between Mary, Joseph and their garrulous, spinsterish donkey is saved from frightful excesses of cuteness and sentimentality by its brevity, by its native wit, and by Wilder's refusal to permit his actors to provide the characters with more reality of emotion than his design calls for.

This play, *The Flight into Egypt*, can be taken as typical of Wilder's work, and as anticipatory of his later, more mature dramaturgy. Mary, riding on the donkey Hepzibah with Joseph at her side, carries the Christ child toward Egypt. The donkey, refusing to hurry even when the clashing armor of Herod's pursuing soldiers sounds from the wings, talks incessantly, of her legs and theology and points of interest on the route. Behind her, the scenery unrolls on a revolving cyclorama, like the vistas in the mechanical wonders of a Dime Museum. The Tigris and Euphrates pass by; then the pyramid and the Sphinx; and it is only when the Donkey realizes that Mary carries the child who was born in the stable where she was formerly tethered that she hurries and completes the journey successfully.

Clearly this is dangerous ground for a dramatist. It is a combination of cliché concepts assembled in a way that to audiences trained in realistic theater might seem novel. Yet the treadmill on which Hepzibah walks and the unrolling scenery were staple commodities of the nineteenth century spectacles, such as *Ben Hur*; the balky donkey is comic strip material even today, and the talkative spinster who becomes capable in a crisis is routine theatrical fare. The application of these elements to Christian story is the only novelty, and this, in view of the play's evidently traditional moral, is unimportant.

The effect of the whole when it is produced is exactly as Wilder's scenic description suggested it should be: a charming mechanical toy, which when wound tightly and the proper springs pressed, endlessly reiterates its story. Character does not obtrude on the sense of the remote and the miniature. The machinery of the setting and the cliché characterizations prohibit any particularization. The Holy Family is separated artfully from reality, held at a distance, turned by Wilder's control of the cliché into myth. Compared with the tedious amateurism of many of the experimental one-act plays of the early twentieth century American theater, *Flight into Egypt*, like its companion plays, reveals a young dramatist with an instinctive mastery of theatrical essentials.

In 1931, six more ambitious one act plays appeared in the volume *The Long Christmas Dinner*. It is an uneven volume. Three of the plays, *Queens of France, Love, and How to Cure It*, and *Such Things Only Happen in Books* suggests that Wilder made some effort to come to terms with the theater as he found it and to work with relatively realistic techniques. The results are charming in certain romantic details and amusing in their tricks of plots, but the plays seem slight beside such shorter works as *The Flight into Egypt*.

The remaining half of the volume is of a different order. Taking his direction from the first little plays, Wilder affirmed what was to become his characteristic dramatic manner and found ways to increase the emotional and thematic substance without losing scope or imaginative freedom. The plays in question are the title play, *The Happy Journey to Trenton and Camden*, and *Pullman Car Hiawatha*.

Like *Flight into Egypt*, each of these longer plays is a journey play. *The Long Christmas Dinner* does not move in space, but involves a progress through time, as a family's several generations act their typical stories around a Christmas-dinner table—being born, maturing, and dying at a ninety year long ceremonial feast. *The Happy Journey* describes a motor trip from Newark to Camden, New Jersey, and *Pullman Car Hiawatha* encompasses a night's train trip from New York to Chicago.

Flight into Egypt, like its companion plays, required an elaborate production scheme to achieve the distance and the freedom in space and time. For these later plays the requirement remains, but the theatrical means are refined and simplified. The primary restriction on space, time, and distance in drama is setting. If there is furniture, it must be used; if people live in houses, they must relate to its windows and doors; if visual reality is desired in a production, then the characters must also seem real and work as real people do, within the bounds of seemingly real time and place. But if this is not the end, then setting and furniture can be dispensed with, and, with a stroke, the problem is solved.

The Long Christmas Dinner has a purely functional setting: the table and chairs of the dinner itself and two portals, one through which characters enter as they are born, the other the portal to death. Setting is here reduced and turned to symbol with a simple theatrical directness reminiscent of the door to the grave in the medieval morality play, *Everyman*. Undetailed and stark, the setting establishes no limit to the play's sense of the passing of years, and it requires no more than token use by the actors whose common mortality is more vital than their traits of character as individuals.

The settings of *Pullman Car Hiawatha* and *The Happy Journey* are more openly theatrical, less symbolic. In these, the stage is stripped. A platform with lights and chairs, plus a few flats to insist visually that the stage *is* a stage replace the trappings of ordinary theatrical illusions. Here, for the first time in Wilder's work, the Stage Manager is brought before the audience to arrange the furnishings, to describe the effect the setting is supposed to have, and to sustain in his own person the concept of non-illusory drama, which permits the plays to describe their journeys.

What led Wilder to develop these devices is less to the purpose than the consequences of such innovations. A boyhood in the Orient had undoubtedly taught him something of the freedom and scope of the oriental drama, and had perhaps conditioned him to the charming utilitarian values of the formalized acting styles and the ubiquitous, visible-invisible functionaries allied to his Stage Manager. Similarly, his interest in theater would have led him to consider the value of the expressionist experiments of the followers of Strindberg. In the same years as he wrote, the theatrical waters were stirred with experiments similar to his. In Germany, Bertolt Brecht was becoming acquainted with Oriental theater and adapting its methods to his style of Epic Theater. In America, the experiments of O'Neill, John Howard Lawson, and many others had suggested the possibility and the desirability of a break from the realistic unities of Ibsen.

Yet, as his first collection suggested, if Wilder were to write drama at all he would have to move toward a nonrealistic dramatic manner. The development of such enabling techniques were essential so long as he held to his attempt to depict the individual in terms that would call to mind the ultimate destiny of all mankind. And this was his theme. In a sense, perhaps, all of Wilder's plays are about the Day of Judgment, imaging human character as a bubble rising to burst on the surface of eternity. There undoubtedly were influences on his experimental style, but, in the last analysis, Wilder's innovations are important consequences of his point of view and of his way of commenting on experience.

The results of the stylistic developments are important. To take *Pullman Car Hiawatha* as a single example: As the train runs westward through the night, like the mechanical Tigris and Euphrates in *The Flight into Egypt*, fields and towns (including Grover's Corners, Ohio) appear and state their relation to it; trackworkers and others concerned with the train's operation step forward to speak their pieces, like graduates of a School of Elocution, awkwardly stilted in speech, paralyzed with stage-fright; and ultimately, guided by the Stage Manager, the hours of the night and the planets pronounce, through wise saws of the ages, a kind of benediction on the train and on its passengers, who restlessly mutter their night thoughts. The sense is of many voices, half heard at a distance, joining in a chorus somehow relevant to man's destiny, somehow in harmony with the singing planets and with a vast but living immensity. In the end, the train does not click along tracks to a purely local destination. It becomes part of the entire westering turn of the earth, part of the movement of life in space.

The production scheme permits Wilder to hold a view of man that takes into account individual differences, but in the end reduces them in size. Characters are sufficiently drawn to reveal particular human dilemmas, yet nothing that anyone does is important in its own right. Again, the human characters are cliché figures, but as their individual characteristics slip from them, as their passions are shown to be symptomatic of the kinds of emotions each of these kinds of people would feel, and as individual will remains powerless before final destiny, the cliché figures form into a pattern whose sense is of a typical assortment of men and women, no one worthier of attention than any other. Because they are cliché images of men, they hold an anonymity entirely suitable to Wilder's larger design.

This is not to say that man is unimportant in the total design. If anything, his importance is increased in relation to the wide scheme against which he is projected. Man's will, passion, and suffering, however, are not his most important characteristics. Rather, his importance emerges through his relationship with nature's cyclic movement. He is measured by what he touches, rather than by what he does, and these points of wide-ranging contact are only revealed by maintaining the broadest perspective on his action. Through this perspective, the dramatist found his most characteristic means of expressing his sense of life, and it may have been these means, the theatrical cliché combined with a startlingly simplified stagecraft, that permitted him to become—in his full-length plays—the only important American writer of comedy.

In comedy, when it has not been scraped and sharpened by an informing satiric intelligence, man is shown as the inhabitant of a basically benevolent world. The sense is that he lives within a charmed circle where nothing ultimately painful or evil can happen. The man who slips on the banana peel does not damage his sacro-iliac, lovers forced to spend a damp and foggy night on the ground in a wood near Athens do not suffer from over-exposure, heartbreak returns to laughter, and *hubris* leads only to a reasoned acceptance of society's norms. The benevolent limits on action and its conse-quences affect character, as well. The range of emotion in comedy tends to be smaller. Passionate outbursts with far-reaching conse-quences, pain, even violent excesses of love are gentled, narrowed, reduced in size and kind and rendered more artificial than real.

In Wilder's first full-length play, *Our Town* (1938) the tech-niques of the comic artist emerge clearly. The characters are limited, held within the benevolent social framework of a turn-of-the-century small town. Their ambitions are unimportant, their suffering is never great and its consequences are muted. They do not quarrel nor lust. They have no thought for their past or their future. They are bounded by reassuring statistical summaries, by familiar occurrences —the night train, the round of the milkman and the paperboy, the homeward stumbling of the drunken organist—and by familiar places—the kitchen, the soda fountain, the graveyard on the hill.

Significantly, they do not look beyond this bounded township at the nation, the world-at-large, nor at the universal scheme in which they figure. They are not inquirers into destiny, and it is clear that nothing they say or do will ever attempt to alter the nature of things. Instead, they maintain the daily, pious rounds of activity, keeping place within set limits. The result is that they are not called upon to express passion of any violent kind, nor are they permitted to cry out in pain. Wilder removes from his stage even scenes of sickness, although instances are reported in passing. Thus, without important action of will, curiosity or awareness, Wilder's characters are brought to a condition of emotional gentleness. At its farthest range, their wonder achieves only a childlike awe at the concept expressed in an envelope's address:

Jane Crofut
The Crofut Farm
Grover's Corners
Sutton County
New Hampshire
The United States of America
Continent of North America
Western Hemisphere
The Earth
The Solar System
The Mind of God

To Rebecca Gibbs, who tells of the letter, what is most remarkable is that "the postman brought it just the same."

It is odd, perhaps, that these inherently docile creatures, incapable of heroism or villainy, are not to be blamed for refusing to attempt to shape their destinies, but Wilder protected his villagers from a charge of spinelessness partly by admitting no occasion to test them. Later, in *The Skin of Our Teeth*, where every moment is a crisis of huge dimension, Wilder buries the individual response in farcical vaudeville, again relieving the characters from becoming involved as individuals in any moral or spiritual dilemmas. What is left in *Our Town* moves perilously close to the sentimental, and would perhaps commit itself irrevocably to saccharine patriotic images were it not that Wilder measures humanity from a distance.

The essential difference between *Our Town* and the bulk of American folk drama is that Wilder attempts to convince no one of his truth by insisting that what he presents is the reality itself. If his story had been developed realistically, carefully plotted, decorated so as to attempt to convince the audience that it was seeing living human beings, much of its truth would have drained from the play, and all of it would have seemed sentimental and unconvincing. But Wilder, as his earlier plays suggested he might, avoids this and with it much of the fraudulence of American folk drama. He insists that the actors are only pretending to be characters. They are stage-managed; they are in rehearsal, so to speak. Above all, they are not attempting to convince anyone of the reality of their illusionary comings and goings. They are deliberately depicted as theatrical stereotypes.

The result is that Wilder's characters become emblems of reality, not reality itself. They are there to remind audiences of familiar things in whose recognition there is pleasure and security. Like the statistics quoted in the opening sequences of the play, the things the characters do are ways of naming blessings.[1] The characters seem a little like priests, the guardians of a shrine whose rituals they only dimly comprehend. In their appointed rounds, they touch familiar things and receive a kind of blessing from the act. They are secure in eternity, and what they do is a ritual enactment of realities which do not need analysis. And because they are deliberate artifices, they escape the merely sentimental. What they touch has the power of a propitiatory charm, a tribal totem, warding off any invasion of evil or doubt.

The distance provided by the artifice permits the drama to move through broken scenes, fragmentarily tracing the lives of George and Emily and their families and their neighbors. Its primary emotion is the joy of discovery and remembering the discovery of the limited world. Moving backward and forward in time and place, the scenes form, in the end, a whole and describe man's course in the timeless cycle of eternity. Even the moment of greatest agony, when Emily returns to earth and cries out that man is unaware of joy as it passes, diminishes in the free slip of time. Tears drain into the earth and memory lies light as the flesh disappears and as thought releases its hold on dead limbs.

For an audience, this is the value of the play: that it reminds men of the good underlying their hesitation, doubts and agony. It promises no salvation, but, equally, in *Our Town* no one is damned. Wilder does not deny the reality of suffering, the necessity of questing and inquiry, but he sees that all such passion and acts of will shall pass away in the surcease of eternity.

In *Our Town*, the open theatricalism acts to diminish the sentimental cliché latent in the subject matter in much the same way that the convention of the boy actress permitted the artificial and improbable plotting of *As You Like It* to become effective. Character is kept at a distance by the stress on the theatrical means. In *Our Town*, the device obviates the necessity for sustained narrative and, while still permitting character to move and to hold an audience's interest, reduces it to something like norms of the experience Wilder is presenting.

In *The Merchant of Yonkers* (1938), Wilder experimented with another device for attaining the same end. Based on Johann

Nestroy's *Einen Jux will es sich Machen,* a German adaptation of
a 19th century English farce, John Oxenford's *A Day Well Spent,*
the play might well be called the Complete Farce, centering on
farce's basic concerns, folly, money and love, developing its story
with complex and improbable plotting, filled with "screen scenes"
involving sudden discoveries and disguises, and with characters
brought on stage for the primary purpose of engineering the story
to its close. Even in his use of typical 19th century stage costume,
Wilder is trying to make his play a reproduction of an older style
of dramaturgy. He succeeds so well that the play seems as good as
any of its models; unfortunately, it seems no better. Old-style farce
permits him to use cliché figures cleverly, and to stress the theatricalism which seem an essential part of his theatrical style. Yet in
the empty trivialities of the story, the amorous escapades of the
Merchant and his apprentices, Wilder deserts the long view of the
human scene which justified the similar effects in *Our Town.* Farce,
as farce always does, diminishes humanity, belittles the human scene,
and commits itself only to the mechanics of laughter. *The Merchant
of Yonkers,* even under the direction of the noted German pro-
ducer, Max Reinhardt, failed when it was first produced. Engaging
as it was, set against *Our Town* it meant little because its effects
were produced for so little purpose.

The farcical theatricalism of *The Merchant of Yonkers* was combined with the more purposive antirealistic techniques in Wilder's
next play, *The Skin of Our Teeth* (1942). *Our Town's* stage manager is banished behind the wings, to be sure, but his anxious voice
is heard in moments of production crisis, and his presence is felt
everywhere. As in *Our Town,* the audience is continually reminded
of itself by intrusive voices from the auditorium, by ushers participating in the destruction of the theater to "save the human race"
from the Ice Age, and by the many kinds of free vaudeville which
occur in the action. From backstage come dressers and stage hands
to duplicate the passing of the planets and the hours, as in *Pullman
Car Hiawatha,* and the swaying flimsiness of the scenery continually
stresses the essentially illusory nature of the theatrical experience.

Added to this is the element of ancient theatrical farce, notably
in Sabina's opening and closing soliloquy, where she is permitted
to enact the part of the traditional comic maid delivering the
exposition. The effect is to dispel illusion in a burlesque of antiquated stage conventions which emphasizes continually the theater's
false face.

As in *Our Town* and, to a lesser extent, *The Merchant of Yonkers*, the devices minimize the particular psychology of the characters, turning them into figures in a charade who perform before a symbolic setting a deliberately unconvincing enactment of man's progress through the ages. Again, the temporal and spatial freedom permitted by the setting enables the action to move in fragmentary symbolic configurations forward and backward in time.

The Antrobus family is several specific families: it is the family unit of the cave-dwellers; it is Adam, Eve, Lilith; it is the family of Noah; it is the family of the average present-day suburban commuter. Its many specific identifications, however, combine to make it the archetype of all families in all times. It becomes "Every Family," the norm of the concept, much as the configurations in *Our Town* become norms. All images are blended in a composition of universal significance.

Thus far, Wilder develops what he has done before, holding his characters at a distance, that they may become symbols. But now, perhaps taking a hint from the stage manager's relations to his actors in *Pullman Car Hiawatha*, he also stresses that his actors are in fact actors, and he does with them what he had not done in *Our Town* or *The Merchant of Yonkers*—he gives them personal stories to enact within the larger frame of the drama.

The effect is a little like the infinity to be found in barbershop mirrors: Lilith, the eternal temptress, is a maid named Sabina, who is played by an actress named Miss Fairweather, who, in turn—once this aperture has been opened—was played by an actress named Tallulah Bankhead. Essentially a comic device, refined and put to more significant service than usual, the technique is similar to that which Shakespeare developed with his original Rosalind: a boy, pretending to be a girl, pretending to be a boy, pretending to be a girl, to the ultimate negation of any reality of character.

In Wilder's play, the device allows him to maintain the sense of comedy even when he portrays situations involving world cataclysm. Yet it is also true that this illumination behind the mask tends at certain points in the action to increase the audience's sense of identification with his characters at the same time that it maintains the long view. At its easiest level, the play has the delights of vaudeville. Thus, when Miss Bankhead read the line, "The Ten Commandments, faugh!" and added in a throaty aside what was evidently a deep personal conviction, "That's the worst line I ever had to say on any stage!" the Bankhead personality broke through layers of Fairweather and Sabina with an effect reminiscent of Hogarth's drawings of false perspective.

Not only serviceable for comic purposes, the device provides Wilder with the empassioned climax of his play. In Act III, when Cain's murderous frenzy becomes the actor's reality, when the artificial enactment of a symbolic gesture becomes the particular actor's truth, illusion and reality merge in a way that neither negates the effect of the passion nor permits the passion to come too close so as to destroy the essential perspective of the play. It is Wilder's particular ability to superimpose artifice on reality in this way, projecting life through his imagery.

In the end what Wilder achieves by his technical experiments with point of view and identification is freedom to depict man moving in great gaps of time, of the limited terrestrial animal who has a dim vision of eternity and, because of it, somehow musters the will to survive.

After *The Skin of Our Teeth*, Wilder turned to matters other than the stage [2] until 1954, when his rewritten version of *The Merchant of Yonkers* opened under its new title, *The Matchmaker*. As directed by Sir Tyrone Guthrie, the play, no longer overshadowed by the success of *Our Town*, came into its own as an amiable piece of tomfoolery. The revisions are very slight, amounting in effect only to the kind of judicious pruning and tightening which any play may expect to undergo in production. At only one moment does Wilder make a significant alteration. Mrs. Levi's soliloquy at the end of Act IV which begins "Ephraim Levi, I'm going to get married again. . . ." contains in its original version a lengthy analysis of the people who refuse to accept the human race:

> You and I have known lots of people who've decided—like Horace Vangelder—not to live among human beings. Yes, they move about among them, they talk to them, they even marry them; but at heart they've decided not to have anything to do with the human race.
>
> They become secret.
>
> They ask nothing and they give nothing.
>
> They've refused the human race and perhaps they're right.
>
> And the first sign that a person's refused the human race is that he makes plans to improve and restrict the human

race according to patterns of his own. It looks like love of
the human race, but believe me, it's the refusal of the
human race,—those blue-print worlds where everyone is
supposed to be happy, and no one's allowed to be free.

If you accept human beings and are willing to live among
them, you acknowledge that every man has a right to his
mistakes. . . .

The lines state clearly enough one of Wilder's creeds, and perhaps
provide a partial explanation of his insistence that man is better
off not knowing the nature of his destiny. Yet they are repetitious
and overly explicit, and in their sociological implications a little
heavy for the tone of the farce.

In the revision, the lines are altered:

After my husband's death I retired into myself. Yes, in
the evenings, I'd put out the cat, and I'd lock the door,
and I'd make myself a little rum toddy; and before I went
to bed I'd say a little prayer, thanking God that I was independent—that no one else's life was mixed up with mine.
And when ten o'clock sounded from Trinity Church tower,
I fell off to sleep and I was a perfectly contented woman.
And one night, after two years of this, an oak leaf fell out
of my Bible. I had placed it there on the day my husband
asked me to marry him; a perfectly good oak leaf—but
without color and without life. And suddenly I realized
that for a long time I had not shed one tear; nor had I
been filled with the wonderful hope that something or
other would turn out well. I saw that I was like that oak
leaf, and on that night I decided to rejoin the human race.

The difference is partly in the tone, in the use of the concrete
rather than the general, but mostly in the quality of the imagery.
In its stress on growth and on the value of life, the imagery of this
one speech is almost sufficient in itself to lift the farce from its
emptiness, to turn it in the end to comedy.

Comedy should be distinguished from farce in two respects. First,
it is not centrally satiric. Comic satire in drama always results in
farce. In plays by Aristophanes, Ben Jonson, Molière, and Shaw,
the generic form which their satire develops is that funny pattern

of humanly improbable action where event is significantly separated from character. The work of Beckett and Ionesco has taught the playgoer once again that farce is capable of serious statement. As all drama can be, farce is a way of looking at life, and at times its particular distortions have no equal for reflecting an inherently distorted world. But farce in the hands of a great playwright is possessed by a demon. It is raised from a sterile existential hell and forced to caper insanely before laughing multitudes. In itself it generates no emotion. An audience for farce is a little like the farce itself—possessed by the attitudes of the playwright. The emotion is applied to the work, not developed within it. An audience is called to share Aristophanes' ribald rage and Molière's scorn but not primarily to understand or sympathize with the characters. What the characters mean is more important than what they do, because their every action only reiterates their hopelessness and their folly. With Ionesco, farce again antiseptically applies a styptic to emotion; with Beckett, although farce is often betrayed by sentimentalism, the end result is more likely to be a sense about Gogo, Didi, and Krapp than a feeling for them.

A second distinction between comedy and its grotesque counterpart follows from the first: that comedy is essentially positive and optimistic, whereas farce is negative in its view of the human condition. Its soulless comedians are generally not permitted any higher good than the merry and notable frauds of Aristophanes' Pisthetairos or Jonson's Volpone. Its world is the artificial construct of the cozener, tales told by a con man to deceive and delight. Whether the cheater be active for love, money, or both, in the end his actions ask no further commitment than that his audience share the dramatist's point of view toward the absurdity he has imaged onstage. The dramatist's truth is local and particular, framed in relationship to temporal criticism and manners, and his characters live, if at all, because folly persists, and in all times cheating is the immediate consequence of folly. Without these particular polarities, so essential in *The Matchmaker*, farce dies and is forgotten despite its wit, its structured cleverness, its frail memorials to the laughter of the dead.

But comedy is a testament to life. Its commitment is to the great regenerative cycle, following man's course from birth through nature to death. By no accident, comedy's main concern is often with love, courtship, and marriage. Comedy's laughter rises from the complications of wooing and of man's stumbling efforts to dominate the life process which grips him. In the great Shakespearean comedy, the laughter arises when the lovers for one reason or another pull away from nature, out of the cyclic process: when the girl destined for love disguises herself as a man, when a woman in obsessive mourning walls herself and her garden away from love. Such spinsters—Olivias, Violas, Rosalinds—and their masculine counterparts, the determined bachelors—the Berownes and Benedicks—as they separate from life, become guilty of folly and move, ironically enough, in the sterile patterns of farce. So Congreve's Mirabel and Millamant, before they "dwindle" into matrimony, move in a maze "like a dog in a dancing school." Yet nature and comedy make short work of the would-be farceurs, overwhelming them in the end and tossing them back to the living source of their blessing, to love, and its vital fulfillment.

It is truistic to acknowledge that in the twentieth century there has been no tragedy to compare with that of the Greek and Renaissance theaters. Often, the most serious criticism of both the contemporary theater and contemporary man is that they are incapable of tragic perception. Yet the point may equally well be made that there is today no comic perception either—a point which may suggest that unalloyed comedy and tragedy are alike in their central point of view and in their final assertion. Although comedy finds its fulfillment in life and tragedy its fulfillment in death, weddings and funerals celebrate the same natural process and both ceremonially testify to the value of the force and of the lives it controls.

For reasons apparent to any watcher of twentieth century skies, such unqualified testimony, such essentially religious testimony as tragedy and comedy have traditionally offered cannot be easily found or readily accepted. The ceremonials which signify joining with or separating from life bring little assurance of sanctity. Men marry and die in haste, and comedy and tragedy have lost their affirmative assurance of life's lasting fulfillments. Both have been hollowed out with farce and sentimentality leaving the form of the thing without its essence, a partial and adulterate perception lacking boldness and wisdom. At the best, a few dramatists have sought after modern equivalents of the tragic and comic values in mixed forms, which by their very impurity testify to the puzzling complexity of an irresolute, modern evaluation of life.

Thus far, in twentieth century American Drama, only two playwrights have proved durable beyond their season. In Eugene O'Neill, there developed a tragedian of stature—awkward, gifted with a giant's strength, sometimes guilty of using it like a giant, yet an artist who saw with the clarity occasionally granted to the pessimist the way man's life can be justified through suffering. At the same time, and conveying something of the same sense of being a little out of the stream of the main direction of American drama as O'Neill's work conveys, Thornton Wilder wrote the three plays which have adhered most closely in this country to the traditional vision and the affirmative concept of great comedy.

In a foreword to *The Angel that Troubled the Waters*, Wilder revealed clearly why this is so. He wrote:

> The art of literature springs from two curiosities, a curiosity about human beings pushed to such an extreme that it resembles love, and a love of a few masterpieces of literature so absorbing that it has all the richest elements of curiosity. I use the word *curiosity* in the French sense of a tireless awareness of things. (It is too late to arrest the deterioration of our greatest English words. We live in an age where *pity* and *charity* have taken on the colors of condescensions; where *humility* is foolishness and *curiosity* is interference. Today *hope*, and *faith* itself, implies deliberate self-deception.

Wilder is right, of course. The sympathies which came so readily and strongly to men in the past are now perplexing and adulterate, unable to abide questioning. Eugene O'Neill constructed an entire scheme of tragedy on the hope that implies deliberate self-deception. Yet Wilder, as his revision of Dolly Levi's soliloquy suggests, is not quite willing to give over the polarities of past assurance: pity, charity, humility, simplicity, hope, faith and the curiosity that leads to wonder. That he cannot deal with them as they essentially are but must cast them in terms of cliché images from old theatrical modes is a consequence of the human condition, not a necessary element in Wilder's faith. Of his first plays he remarked that they are almost all religious plays, but, he added, "religious in that dilute fashion that is a believer's concession to a contemporary standard of good manners."

The concessions must be made. Perhaps, in dealing with religious themes in theatrical terms they have always to be made. Yet it is evident that the concessions are in the form of technical experimentations, of the way of presenting the themes, rather than in the themes themselves. At the center of his dramas, at least, Wilder makes no concession. That he does not explains much of his present pre-eminence and suggests why his work may survive the more ephemeral drama of his time.

NOTES

1. Detailed biographical evidence is lacking in substantiation, but his plays suggest that Wilder himself touched reality as firmly and as often as he could. For instance, in *The Happy Journey to Trenton and Camden* he names a high school principal, Mr. Biedenbach, who was in fact the principal of the Berkeley (California) High School which Wilder attended. In the same play, the characters pass and comment on the Lawrenceville Academy where Wilder was teaching as he wrote the play. A sudden blurring of artifice and reality occur, as if the characters were watching Wilder watching them.

2. Omitted from consideration here are his early play, *The Trumpet Shall Sound* (1927), his translation of Andre Obey's *Lucrèce* which Katherine Cornell played in 1932, and his version of the Alcestis story, variously titled *The Alcestiad, The Drunken Sisters,* and *A Life in the Sun.* The latter was first staged at the Edinburgh Festival in 1955, but was withdrawn from the English stage thereafter. It has been published in German translation. Its first general appearance in English was as the libretto of an opera by Louise Talma. Wilder has been at work for some years on two cycles of one-act plays concerned with the Seven Deadly Sins and the Seven Ages of Man. When completed they are intended to be played in varying combinations over a series of evenings. Three of these plays were staged off-Broadway in 1962.

JOHN GASSNER

A *Streetcar Named Desire*: a Study in Ambiguity

1   AN EVALUATION

Among the new plays of the 1947–48 season A *Streetcar Named Desire* was not only the best but the most indicative of the flexibility of realism. Strongly rooted in the reality of character and environment, and replete with stinging naturalistic detail, this tragedy of a fallen member of the Southern landed aristocracy, nevertheless, abounds in poetic overtones. These are justified, in part, by Blanche's refinement of language. She is well bred and she has had sufficient education to have taught school for a while. Her consuming need, moreover, is to make herself and others constantly aware of her refinement. She is concealing her tawdry past of alcoholism, incontinence, and common prostitution. She is compensating for her fallen estate. Her memories being as unbearable as her present circumstances, she must transform both by building a dream-world for herself. Obviously, this world contains a large measure of self-delusion, as well as a good deal of pretentious public behavior. She makes "poetry," which her cultural background enables her to "activize" in the form of "manners" and to articulate in dialogue. Her drama becomes "poetic drama." Not realistic drama with poetic varnish, but realistic drama naturally and necessitously poetic. How necessitously, we can realize from the fact that her very refinement

From *The Theatre in Our Times* by John Gassner. Reprinted by permission of Crown Publishers, Inc. Copyrighted 1954 by John Gassner.

betrays her by becoming excessive—hysterically fastidious rather than natural. Her manners become mannerisms, and her speech verges on preciosity. As if in atonement, she crucifies herself on a cross of culture. In *Streetcar*, poetic drama becomes psychological reality.

For Williams, in this play, there can be no borderline between prose and poetry any more than there can be between reality and fantasy. This was also true in the case of Amanda and Laura in *The Glass Menagerie*, as well as, to some degree, in the case of Tom the Narrator when he remembers and ponders upon their world, so fantastic in its ineffectual twilight reality by contrast with the realities of the Second World War. (And, like Blanche, Tom is a poet *manqué*, as his narrations prove; though inadvertently, I suspect, since the author of these speeches is Williams, not Tom, and it is Williams who becomes "literary.") Alma's story in *Summer and Smoke* would, later in Williams' career, also make "poetry" as an extension of her life and as a defense against it. The fusion of poetry and prose began, indeed, early for Williams, in *Battle of Angels* and in such one-act plays as *Portrait of a Madonna* and *The Lady of Larkspur Lotion*. The fusion is a necessary one not only in his treatment of character, but in the development of conflict. *Streetcar* establishes a contrast between Blanche's mask of inviolable gentility and the opinion of her that others must form. This fact provides a major conflict in *Streetcar*. Characterization in *Streetcar* is indistinguishable from this particular tension, as well as from that which already exists within her. *Characterization as tension* is undoubtedly the best kind of dramatic characterization. We find it, for example, in *Hippolytus, Hamlet, Phaedra*—and *Desire Under the Elms*.

At the same time, there is an ambiguity in Blanche's situation— or, rather, we have here a series of ambiguities. Placed in opposition to Stanley Kowalski at the beginning of the play, she is the aristocrat who condescends to the plebeian when she is not actually scorning him. This is compulsive conduct on her part, because she must feel superior to her sister's husband if she is not to feel inferior in view of her helplessness. But her behavior does not commend her to us. She is also an element of disease threatening the healthiness of her sister's relations with Stan. We can be grateful at first when Stan, disconcerted by Blanche, tries to take Blanche down a peg. Yet there is a certain splendor in Blanche's personality—a tragic splendor until the clinical aspects of her character dim it. Her sister avoided shipwreck by compromise—by marrying Stan and by satiating herself at the trough of commonplace gratifications in marriage. Stella is fortunate in this respect, as ordinary people, who have an aptitude for "the blisses of the commonplace," are fortunate. Blanche, on the contrary, cannot renounce her view of herself as a rare individual. Like other tragic characters, she *longs* for "the blisses of the commonplace" but is as incapable of accepting them as she is incapable of courting them efficiently. Tragic characters are "efficient" only in courting, suffering and encompassing their own destruction. Antigone, Oedipus, Hamlet, and Lear are tremendously efficient in this respect. Therein lies their *arête*, their specialness and stature, even when it is wrapped in folly, as in the case of Lear's dotage. Therein lies also their ultimate *hamartia*, or tragic flaw, which is, above all, their inability to recognize, in the words of Keats, that life has its impossibilities.

Thus far the ambiguities are dramatically, indeed tragically, fruitful. Reality is encountered meaningfully when it becomes plain that Blanche comes to a haven to which she will be unable to *decline* and therefore "adjust." She must turn safety into hell, given the necessities of her character. Also, those who can provide the haven must either eject her from it or turn it into hell for her. Overabundant in animal health and devoid of tender-mindedness, Stan must try to eject her; and, failing to eject her, to quarantine her psychologically (by proving her to have been a harlot), because she has brought unease, if not indeed disease, into his home. And her sister Stella must eject her as an insane accuser of Stan, after the latter has violated Blanche. Otherwise Stella could not remain with Stan, to whom she is bound by sexuality, love, and economic convenience, especially now that she has borne a child. Stan must also turn the haven into hell for Blanche as a necessity of his brutish inclinations, which have been inflamed by the sex-duel that has arisen between them—not without necessitous, if perhaps only half-conscious, initiative on her part. And these ambiguities, too, produce "poetry"—as dialogue, character insight, and atmosphere.

Williams, however, not only enriched but muddled his play with his ambiguities; they are at times only *melodramatically* fruitful. He reduced potential tragedy to psychopathology. Blanche's psychological situation, indeed, is already so untenable when she enters the home of Stan and Stella that she should be receiving psychiatric care. Williams, moreover, muddled the social basis for Blanche's drama, which he himself underscored with references to her Southern plantation. The aristocratic family's fortunes declined, it is true, and left her economically insecure; but she could have supported herself honorably as a teacher had she not become a victim of neurosis. Her plight is attributed to the bizarre—and to me specious —circumstance that her husband killed himself after realizing that he was a hopeless homosexual. As the daughter of a Southern "Cherry Orchard" family, she might have become quite credibly ill adjusted to reality by overrefinement and pride. But Williams, unsatisfied with normal motivations, adds the causative factor of marriage to a homosexual which has not been established as inevitable. Nor is it convincing that the young husband's death should have led her to seduce schoolchildren and take up with soldiers in a neighboring camp. *The Cherry Orchard* is pyramided upon normal motivation. Therefore the characters, their failure, and their social reality, or their symbolic value as representatives of a dying aristocracy, are equally believable. In *Streetcar*, in so far as Blanche's role is concerned, only her illness is believable—and even that is suspect, in so far as its inevitability is questionable.

It is also curious how Stan's role changes from that of an opponent who has reason to guard his marriage against Blanche to the role of a brute who in violating Blanche also violates his marriage. And if it is argued that the point of the play is precisely that Blanche, who needs every consideration, is thrust into a brute world that gives her no consideration, then, I say, Williams has destroyed the tragic possibilities of *Streetcar* in another way: He has settled for pathos whereas the ambience of his characterization of Blanche suggests a play possessed of a sharper, more equitable, and harder insight— namely, that of tragedy. I would argue, indeed, that having missed that insight—which is surely a defect or insufficiency in the author's thinking—Williams *had* to turn Stan into a brute. Stan was not a mere brute at the beginning of the play; and, later, he could claim the right to warn his wartime-buddy Mitch against marriage with Blanche because she had been a harlot. But Stan became a brute unmistakably in the rape scene toward the end of the play.

Williams, indeed, seems to have succumbed to a generally jaundiced view of normality by giving the impression that the common world is brutish, as if life in a poor neighborhood and Stan and Stella's sexually gratifying marriage were brutish. That is hardly the case, of course, and Williams himself contradicts this view, here and there, in his picture of the New Orleans Latin Quarter and of some aspects of the sister's life with Stan. But *Streetcar* exhibits a good deal of ambivalence on the author's part. The realist and the esthete are at odds with each other in this play. Enough variation in emphasis is possible, given the individual actor and the individual director, to make different stage productions yield different impressions, if not indeed somewhat different themes. But *Streetcar*, for all its dramatic momentum and surge, is a divided work. Ambiguities split the emphasis between realistic and decadent drama, between normal causation and accident, between tragedy and melodrama. Although *Streetcar* crackles with dramatic fire, it lacks a steady flame. Its illumination flickers.

2   "SPINES" FOR DRAMA

An important question arises. If *A Streetcar Named Desire* is so divided a play, how can it be staged satisfactorily?

The answer is that the unifying impulse and intelligence begin to operate. The director arrives at an over-all meaning or "spine" for the play, and for each of the characters—especially for the important ones. To prove the absolute validity of the "spine," assuming that this were always possible or could be done without endless disputation, is unnecessary. It is necessary only to make enough sense of the play and its acting parts to have confidence that one knows where one is going as a director in guiding the actor, determining the stage business, calling for a certain kind of setting, and so on. Likewise, the actor: the "spine" he finds for his role, with or without the director, is not absolute. It can only accord with the actor's personality and temperament, and with his understanding of the part and of its relationship to the other parts in the play.

"Spine" is an approximation of the meaning of the play and the meaning of the part. "Spine" is relative to the director and the actor, who brings himself to the stage production—and in bringing himself brings also, let us note, his education, taste, bias, etc., to it. It is possible, therefore, for different directors to stage *Streetcar* differently, and for different actors (Jessica Tandy and Uta Hagen, for example, in the same role of Blanche Du Bois) to play the same part differently and, nevertheless, to give it cohesion or logic—provided there is enough intelligence operating in the work, as there is in *Streetcar*.

It is also possible for the same play to be produced differently in different places and times. The important factor is this: if the play makes sense to those who perform it, there is the likelihood that it will make much the same sense to their audiences. That is, if these audiences are in accord with the director's and author's taste and viewpoint, or values. (It was noticed after *Streetcar* had been running for some time on Broadway that audiences, no longer typically a New York playgoing public, reacted to the play as though it were rather comic and prurient.)

In the case of Elia Kazan's production of *A Streetcar Named Desire*, we have the director's notes to himself. (They are reproduced by Toby Cole and Helen Krich Chinoy in their useful book, *Directing the Play*, Bobbs-Merrill.) Kazan told himself that Blanche's "spine" was "to find Protection." Concerning the theme of the play, he wrote: "This little twisted, pathetic, confused bit of light and culture puts out a cry." Then it is destroyed by factors which Kazan described as "the crude forces of violence, insensibility and vulgarity which exist in our South—and this cry is the play." Whether we agree with this definition or not (and I quarrel with both the reference to "in our South" here and to the charge of insensibility with reference to all characters except Stan), Kazan made *Streetcar* matter sufficiently to most playgoers on the basis of this effort at unifying its action.

The critic's function is, of course, to discover whether the play is artistically solvent. Neither the playwright's nor the director's (nor the actor's) definitions may be valid in the critic's opinion— or more than only partially valid. But, then, the critic's function is not that of an agent of the theatre whose business it is to make a play succeed. His business is to evaluate or judge the work rather than put it "across." He is a detached, disinterested party in this respect. For him the "spine" found for the play by the playwright's collaborators in the theatre may *not* pull together the elements of the work that have been left unfused or inharmonious.

The reviewer—in so far as he can be distinguished from the critic —will submit to the spell of the production, if it is an effective one. He is more susceptible, so to speak, to the conspiracy of playwrights, director, actors, and others to put the play "across" on the stage. Moreover, he *should* be susceptible, even when he carries his faculty of judgment with him; otherwise he will be a stick of wood in an audience full of live people. It should be possible (and it is usually possible) to work on his sensibilities with all the potency of theatre craftsmanship. That being the case, the reviewer, like any other responsive member of the audience, also organizes impressions or finds a "spine," which is sufficient to make the play mean something to him—unless, of course, the play or the production is hopelessly disorganized and meaningless.

3 PLAY REVIEW

The result is a "review," and, with all its partial insights, oversights, and hastily formed impressions, it pertains importantly to the work that is being reviewed. The reviewer records the effect that the play in a particular production was able to exert on one impressionable individual. If his impressions are not flagrantly at variance with those formed by most other reviewers or experienced playgoers who saw the same production, his report tells us something about the dramatic quality of the work. In the case of *Streetcar*, a consensus established this much with certainty: It was a stirring and anything but meaningless work, if not indeed a work of genius, regardless of my analysis of its ambivalences or ambiguities and consequent shortcomings, upon which I could have, indeed, enlarged. (The same judgment can be also rendered on *Death of a Salesman*, in spite of an unsuccessful fusion of social and individual causation in Willy Loman's drama.)

The fact that a play could make such an impression is certainly relevant to what the play is, if we can assume that the reviewer was not naturally eccentric or willfully perverse. (Or willfully "superior," out of youthful *hybris* or out of a calculated effort to call attention to himself and his predilections rather than to the play in question!) The fact that the work enabled the reviewer—an individual who has written down his reactions for publication—to discover a "spine" of some magnitude and interest tells us that the playwright and the performers managed to exert a certain degree of power and persuasion.

With this in view, and as an example of two levels of judgment which sometimes more or less coincide and sometimes do not, I reproduce here my very first review of *Streetcar*, almost exactly as it was published in *Forum* magazine and subsequently in periodicals abroad.

When *The Glass Menagerie* opened on a memorable spring evening in 1945, New York critics had the pleasure of acclaiming the arrival of a promising new playwright in Tennessee Williams. On December 3, 1947, when A *Streetcar Named Desire* opened at the Ethel Barrymore Theatre, they made the always welcome discovery that their expectations had been met with indisputable certainty. If, in addition, they cast a backward glance at the thirty-three-year-old author's numerous one-acters of unmistakable distinction, as well as the published text of his full-length *Battle of Angels*, which the Theatre Guild was forced to withdraw after its opening in Boston, there could be no doubt that America had a new major dramatist. When the recording angel writes, he will have Tennessee Williams to add to the good deeds America has piled up for herself in heaven as on earth.

In a stirring and beautiful production directed by Elia Kazan, who has a number of brilliant jobs of stage and film directing to his credit, A *Streetcar Named Desire* emerges as the most moving American play of the past dozen years. It is, moreover, a play that needs no erudite exegesis, no coterie support, no apologetics to make it acceptable.

Blanche Du Bois, a young woman bred on a rich plantation that had gone to seed, arrives at a disreputable quarter of New Orleans to stay with her sister Stella, who has married the rough-hewn Polish laborer, Stanley Kowalski. Blanche is not well; she is extremely nervous and hears strange music when distressed. Her distress increases when she surveys the sordid surroundings, when she observes that she will be sleeping next to her sister's bedroom with only a curtain between the rooms, and when she meets her strange and gruff brother-in-law. She has been a schoolteacher as well as a belle. She exudes the spirit of refinement in her speech and comportment, and clings pathetically to her clothing and furs, mementoes of a life to which her present environment makes a garish contrast. Her sister Stella has an earthy simplicity and sound animal instincts; she is happy with her exuberant and violently virile Pole, But she, poor Blanche, who is in such need of quiet and comfort, has entered the strange precincts of the uninhibited, uncomfortably hearty proletariat. Her delicate scorn and wincing aristocratic superiority cannot be mistaken. One cannot help pitying her, and also laughing at her because the life she affects to despise seems so invincibly alive while her eyes seem fixated on a decadent past. But pity claims priority because her helplessness is so palpable, and because she is so evidently concealing a wounded past. Pity, however, is precisely what she cannot incite in Kowalski, to whom her refinement is both comic and affronting, in whom curiosity about this strange woman becomes an obsession, and for whom her presence is a disturbing element. He had been happy with Stella in a rough-and-tumble manner, and now he must defer to Blanche's delicacy, her nerves, and her disdain of his uncouth conduct and animal spirits.

He begins to unravel her past, thread by thread, from the suspiciousness of her conduct and from chance bits of information. It is not long before he discovers that she had been compelled to leave her home town after seducing one of her boy students, and that subsequently she had spent some time in a disreputable house. This is the woman for whom the slightest indelicacy is a torment! And his suspicions are only too well substantiated by her birdlike attempts at sexual intimacy. Her whole pitiful story unrolls before the audience, which the omniscient author involves in an understanding and sympathy that must remain a sealed book to the elemental and lively fellow who is her brother-in-law. In her golden girlhood Blanche had deeply loved and then married a lovable young man who turned out to be a homosexual and who killed himself when his sense of guilt became unbearable. Her seduction of young students became a compensatory and compulsive measure; and her masquerade of fastidiousness was a necessary defense against the gross reality of her desires, as well as against the sordid world into which she had been thrown.

Blanche, we realize, is pretty far gone after the shipwreck of her ego, but she finds one unexpected straw to cling to—that is, in addition to the delusion or pretense that a wealthy man in Florida is ready to leave his wife for her. The straw is Harold Mitchell, a friend of Kowalski's and an innocent, mother-coddled lad who is strongly attracted to the fey creature. After a few affecting encounters he is even ready to marry her, with his mother's permission, and Blanche is eagerly awaiting him on the evening of her birthday, an occasion that is being observed with cake and candles by her pitying sister. But the suitor does not arrive, and Kowalski bluntly admits that he had revealed Blanche's past to his friend; he wasn't going to let his best friend marry a tart. This is the crisis, and thereafter every event contributes torments to unsettle an already badly jolted mind. Valiantly Blanche continues to spin threads of romantic illusion as an anchor to life, but the last threads are severed when her brother-in-law, whom she has been vaguely enticing, violates her, and Stella reluctantly consents to committing her sister to an asylum. The concluding scene is as heartrending as any one of a half a dozen other preceding scenes. The matron from the asylum knocks her down on the floor when she struggles; the physician from the asylum takes one quick look at her and resolves to salvage her self-respect. He removes his hat, speaks to her in courtly accents, and raises her from the floor. Instantly she radiates pleasure and walks out with him, her head high as if she were following a gentleman who has shown her the extreme courtesy which befits a lady.

I have told this story at some length, but even so the narration is the merest summary. The Mielziner setting, which combines sharp realism with poetic beauty, adds the dimensions of environment to the plot. The characterization is vastly enriched by the performances of Jessica Tandy, who plays Blanche with great virtuosity, as well as conviction, and of Marlon Brando, whose Kowalski is a masterful realization of innocence, animality, and shrewdness. The story itself is many-faceted. And here we may find the true measure of the play's compelling power, aside from the variety and magic of the dialogue. Tennessee Williams has accomplished what is seldom achieved in contemporary dramaturgy; unlike most of his fellow-craftsmen, he has not only built a play well but he has built it with the steel and brick of narrative and characterizing substance.

What *A Streetcar Named Desire* has is the abundance of a good novel. It might have actually been elaborated into a novel, which book critics, with customary enthusiasm, would have hailed as indicative of the combined capacities of a Faulkner and Dostoevsky, without being fundamentally more substantial than Williams' play is on the stage. Life has density in this drama of a woman's tragic effort to clothe her nakedness. (The nearest modern parallel in playwriting is perhaps Pirandello's more cerebral play *Naked*.) The theme is one of the universals of human experience, and it has been managed in a variety of ways by such novelists as Conrad, Dostoevsky, Gogol, Flaubert, and De Maupassant. The author's viewpoint combines a sharp sense of reality, a naturalistic fearlessness in the face of what is gross in individual life and society, and a just compassion. The handling of the dramatic elements is remarkably astute, since the author keeps wave after wave of revelation hurtling through the play. He balances humor and pathos as surely as he balances Blanche's illusions and the objective realities. He distributes effects in the right proportions and at the right time (for dramatic writing, more than fiction, is dependent upon the proportion of the parts and the timing of impressions), and plays upon the impressionableness of an audience as a concert pianist plays upon the black and white keys. But what stands out as most contributory to the making of a memorable play is the total effect of humanity seen in the round. This has been unnecessarily left to the novelists by playwrights who think more of construction than of the material with which they are building.

THOMAS PARKINSON

The Later Plays of W. B. Yeats

Criticism of Yeats's later plays tends to stress their relation to his lyric poems on the one hand and his philosophy on the other. Their usefulness in this respect has been elaborately demonstrated in F. A. C. Wilson's recent *W. B. Yeats and Tradition*,[1] in which the five last plays are intensively analyzed as philosophical structures that, in turn, illuminate certain of the later poems. But Mr. Wilson follows a stultifying habit in Yeats criticism by ignoring the theatrical tradition, the idea of a theater, that motivated the plays from about 1916 on. Hence once again the actual texture, the stage potentialities, the theatricality of the plays have been depreciated, and their relevance to the needs of the modern theater remains unexamined. In part the general distaste for Yeats's later plays as theatrical vehicles has been strengthened by Yeats's criticism, his denial of the role of "character" in drama, his lofty refusal in his late years to concern himself with "public" theater, his ironic insistence on the specialized reference of his fables and plots. Much of this can be dismissed as exasperated pose—his dislike of "character" in drama came from the special use of the term in the Irish press to indicate a type of personage that he and Synge were not interested in treating—and it seems to me that the current literary habit might put us in a frame of mind more receptive to the great experiments of Yeats's later dramas. At any event, it might help if for a moment we looked not at what Yeats wrote *about* his plays but what he wrote *in* them.

Yeats's later drama began after he had turned over the management of the Abbey Theatre to Lennox Robinson as representative of the young, rising realists of Ireland. The publication of Yeats's *Plays for an Irish Theatre* in 1911 marked the end of his early, or Abbey, dramatic period, and from 1911 through 1915 his energies were diverted from the theater to the writing of essays, his autobiography, and non-dramatic verse. He still worked on one play, *The Player Queen*, but until Ezra Pound introduced him to the notes of Ernest Fenollosa that eventuated in Pound's *Noh or Accomplishment* and *Certain Noble Plays of Japan*, he saw no way of shaping a dramatic form that would satisfy his need for a theater without getting him once more involved in "theatre business, management of men," that had for so long exhausted his capacity for patience and calm. With the help of the Pound adaptations, he then wrote, ". . . I have invented a form of drama, distinguished, indirect, and symbolic, and having no need of mob or press to pay its way. . . ." [2] And when Pound wrote to his parents about Yeats's motives he stressed the liberation from commercialism that the form of *At the Hawk's Well* allowed:

> Yeats . . . has done a play of his own on the Noh model, and is preparing a new dramatic movement, plays which won't need a stage, and which won't need a thousand people for 150 nights to pay the expenses of production. Yeats seems to expect the new drama to do something, at least there will be no compromise, actors will wear masks, scenery will be mostly imagined, at most a cloth or a screen. . . . [3]

Yeats was not so eager for a dramatic "movement" as was Pound. He agreed with him only in his belief that these "chamber" plays would liberate him from attempting to please the belligerent Abbey pit.

Yeats could not literally adapt Noh form, which is dependent on traditional associations that come from common beliefs shared by writer, actors, and audience and embodied in conventions comprehended in such detail that the most minute gesture is endlessly significant. It seems to me that the "influence" of the Noh on Yeats can easily be exaggerated; the Japanese forms sanctioned and strengthened motives already existent in Yeats's dramaturgy. As he and Pound worked on the Fenollosa manuscripts at Stone Cottage, Pound relied on Yeats's knowledge of spiritism, and on his skill in rendering dialogue. Any reader coming to Pound's versions of the Noh drama must be impressed by their proximity to the earlier plays that Yeats wrote for the Abbey, not only in general form but also in texture of speech. The Japanese characters frequently sound like figures left over from the early dialect plays of Lady Gregory and Yeats:

> WAKI: There never was anybody heard of Mount Shinobu but had a kindly feeling for it; so I, like any other priest that might want to know a little bit about each one of the provinces, may as well be walking up here along the much travelled road.[4]

Later:

> WAKI: Yes, I know that the cloth of this place and the lacquers are famous things. I have already heard of their glory, and yet I still wonder why they have such great reputation.

> TSURE: Ah well now, that's a disappointment.[5]

And to this an audience schooled in the dialect of Galway might well reply, "Sure, and it is."

Something more than accident causes this strange use of Western Irish dialect in these medieval Japanese settings. Yeats's involvement in the Pound redactions was greater than has been supposed: he was in on the process of rendering, especially in one Noh play, *Nishikigi*, that presented him with the plot of *The Dreaming of the Bones*. Although his contribution to the translations came largely through discussion and, in a few instances, rendering of dialogue, he certainly had already a clear sense of the stagecraft behind these short plays written largely in verse. The general structure of the Noh plays did not differ radically from several of his earlier *Plays for an Irish Theatre*, and the curious mixture of extreme simplicity of spectacle with elaborateness of costuming had a genuine attraction for him. The financial and technical limits of the Abbey had forced him to use minimal scenery, and he had gradually come to prefer the simplest of screens and backdrops as background, as the evolution of staging of *The Countess Cathleen* reveals, the movement from early versions in the elaborate nineteenth-century manner to the 1911 version with its simple painted cloth for backdrop. The example of Gordon Craig had also evoked possibilities, and partly through Craig and partly through his own speculations on the occult, he had been considering the stage possibilities of masks. The Noh used ceremonious costumes and especially masks to represent the forms of gods and spirits; and to Yeats, with his abiding preoccupation with the relation between temporal and eternal, it was an exciting confirmation of an emergent dramatic motive to discover that in Noh drama the crises often came with the revelation that one of the characters was in fact a god or ghost.

What the Noh plays did for him was to stabilize a design in his plays that had already been present in, for example, *Deirdre*, though not so formally or ritualistically fixed. In *Deirdre*, the action opens with songs by two musicians. A subsidiary character then enters and with occasional asides to and from the musicians makes an exposition of prior relevant action. The two main characters then enter to take up the action from the point that the expositor has reached, the expositor remaining on the stage as commentator on the action of the principals. Their dialogue moves toward a solution of their problem, and, at the moment of climax, the supernatural emerges upon the scene. With the action brought to completion, the singers conclude with choral comment. *Deirdre* is a much more cluttered play than any of the *Plays for Dancers*, but seen at such a level of abstraction, the action of *Deirdre* is clearly analogous to that of *At the Hawk's Well* or *The Only Jealousy of Emer* or *The Dreaming of the Bones*—or *Nishikigi*.

The Noh plays translated by Pound and, I would suggest, Yeats validated motives already strong in Yeats's dramaturgy. One motive in particular, held in check by his unstable relation with the Abbey audience, was liberated: his belief in the essentially religious function of drama, and his attendant sense of theater as ritual. In the Abbey plays he had satisfied himself with the merest suggestion of supernatural apparition, but from *At the Hawk's Well* (1916) onward he no longer contented himself with dramatizing a heroic human design but placed his chief figures directly in relation to a supernatural paradigm. He could find in the Noh plays the origin of cultural values that would aid him to shoulder aside the detritus of a crumbling civilization. Both Arthur Waley and Fenollosa asserted that the Noh drama was analogous to both Greek and Elizabethan in its religious origins, and it was an appropriate form to render his ambitious articulation of a new religious vision that would integrate the pre-Christian imagination of Europe with the grand insights of the East. The forms of Irish myth, the ideas and cosmology of Buddhism, and the dramaturgy of Noh would restore drama to its original sources and theater to its only valid function, the evocation of a sacred presence. Then he might see what he so missed in West End and Abbey theater, an audience exalted by the contemplation of glorious images of possibility and attainment. The quality to be restored could only be embodied by all the devices of ceremonious mystery, the shapes of dance and poetry fashioning with the art of the designer an image of mankind ritualized and liberated.

The décor, and particularly the masks, allowed him to treat directly possibilities of life that his heroic plays written for the Abbey Theatre could only suggest. In *The Only Jealousy of Emer* he could treat action that took place after Cuchulain's death, and by the use of the mask he could present the remote, stylized, supernatural reality of Fand and Bricriu, and by giving Cuchulain a mask he could establish his community with the spirits of the Sidhe. The use of the mask allowed him to distinguish the vulnerable shifting humanity of Cuchulain's wife Emer and mistress Eithne Inguba from the fixed personifications of universal paradigm that were Bricriu and Fand. What he could not directly present in unmeasured human movement could be obliquely suggested in the stabilized, plotted design of a dancer's steps. Through these devices he could present not merely the posture of calm in the chess-playing of Naisi and Deirdre or the sudden mad remorse of Cuchulain but a serious act of choice between supernatural possibility and human limit. The rejection of divine illumination in favor of life is the constant tragic pattern of the plays, so that Cuchulain's ultimate apotheosis in *The Death of Cuchulain* comes from his earlier refusal of godhood out of loyalty to the human claim exerted by his wife.

The later plays are not all tragic, as we shall shortly see, but they do all exhibit the finest sense of poetic drama. The various versions of *The Only Jealousy of Emer* and of *A Full Moon in March* show the same control over stage possibilities that marks Yeats's drama in general. We tend to forget sometimes that Yeats had more intimate experience of the theater than any other important English poet since Dryden. Plays did not come easily to him, as the manuscripts show, and as some of the published versions reveal. The early version of *A Full Moon in March—The King of the Great Clock Tower—* was dreadfully confused by the presence of the King, who seemed bewildered by the action and not at all sure that his presence was proper and desirable. The later version left him out, so that the stage was occupied by only two figures, Queen and Stroller; as a result the dramatic tension was not muddled by the King's perpetual uneasiness and astonishment. And in *The Only Jealousy of Emer* the first version did not fulfill the possibilities of the material. In this version the conflict is between Cuchulain and the woman of the Sidhe, and this conflict is presented as unrelated to any conflict appearing at the level of the stage itself, where Bricriu and Emer are talking. Cuchulain and Fand appear in visionary form, and their lives and arguments are independent of the immediate issue between Cuchulain's wife and Fand's enemy. In the final version of the play, the conflicts at both levels are interrelated and the ultimate rejection of Cuchulain's love by Emer parallels the failure of Fand to win Cuchulain. The tragedy is deepened by the double rejection, and the double affirmation of human life over the divine underscores the terror of ultimate human loneliness and loss. What remains is the ignorance of Eithne Inguba, who is free of knowledge as she is free of terror, living a life essentially natural and therefore untroubled by apprehension of the human condition torn between nature and super-nature. *Calvary* too displays the same terror of the human condition, and in its original manuscript form the play stressed every element that showed men living in a void between nature and super-nature, so that the birds in the chorus's opening and closing songs were not—as Yeats later declared them to be—symbols of the "subjective" life but quite simply images of a life freed from the perplexities and intricacies of remorse, betrayal, sacrifice, and salvation: their state was not unregenerate but unequivocally natural, i.e., fitting.

In addition to the tragedies—the three plays of the Cuchulain cycle, *The Dreaming of the Bones, Purgatory, The Herne's Egg*—Yeats wrote several other plays that exploit possibilities utilized in the Noh drama and in his *Plays for Dancers*. In these plays he required the aid of Ninette de Valois and a mask designer as well as musicians, but their tone differs. Here the concern is not so much with the heroism of men but with the reality of gods and spirits; they are plays of revelation primarily, and they attempt to assert an imposing reality rather than to create an arena where there is significance in choice. Yet the theatricality is no less, is even increased by the strain of presentation, the deliberate creation of an irrational atmosphere in which the emergence of the god seems inevitable and real.

Of these plays the most compelling is the very short play in prose,

Resurrection, which is perhaps best known for the "Two Songs from a Play" that introduce and conclude its action. It began as a dialogue, and the dialogue originally was completely free of any dramatic tension, any reference to any world outside the minds of the Greek and Hebrew who carry the burden of the finished play. The Greek spoke in tones that one would consider appropriate to a student of Jane Harrison or Frazer or Cornford, if that student had been immersed in the lore of Thrice-Greatest Hermes. He explained endlessly, with almost professorial patience, the way in which a real spirit could manage to persuade Mary—Christ's mother—that he was substantial flesh and blood. His Egyptian experience granted him such knowledge. And all the elements that make the ultimate appearance of Christ credible, the steady movement toward hysteria that begins with the Greek's first outburst of laughter at the sight of Calvary through the window and culminates in the Syrian's possession by laughter from a source beyond his consciousness—all these elements are either not present or buried under ancillary material in the original draft. In their place we find excurses on the difference between men and women in their capacity for deception and self-deception, examinations of Judas's hypothetical state of mind—in short, talk.

In the final version of the play something else comes through. Each moment of tension is underlined and clarified. In the original draft the Syrian is absent from the dialogue between Greek and Hebrew for no particular reason, but in the final play his absence is the occasion for an outburst against the Greek by the Hebrew: "You knew the danger we were all in and yet you weakened our guard?" And the concluding scene arranges an ascending order of terror from the sudden silence of the Dionysian revellers through the various signs of a new presence in the room to the ultimate emergence of the masked figure of Christ.

In this play the motives of these later plays are developed with a thorough brilliance that dazzles. For it was, of course, not the Greek but Yeats himself who had been buried in the study of the ritual origins of drama, who had constructed in the *Resurrection* a play that analogizes the form of Greek tragedy as described in Gilbert Murray's analysis. While the Greek and Hebrew are discussing the divinity and humanity of Christ, a decadent Dionysiac street revel is taking place. The Agon of Greek and Hebrew is paralleled by the actions of the revellers. The Greek disdainfully reports the sacrificial symbolic death of Dionysus as the Agon moves on to the Pathos, and the Messenger—the Syrian—appears to announce not the death of the God (Christ) but the emptiness of the tomb. This to the Greek is proof that Christ was no man, no being of flesh and blood, so that to him it is the death of the idea of Jesus Christ true god and true man. But at this precise point when the Threnos or Lamentation is appropriate, the figure of Christ appears, and when the Greek challenges Him, attempting to prove that He never was anything but a spirit form, he finds that Christ is indeed there in the flesh, that His heart is beating, so that this is the stage of Anagnorisis or recognition. Christ passes through the room to be reunited with The Eleven, and off-stage comes the ultimate Perepiteia, in which the grief of the apostles is transformed into joy. The Dionysiac street revel, conducted not by whores for Eleusis but by female impersonators, ironically accompanies the actual resurrection of a new God. So, through Agon, Pathos, Messenger, Threnos, Anagnorisis, and Perepiteia, the play follows the design of the Greek drama. A sacred presence is evoked almost in spite of all the participants, from the Alexandrian Greek and the worldly Hebrew and hysterical Syrian to the woman giving herself to some stranger in the street.

What *Resurrection* and Yeats's other tragic plays represent is not a mere archaic reconstruction of a posited archetype but the expression of a sensibility that genuinely approximated the originating tragic mind of world civilization. By years of study and meditation, Yeats constructed in his own being a voice that allowed the primitive voice to speak through layers of civilization. His lyrics and plays hence tap a reservoir of feeling that current dramatic literature seldom reaches in depth and intensity. Perhaps, seeing *Waiting for Godot* with its terrible-tender parody of human religious hope, we might observe a similarity of motive that would lead us to remember that the man who first among modern authors set an action of doomed spiritual attendance by an ancient tree (in *At the Hawk's Well*) was also Irish. I don't think it unreasonable to assume that the theatrical tradition of *Godot* and *Fin de partie* derives from *At the Hawk's Well*, *The Cat and the Moon*, and *The Herne's Egg*. The same savagery and tenderness are at work, and the same basically religious motivation.

The current literary state of mind might well be more receptive to Yeats's later plays than that of preceding decades. We are more ready to accept arbitrary conventions, more aware of the liberation of spirit attendant on formalized, even ritualized, presentation. The baroque and rococo do not seem to us effete because over-formalized, and Giorgio Melchiori has gone so far as to describe our age as the age of the tightrope walker, the delicate keeping of balance through formal observance being a dominant thread of our life.[6] Certainly in lyric poetry this is an age of elegance, even dandyism, in one of its aspects. This was not Yeats's motive: a passion for knowledge, for truth, drove him past the qualities that Mr. Melchiori finds in the theater of Christopher Fry, for example, but the fact that we are ready to accept the cloying artifice of Fry might indicate that we are at last ready to accept the possibilities revealed through the later great plays of Yeats. We should find in them what we cannot find in other elegant products of our theatrical and poetic imagination, that is, a recognition of the genuine terror of the human condition, of the need for a fresh start, the requirements of a new form that will not merely fit our nostalgia for preciousness but transmute our empty hearts.

NOTES

1. F. A. C. Wilson, W. B. Yeats and Tradition, London, 1958.
2. W. B. Yeats, Essays and Introductions, London, 1961, p. 221.
3. Letter to Homer Pound, unpublished manuscript, Yale University Library.
4. Certain Noble Plays of Japan: From the Manuscripts of Ernest Fenollosa, Chosen and Finished by Ezra Pound, with an Introduction by William Butler Yeats, The Cuala Press, Churchtown, Dundrum, 1916, p. 1.
5. Ibid., p. 3.
6. Giorgio Melchiori, The Tightrope Walkers, London, 1956.